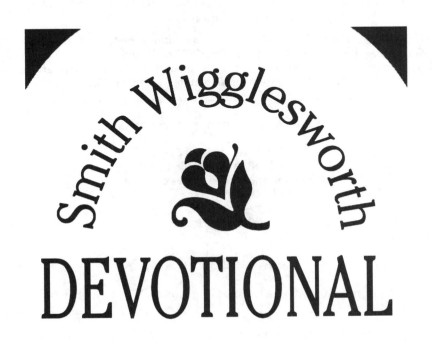

Smith Wigglesworth

DEVOTIONAL

Whitaker House

Whitaker House gratefully acknowledges and thanks Glenn Gohr and the entire staff of the Flower Pentecostal Heritage Center in Springfield, Missouri, and Rev. Desmond Cartwright of the Donald Gee Centre for Pentecostal and Charismatic Research in Mattersey, England, for graciously assisting us in compiling Smith Wigglesworth's works for publication in this book.

SMITH WIGGLESWORTH DEVOTIONAL

ISBN-10: 0-88368-574-4
ISBN-13: 978-0-88368-574-7
Printed in the United States of America
© 1999 by Whitaker House

Whitaker House
1030 Hunt Valley Circle
New Kensington, PA 15068
www.whitakerhouse.com

Compiled by Patricia Culbertson, Editor, Whitaker House

Library of Congress Cataloging-in-Publication Data

Wigglesworth, Smith, 1859–1947
Smith Wigglesworth devotional / by Smith Wigglesworth
p.   cm.
ISBN 0-88368-574-4 (pbk.)
1. Devotional calendars—Pentecostal churches.
2. Christian life—Pentecostal authors.   I. Title.
BV4811.W5924   1999
242'.2—dc21
99-23662

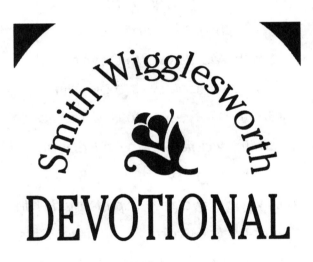

Smith Wigglesworth

DEVOTIONAL

Titles by Smith Wigglesworth

Contents

Contents

Contents

Contents

Introduction

An encounter with Smith Wigglesworth was an unforgettable experience. This seems to be the universal reaction of all who knew him or heard him speak. Smith Wigglesworth was a simple yet remarkable man who was used in an extraordinary way by our extraordinary God. He had a contagious and inspiring faith. Under his ministry, thousands of people came to salvation, committed themselves to a deeper faith in Christ, received the baptism in the Holy Spirit, and were miraculously healed. The power that brought these results was the presence of the Holy Spirit, who filled Smith Wigglesworth and used him in bringing the good news of the Gospel to people all over the world. Wigglesworth gave glory to God for everything that was accomplished through his ministry, and he wanted people to understand his work only in this context, because his sole desire was that people would see Jesus and not himself.

Smith Wigglesworth was born in England in 1859. Immediately after his conversion as a boy, he had a concern for the salvation of others and won people to Christ, including his mother. Even so, as a young man, he could not express himself well enough to give a testimony in church, much less preach a sermon. Wigglesworth said that his mother had the same difficulty in expressing herself that he did. This family trait, coupled with the fact that he had no formal education because he began working twelve hours a day at the age of seven to help support the family, contributed to Wigglesworth's awkward speaking style. He became a plumber by trade, yet he continued to devote himself to winning many people to Christ on an individual basis.

In 1882, he married Polly Featherstone, a vivacious young woman who loved God and had a gift of preaching and evangelism. It was she who taught him to read and who became his closest confidant and strongest supporter. They both had compassion for the poor and needy in their community, and they opened a mission, at which Polly preached. Significantly, people were miraculously healed when Wigglesworth prayed for them.

In 1907, Wigglesworth's circumstances changed dramatically when, at the age of forty-eight, he was baptized in the Holy Spirit. Suddenly, he had a new power that enabled him to preach, and even his wife was amazed at the transformation. This was the beginning of a worldwide evangelistic and healing ministry that reached

Introduction

thousands. He eventually ministered in the United States, Australia, South Africa, and all over Europe. His ministry extended up to the time of his death in 1947.

Several emphases in Smith Wigglesworth's life and ministry characterize him: a genuine, deep compassion for the unsaved and sick; an unflinching belief in the Word of God; a desire that Christ should increase and he should decrease (John 3:30); a belief that he was called to exhort people to enlarge their faith and trust in God; an emphasis on the baptism in the Holy Spirit with the manifestation of the gifts of the Spirit as in the early church; and a belief in complete healing for everyone of all sickness.

Smith Wigglesworth was called "The Apostle of Faith" because absolute trust in God was a constant theme of both his life and his messages. In his meetings, he would quote passages from the Word of God and lead lively singing to help build people's faith and encourage them to act on it. He emphasized belief in the fact that God could do the impossible. He had great faith in what God could do, and God did great things through him.

Wigglesworth's unorthodox methods were often questioned. As a person, Wigglesworth was reportedly courteous, kind, and gentle. However, he became forceful when dealing with the Devil, whom he believed caused all sickness. Wigglesworth said the reason he spoke bluntly and acted forcefully with people was that he knew he needed to get their attention so they could focus on God. He also had such anger toward the Devil and sickness that he acted in a seemingly rough way. When he prayed for people to be healed, he would often hit or punch them at the place of their problem or illness. Yet no one was hurt by this startling treatment. Instead, they were remarkably healed. When he was asked why he treated people in this manner, he said that he was not hitting the people but that he was hitting the Devil. He believed that Satan should never be treated gently or allowed to get away with anything. About twenty people were reportedly raised from the dead after he prayed for them. Wigglesworth himself was healed of appendicitis and kidney stones, after which his personality softened and he was more gentle with those who came to him for prayer for healing. His abrupt manner in ministering may be attributed to the fact that he was serious about his calling and got down to business quickly.

Although Wigglesworth believed in complete healing, he encountered illnesses and deaths that were difficult to understand. These included the deaths of his wife and son, his daughter's lifelong deafness, and his own battles with kidney stones and sciatica.

Introduction

He often seemed paradoxical: compassionate but forceful, blunt but gentle, a well-dressed gentleman whose speech was often ungrammatical or confusing. However, he loved God with everything he had, he was steadfastly committed to God and to His Word, and he didn't rest until he saw God move in the lives of those who needed Him.

In 1936, Smith Wigglesworth prophesied about what we now know as the charismatic movement. He accurately predicted that the established mainline denominations would experience revival and the gifts of the Spirit in a way that would surpass even the Pentecostal movement. Wigglesworth did not live to see the renewal, but as an evangelist and prophet with a remarkable healing ministry, he had a tremendous influence on both the Pentecostal and charismatic movements, and his example and influence on believers is felt to this day.

Without the power of God that was so obviously present in his life and ministry, we might not be reading excerpts of his sermons, for his spoken messages were often disjointed and ungrammatical. However, true gems of spiritual insight shine through them because of the revelation he received through the Holy Spirit. It was his life of complete devotion and belief in God and his reliance on the Holy Spirit that brought the life-changing power of God into his messages.

As you read this book, it is important to remember that Wigglesworth's works span a period of several decades, from the early 1900s to the 1940s. Originally these messages were spoken rather than written. Because of Wigglesworth's unique style, the devotionals in this book have been edited for clarity, and archaic expressions that would be unfamiliar to modern readers have been updated. These devotionals have been taken from seven books of Wigglesworth's sermons published in 1998–1999 by Whitaker House. These thematically arranged books of sermons include *Smith Wigglesworth on Faith, Smith Wigglesworth on Spirit-Filled Living, Smith Wigglesworth on Power to Serve, Smith Wigglesworth on God's Transforming Power, Smith Wigglesworth on Healing, Smith Wigglesworth on the Holy Spirit,* and *Smith Wigglesworth on Spiritual Gifts.*

In conclusion, we hope that as you read these words of Smith Wigglesworth, you will truly sense his complete trust and unwavering faith in God and take to heart one of his favorite sayings: "Only believe!"

January 1

God's Plan Is Best

For as the heavens are higher than the earth, so are My ways higher than your ways, and My thoughts than your thoughts.
—Isaiah 55:9

Scripture reading: Genesis 28:10–22

Looking back on our spiritual journeys, we will see that we have held on to our own way too much of the time. When we come to the end of ourselves, God can begin to take control. The Scripture asks, *"Can two walk together, unless they are agreed?"* (Amos 3:3). We cannot enter into the profound truths of God until we relinquish control, for *"flesh and blood cannot inherit the kingdom of God; nor does corruption inherit incorruption"* (1 Cor. 15:50).

Jacob's name means "supplanter." When Jacob came to the end of his plans, God had a better plan. How slow we are to see that there is a better way.

The glory is never so wonderful as when we realize our helplessness, throw down our sword, and surrender our authority to God. Jacob was a diligent worker, and he would go through any hardship if he could have his own way. In numerous situations, he had his way; all the while, he was ignorant of how gloriously God had preserved him from calamity.

God has a plan beyond anything that we have ever known. He has a plan for every individual life, and if we have any other plan in view, we miss the grandest plan of all. Nothing in the past is equal to the present, and nothing in the present can equal the things of tomorrow. Tomorrow should be so filled with holy expectations that we will be living flames for Him. God never intended His people to be ordinary or commonplace. His intentions were that they should be on fire for Him, conscious of His divine power, realizing the glory of the Cross that foreshadows the crown.

Jacob and his mother had a plan to secure the birthright and the blessing, but God planned the ladder and the angels. Isaac, Jacob's father, agreed that Jacob should go *"to Padan Aram, to the house of Bethuel* [his] *mother's father"* (Gen. 28:2). On his way there, Jacob rested his head on a stone. In his dream, he saw a *"ladder...and its top reached to heaven"* (v. 12). Above the ladder,

13

January 1

Jacob saw God and heard Him say, *"The land on which you lie I will give to you and your descendants"* (v. 13). He also heard God tell him, *"I am with you and will keep you wherever you go, and will bring you back to this land; for I will not leave you"* (v. 15). What a good thing for Jacob that in the middle of carrying out his own plan, God found him at the right place. The trickery to obtain the birthright had not been the honorable thing to do, but here at Bethel, he found that God was with him.

Many things may happen in our lives, but when the veil is lifted and we see the glory of God, His tender compassion covers us all the time. How wonderful to be where God is. Jacob experienced twenty-one years of wandering, fighting, and struggling. Listen to his conversation with his wives: *"Your father has deceived me and changed my wages ten times, but God did not allow him to hurt me"* (Gen. 31:7). To his father-in-law, Jacob said,

> *Unless the God of my father...had been with me, surely now you would have sent me away empty-handed. God has seen my affliction and the labor of my hands.* (Gen. 31:42)

There is a way that God establishes. In our human planning, we may experience blessings of a kind, but we also undergo trials, hardships, and barrenness that God would have kept from us if we had followed His way. I realize through the anointing of the Holy Spirit that there is a freshness, a glow, a security in God where you can know that God is with you all the time. There is a place to reach where all that God has for us can flow through us to a needy world all the time.

Thought for today: There is a good; there is a better; but God has a best, a higher standard for us than we have yet attained. It is a better thing if it is God's plan and not ours.

January 2

Equipped with Power

Seek out from among you seven men of good reputation,
full of the Holy Spirit and wisdom, whom we may appoint
over this business.
—Acts 6:3

Scripture reading: Acts 6:1–10

*D*uring the time of the inauguration of the church, the disciples were pressured by many responsibilities. The practical things of life could not be attended to, and many were complaining concerning the neglect of their widows. Therefore, the disciples decided to choose seven men to do the work of caring for the needs of these widows—men who were *"full of the Holy Spirit."* What a divine thought. No matter what kind of work was to be done, however menial it may have been, the person chosen had to be *"full of the Holy Spirit."* The plan of the church was that everything, even everyday routines, must be sanctified to God, for the church had to be a Holy Spirit church. Beloved, God has never ordained anything less.

The heritage of the church is to be so equipped with power that God can lay His hand upon any member at any time to do His perfect will. There is no stopping point in the Spirit-filled life. We begin at the Cross, the place of disgrace, shame, and death, and that very death brings the power of resurrection life. Then, being filled with the Holy Spirit, we go on *"from glory to glory"* (2 Cor. 3:18). Let us not forget that possessing the baptism in the Holy Spirit means that there must be an ever increasing holiness. People know when the tide is flowing; they also know when it is ebbing. How the church needs divine anointing. It needs to see God's presence and power so evidenced that the world will recognize it.

Thought for today: When we please God in our daily service, we will always find that everyone who is faithful in the little things, God will make ruler over much (Matt. 25:21).

January 3

Above the Ordinary

They chose Stephen, a man full of faith and the Holy Spirit.
—Acts 6:5

Scripture reading: Acts 6:8–15; 7:55–60

God has privileged us in Christ Jesus to live above the ordinary human plane of life. Those who want to be ordinary and live on a lower plane can do so, but as for me, I will not. The same anointing, the same zeal, the same Holy Spirit power is at our command as it was at the command of Stephen and the apostles. We have the same God that Abraham and Elijah had, and we do not need to lag behind in receiving any gift or grace. We may not possess all the gifts as abiding gifts, but as we are full of the Holy Spirit and divine anointing, it is possible, when there is a need, for God to make evident every gift of the Spirit through us as He may choose.

Stephen, an ordinary man, became extraordinary under the Holy Spirit's anointing until, in many ways, he stands supreme among the apostles. *"And Stephen, full of faith and power, did great wonders and signs among the people"* (Acts 6:8). As we go deeper in God, He enlarges our capacity for understanding and places before us a wide-open door. It is not surprising that this man chosen to serve tables was later called to a higher plane.

You may ask, "What do you mean? Did he stop taking care of his responsibilities?" No, but he was lost in the power of God. He lost sight of everything in the natural and steadfastly fixed his gaze on Jesus, *"the author and finisher of our faith"* (Heb. 12:2), until he was transformed into a shining light in the kingdom of God. May we be awakened to believe His Word and to understand the mind of the Spirit, for there is an inner place of purity where we can see God. Stephen was an ordinary person, but he was in the place where God could move him so that he, in turn, could affect those around him. He began in a humble place and ended in a blaze of glory. Dare to believe Christ.

Thought for today: Chosen for menial service, Stephen became mighty for God.

January 4

Opportunity for Action

Whatever you do, do all to the glory of God.
—1 Corinthians 10:31

Scripture reading: Proverbs 15:28–16:9

On a ship one day, some people said to me, "We are going to have a program. Would you be a participant in the entertainment?"

I replied, "Come in a quarter of an hour, and I will tell you."

They came round again and said, "Are you ready?"

"Yes," I told them, "I have got a clear witness that I have to be in the entertainment."

So they said to me, "What can you do?"

"I can sing," I offered.

They said, "Where would you like to be scheduled in the entertainment? We are going to have a dance."

I said, "Put me down just before the dance."

I went to the entertainment, and when I saw the clergymen trying to please the people, it turned me to prayer. My turn came, and I went up to the piano with my "Redemption Songs." When the lady saw the music, she said, "I cannot play this kind of music."

I said, "Be at peace, young lady. I have music and words inside." So I sang:

> If I could only tell Him as I know Him.
> My Redeemer who has brightened all my way;
> If I could tell how precious is His presence,
> I am sure that you would make Him yours today.
> Could I tell it, Could I tell it,
> How the sunshine of His presence lights my way.
> I would tell it, I would tell it,
> And I'm sure that you would make Him yours today.

I sang the song, and when I finished, the people said, "You have spoiled the dance." Well, I was there for that purpose, to spoil the dance. From the least to the greatest, they were weeping. They never had a dance, but they had a prayer meeting. Six young men were saved by the power of God in my cabin.

17

A preacher came to me afterwards and said, "How dare you sing that?" "Why," I said, "how dare I not sing it?" It was my opportunity. He was going to India, and when he got there, he wrote in his periodical and mailed it to England. He said, "I did not seem to have any chance to preach the Gospel, but there was a plumber on board who seemed to have plenty of opportunities to preach to everybody. He said things that continue to stick with me. He told me that the book of Acts was written only because the apostles acted."

You see, I was in the drama of acting in the name of Jesus. And so that opened the door and provided me a place that I could speak all the time. The door was open in every way. Glory to God!

Thought for today: You are in the right position when you allow the glory of the new life to cause you to act. Live in the Acts of the Apostles, and every day you will see some miracle worked by the power of the living God.

Alone with God

*Then Jacob was left alone; and a Man wrestled
with him until the breaking of day.*
—Genesis 32:24

Scripture reading: Psalm 62:5–63:4

*J*acob was given time to think. Oh, to be left alone with God! In the context of the Scripture, we read that several things had preceded his being alone. His wives and his children had been sent ahead. His sheep, oxen, camels, and donkeys had gone ahead. He was alone.

Often, you will find that you are left alone. Whether you like it or not, you will be left alone as Jacob was left alone. His wives could not make atonement for him; his children could not make atonement for him; his money was useless to help him.

What made Jacob come to that place of loneliness, weakness, and knowledge of himself? He recalled the grace with which God had met him twenty-one years before, when he saw the ladder and the angels and heard the voice of God: *"Behold, I am with you and will keep you wherever you go, and will bring you back to this land; for I will not leave you until I have done what I have spoken to you"* (Gen. 28:15). He remembered God's mercy and grace.

He was returning to meet his brother Esau, who had become very rich. Esau had been blessed abundantly in the things of this world. He had authority and power to take all that Jacob had and to take vengeance upon him. Jacob knew this. He also knew that there was only one way of deliverance. What was it? Only God could keep Jacob safe. God had met him twenty-one years before when he had left home empty-handed. Now, he was returning with wives, children, and goods, but he was lean in soul and impoverished in spirit. Jacob said to himself, "If I do not get a blessing from God, I can never meet Esau," and he made up his mind he would not go on until he knew that he had favor with God. Jacob was left alone. Unless we get alone with God, we will surely perish. God intervenes when conflict exists. The way of revelation is plain. The Holy Spirit's plan is so clear that we have to say God was in it after all.

Jacob was left alone. He knelt alone. The picture is so real to me. Alone! He began to think. He thought about the ladder and the angels. I think as he began to pray, his tongue stuck to the roof of his mouth. Jacob had to get rid of a lot of things. It had all been Jacob! As he got alone with God, he knew it. If you get alone with God, you will find it to be a place of revelation. Jacob was left alone, alone with God. We stay too long with our relations, our camels, and our sheep. Jacob was left alone. Hour after hour passed. He began to feel the presence of God, but he still had not received the desired blessing.

Jacob said, *"I will not let You go unless You bless me!"* (Gen. 32:26). And God blessed him: *"Your name shall no longer be called Jacob, but Israel"* (v. 28). The change of Jacob to Israel was wonderful! Israel! Victory all the time! God is building all the time. God is sufficient all the time. Now Jacob had power over the cattle, power over Esau, power over the world. All was in subjection as he came out of the great night of trial. The sun rose upon him. Oh, that God may take us on in the same way.

Thought for today: God intends for people to be severed by the force of His power, so hold fast; He will never let go. If we let go, we will fall short.

January 6

The Way to Victory

Hold fast to the LORD your God.
—Joshua 23:8

Scripture reading: Genesis 32:24–33:11

*I*f God is ever disappointed when you wait in His presence, it will be because you are not fervent. If you are not serious and intense, you disappoint God. If God is with you and you know it, be in earnest. Pray and believe: *"Hold fast the confidence and the rejoicing of the hope firm to the end"* (Heb. 3:6). If you do not, you disappoint God.

Jacob was that way. God said, "You are not real enough; you are not hot enough; you are too ordinary; you are no good to Me unless you are filled with zeal—white hot!" The Angel of the Lord said, *"Let Me go, for the day breaks"* (Gen. 32:26). Jacob knew if God went without blessing him, he could not meet Esau. If you are left alone with God and you cannot get to a place of victory, it is a terrible time. You must never let go, whatever you are seeking— fresh revelation, light for your path, some particular need—never let go. Victory is ours if we are earnest enough.

You must always master that with which you are wrestling. If darkness covers you, if a fresh revelation is what you need, or if your mind needs to be relieved, always get the victory. God says you are not earnest enough. You say, "The Word does not say that." But it was in God's mind. In wrestling, the strength is in the neck, chest, and thigh; the thigh is the source of strength. So God touched Jacob's thigh. With that strength gone, defeat is sure. What did Jacob do? He hung on.

Jacob said, *"I will not let You go unless You bless me!"* (v. 26). And God blessed him: *"Your name shall no longer be called Jacob, but Israel"* (v. 28). The change of Jacob to Israel was wonderful! Now Jacob had power.

What happened after that? Read how God blessed and honored him. Esau met him. There was no fighting now. What a blessed state of grace! They kissed each other: *"When a man's ways please the LORD, He makes even his enemies to be at peace with him"* (Prov. 16:7).

"What about all these cattle, Jacob?"

21

"Oh, they are a present."

"I have plenty; I don't want your cattle. What a joy it is to see your face again!"

What a wonderful change! Who caused it? God.

Could Jacob hold God? Can you hold God? Yes, you can. Sincerity can hold Him, dependence can hold Him, weakness can hold Him, for *"when* [you are] *weak, then* [you are] *strong"* (2 Cor. 12:10). I'll tell you what cannot hold Him: self-righteousness cannot hold Him; pride cannot hold Him; assumption cannot hold Him; high-mindedness cannot hold Him—thinking you are something when you are nothing, puffed up in your imagination. You can hold Him in your prayer closet, in the prayer meeting, everywhere: *"If anyone hears My voice and opens the door, I will come in to him and dine with him, and he with Me"* (Rev. 3:20).

Can you hold Him? You may sometimes think that He has left you. Oh, no! He does not leave Jacob, Israel. What changed his name? Jacob obtained the blessing because of the favor of God and his yieldedness to God's will. God's Spirit was working in him to bring him to a place of helplessness. God worked to bring him to Bethel, the place of victory. Jacob remembered Bethel, and through all the trying circumstances, he had kept his vow. (See Genesis 28:20–22.) When we make vows and keep them, God helps us and leads us to victory.

Thought for today: Let us in all our seeking see that we have the favor of God. Keep His commandments. Walk in the Spirit. Be tenderhearted and lovable. If we do these things, our ministry will be a blessing to others.

January 7

The Living Word

When He had come down from the mountain, great multitudes followed Him. And behold, a leper came and worshiped Him, saying, "Lord, if You are willing, You can make me clean." Then Jesus put out His hand and touched him, saying, "I am willing; be cleansed." Immediately his leprosy was cleansed.
—Matthew 8:1–3

Scripture reading: Isaiah 53:1–11

When I read these words, my heart is moved, for I realize that Jesus is just as much present with us as He was in Jerusalem when He walked the earth. How it changes our whole nature as we comprehend what Jesus meant when He said, *"You search the Scriptures, for in them you think you have eternal life; and these are they which testify of Me"* (John 5:39). This living Word is not given to us just because of the narratives or the wonderful parables that Jesus taught, but so that we, through it, might be changed. Beloved, His presence is so remarkable that if we will but call on Him, believing that He has the power to give eternal life at His command, we will be changed in body, soul, and spirit.

When Jesus was on earth and beheld suffering humanity, He was moved with compassion. He met the most difficult problems; one of the hardest conditions to meet was leprosy. The moment that leprosy was pronounced upon a person, it meant that he was doomed. Just as there was no remedy at that time for a leper, there is no earthly power that can deliver us from sin. Leprosy was the disease that had a death sentence, and sin means death to the spiritual man unless it is cleansed by the blood of Jesus. Here was a leper with the seal of death on him, and there was only one hope. What was it? If he could come to Jesus, he would be healed. But how could a leper come to Jesus? When a leper came near other people, he had to cry out: *"Unclean! Unclean!"* (Lev. 13:45)—so how could a leper ever get near to Jesus?

The difficulty was tremendous, but when faith lays hold, impossibilities must yield. When we touch the Divine and believe God, sins will be forgiven; diseases will go; circumstances will change. I can almost read the thoughts of the people as they passed by the leper: "You poor leper! If you had been where we were, you would

23

have seen the most remarkable things happen, for people were delivered from all kinds of diseases today." The leper might have asked, "Where were you?" They would have answered, "We have been with Jesus!" Oh, the thrill of life when we have been with Jesus.

Let me give you a little picture. Every night when Jesus left the disciples and made His way up the mountainside, they would watch Him as far as the eye could see, until He disappeared. On the next day, the crowds would gather and watch for His appearing. They were so taken up with watching for Jesus that when they saw Him coming down the mountain, they could not keep quiet. Their hearts were full of the thought of seeing Him, but where was the leper? The leper, too, had come, but the eyes of the people were not on the leper now. They were watching for Jesus. The leper kept close to the crowd, and as Jesus drew nearer, he began his chant, *"Unclean! Unclean!"*

The crowd immediately moved away from him, leaving the path clear for the leper to be the first to get to Jesus. No one could turn him back. No one could stop a man whose heart was set on reaching Jesus. No power on earth can stop a sinner from reaching the side of the Master, if he has faith that will not be denied. Perhaps some have awful diseases in their bodies, or their souls are far away from God. They have been prayed for, and have prayed themselves, but the thing is not removed, and they are in the place where the leper was. He knew that Jesus could heal him. All he had to do was get close enough to Jesus.

Jesus makes one great sweeping statement from that day to this as He says, *"I am willing; be cleansed."* Immediately, the man's leprosy was cleansed.

Thought for today: When you are in the place God wants you to be, you will be healed.

24

Faith's Commanding Position

Now faith is the substance of things hoped for,
the evidence of things not seen.
—Hebrews 11:1

Scripture reading: Psalm 20

*P*aul related his conversion many times over, and I believe it is good to rehearse what God has done for you. I have been privileged to travel to every part of the world and have seen that God has arranged a plan for me. I said to my congregation, "The Lord is moving me to go out through the States and Canada." When the Lord told me, I said, "Lord, You have three things to do: You have to find money for home and find money to go, and You have to give me a real change, for You know that sometimes my mind or memory is no good at all to me."

Right away money came from all over, and I said, "It is true God is sending me. I already have fifty pounds." My son George said, "Father, Mother's gone to heaven, and you are leaving us; what will we do?" I said, "George, you open the next letter." In it was twenty-five pounds. He saw that God would provide.

I went to Liverpool, and a man said, "Here is five pounds for you." When I was on the ship, a poorly dressed lady gave me a red sugar bag, and there were twenty-five gold coins in it. Just as I was getting on the ship, a man came and gave me a book and said, "There is a page for every day in the year." And the Lord said to me, "Put down everything that takes place in the month." I did so, and I had a memory like an encyclopedia. You see, I never learned geography, and God sent me all over the world to see it.

Do not fail to claim your holy position—the commanding position of faith—so that you will overcome the power of the Devil. The best time you have is when you are in the most difficult position.

Thought for today: Ask God to give you the grace to use the faith you have. God will work the miracle if you dare to stand upon the Word.

Testimony of Faith

"What shall we do, that we may work the works of God?"
Jesus answered and said to them, "This is the work of God,
that you believe in Him whom He sent."
—John 6:28–29

Scripture reading: Psalm 4

I was healed of appendicitis, because of faith based on the knowledge of the experience of faith. When I have ministered to others, God has met and answered according to His will. We know that God will not fail us when we believe and trust in His power. The centurion had this faith when he said to Jesus, *"Speak a word, and my servant will be healed"* (Matt. 8:8). Jesus answered him, *"'Go your way; and as you have believed, so let it be done for you.' And his servant was healed that same hour"* (v. 13).

In one place where I was staying, a young man came in telling us that his sweetheart was dying; there was no hope. I said, "Only believe." This was faith based on knowledge. I knew that what God had done for me He could do for her. We went to the house. Her sufferings were terrible to witness. I said, "In the name of Jesus, come out of her." She cried, "Mother, Mother, I am well." Then I said that the only way to make us believe it was for her to get up and dress. Soon she came down dressed. The doctor came in and examined her carefully. He said, "This is of God; this is the finger of God." It was faith based on knowledge.

If I were to receive a check for a thousand pounds and knew only imperfectly the character of the man who sent it, I would be careful of him. I would not rely on the money until the check was honored. Jesus, on the other hand, did great works because of His knowledge of His Father. He knew He could count on the character of God. Faith begets knowledge, fellowship, and communion. If you see imperfect faith, full of doubt, a wavering condition, it always comes because of imperfect knowledge.

Thought for today: God is more eager to answer than we are to ask.

January 10

Victory over Difficult Circumstances

He is able even to subdue all things to Himself.
—Philippians 3:21

Scripture reading: Matthew 4:16–25

I have come across several mental cases. How difficult they are naturally, but how easy for God to deal with. One lady came saying, "Just over the way there is a young man terribly afflicted, with no rest day or night." I went with a very imperfect knowledge as to what I had to do, but in the weak places, God helps our infirmities. I rebuked the demon in the name of Jesus, and then I said, "I'll come again tomorrow." The next day when I went, he was quite well and with his father in the field.

Fifty miles away, there was a fine young man, twenty-five years of age. He had lost his reason, could have no communication with his mother, and was always wandering up and down. I knew God was waiting to bless. I cast out the demon power and heard later that he had become quite well.

Thus the blessed Holy Spirit takes us on from one place to another. So many things happen; I live in heaven on earth. Do not wait for inspiration if you are in need; the Holy Spirit is available, and you can have perfect deliverance.

I was taken to three persons, one in the care of an attendant. As I entered the room, there was a terrible din and quarreling. It was such a noise it seemed as if all the powers of hell were stirred. I had to wait for God's time. The Holy Spirit rose in me at the right time, and the three were delivered. That night, they were singing praises to God.

Christ is the same today. When He reigns in you, you know how to obey and how to work in conjunction with His will, His power, His light, and His life. When we have faith based on knowledge, we know He has come. *"You shall receive power when the Holy Spirit has come upon you"* (Acts 1:8). God is with the person who dares to stand upon His Word.

Thought for today: How bountiful God is when we depend on Him! He gives us enough to spare for others.

Faith Based on Knowledge

*Jesus answered and said to them, "This is the work of God, that
you believe in Him whom He sent."*
—John 6:29

Scripture reading: Luke 9:1–11

I remember a person who had not been able to smell anything for four years. I said, "You will smell now if you believe." She went about smelling everything and was quite
excited. The next day she gave her testimony.

Another came and asked, "Is it possible for God to heal my
ears?" The eardrums had been removed. I said, "Only believe." She
went down into the audience in great distress; others were healed,
but she could not hear. The next night she came again. She said, "I
am going to believe tonight." The glory fell. The first time she
came feeling; the second time she came believing.

At one place, there was a man anointed with oil for a rupture.
He came the next night and rose in the meeting saying, "This man
is an impostor. He is deceiving the people. He told me last night I
was healed; I am worse than ever today." I spoke to the evil power
that held the man and rebuked it, telling the man he was indeed
healed. He was a stonemason. The next day, he testified to lifting
heavy weights and that God had met him. *"By His stripes we are
healed....And the LORD has laid on Him the iniquity of us all"* (Isa.
53:5–6). He was against the Word of God, not me.

*"'What shall we do, that we may work the works of God?' Jesus
answered and said to them, 'This is the work of God, that you believe in Him whom He sent'"* (John 6:28–29). Anything else? Yes.
He took our infirmities and healed all our diseases. I myself am a
marvel of healing. If I fail to glorify God, the stones will cry out.
(See Luke 19:37–40.) Salvation is for all. Healing is for all. The
baptism of the Holy Spirit is for all.

Consider yourselves dead indeed unto sin, but alive unto God
(Rom. 6:11). By His grace you will get the victory every time. It is
possible to live a holy life.

Thought for today: The Holy Spirit has the latest news from the
Godhead and has designed for us the right place at the right time.

The Fullness of His Word

Faith is the substance of things hoped for,
the evidence of things not seen.
—Hebrews 11:1

Scripture reading: Hebrews 11:1–10

We may be in a very low ebb of the tide, but it is good to be in a place where the tide can rise. Everything depends on our being filled with the Holy Spirit. If He can only get us in readiness for His plan to be worked out, it will be wonderful.

Everything depends on our believing God. If we are saved, it is only because God's Word says so. We cannot rest upon our feelings. We cannot do anything without a living faith. It is surely God Himself who comes to us in the person of His beloved Son and strengthens us so that we realize that our bodies are surrounded by His power. All things are possible for us in God.

God purposes that we might be on the earth to manifest His glory, that every time satanic power is confronted, God might be able to say of us as He did of Job, "What do you think about him?" (See Job 1:8.) The joy of the Lord can be so clearly evidenced in us that we will be filled with God and able to rebuke the Devil.

God has shown me in the night watches that everything that is not of faith is sin (Rom. 14:23). God wants to bring us into harmony with His will so that we will see that if we do not believe all of the Word of God, something in us is not purely sanctified to accept the fullness of His Word. Many people put their human wisdom in the place of God, and God is not able to give the best because the human is confronting God in such a way. God is not able to get the best through us until the human will is dissolved.

People say, "I want things to be tangible. I want something to appeal to my human reasoning." My response is that everything that you cannot see is eternal. Everything you see now will fade away and will be consumed, but what you cannot see, what is more real than you, is the substance of all things: God in the human soul, mightier than you by a million times.

Thought for today: There is nothing we can come short of if the Holy Spirit is the prime mover in our thoughts and lives, for He has a plan greater than ours.

Faith at Work

He...gave some to be apostles, some prophets, some evangelists,
and some pastors and teachers, for the equipping of the saints
for the work of ministry...till we all come to the unity of the faith
and of the knowledge of the Son of God.
—Ephesians 4:11–13

Scripture reading: Ephesians 4:7–5:1

A man traveled with me from Montreal to Vancouver and then on ship to New Zealand. He was a dealer of race-horses. It seemed he could not leave me. He was frivolous and talked about races, but he could not keep up his end of the conversation. I did not struggle to keep my end up because mine is a living power. No person who has Jesus as the inward power of his body needs to tremble when Satan comes around. All he has to do is to *"stand still, and see the salvation of the LORD"* (Exod. 14:13).

This man entered into a good deal of frivolity and talk of this world. Coming upon a certain island of the Fiji group, we all disembarked, and God gave me wonderful liberty in preaching. The man came back afterwards; he did not go to meet his racing and card-playing chums; instead, He came stealing back to the ship. With tears in his eyes, he said, "I am dying. I have been bitten by a snake." His skin had turned to a dark green, and his leg was swollen. "Can you help me?" he asked.

If we only knew the power of God! If we are in a place of substance, of reality, of ideal purpose, it is not human; we are dealing with almightiness. I have a present God. I have a living faith, and the living faith is the Word. The Word is life, and the Lord is *"the same yesterday, today, and forever"* (Heb. 13:8). Placing my hands upon the serpent bite, I said, "In the name of Jesus, come out!" He looked at me, and the tears came. The swelling went down before his eyes, and he was perfect in a moment.

Yes, *"faith is the substance of things hoped for, the evidence of things not seen"* (Heb. 11:1). Faith is what came into me when I believed. I was born of the incorruptible Word by the living virtue, life, and personality of God. I was instantly changed from nature to grace. I became a servant of God, and I became an enemy of unrighteousness.

January 13

The Holy Spirit wants us to clearly understand that we are a million times bigger than we know. Most Christians have no conception of what they are. Oh, that God would bring us into divine attractiveness by His almightiness so that all our bodies would wake up to resurrection force, to the divine, inward flow of eternal power coursing through our human frames.

God took you into His pavilion and began to clothe you and give you the gifts of the Spirit. He did this so that in that ministry, by the power of God, you would bring all the church into the perfect possession of the fullness of Christ. Oh, the wonder of it! Oh, the adaptability of His equipment!

I believe God wants something to be in you that could never be unless you cease to live for yourself. God wants you to live for Him, to live for others. But, oh, to have the touch of God! Beloved, the Holy Spirit is the Comforter. The Holy Spirit did not come to speak of Himself, but He came to unveil Him who said, *"Take My yoke upon you and learn from Me, for I am gentle and lowly in heart, and you will find rest for your souls"* (Matt. 11:29). The Holy Spirit came to thrill you with resurrection power, and He came so that you would be anointed with fresh oil that overflows in the splendor of His almightiness. Then right through you will come forth a river of divine anointing that will sustain you in the bitterest place. It will give life to the deadest formality and say to the weak, "Be strong," and to them who have no might, "The Lord of Hosts is here to comfort you." (See Isaiah 40:29; Zechariah 1:17.) Possibility is the greatest thing of your life.

Thought for today: God wants us to be like the rising of the sun, filled with the rays of heaven, all the time beaming forth the gladness of the Spirit of the Almighty.

Faith Is the Victory

This is the victory that has overcome the world; our faith.
—1 John 5:4

Scripture reading: 1 John 5:4–15

When I was ministering to the sick, a man came who was shriveled and weakened; his cheek bones were sticking out, his eyes sunken, and his neck all shriveled. He was just a form of a man. He whispered, for he could only speak with a weak voice, "Can you help me?"

I asked "What is it?" He said that he had had surgery to remove stomach cancer. As a result of the operation, he could not swallow.

He said, "I have tried to take some juice today, but it would not go down." He whispered, "I have a hole in my stomach. As I pour liquid in through a tube, my stomach receives that. I have been living this way for three months."

You could call it a shadow of life he was living. Could I help him? Look! This Book can help anybody. This Book is the essence of life. God moves as you believe. This Book is the Word of God. Could I help him? I said, "On the authority of this Word, this night you will have a big supper."

But he said he could not eat. "Do as I tell you," I answered.

"How can it be?"

"It is time," I said, "to go and eat a good supper." He went home and told his wife.

She could not understand it. She said, "You cannot eat. You cannot swallow."

But he whispered, "The man said I had to do it." He became hungry and ventured, "I will try it." His wife prepared his supper. He took a mouthful, and it went down just as easy as possible. He went on eating food until he was full. Then he and his wife had one of the best times of their lives. The next morning he was so full of joy because he had eaten again. He looked down out of curiosity to see the hole and found that God had closed it up!

But you ask, Can He do it for me? Yes, if you believe it. Let God have His way. Touch God now. Faith is the victory.

Thought for today: The Word of God is marrow to your bones. It is resurrection from every weakness; it is life from the dead.

The Foundation of Faith

In the beginning was the Word, and the Word was with God,
and the Word was God. He was in the beginning with God.
All things were made through Him, and without Him
nothing was made that was made.
—John 1:1–3

Scripture reading: Luke 6:27–49

*I*f we are ever going to make any progress in the divine life, we will have to have a real foundation. There is no foundation except the foundation of faith for us. All our actions and all that ever will come to us that is of any importance will be because we have a Rock. If you are on the Rock, no power can move you. In any area or principle of your faith, you must have something established in you to bring it forth. There is no establishment outside God's Word. Everything else is sand. Everything else will break apart. If you build on anything else but the Word of God—on imaginations, sentimentality, or feelings—it will mean nothing without the foundation, and the foundation will have to be in the Word of God.

I was once going on a train to Blackpool. It is a fashionable resort, and many people go there because of the high tides and the wonderful sights they see as the ocean surges up in large, massive mountains of sea. As I traveled, I looked over and said to a builder, "Those men are building houses upon sand."

"Oh," he said, "you don't know. You are not a builder. Don't you know that we can pound that sand until it becomes like rock?"

I said, "Nonsense!" I saw the argument was not going to profit, so I dropped it. By and by, we reached Blackpool, where the mountainous waves come over. I saw a row of houses that had fallen flat, and drawing the attention of this man, I said, "Oh, look at those houses. See how flat they are." He forgot our previous conversation and said, "You know here we have very large tides, and these houses, being on the sand when the floods came, fell."

Our foundation must be something better than sand, and everything is sand except the Word. There isn't anything that will remain. We are told that heaven and earth will be melted with fervent heat (2 Pet. 3:10). But we are told that the Word of God will be forever, and not one jot or tittle of the Word of God will fail (Matt. 5:18). If there is anything that satisfies me, it is in knowing that *"Your word is settled in heaven"* (Ps. 119:89). Another passage in Psalm 138 says, *"You have magnified Your word above all Your name"* (v. 2). The very establishment for me is the Word of God.

Here we have the foundation of all things, which is the Word. It is a substance; it is a power. It is more than relationship; it is personality. To every soul that enters into this privilege, it is a divine injunction to be born of this Word. What it means to us will be very important. For remember, it is *"substance"*; it is an *"evidence of things not seen"* (Heb. 11:1). It brings about what you cannot see and brings forth what is not there.

God took the Word and made the world. We live in the world that was made by the Word of God, and it is inhabited by millions of people. You say it is a substance. Jesus, the Word of God, made it with the things that did not appear. And nothing has been made that has not been made by the Word (John 1:3). When we come to the truth of what that Word means, we will be able not only to build, but also to know; not only to know, but also to have. Live and operate in the fact of the Word; rest in the knowledge of the principles of the Most High.

Thought for today: *"Man shall not live by bread alone, but by every word of God"* (Luke 4:4). Feast on the Word of God; discover its richness.

January 16

Always Advancing

As newborn babes, desire the pure milk of the word,
that you may grow thereby.
—1 Peter 2:2

Scripture reading: 1 Peter 1:13–2:5

*B*eloved, don't forget that every day must be a day of advancement. If you have not made any advancement since yesterday, in a measure, you are a backslider. There is only one way for you between Calvary and glory, and it is forward. It is every day forward. It is no day back. It is advancement with God. It is cooperation with Him in the Spirit.

We must see these things, because if we live on the same plane day after day, our vision becomes stale; the principles lose their earnestness. But we must be like those who are catching the vision of the Master day by day. We must make inroads into every passion that would interfere, and we must bring everything to the slaughter that is not holy. For in these days, God wants us to know that He wishes to seat us on high.

Often the most trying times are the most beneficial to our Christian growth. Consider Daniel, Shadrach, Meshach, and Abednego. Remember Moses and the trials he faced. Beloved, if you read the Scriptures, you will never find anything about the easy times. All the glories came out of hard times.

If you are to be really reconstructed, it will be in a hard time. It won't be in a singing meeting, but at a time when you think all things are dried up, when you think there is no hope for you and you have passed up everything. That is the time that God makes the person. And out of the experience, we will have a story to tell about what God has done for us. When the trial is severe; when you think that no one is being tried as much as you; when the trial is so hard that you cannot sleep and you do not know what to do; *"count it all joy"* (James 1:2). You are in a good place when you do not know what to do; look to God for the answer.

Thought for today: It is when you are tried by fire that God purges you, takes the dross away, and brings forth pure gold.

Say Amen to Jesus

Peter...said, "Now I know for certain that the Lord has sent His angel, and has delivered me from the hand of Herod and from all the expectation of the Jewish people."
—Acts 12:11

Scripture reading: Acts 12:1–17

There is a lot in an amen. I find that you can have zeal without faith. The Scripture reading shows the difference between the amen of faith and having zeal without faith.

When Peter was imprisoned by Herod, the church was in constant prayer for his release. They were even praying all night. They had zeal, but they did not have faith. Although there is much that could be commended to us from this passage, one thing is missing: faith. Young Rhoda had more faith than all the rest of them. When the knock came at the door, she ran to answer it. The moment she heard Peter's voice, she was so excited to share the good news that she didn't even unlock the gate so that Peter could come in. She ran with joy to tell those praying that Peter stood at the gate.

All the people said, "You are mad. It isn't so." She insisted that she had seen Peter, but the people had no faith at all. They said, "Perhaps God has sent an angel."

But Rhoda said, "It is Peter." And Peter continued knocking. They went and found him at the door. They had zeal but no faith. God wants to bring us to the place where we will take hold of Him in a living way. We need to rest and always trust the plan of God.

There was such a difference between Zacharias and Mary. Zacharias definitely wanted a son, but even when the angel came and told him that he would be a father, he was full of unbelief. The angel said, *"You will be mute and not able to speak...because you did not believe"* (Luke 1:20). But when the angel came to Mary, she said, *"Let it be to me according to your word"* (v. 38). This was the beginning of the amen.

God wants us to have an inward amen, a mighty moving amen. This amen says, "It is," because God has spoken.

Thought for today: Believe that there can be a real amen in your life.

A Divine Faith

Have faith in God.
—Mark 11:22

Scripture reading: Psalm 9

*T*here is a great difference between our faith and the faith of Jesus. Our faith comes to an end. Most people have come to the place where they have said, "Lord, I have gone so far; now I can go no further. I have used all the faith I have, and I just have to stop now and pray for more faith."

Thank God that we have the faith we do, but there is another faith. I remember one day being in northern England and visiting some sick people. I was taken to a house where a young woman was lying on her bed. Her reason had gone, and many things were manifested there that were satanic, and I knew it.

She was only a young woman, a beautiful child. Then the husband, a young man, came in with a baby, and he leaned over to kiss his wife. The moment he did, she threw herself onto the other side of the bed, just as a lunatic would do, with no consciousness of the presence of her husband. That was very heartbreaking. Then he took the baby and pressed the baby's lips to the mother. Again, she responded wildly. I said to a sister who was attending her, "Have you had anyone to help?"

"Oh," she said, "we have had everything."

But I said, "Have you no spiritual help?"

Her husband stormed out and said, "Help? You think that we believe God after we have had seven weeks of no sleep and of maniac conditions? You are mistaken. You have come to the wrong house."

That brought me to a place of compassion that something had to be done for this woman. Then with my faith, I began to penetrate the heavens with my prayers. I never saw anyone get anything from God who prayed with an earthly focus. If you receive anything from God, you will have to pray into heaven, for the answers are all there.

As I saw in the presence of God the limitations of my faith, there came another faith, a faith that could not be denied, a faith that took the promise, a faith that believed God's Word. And I came from that presence back again to earth, but I was not the same man under the same conditions that had confronted me before. In the name of Jesus, I was a man with a faith that could shake hell.

I said, "Come out of her in the name of Jesus!" She rolled over, fell asleep, and wakened in fourteen hours, perfectly sane and perfectly whole. Oh, there is faith, but Jesus wants to bring us all into a place in line with God where we cease to be, and His faith takes over. God must have the right of way, of thought and of purpose. God must have control.

Thought for today: You cannot know God by nature; you get to know Him by an open door of grace. The way to God is the way of faith; there isn't any other way.

January 19

Trusting in God's Promises

So Abram departed as the LORD had spoken to him.
—Genesis 12:4

Scripture reading: Genesis 12:1–9

or twenty-five years, Abraham believed the promise that God would give him a son. For twenty-five years, he stood face-to-face with God on the promise, every year expecting to have a son. Sarah was becoming weaker, and Abraham's own stamina and body were becoming frailer. Natural conditions were changing both Sarah and him so that, as far as they could see, it would be humanly impossible for them to bring forth fruit. But Abraham dared not look either at Sarah or himself in that respect. He had to look at God. You cannot find anywhere that God ever failed. He wants to bring us into that blessed place of faith, changing us into a real substance of faith, until we are so like-minded that whatever we ask, we believe we receive, and our joy becomes full because we believe. I want you to see how God covered Abraham because he believed.

Hear what God said to Abraham, and then see how Abraham acted. He was among his own people and his own kindred, and God said to him, "Come out, Abraham, come out!" And Abraham obeyed and came out, not knowing where he was going. You will never go through with God in any area except by believing Him. It is "Thus says the Lord" every time, and you will see the plan of God come right through when you dare to believe. Abraham left his own country, and God was with him. Because he believed God, God overshadowed him.

When God sets His seal upon you, the Devil will not dare to break it. You know what a seal is, don't you? Now, then, when God puts His seal upon you, the Devil has no power there. He will not dare to break that seal and go through, and God puts His seal on the people who believe Him.

There are two kinds of righteousness. There is a righteousness that is according to the law, the keeping of the law, but there is a better righteousness than that. You ask, "What could be better than keeping the law?" The righteousness that sees God and obeys Him in everything is better. The righteousness that believes that every prayer uttered is going to bring the answer from God is better. There is a righteousness that is made known only to the heart that knows God. There is a side to the inner man that God can reveal only to the one who believes Him.

We have many scriptural illustrations as well as personal ones to show us how God works with those who believe Him. One of the greatest examples of all is where God worked in Abraham. There were many good points about Sarah, but she had not reached the place of trusting fully in God. She laughed and then denied having done so (Gen. 18:12, 15). Before that, when they had waited a time and she had seen that their bodies were growing frailer, she had said, "It will be just as good for you to take Hagar for a wife and bring forth a son through her." (See Genesis 16:1–2.) But that was not the seed of Abraham that God had spoken about, and that caused a great deal of trouble in the house of Abraham.

The one who walks with God can only afford to follow God's leadings, and when He leads you, it is direct and clear. The evidence is so real that every day you know that God is with you, unfolding His plan to you. It is lovely to be in the will of God.

There is a higher order than the natural man, and God wants to bring us into this higher order where we will believe Him. In the first place, God promised Abraham a son. Could a child be born into the world, except through the natural law? It was when all natural law was finished and when there was no substance in these two persons, Abraham and Sarah, that the law of the Spirit brought forth a son. It was the law of faith in the God who had promised.

Thought for today: Prayer not only changes things but also changes you. The person of prayer recognizes his great inheritance of faith.

January 20

Born of God

*As many as received Him, to them He gave the right to become
children of God...born, not of blood, nor of the will of the flesh,
nor of the will of man, but of God.*
—John 1:12–13

Scripture reading: Romans 4:8–5:2

I see before me faces I know, and I can tell that these people
are born of God (John 1:13). Sometimes I see that this
power of God within us is greater when we are weak than
when we are strong, just as this power in Abraham grew stronger
as his body grew weaker.

Looking at him, Sarah would shake her head and say, "I never
saw anybody so thin and weak and helpless in my life. No, Abraham, I have been looking at you, and you seem to be going right
down." But Abraham refused to look at his own body or Sarah's; he
believed that the promise would happen.

Suppose you come for healing. You know as well as possible
that, according to the natural life, there is no virtue in your body to
give you that health. You also know that the ailment from which
you suffer has drained your life and energy so that there is no help
at all in you, but God says that you will be healed if you believe. It
makes no difference how your body is. It was exactly the helplessness of Sarah and Abraham that brought the glorious fact that a
son was born, and I want you to see what sort of a son he was.

He was the son of Abraham. His seed is the seed of the whole
believing church—innumerable as the sands on the seashore. God
wants us to know that there is no limitation with Him, and He
wants to bring us to a place where there will be no limitation in us.
This state would be brought about by the working of the Omnipotent in the human body, working in us continually—the One who is
greater than any science or any power in the world—and bringing
us into the place to comprehend God and man.

Some of you would like a touch in your bodies; some would like
a touch in your spirit; some would like to be baptized in the Holy
Spirit; some want to be filled with all God's power. It is there for
you.

41

Now come into a position of faith. I want you to see that you can be healed if you will hear the Word. Some people want healing; maybe some need salvation; maybe others want sanctification and the baptism of the Spirit. Romans 5:2 says that it is by faith that we have access into grace. Grace is omnipotence; it is activity, benevolence, and mercy. It is truth, perfection, and God's inheritance in the soul that can believe. Grace is God. You open the door by faith, and God comes in with all you need and want. It cannot be otherwise, for it is *"of faith that it might be according to grace"* (Rom. 4:16). It cannot be by grace unless you say it will be so.

This is believing, and most people want healing by feeling. It cannot be. Some even want salvation on the same lines, and they say, "Oh, if only I could feel I was saved!" It will never come that way. So God brings you to hear the Scriptures, which can make you *"wise unto salvation"* (2 Tim. 3:15), which can open your understanding and make you so that if you will hear the truth, you will go out with what you want. Then you have power to shut the door and power to open the door to healing.

Thought for today: Three things work together. The first is faith. Faith can always bring the second thing—fact—and fact can always bring the third thing—joy.

January 21

Dare to Believe!

As it is written, "I have made you a father of many nations."
—Romans 4:17

Scripture reading: Genesis 15:3–6; 18:9–15

Here are Sarah—her body is almost dead—and Abraham—his body is almost dead. "Now," says Abraham, "God has made me a father of many nations, and there is no hope of a son according to the natural law, no hope whatever." Here God says, *"I have made you a father of many nations,"* yet Abraham has no son. During the past twenty years of waiting, conditions had grown more and more hopeless, yet the promise had been made.

How long have you believed and still suffered from some disease? How long have you been waiting for the promise, and it has not come? Did you need to wait? Look here! I want to tell you that all the people who are saved are blessed with faithful Abraham (Gal. 3:9). Abraham is the great substance of the whole keynote of Scripture; he is a man who dared for twenty-five years to believe God when everything got worse every day. I do not know anything in the Scriptures as marvelous, as far-reaching, and as full of the substance of living reality to change us if we will believe God. He will make us so different. This is a blessed incarnation of living faith that changes us and makes us know that *"[God] is, and that He is a rewarder of those who diligently seek Him"* (Heb. 11:6). God is a reality. God is true, and in Him there is no lie or *"shadow of turning"* (James 1:17). Oh, it is good! I do love to think about such truths as these.

No subject in the whole Bible makes my body aflame with passion after God and His righteousness as this one does. I see that He never fails. He wants man to believe, and then man will never fail. Oh, the loveliness of the character of God!

"A father of many nations." You talk about your infirmities—look at this! I have never felt I have had an infirmity since I understood this chapter. My cup runs over as I see the magnitude of this living God.

It is almost as if Abraham had said, "I won't look at my body. I won't look at my infirmities. I believe God will make the whole thing right." Some of us can say, "What does it matter if I have not heard for over twenty years? I believe my ears will be perfect." God is reality and wants us to know that if we will believe, it will be perfect. *"God...gives life to the dead and calls those things which do not exist as though they did"* (Rom. 4:17).

Then God tested Abraham and Sarah still further than that. Oh, it is blessed to know you are tested. It is the greatest thing in the world to be tested. Some people say, "Oh, I don't know why my lot is such a heavy one," and God puts them into the fire again. He knows how to do it. I can tell you, He is a blessed God. There is no such thing as a groan when God gets hold of you. There is no such thing as lack to those who trust the Lord. When we really get in the will of God, He can make our enemies to be at peace with us (Prov. 16:7). It is wonderful.

I wonder if you really believe that God can quicken what is dead. I have seen it many times. The more there was no hope, Abraham believed in hope. Sometimes Satan will cloud your mind and interfere with your perception so that the obscure condition is brought right in between you and God, but God is able to change the whole position if you will let Him have a chance. Turn your back on every sense of unbelief, and believe God. There are some who would like to feel the presence of the touch of God; God will bring it to you. I wish people could come to this place.

Abraham had a good time. The more he was squeezed, the more he rejoiced:

> *And not being weak in faith, he did not consider his own body, already dead (since he was about a hundred years old), and the deadness of Sarah's womb. He did not waver at the promise of God through unbelief, but was strengthened in faith, giving glory to God.* (Rom. 4:19–20)

God knows. He has a plan; He has a way. Do you dare trust Him?

Thought for today: You never know what you are made of until you are tested.

January 22

The Promise Fulfilled

Sarah conceived and bore Abraham a son in his old age,
at the set time of which God had spoken to him.
—Genesis 21:2

Scripture reading: Genesis 21:1–20

*R*ight in that house where Isaac and Ishmael lived were the seed of promise and the seed of flesh. There was strife and trouble there, for Ishmael was teasing Isaac. You will find that there is nothing that is going to hold you except the Isaac life—the seed of Abraham. You will find that the flesh life will always have to be cast out. And Sarah said, *"Cast out [Hagar] and her son"* (Gen. 21:10). It was very hard to do, but it had to be done. You may say, "How hard!" Yes, but how long did it have to be? It had to be until submission came. There will always be jealousy and strife in your hearts and lives until flesh is destroyed, until God controls and rules in authority over the whole body. When His power reigns over you, you will find that your whole life is full of peace and joy.

Isaac grew up to be a fine young man, perhaps twenty years of age—we are not told—but then came another test. God said to Abraham, "Take your son Isaac, and offer him to Me upon the mount that I will show you." (See Genesis 22:2.) Do you think that Abraham told anybody about that? No, I am sure he didn't. Isaac was near to his heart, and God said he had to offer him on the altar, and there he was—Isaac, the heart of his heart—and God said he was to be the seed of all living. What did he have to do but believe that, just as miraculously as Isaac came into the world, God could raise him even if he were slain? Did he tell Sarah about the thing? No, I am certain he did not, or else he would not have gotten away with that boy. There would have been such a trial in the home. I believe he kept it to himself. When God tells you a secret, don't tell anyone else. God will possibly tell you to go and lay hands on some sick one. Go, do it, and don't tell anyone.

I know that Satan does not know my thoughts; he only knows what I let out of my mouth. Sometimes he suggests thoughts in order to get to know my thoughts, but I can see that God can captivate my thoughts in such a way that they may be entirely for Him.

When God rules in your heart, you will see that every thought is captive, that everything is brought into obedience and is brought into a place where you are in dominion because Christ is enthroned in your life (2 Cor. 10:4–5). God reveals deep and special things to some people. Keep your counsel before God.

I see this: Abraham could offer Isaac. I believe that God wants me to tell you how so that you may know something about your trials. Some people think they are tried more than other people. Trials are used to purify you; it is the fiery furnace of affliction that God uses to get you in the place where He can use you. The person who has no trials and no difficulties is the person whom God does not dare allow Satan to touch because this person could not stand temptation. But Jesus will not allow any man to be tempted more than he is able to bear (1 Cor. 10:13). Before Abraham offered Isaac, he was tried, and God knew he could do it. Before God puts you through the furnace of afflictions, He knows you will go through.

If you know you need the baptism of the Holy Spirit, and you know it is in the Scriptures, never rest until God gives it to you. If you know it is scriptural for you to be healed of every weakness, never rest until God makes the healing yours. If you know that the Scriptures teach holiness, purity, and divine likeness—overcoming under all conditions—never rest until you are an overcomer. If you know that men who have gone in and have seen the face of God have had the vision revealed and have had all the Scriptures made to be life in their lives, never rest until you come to it.

We must live in the fire. We must hate sin; we must love righteousness. We must live with God, for He says we have to be blameless and harmless amid the crooked positions of the world (Phil. 2:15). I look at you now, and I say God is able to confirm all I have been saying about trials and testings, which are the greatest blessings you can have.

What a redemption! What a baptism! What an anointing! It is ecstasies of delight beyond all expression for the soul to live and move in Him who is our being (Acts 17:28).

Thought for today: If you knew the value of trials, you would praise God for them more than for anything.

The Master's Touch

Do all things without complaining and disputing,
that you may become blameless and harmless, children of God
without fault in the midst of a crooked and perverse generation,
among whom you shine as lights in the world.
—Philippians 2:14–15

Scripture reading: James 1:16–27

I see many remarkable things in the life of Stephen. One thing moves me, and that is the truth that I must live by the power of the Spirit at all costs. God wants us to be like Stephen: *"full of faith and the Holy Spirit"* (Acts 6:5). You can never be the same again after you have received this wonderful baptism in the Holy Spirit. It is important that we should be full of wisdom and faith day by day and full of the Holy Spirit, acting by the power of the Holy Spirit. God has set us here in the last days, these days of apostasy, and wants us to be burning and shining lights in the midst of an indecent generation. God is longing for us to come into such a fruitful position as the children of God, with the marks of heaven upon us and with His divinity bursting through our humanity, that He can express Himself through our lips of clay. He can take clay lips and weak humanity and make an oracle for Himself of such things. He can take frail human nature and by His divine power make our bodies suitable to be His holy temple, washing our hearts whiter than snow.

Our Lord Jesus says, *"All authority has been given to Me in heaven and on earth"* (Matt. 28:18). He longs that we would be filled with faith and with the Holy Spirit, and He declares to us, *"He who believes in Me, the works that I do he will do also; and greater works than these he will do, because I go to My Father"* (John 14:12). He has gone to the Father. He is in the place of power, and He exercises His power not only in heaven but also on earth, for He has all power on earth as well as in heaven. Hallelujah! What an open door to us if we will only believe Him!

The disciples were men after our standard as far as the flesh goes. God sent them forth, joined to the Lord and identified with Him. How diverse Peter, John, and Thomas were! Impulsive Peter was always ready to go forth without a stop. John, the beloved, leaned on the Master's breast (John 21:20). Thomas had a hard nature and defiant spirit: *"Unless I...put my finger into the print of the nails, and put my hand into His side, I will not believe"* (John 20:25). What strange flesh! How peculiar they were! But the Master could mold them. There was no touch like His.

Under His touch, even stony-hearted Thomas believed. Oh, my God, how You have had to manage some of us! Have we not been strange and very peculiar? But when God's hand comes upon us, He can speak to us in such a way; He can give us a word or a look, and we are broken. Has He spoken to you? I thank God for His speaking. Behind all of His dealings, we see the love of God for us. He sees our bitter tears and our weeping night after night. There is none like Him. He knows; He forgives. We cannot forgive ourselves; we oftentimes would give the world to forget, but we cannot. The Devil won't let us forget. But God has forgiven and forgotten. Do you believe self or the Devil or God? Which are you going to believe? Believe God. I know the past is under the blood of Christ and that God has forgiven and forgotten, for when He forgives, He forgets. Praise the Lord! Hallelujah! We are baptized to believe and to receive.

Thought for today: It is not what we are that counts, but what we can be as He disciplines, chastens, and transforms us by His all-skillful hands.

Full of Faith and Power

Stephen, full of faith and power, did great wonders and signs.
—Acts 6:8

Scripture reading: Luke 4:1–19

*I*n the early days of the church, all who did the work of serving had to be full of the Holy Spirit. The greatest qualification for ministry is to be filled with the Spirit.

Stephen was a man *"full of faith and the Holy Spirit"* (Acts 6:5). God so manifested Himself in Stephen's body that he became an epistle of truth, known and read by all. He was full of faith! Such men never talk doubtfully. You never hear them say, "I wish it could be so," or "If it is God's will." They have no *ifs;* they know. You never hear them say, "Well, it is not always so." They say, "It is sure to be." They laugh at impossibilities and cry, "It will be done!" They shout while the walls are up and when they come down. God has this faith for us in Christ. We must be careful that no unbelief and no wavering are found in us.

"Stephen, full of faith and power, did great wonders and signs among the people" (Acts 6:8). The Holy Spirit could do mighty things through him because he believed God, and God is with the man who dares to believe His Word. All things were possible because of the Holy Spirit's position in Stephen's body. Because Stephen was full of the Holy Spirit, God could fulfill His purposes through him. When a child of God is filled with the Holy Spirit, the Spirit *"makes intercession for the saints according to the will of God"* (Rom. 8:27). He fills us with longings and desires until we are in a place of fervency like a glowing fire. When we do not know what to do, the Holy Spirit begins to work. When the Holy Spirit has liberty in the body, He conveys all prayers into the presence of God. Such prayers are always heard. Such praying is always answered; it is never bare of result. When we are praying in the Holy Spirit, faith is evident, and as a result the power of God can be manifested in our midst.

When some of the various synagogues arose to dispute with Stephen, *"they were not able to resist the wisdom and the Spirit by which he spoke"* (Acts 6:10). When we are filled with the Holy Spirit, we will have wisdom.

Thought for today: A man full of faith hopes against hope.

January 25

The Power of the Spirit

And they were all filled with the Holy Spirit.
—Acts 2:4

Scripture reading: Acts 2:1–21

One night I was entrusted with a meeting, and I was guarding my position before God. I wanted approval from the Lord. I saw that God wants men full of the Holy Spirit, with divine ability, filled with life, a flaming fire. In the meeting a young man stood up. He was a pitiful object with a face full of sorrow. I said, "What is it, young man?"

He said he was unable to work, and he could scarcely walk. He said, "I am so helpless. I have tuberculosis and a weak heart, and my body is full of pain."

I said, "I will pray for you." I said to the people, "As I pray for this young man, you look at his face and see it change."

As I prayed, his face changed. I said to him, "Go out, run a mile, and come back to the meeting."

He came back and said, "I can now breathe freely."

The meetings were continuing, and I missed him. After a few days, I saw him again in a meeting. I said, "Young man, tell the people what God has done for you."

"Oh," he said, "I have been able to work and make money."

Praise God, this wonderful stream of salvation never runs dry. You can take a drink; it is close to you. It is a river that is running deep, and there is plenty for all.

In a meeting, a man rose and said, "Will you touch me? I am in a terrible situation. I have a large family, but because of an accident in the pit, I have had no work for two years. I cannot open my hands." I was full of sorrow for this poor man, and something happened that had never happened before. We are in the infancy of this wonderful outpouring of the Holy Spirit, and there is so much more for us. I put out my hand, and before my hands reached his, he was loosed and made perfectly free.

I see that Stephen, full of faith and of power, did great wonders and miracles among the people. This same Holy Spirit can fill you, too, and then right things will be accomplished. God will grant it. God is ready to touch and transform you right now.

Once a woman rose in the meeting asking for prayer. I prayed for her, and she was healed. She cried out, "It is a miracle! It is a miracle! It is a miracle!" That is what God wants to do for us all the time. As surely as we get free in the Holy Spirit, something will happen. Let us pursue the best things, and let God have His right-of-way.

May the Lord open our eyes to see Him and to know that He is deeply interested in all that concerns us. He is *"touched with the feeling of our infirmities"* (Heb. 4:15 KJV).

All things are naked and open to the eyes of Him with whom we are connected (v. 13). He knows about that asthma. He knows about that rheumatism. He knows about that pain in the back, head, or feet. He wants to loose every captive and to set you free just as He has set me free. I hardly know that I have a body today. I am free from every human ailment, absolutely free. Christ has redeemed us. He has power over all the power of the Enemy and has worked out our great victory. Will you have it? It is yours; it is a perfect redemption.

It is God's desire to make us a new creation, with all the old things passed away and all things within us truly of God; to bring in a new, divine order, a perfect love and an unlimited faith. (See 2 Corinthians 5:17.) Will you accept God's plan for you? Redemption is free. Arise in the activity of faith, and God will heal you as you rise. Only believe, and receive in faith. Stephen, full of faith and of the Holy Spirit, did great signs and wonders (Acts 6:8). May God bless this passage and fill us full of His Holy Spirit. Through the power of the Holy Spirit, may He reveal Christ in us more and more.

The Spirit of God will always reveal the Lord Jesus Christ. Serve Him; love Him; be filled with Him. It is lovely to hear Him as He makes Himself known to us. He is the same yesterday, today, and forever (Heb. 13:8). He is willing to fill us with the Holy Spirit and faith just as He filled Stephen.

Thought for today: We may be very ordinary, but God wants to make us extraordinary in the Holy Spirit.

God's Word Is Sure

Whoever says to this mountain, "Be removed and be cast into the sea," and does not doubt in his heart, but believes that those things he says will be done, he will have whatever he says. Therefore I say to you, whatever things you ask when you pray, believe that you receive them, and you will have them.
—Mark 11:23–24

Scripture reading: Mark 10:13–31

These are days when we need to have our faith strengthened, when we need to know God. God has designed that the just will live by faith (Rom. 1:17), no matter how they may be fettered. I know that God's Word is sufficient. One word from Him can change a nation. His Word is *"from everlasting to everlasting"* (Ps. 90:2). It is through the entrance of this everlasting Word, this incorruptible seed, that we are born again and come into this wonderful salvation. *"Man shall not live by bread alone, but by every word that proceeds from the mouth of God"* (Matt. 4:4). This is the food of faith. *"Faith comes by hearing, and hearing by the word of God"* (Rom. 10:17).

Everywhere people are trying to discredit the Bible and remove its miracles. One preacher says, "Well, you know, Jesus arranged beforehand to have that colt tied where it was and for the men to say just what they did." (See Matthew 21:2–3.) I tell you, God can arrange everything. He can plan for you, and when He plans for you, all is peace. All things are possible if you will believe.

Another preacher says, "It was an easy thing for Jesus to feed the people with five loaves. The loaves were so big in those days that it was a simple matter to cut them into a thousand pieces each." (See John 6:5–13.) But he forgets that one little boy brought those five loaves all the way in his lunch basket. There is nothing impossible with God.

Thought for today: All the impossibility is with us when we measure God by the limitations of our unbelief.

Reaching Out in Faith

*Jesus said to him, "If you can believe,
all things are possible to him who believes."*
—Mark 9:23

Scripture reading: Mark 9:1–29

We have a wonderful God, a God whose ways are *"past finding out"* (Rom. 11:33) and whose grace and power are limitless.

I was in Belfast one day and saw one of the brothers of the assembly. He said to me, "Wigglesworth, I am troubled. I have had a good deal of sorrow during the past five months. I had a woman in my church who could always pray the blessing of heaven down on our meetings. She is an old woman, but her presence is always an inspiration. Five months ago she fell and broke her leg. The doctors put it into a cast, but when they removed the cast, the bones were not properly set, and she fell and broke the leg again."

He took me to her house, and there was a woman lying in a bed on the right-hand side of the room. I said to her, "Well, what about it now?"

She said, "They have sent me home incurable. The doctors say that I am so old that my bones won't knit. There is no strength in my bones. They could not do anything for me, and they say I will have to lie in bed for the rest of my life."

I said to her, "Can you believe God?"

She replied, "Yes, ever since I heard that you had come to Belfast, my faith has been quickened. If you will pray, I will believe. I know there is no power on earth that can make the bones of my leg knit, but I know that nothing impossible with God."

I said, "Do you believe He will meet you now?"

She answered, "I do."

It is grand to see people believe God. God knew all about this leg and that it was broken in two places. I said to the woman, "When I pray, something will happen."

Her husband was sitting there; he had been in his chair for four years and could not walk a step. He called out, "I don't believe. I won't believe. You will never get me to believe."

I said, "All right," and laid my hands on his wife in the name of the Lord Jesus.

The moment hands were laid upon her, she cried out, "I'm healed."

I said, "I'm not going to assist you to rise. God will do it all." She arose and walked up and down the room, praising God.

The old man was amazed at what had happened to his wife, and he cried out, "Make me walk, make me walk."

I said to him, "You old sinner, repent."

He cried out, "Lord, You know I believe."

I don't think he meant what he said; anyhow the Lord was full of compassion. If He marked our sins, where would any of us be? If we will meet the conditions, God will always meet us if we believe all things are possible.

I laid my hands on him, and the power went right through the old man's body. For the first time in four years, those legs received power to carry his body. He walked up and down and in and out of the room. He said, "Oh, what great things God has done for us tonight!"

Did you believe before you were saved? So many people want to be saved, but they want to feel saved first. There never was a man who felt saved before he believed. God's plan is always the following: if you will believe, you will see the glory of God (John 11:40). I believe God wants to bring us all to a definite place of unswerving faith and confidence in Himself.

In our text from Mark, Jesus uses the illustration of a mountain. Why does He say a mountain? If faith can remove a mountain, it can remove anything. The plan of God is so marvelous that if you will only believe, all things are possible (Mark 9:23).

Thought for today: Desire God, and you will have desires from God.

Love Has No Doubts

Whoever...does not doubt in his heart,
but believes..., he will have whatever he says.
—Mark 11:23

Scripture reading: James 1:2–15

*I*magine a young man and woman who have fallen in love. In a short while, there is a strong love for each other. What is a heart of love? It is a heart of faith. Faith and love are kin. In the measure that the young man and young woman love one another, they are true. One may go North and the other South, but because of their love, they will be faithful to one another.

It is the same when there is a deep love toward the Lord Jesus Christ. In this new life into which God has brought us, Paul told us that we *"have become dead to the law through the body of Christ, that* [we] *may be married to another; to Him who was raised from the dead"* (Rom. 7:4). God brings us into a place of perfect love and perfect faith. A person who is born of God is brought into a loyalty to the Lord Jesus that shrinks from anything impure. You see the purity of a man and woman when there is a deep natural affection between them; they disdain the very thought of either of them being untrue. In the same way, in the measure that a person has faith in Jesus, he is pure.

We cannot doubt in our hearts. As we read His Word and believe the promises that He has so graciously given to us, we are made partakers of His very essence and life. The Lord is made a Bridegroom to us, and we are His bride. His words to us are spirit and life (John 6:63), transforming us and changing us, expelling what is natural and bringing in what is divine.

It is impossible to comprehend the love of God as we think in human terms. We must have a revelation from the Spirit of God. It was the love of God that brought Jesus, and it is this same love that helps you and me to believe. God will be your strength in every weakness. You who need His touch, remember that He loves you. If you are helpless or sick, look to the God of all grace, whose very essence is love, who delights to give liberally all life and strength and power that you need.

Thought for today: As we have heart fellowship with our Lord, our faith cannot be daunted.

January 29

Be Cleansed Today

*If you bring your gift to the altar, and there remember that your
brother has something against you, leave your gift there before the
altar, and go your way. First be reconciled to your brother, and then
come and offer your gift.*
—Matthew 5:23–24

Scripture reading: Matthew 5:13–26

When I was in Switzerland, the Lord was graciously working and healing many of the people. I was staying with
Brother Reuss of Goldiwil, and two policemen were sent
to arrest me. The charge was that I was healing the people without
a license. Mr. Reuss said to them, "I am sorry that he is not here
just now; he is holding a meeting about two miles away, but before
you arrest him I would like to show you something."

Brother Reuss took these two policemen down to one of the
lower parts of that district, to a house with which they were famil-
iar, for they had often gone to that place to arrest a certain woman
who was constantly an inmate of the prison because of continually
being engaged in drunken brawls. He took them to this woman and
said to them, "This is one of the many cases of blessing that have
come through the ministry of the man you have come to arrest.
This woman came to our meeting in a drunken condition. Her body
was broken, for she was ruptured in two places. While she was
drunk, the evangelist laid his hands on her and asked God to heal
her and deliver her."

The woman joined in, "Yes, and God saved me, and I have not
tasted a drop of liquor since."

The policemen had a warrant for my arrest, but they said with
disgust, "Let the doctors do this kind of thing." They turned and
went away, and that was the last we heard from them.

We have a Jesus who heals the brokenhearted, who lets the
captives go free (Isa. 61:1), who saves the very worst. Do you dare
spurn this glorious Gospel of God for spirit, soul, and body? Do you
dare spurn this grace? I realize that this full Gospel has in great
measure been hidden, this Gospel that brings liberty, this Gospel
that brings souls out of bondage, this Gospel that brings perfect
health to the body, this Gospel of entire salvation. Listen again to

the words of Him who left heaven to bring us this great salvation: *"Assuredly, I say to you, whoever says to this mountain, 'Be removed'...he will have whatever he says"* (Mark 11:23). Whatever he says!

I realize that God can never bless us when we are being hard-hearted, critical, or unforgiving. These things will hinder faith quicker than anything. I remember being at a meeting where there were some people waiting for the baptism and seeking to be cleansed, for the moment a person is cleansed the Spirit will fall. There was one man with red eyes who was weeping bitterly. He said to me, "I will have to leave. It is no good my staying unless I change things. I have written a letter to my brother-in-law and filled it with hard words, and this thing must first be straightened out." He went home and told his wife, "I'm going to write a letter to your brother and ask him to forgive me for writing to him the way I did."

"You fool!" she said.

"Never mind," he replied, "this thing is between God and me, and it has got to be cleared away." He wrote the letter, came again to the meeting, and immediately God filled him with the Spirit.

I believe a great many people want to be healed, but they are harboring things in their hearts that are like a blight. Let these things go. Forgive, and the Lord will forgive you. There are many good people, people who mean well, but they have no power to do anything for God. Some little thing came in their hearts years ago, and their faith has been paralyzed ever since. Bring everything to the light. God will sweep it all away if you will let Him. Let the precious blood of Christ cleanse you from all sin. If you will only believe, God will meet you and bring into your lives the sunshine of His love.

Thought for today: Always be in tune with God, and then the music will come out as sweetly as possible.

The Blessing of the Lord's Supper

*This cup is the new covenant in My blood. This do,
as often as you drink it, in remembrance of Me.*
—1 Corinthians 11:25

Scripture reading: Luke 22:7–39

No service is so wonderful to me as the service of partaking in the Lord's Supper, the Holy Communion. I would love to see the saints gather together at every meeting in order to remember Christ's death, His resurrection, and His ascension. What a thought that Jesus Himself instituted this glorious memorial for us. Oh, that God would let us see that it is *"as often"* as we do it. It is not weekly, not monthly, not quarterly, but *"as often"* as we do it. What a blessed remembrance it is to know that He took away our sins.

I am sure that every Christian has a great desire to do something for Jesus, and what He wants us to do is to keep in remembrance the cross, the grave, the Resurrection, and the Ascension; the memory of these four events will always bring us into a place of great blessing. You do not need, however, to continually live on the cross, or even in remembrance of the cross, but what you need to remember about the cross is, *"It is finished"* (John 19:30). You do not need to live in the grave, but only keep in remembrance that *"He is risen"* (Matt. 28:6) out of the grave and that we are to be seated *"with Him in glory"* (Col. 3:4).

The institution of the Lord's Supper is one of those settings in Scripture, a time in the history of our Lord Jesus Christ, when the mystery of the glories of Christ was being unveiled. As the Master walked on this earth, the multitudes would gather with eagerness and longing in their hearts to hear the words that dropped from His gracious lips. But there were also those who had missed the vision. They saw the Christ, heard His words, but those wonderful words were like idle tales to them.

When we miss the vision and do not come into the fullness of the ministry of the Spirit, there is a reason. Beloved, there is a deadness in us that must have the resurrection touch. Today we have the unveiled truth, for the dispensation of the Holy Spirit has come to unfold the fullness of redemption so that we might be clothed with power. What brings us into the state where God can pour His blessing upon us is a broken spirit and a contrite heart (Ps. 51:17). We need to examine ourselves to see what state we are in, whether we are just religious or whether we are truly in Christ.

The human spirit, when perfectly united with the Holy Spirit, has but one place, and that is death, death, and deeper death. In this place, the human spirit will cease to desire to have its own way, and instead of "My will," the cry of the heart will be, "May Your will, O Lord, be done in me."

Thought for today: Jesus is interceding for us to keep us right, holy, ready, mighty, and filled with Himself so that we might bring the fragrance of heaven to the world's needs.

A Living Epistle

You are our epistle written in our hearts, known and read
by all men; clearly you are an epistle of Christ.
—2 Corinthians 3:2–3

Scripture reading: Matthew 8:14–27

*E*very believer should be a living epistle of the Word, one who is read and known by all. Your very presence should bring such a witness of the Spirit that everyone with whom you come in contact will know that you are a sent one, a light in the world, a manifestation of Christ, a biblical Christian.

Jesus' disciples had to learn that whatever He said must come to pass. Jesus said—very slowly and thoughtfully, I believe—the following:

> *Behold, when you have entered the city, a man will meet you carrying a pitcher of water; follow him into the house which he enters. Then you shall say to the master of the house, "The Teacher says to you, 'Where is the guest room where I may eat the Passover with My disciples?'"* (Luke 22:10–11)

Beloved, let me say this, there was no person in Palestine who had ever seen a man bearing a pitcher of water. It is an unknown thing. Therefore, we find Jesus beginning with a prophecy that brought that inward knowledge to them that what He said must come to pass. This is the secret of the Master's life: prophecy that never failed. There is no power that can change the Word of God. Jesus was working out this great thought in the hearts of His disciples so that they might know that what He said would come to pass. After Jesus had given that wonderful command to Peter and John, those disciples were walking into the city, no doubt in deep meditation, when suddenly they cried out in amazement, "Look! There he is! Just as the Master has said."

When I was in Jerusalem, I was preaching on Mount Olivet, and as I looked down to my right I saw where the two ways met, where the donkey was tied. I could see the Dead Sea, and while I was preaching, I saw at least 150 women going down with pitchers and then carrying them back on their heads, full of water. But I did not see one man. However, Jesus said that it had to be a man, and so it was, for no one could change His word.

Some have said to me that He had it all arranged for a man to carry a pitcher of water. I want to tell you that God does not have to arrange with mortals to carry out His plans. God has the power to hear the cry of some poor needy child of His who may be suffering in England, Africa, China, or anywhere else, saying, "O God, You know my need." And in New York, Germany, California, or some other place, there is a disciple of His on his knees, and the Lord will say to him, "Send help to that brother or sister, and do not delay." And the help comes. He did not need to arrange for a man to help Him out by carrying a pitcher of water. He works according to His Word, and Jesus said a man would carry water.

What did those disciples do as they saw the man? Did they go forward to meet him? No, they waited for the man, and when he came up, they probably walked alongside of him without a word until he was about to enter the house. Then I can hear one saying to him, "Please, sir, the Master wants the guest chamber!" "The guest chamber? Why, I was preparing it all day yesterday but did not know whom it was for." With man things are impossible, but God is the unfolder of the mysteries of life and holds the universe in the hollow of His hand. What we need to know now is that *"the LORD thy God in the midst of thee is mighty"* (Zeph. 3:17 KJV), and He works according to His Word.

Thought for today: We need a faith that leaps into the will of God and says, "Amen!"

February 1

Faith and Remembrance

*The word which they heard did not profit them, not being mixed
with faith in those who heard it.*
—Hebrews 4:2

Scripture reading: Psalm 119:41–50; Luke 22:15–20

he words of Jesus are life—never think they are less. If you
believe them, you will feel quickened. The Word is powerful;
it is full of faith. The Word of God is vital. Faith is established and made manifest as we hear the Word. Beloved, read the
Word of God in quietude, and read it out loud, for *"he who hears
My word"* (John 5:24), to him it gives life.

Listen to these words from Scripture: *"With fervent desire I
have desired to eat this Passover with you before I suffer"* (Luke
22:15); *"The hour has come; behold, the Son of Man is being betrayed into the hands of sinners"* (Mark 14:41). From the beginning
of time, there has never been an hour like this. These words were
among the greatest that Jesus ever spoke: *"The hour has come."*

Time was finished and eternity had begun for every soul that
was covered with the blood. Until that hour, all people lived only to
die, but the moment the sacrifice was made, it was not the end but
only the beginning. The soul, covered with the blood, has moved
from a natural to an eternal union with the Lord. Instead of death
will be the fullness of life divine.

While I was in Jerusalem, I preached many weeks outside the
Damascus Gate, and God mightily blessed my ministry. It is wonderful to be in the place where God can use you. As I was leaving
Jerusalem, some Jews who had heard me preach wanted to travel
with me and stay at the same hotel where I was staying. When we
were sitting around the table eating, they said, "What we cannot
understand is that when you preach we feel such power. You move
us. There is something about it; we cannot help but feel that you
have something different from what we have been used to hearing.
What is it?"

I replied that it was because I preached Jesus in the power of
the Holy Spirit, for He was the Messiah, and He causes a child of
His to live in the reality of a clear knowledge of Himself so that
others know and feel His power. It is this knowledge that the
church today needs so much.

Do not be satisfied with anything less than the knowledge of a real change in your nature, the knowledge of the indwelling presence and power of the Holy Spirit. Do not be satisfied with a life that is not wholly swallowed up in God.

There are many books written about the Word, and we love clear, definite teaching on it. But go to the Book, and listen to what the Master says. You will lay a sure foundation that cannot be moved, for we are born again by the incorruptible Word of God (1 Pet. 1:23). We need the simplicity, the rest of faith, that brings us to the place where we are steadfast and immovable. How wonderful the living Word of God is!

Can you not see that the Master was so interested in you that He would despise the shame of the cross (Heb. 12:2)? The judgment hall was nothing to Him; all the rebukes and scorn could not take from Him the joy of saving you and me. His sacrificial love and joy caused Him to say, "I consider nothing too vile to endure on behalf of Wigglesworth; I count nothing too horrid to bear for Brown; My soul is on the wing to save the world!" How beautiful this is! How it should thrill us! He knew that death was represented in that sacred cup, yet He joyfully said, *"With fervent desire I have desired to eat this Passover with you before I suffer"* (Luke 22:15). Take the bread, drink of the cup, and as often as you take it, remember (1 Cor. 11:24–25). In other words, take the memory of what it means home with you; think on it, and analyze its meaning.

As we come to the time of the breaking of bread, the thought should be, "How should I partake of it?" We should be able to say, "Lord, I desire to eat it to please You, for I want my whole life to be for You!" As the stream of the new life begins to flow through your being, allow yourself to be immersed and carried on until your life becomes a ceaseless flow of the river of life. Then it will be *"No longer I who live...but Christ lives in me"* (Gal. 2:20). Get ready for the breaking of bread and for partaking of the wine, and in doing so, remember Him.

Thought for today: We are no better than our faith.

The Living Word

Man shall not live by bread alone, but by every word of God.
—Luke 4:4

Scripture reading: Luke 8:5–15

God's Word is:
    Supernatural in origin.
    Eternal in duration.
    Inexpressible in valor.
    Infinite in scope.
    Regenerative in power.
    Infallible in authority.
    Universal in application.
    Inspired in totality.

We should:
    Read it through.
    Write it down.
    Pray it in.
    Work it out.
    Pass it on.

The Word of God changes a person until he becomes an epistle of God (2 Cor. 3:3). The Word transforms the mind, changes the character, and gives us an inheritance in the Spirit, until we are conformed—God coming in, dwelling in us, walking and talking through us. There is no God like our God.

God is love. *"He who abides in love abides in God"* (1 John 4:16). God wants to take ordinary men and bring them into extraordinary conditions. God has room for the thirsty man who is crying out for more of Himself. It is not what we are, but it is what God wants us to be. Beloved, let us rededicate ourselves afresh to God!

Thought for today: God has promised to fulfill, fill full, the desire of those who fear Him.

February 3

A Living Faith

Whatever things you ask when you pray, believe that
you receive them, and you will have them.
—Mark 11:24

Scripture reading: Matthew 17:14–21

What will it be like when we get rid of this body of flesh? In the meantime, God means for us to put on the whole armor of God (Eph. 6:11) while we are here. He wants us to be covered with the covering of His Spirit and to grow in grace and the knowledge of God (2 Pet. 3:18).

Oh, what God has laid up for us, and what we may receive through the name of Jesus! Oh, the value of the name, the power of the name; the very name of Jesus brings help from heaven and can bind evil powers and *"subdue all things to Himself"* (Phil 3:21). Thank God for victory through our Lord Jesus Christ.

For the sake of saving us, Jesus *"endured the cross, despising the shame"* (Heb. 12:2). How beautiful it is to say with our whole will, "I will be obedient to God." He is lovely; He is beautiful. I do not remember Him ever denying me anything when I have come to Him; He has never turned me away empty. He is such a wonderful Savior, such a Friend that we can depend upon with assurance, rest, and complete confidence. He can roll away every burden.

Think of Him as the exhaustless Savior, the everlasting Friend, One who knows all things, One who is able to help and deliver us. When we have such a Source as this, we can stretch out our hands and take all that we need from Him.

We may think we have faith in God, but we must not doubt in our hearts. Faith is an inward operation of the divine power that dwells in the contrite heart and can lay hold of things not seen. Faith is a divine act; faith is God in the soul. God operates by His Son and transforms the natural into the supernatural.

Faith is active, never dormant. Faith lays hold; faith is the hand of God; faith is the power of God. Faith never fears; faith lives amid the greatest conflict; faith moves even things that cannot be moved. God fills us with His divine power, and sin is dethroned. *"The just shall live by faith"* (Rom. 1:17). You cannot live by faith until you are just and righteous. You cannot live by faith if you are unholy or dishonest.

65

In order to understand His fullness, we must be filled with the Holy Spirit. God has a measure for us that cannot be measured. When you are in this relationship, sin is dethroned, but you cannot purify yourself. It is by the blood of Jesus Christ, God's Son, that you are cleansed from all sin. We are His life; we are members of His body. The Spirit is in us, and there is no way to abide in the secret place of the Lord except by holiness.

Be filled with the Word of God. Listen, those of you who have stiff knees and stiff arms today, you can get a tonic by the Word of God that will loosen your joints and will divide even your joints and marrow (Heb. 4:12).

One of the greatest things in the Word of God is that it discerns the thoughts and intentions of the heart. Oh, that you may allow the Word of God to have perfect victory in your bodies so that they may be tingling through and through with God's divine power! Divine life does not belong to this world but to the kingdom of heaven, and the kingdom of heaven is within you (Luke 17:21).

God wants to purify our minds until we can bear all things, believe all things, hope all things, and endure all things (1 Cor. 13:7). God dwells in you, but you cannot have this divine power until you live and walk in the Holy Spirit, until the power of the new life is greater than the old life.

God wants us to move mountains. Sometimes things appear as though they cannot be moved, but you can believe in your heart and stand on the Word of God, and God's Word will never be defeated. First, believe that you get them, and then you will have them. That is the difficulty with people. They say, "Well, if I could feel I had it, I would know I had it." But you must believe it, and then the feeling will come. You must believe it because of the Word of God.

Thought for today: Anything that appears to be like a mountain can be moved: the mountains of difficulty, the mountains of perplexity, the mountains of depression or depravity—things that have bound you for years.

Victory through Faith

Increase our faith.
—Luke 17:5

Scripture reading: Luke 18:1–14

*I*nactivity must be brought to a place of victory. Inactivity—what wavers, what hesitates, what fears instead of having faith—closes up everything, because it doubts instead of believes in God. What is faith? Faith is the living principle of the Word of God. It is life; it produces life; it changes life. How great our faith should be, for we cannot be saved except by faith. We cannot be kept except by faith. We can only be baptized by faith, and we will be caught up by faith; therefore, faith in the living God is a blessed reality.

All the wonderful things that Jesus did were done so that people might be changed and made like Him. Oh, to be like Him in thought, act, and plan! He went about His Father's business and was eaten up with the zeal of His house (Ps. 69:9). I am beginning to understand 1 John 3:2: *"Beloved, now we are children of God; and it has not yet been revealed what we shall be, but we know that when He is revealed, we shall be like Him, for we shall see Him as He is."* As I feed on the Word of God, my whole body will be changed by the process of the power of the Son of God.

The Lord dwells in a humble and contrite heart and makes His way into the dry places, so if you open up to Him, He will flood you with His life. You can never cleanse sin; you can never purify sin; you can never be strong if in sin; you will never have a vision while in sin. Revelation stops when sin comes in. The human spirit must come to an end, but the Spirit of Christ must be alive and active. You must die to the human spirit, and then God will quicken your mortal body and make it alive (Rom. 8:11). Without holiness no man will see God (Heb. 12:14).

Thought for today: A little bit of sin will spoil a whole life.

The Substance of Faith

For in [the gospel of Christ] *the righteousness of God is revealed from faith to faith; as it is written, "The just shall live by faith."*
—Romans 1:17

Scripture reading: Romans 1:5–20

What is faith? It is the very nature of God. Faith is the Word of God. It is the personal inward flow of divine favor, which moves in every fiber of our being until our whole nature is so quickened that we live by faith, we move by faith, and we are going to be caught up to glory by faith! Faith is the glorious knowledge of a personal presence within you, changing you from strength to strength, from glory to glory, until you get to the place where you walk with God, and God thinks and speaks through you by the power of the Holy Spirit. Oh, it is grand; it is glorious!

God wants us to have far more than what we can handle and see, and so He speaks of *"the substance of things hoped for, the evidence of things not seen"* (Heb. 11:1). With the eye of faith, we may see the blessing in all its beauty and grandeur. God's Word is *"from everlasting to everlasting"* (Ps. 90:2), and *"faith is the substance"* (Heb. 11:1).

If I would give some woman a piece of cloth, scissors, needle, and thread, she could produce a garment. Why? Because she had the material. If I would provide some man with wood, a saw, a hammer, and nails, he could produce a box. Why? Because he had the material. But God, without material, spoke the Word and produced this world with all its beauty. There was no material there, but the Word of God called it into being by His creative force. With the knowledge that you are born again by this incorruptible Word, which lives and abides forever (1 Pet. 1:23), you know that within you is this living, definite hope, greater than yourself, more powerful than any dynamic force in the world, for faith works in you by the power of the new creation of God in Christ Jesus.

Therefore, with the audacity of faith, we should throw ourselves into the omnipotence of God's divine plan, for God has said to us, *"If you can believe, all things are possible to him who believes"* (Mark 9:23). It is possible for the power of God to be so manifest in your human life that you will never be as you were before; you will be always going forward from victory to victory, for faith knows no defeat.

The Word of God will bring you into a wonderful place of rest in faith. God intends for you to have a clear conception of what faith is, how faith came, and how it remains. Faith is in the divine plan, for it brings you to the open door so that you might enter in. You must have an open door, for you cannot open the door. It is God who does it, but He wants you to be ready to step in and claim His promises of all the divine manifestations of power in the name of Christ Jesus. It is only then that you will be able to meet and conquer the enemy, for *"He who is in you is greater than he who is in the world"* (1 John 4:4).

Living faith brings glorious power and personality; it gives divine ability, for it is by faith that Christ is manifested in your mortal flesh by the Word of God. I do not want you to miss the knowledge that you have heard from God, and I want you to realize that God has changed you so that all weakness, fear, inability—everything that has made you a failure—has passed away.

Thought for today: Faith has power to make you what God wants you to be; only you must be ready to step into the plan and believe His Word.

A Triumphant Position

For by [faith] *the elders obtained a good testimony.*
—Hebrews 11:2

Scripture reading: Hebrews 11:1–13

*T*he first manifestation of God's plan was the cross of Calvary. You may refuse it; You may resist it; but God, who loves you *"with an everlasting love"* (Jer. 31:3), has followed you through life and will follow you with His great grace, so that He may bring you to a knowledge of this great salvation.

God, in His own plan for your eternal good, may have brought something into your life that is distasteful, something that is causing you to feel desperate or to feel that your life is worthless. What does it mean? It means that the Spirit of God is showing you your own weakness so that you might cry out to Him, and when you do, He will show you the cross of redemption. Then God will give you faith to believe, for faith is the gift of God.

God, who has given us this faith, has a wonderful plan for our lives. Do you remember when God brought you to this place of salvation, how the faith He gave you brought a great desire to do something for Him, and then He showed you that wonderful open door? I was saved over sixty-seven years ago, and I have never lost the witness of the Spirit. If you will not allow your human nature to crush your faith and interfere with God's plan in its wonderful divine setting, you will mount up like the eagles (Isa. 40:31). Oh, the wonderful effectiveness of God's perfect plan working in us with the divine Trinity flowing through humanity, changing our very nature to the extent that we cannot disbelieve but must act faith, talk faith, and in faith sing praises to the Lord! There is no room for anything that is not faith, for we have passed beyond the natural plane into a new atmosphere where God encloses us.

Faith is an increasing position, always triumphant. It is not a place of poverty but of wealth. If you always live in fruitfulness, you will always have plenty. What does it say in our text? *"The elders obtained a good testimony."* The man who lives in faith always has a good testimony. The Acts of the Apostles were written because the lives of the apostles bore the fruit of active faith. To them, faith was an everyday fact. If your life is in the divine order, you will not only have a living, active faith, but also a faith that builds up others.

What is the good of preaching without faith? God intends that we should live in this glorious sphere of the power of God so that we will always be in a position to tell people of the act that brought the fact. What is the good of praying for the sick without faith? You must believe that God will not deny Himself, for the Word of God cannot be denied. I believe this message is given in divine order so that you may no longer be in a place of doubt but will realize that *"faith is the substance"* (Heb. 11:1). Beloved, even with all the faith we have, we are not even so much as touching the hem of God's plan for us. It is like going to the seashore and dipping your toe in the water, with the great vast ocean before you. God wants us to rise on the crest of the tide and not keep paddling along the shore. Oh, to be connected with that sublime power, so that human nature may know God and the glory of the manifestation of Christ!

The Word of God is eternal and cannot be broken. You cannot improve on the Word of God, for it is life, and it produces life. Listen! God has begotten you to *"a living hope"* (1 Pet. 1:3). You are born again of the Word that created worlds. If you dare to believe, such belief is powerful. God wants us to be powerful, a people of faith, a purified people, a people who will launch out in God and dare to trust Him in glorious faith, which always takes us beyond what is commonplace to an abiding place in God.

Thought for today: You must act before you can see the fact.

February 7

Faith Is a Sure Foundation

Where is your faith?
—Luke 8:25

Scripture reading: Luke 8:21–39

*T*he Word of God is not only wonderful, but also powerful. Any natural condition can be changed by the Word of God, which is a supernatural power. In the Word of God is the breath, the nature, and the power of the living God, and His power works in every person who dares to believe His Word. There is life through the power of it, and as we receive the Word of faith, we receive the nature of God Himself.

It is as we lay hold of God's promises in simple faith that we become partakers of the divine nature. As we receive the Word of God, we come right into touch with a living force, a power that changes nature into grace, a power that makes dead things live, and a power that is of God, that will be manifested in our flesh. This power has come forth with its glory to transform us by divine acts into sons of God, to make us like the Son of God, by the Spirit of God who moves us on from grace to grace and from glory to glory as our faith rests in this living Word.

It is important that we have a foundational truth, something greater than ourselves, on which to rest. In Hebrews 12:2 we read, *"Looking unto Jesus, the author and finisher of our faith."* Jesus is our life, and He is the power of our life. We see in the fifth chapter of Acts that as soon as Peter was let out of prison, the Word of God came: *"Go...speak...all the words of this life"* (Acts 5:20).

There is only one Book that has life. In this Word we find Him who came that we might have life and have it more abundantly (John 10:10), and by faith this life is imparted to us. When we come into this life by divine faith—and we must realize that it is by grace we are saved through faith, and that it is not of ourselves but *"is the gift of God"* (Eph. 2:8)—we become partakers of this life. This Word is greater than anything else. There is no darkness in it at all. Anyone who dwells in this Word is able under all circumstances to say that he is willing to come to the light so that his deeds may be seen (John 3:21). But outside of the Word is darkness, and the manifestations of darkness will never desire to come to the light

72

because their deeds are evil. But the moment we are saved by the power of the Word of God, we love the light and the truth. The inexpressible divine power, force, passion, and fire that we receive are of God. Drink, my beloved, drink deeply of this Source of life.

"Faith is the substance of things hoped for" (Heb. 11:1). Someone said to me one day, "I would not believe in anything I could not handle and see." Everything you can handle and see is temporary and will perish with the using. But the things not seen are eternal and will not fade away. Are you dealing with tangible things or with the things that are eternal, that are facts, that are made real to faith? Thank God that through the knowledge of the truth of the Son of God, I have within me a greater power, a mightier working, an inward impact of life, of power, of vision, and of truth more real than anyone can know who lives in the realm of the tangible.

Thought for today: God manifests Himself to the person who dares to believe.

February 8

Divine Authority

*Put on the whole armor of God, that you may be able to stand
against the wiles of the devil.*
—Ephesians 6:11

Scripture reading: Ephesians 6:10–18

I am more and more convinced every day I live that very few who are saved by the grace of God have a right conception of how great their authority is over darkness, demons, death, and every power of the Enemy. It is a real joy when we realize our inheritance.

I was speaking like this one day, and someone said, "I have never heard anything like this before. How many months did it take you to think up that sermon?"

I said, "My brother, God pressed my wife from time to time to get me to preach, and I promised her I would preach. I used to labor hard for a week to think something up, then give out the text and sit down and say, 'I am done.' Oh, brother, I have given up thinking things up. They all come down. And the sermons that come down, stop down, then go back, because the Word of God says His Word will not return to Him void (Isa. 55:11). If you get anything up in your own power, it will not stay up very long; when it goes down, it will take you down with it."

The sons of God are made manifest in this present earth to destroy the power of the Devil. To be saved by the power of God is to be brought from the realm of the ordinary into the extraordinary, from the natural into the divine.

Do you remember the day when the Lord laid His hands on you? You say, "I could not do anything except praise the Lord." Well, that was only the beginning. Where are you today? The divine plan is that you increase until you receive the measureless fullness of God. You do not have to say, "I tell you it was wonderful when I was baptized with the Holy Spirit." If you have to look back to the past to make me know you are baptized, then you are backslidden.

If the beginning was good, it ought to be better day by day, until everybody is fully convinced that you are filled with the might of God in the Spirit, *"filled with all the fullness of God"* (Eph. 3:19). *"Do not*

74

be drunk with wine, in which is dissipation; but be filled with the Spirit" (Eph. 5:18). I don't want anything other than being full and fuller and fuller, until I am overflowing like a great big vat. Do you realize that if you have been created anew and born again by the Word of God that there is within you the word of power and the same light and life as the Son of God Himself had?

God wants to flow through you with measureless power of divine utterance and grace until your whole body is a flame of fire. So many people have been baptized with the Holy Spirit; there was a movement, but they have become monuments, and you cannot move them. God, wake us out of sleep lest we should become indifferent to the glorious truth and the breath of Your almighty power. We must be the light and salt of the earth (Matt. 5:13–14), with the whole armor of God upon us (Eph. 6:11). It would be a serious thing if the enemies were about and we had to go back and get our shoes. It would be a serious thing if we had on no breastplate.

How can we be furnished with the armor? Take it by faith. Jump in, stop in, and never come out, for this is a baptism to be lost in, where you only know one thing and that is the desire of God at all times. The baptism in the Spirit should be an ever increasing endowment of power, an ever increasing enlargement of grace. Oh, Father, grant us a real look into the glorious liberty You have designed for the children of God, who are delivered from this present world, separated, sanctified, and made suitable for Your use, whom You have designed to be filled with all Your fullness.

Thought for today: God intends each soul in Pentecost to be a live wire—not a monument, but a movement.

February 9

Just Believe

If you can believe, all things are possible to him who believes.
—Mark 9:23

Scripture reading: Mark 9:17–29

Nothing has hurt me so much as seeing so-called believers have so much unbelief in them. Suppose that all the people in the world did not believe; that would make no difference to God's Word; it would be the same. You cannot alter God's Word. It is *"from everlasting to everlasting"* (Ps. 90:2).

I was preaching on faith one time, and a man in the audience said three times, "I won't believe." I kept right on preaching because that made no difference to me. I am prepared for a fight any day, the fight of faith. We must keep the faith that has been committed to us. I went on preaching, and the man shouted out, "I won't believe." As he left, he cried out again, "I won't believe."

Later, a message came saying that as soon as he got outside, the Spirit said to him, "You will be mute because you did not believe." It was the same Spirit that came to Zacharias and said, *"You will be mute and not able to speak until the day these things take place, because you did not believe my words"* (Luke 1:20).

I believe in a hell. Who is in hell? Unbelievers. Thank God they are there, for they are no good for any society. I said to the leader of that meeting, "You go and see this man and find out if these things are so."

He went to the house, and the first to greet him was the man's wife. He said, "Is it true that your husband declared three times in the meeting that he would not believe and now he cannot speak?"

She burst into tears and said, "Go and see." He went into the room and saw the man's mouth in a terrible state. The man got a piece of paper and wrote, "I had an opportunity to believe. I refused to believe, and now I cannot believe and cannot speak." The greatest sin in the world is to disbelieve God's Word. We are not of those who draw back, but we are of those who believe (Heb. 10:39); for God's Word is a living Word, and it always acts.

Thought for today: If you want to go to hell, all you need to do is to disbelieve the Word of God.

February 10

A Divine Touch

[The Lord] *heals all your diseases.*
—Psalm 103:3

Scripture reading: Psalm 103

One day a stylishly dressed lady came to our meeting and on up to the platform. Under her arm, going down underneath her dress, was a crutch that nobody could see. She had been helpless in one leg for twenty years, had heard of what God was doing, and wanted to be prayed for. As soon as we prayed for her, she exclaimed, "What have you done with my leg?" Three times she said it, and then we saw that the crutch was loose and hanging and that she was standing straight up.

The lady who was interpreting for me said to her, "We have done nothing with your leg. If anything has been done, it is God who has done it."

She answered, "I have been lame and used a crutch for twenty years, but my leg is perfect now." We did not suggest that she kneel at the altar and thank God; she fell down among the others and cried for mercy. I find that when God touches us, it is a divine touch of life and power; it thrills and quickens the body so that people know it is God. Then conviction comes, and they cry for mercy.

God heals by the power of His Word. But the most important thing is, Are you saved? Do you know the Lord? Are you prepared to meet God? You may be an invalid as long as you live, but you may be saved by the power of God. You may have a strong, healthy body but may go straight to hell because you know nothing of the grace of God and salvation. Thank God I was saved in a moment, the moment I believed, and God will do the same for you.

God means by this divine power within you to make you follow after the mind of the Spirit by the Word of God until you are entirely changed by the power of it. You might say, "Wigglesworth, is there anything you can look up to God and ask Him for in your body?" I will say now that I have a body in perfect condition and have nothing to ask for, and I am sixty-five. It was not always so. This body was a frail, helpless body, but God fulfilled His Word to me: He took my infirmities and my sicknesses, and by His stripes I am healed (Matt. 8:17; Isa. 53:5).

It is wonderful to go here and there and not even notice that you have a body because it is not a hindrance to you. He took our infirmities. He bore our sickness; He came to heal our broken-heartedness. Jesus wants us to come forth in divine likeness, in resurrection force, in the power of the Spirit, to walk in faith and understand His Word. That is what He meant when He said He would give us power over all the power of the Enemy. He will subdue all things until everything comes into perfect harmony with His will. Is He reigning over your affections, desires, and will? If so, when He reigns, you will be subject to His reigning power. He will be the authority over the whole situation. When He reigns, everything must be subservient to His divine plan and will for us.

See what the Word of God says, *"No one can say that Jesus is Lord except by the Holy Spirit"* (1 Cor. 12:3). *"Lord!"* Bless God forever. Oh, for Him to be Lord and Master! For Him to rule and control! For Him to be filling your whole body with the plan of truth! Because you are in Christ Jesus, all things are subject to Him. It is lovely, and God wants to make it so to you. When you get there, you will find divine power continually working. I absolutely believe that no person comes into the place of revelation and activity of the gifts of the Spirit except by this fulfilled promise of Jesus that He will baptize us in the Holy Spirit.

Thought for today: Praise God for anything that brings people to the throne of grace.

God Knows and Can Heal

Jesus went about all the cities and villages, teaching in their synagogues, preaching the gospel of the kingdom, and healing every sickness and every disease among the people.
—Matthew 9:35

Scripture reading: Psalm 147

I was taken to see a beautiful nine-year-old boy who was lying on a bed. The mother and father were distraught because he had been lying there for months. They had to lift and feed him; he was like a statue with flashing eyes. As soon as I entered the place, the Lord revealed to me the cause of the trouble, so I said to the mother, "The Lord shows me there is something wrong with his stomach."

She said, "Oh no, we have had two physicians, and they say it is paralysis of the mind."

I said, "God reveals to me it is his stomach."

"Oh, no, it isn't. These physicians ought to know, they have X-rayed him."

The gentleman who brought me there said to the mother, "You have sent for this man; you have been the means of his coming; now don't you stand out against him. This man knows what he has got to do."

But Dr. Jesus knows more than that. He knows everything. All you have to do is call for Jesus, and He will come. Divine things are so much better than human things. Who will interfere with the divine mind of the Spirit that has all revelation, that understands the whole condition of life? The Word of God declares He knows all things (1 John 3:20) and is well acquainted with the manifestation of our bodies, for everything is naked and open before Him to whom we must give account (Heb. 4:13). Having the mind of the Spirit, we understand what the will of God is. I prayed over this boy and laid my hands on his stomach. He became sick, vomited a worm thirteen inches long, and was perfectly restored.

Thought for today: When will we come into the knowledge of God? When we cease from our own minds and allow ourselves to become clothed with the mind and authority of the mighty God.

February 12

Unbelief Hinders God's Power

*Now He did not do many mighty works there
because of their unbelief.*
—Matthew 13:58

Scripture reading: Hebrews 3:8–19

The Spirit of God wants us to understand there is nothing that can interfere with our coming into perfect blessing except unbelief. Unbelief is a terrible hindrance. As soon as we are willing to allow the Holy Spirit to have His way, we will find that great things will happen all the time. But oh, how much of our own human reason we have to get rid of, how much human planning we have to become divorced from. What would happen right now if everybody believed God? I love the thought that God the Holy Spirit wants to emphasize the truth that if we will only yield ourselves to the divine plan, He is right there to bring forth the mystery of truth.

How many of us believe the Word? It is easy to quote it, but it is more important to have it than to quote it. It is very easy for me to quote, *"Now we are children of God"* (1 John 3:2), but it is more important for me to know whether I am a son of God. When the Son was on the earth, He was recognized by the people who heard Him. *"No man ever spoke like [Him]"* (John 7:46). His word was with power, and that word came to pass. Sometimes you have quoted, *"He who is in you is greater than he who is in the world"* (1 John 4:4), and you could tell just where to find the verse. But brother, is it so? Can demons remain in your presence? You have to be greater than demons. Can disease lodge in the body that you touch? You have to be greater than the disease. Do we dare stand on the Word of God and face the facts of the difficulties before us?

"Faith is the substance of things hoped for" (Heb. 11:1). Faith is the Word. You were begotten of the Word; the Word is in you; the life of the Son is in you; and God wants you to believe.

Thought for today: Can anything in the world stand against you and hold its place if it is a fact that He who is in you is greater than he who is in the world?

February 13

No Defeat with God

This is the victory that has overcome the world; our faith.
—1 John 5:4

Scripture reading: Romans 10:4–17

I was called to Halifax, England, to pray for a lady missionary. I found that it was an urgent call. I could see there was an absence of faith, and I could see there was death.

I said to the woman, "How are you?"

In a very weak tone of voice she said, "I have faith."

"Faith? Why are you dying? Brother Walshaw, is she dying?"

"Yes."

To a friend standing by, "Is she dying?"

"Yes."

Now I believe there is something in a heart that is against defeat, and this is the faith that God has given to us. I said to her, "In the name of Jesus, now believe, and you'll live." She said, "I believe," and God sent life from her head to her feet. They dressed her, and she lived.

The Bible says, *"Have faith"* (Mark 11:22). It isn't just *saying* you have faith. It is *believing* in your heart. It is grasping the promises of the eternal God. *"This is the victory that has overcome the world; our faith."* He who believes overcomes the world. *"Faith comes by hearing, and hearing by the word of God"* (Rom. 10:17). He who believes in his heart—can you imagine anything easier than that? He who believes in his heart! No one who believes in his heart can live according to the world. He dies to everything worldly. He who loves the world is not of God. You can measure the whole thing and examine yourself to see if you have faith. Faith enables you to lay hold of what is and to get it out of the way for God to bring in something that is not.

Just before I left for home I was in Norway. A woman wrote to me from England saying she had been operated on for cancer three years before but that it was now coming back. She was living in constant dread of the whole thing, since the operation was so painful. She asked if it would it possible to see me when I returned to England. I wrote that I would be passing through London on the twentieth of June. If she would like to meet me at the hotel, I would pray for her.

81

When I met this woman, I saw that she was in great pain, and I have great sympathy for people who have tried to get relief and have failed. I saw how distressed she was. She came to me in a mournful spirit, and her whole face was downcast. I said to her, "There are two things that are going to happen today. One is that you are to know that you are saved."

"Oh, if I could only know I was saved," she said.

"There is another thing. You have to go out of this hotel without a pain, without a trace of the cancer."

Then I began with the Word—oh, this wonderful Word! We do not have to go up to bring Him down; nor do we have to go down to bring Him up (Rom. 10:6–7). *"'The word is near you, in your mouth and in your heart' (that is, the word of faith which we preach)"* (v. 8). I said, "Believe that He took your sins when He died on the cross. Believe that when He was buried, it was for you. Believe that when He arose, it was for you. And now He is sitting at God's right hand for you. If you can believe in your heart and confess with your mouth, you will be saved."

She looked at me saying, "Oh, it is going all through my body. I know I am saved now. If He comes today, I'll go to heaven. How I have dreaded the thought of His coming all my life! But if He comes today, I know I will be ready."

The first thing was finished. Now for the second. I laid my hands upon her in the name of Jesus, believing in my heart that I could say what I wanted and it would be done. I said, "In the name of Jesus, I cast this out."

She jumped up. "Two things have happened," she said. "I am saved, and now the cancer is gone."

> Faith will stand amid the wrecks of time,
> Faith unto eternal glories climb;
> Only count the promise true,
> And the Lord will stand by you.
> Faith will win the victory every time!

Thought for today: Faith is God in the human vessel.

The Way to Overcome

*Who is he who overcomes the world, but he who believes
that Jesus is the Son of God?*
—1 John 5:5

Scripture reading: 1 John 5

The greatest weakness in the world is unbelief. The greatest power is the faith that works by love. Love, mercy, and grace are bound eternally to faith. Fear is the opposite of faith, but *"there is no fear in love"* (1 John 4:18). Those whose hearts are filled with a divine faith and love have no question in their hearts as to being caught up when Jesus comes.

The world is filled with fear, torment, remorse, and brokenness, but faith and love are sure to overcome. God has established the earth and humanity on the lines of faith. As you come into line, fear is cast out, the Word of God comes into operation, and you find bedrock. All the promises are *"Yes"* and *"Amen"* to those who believe (2 Cor. 1:20).

When you have faith in Christ, the love of God is so real that you feel you could do anything for Jesus. Whoever believes, loves. *"We love Him because He first loved us"* (1 John 4:19). When did He love us? When we were in the mire. What did He say? *"Your sins are forgiven you"* (Luke 5:20). Why did He say it? Because He loved us. What for? That He might bring many sons into glory (Heb. 2:10). What was His purpose? That we might be with Him forever.

The whole pathway is an education for this high vocation and calling. How glorious this hidden mystery of love is! For our sins there is the double blessing. *"Whatever is born of God overcomes the world. And this is the victory...our faith"* (1 John 5:4). To believe is to overcome.

I am heir to all the promises because I believe. It is a great heritage. I overcome because I believe the truth, and the truth makes me free (John 8:32). Christ is the root and source of our faith, and because He is in our faith, what we believe for will come to pass. There is no wavering. This is the principle: he who believes is definite. A definite faith brings a definite experience and a definite utterance.

There is no limit to the power God will cause to come upon those who cry to Him in faith, for God is rich to all who will call upon Him. Stake your claim for your children, your families, your coworkers, so that many sons may be brought to glory. As your prayer rests upon the simple principle of faith, nothing will be impossible for you.

The root principle of all this divine overcoming faith in the human heart is Christ, and when you are grafted deeply into Him, you may win millions of lives to the faith. Jesus is the Way, the Truth, and the Life (John 14:6). He is the answer to every hard problem in your heart.

"Love has been perfected among us in this: that we may have boldness in the day of judgment; because as He is, so are we in this world" (1 John 4:17). *"Everyone who has this hope in Him purifies himself"* (1 John 3:3). God confirms this faith in us so that we may be refined in the world, *"not having spot or wrinkle or any such thing"* (Eph. 5:27).

It is the Lord who purifies and brings us to the place where the fire burns up the dross, and there He anoints us with fresh oil, so that at all times we may be ready for His appearing. God is separating us for Himself, just as He separated Enoch for a walk with Himself. Because of a divinely implanted faith, he could testify before his translation that he pleased God (Heb. 11:5). As the Day of the Lord hastens on, we, too, need to walk by faith until we overcome all things. By our simple belief in Jesus Christ, we walk right into glory.

Thought for today: Being more than overcomers is to have a shout at the end of the fight.

February 15

Only Believe

Do not be afraid; only believe.
—Mark 5:36

Scripture reading: Galatians 5:16–6:10

I want you to be full of enough joy to fill a deep well. If you have to make it happen, there is something wrong. If God makes it happen, there is always something right.

I have thought a great deal about momentum. When a train has arrived at a certain place, some people get out, but some go on to the end of the line. Let us go far enough. There is only one thing to do: stay fully aware and always be pressing on. It will not do to trust in the past. Let us go forward. When it comes to the power of momentum, the past will not do. We must have an inflow of the life of God manifested.

> Only believe, only believe,
> All things are possible, only believe.

The importance of that chorus is found in the word *only*. When you can get rid of yourself and everything else you rely on and have *only* God behind you, then you have reached a place of great reinforcement. If you help yourself—in the measure you help yourself—you will find that the life of God and the power of God are diminished.

Many people try to help themselves. What God wants is for us to cling to Him absolutely and entirely. This is the grand plan that God has for us: *"Only believe."* If we believe, we will have absolute rest and perfect submission.

Conditions on God's side are always beyond your asking or thinking. The conditions on your side cannot reach the other side unless you come into a place where you can rest on the omnipotent plan of God; then His plan cannot fail to be successful. *"Only believe"* and you will have absolute rest and perfect tranquillity. You can then say, "God has said it, and it cannot fail." All His promises are *"Yes"* and *"Amen"* to those who believe (2 Cor. 1:20).

Thought for today: Allow God to take absolute charge of the whole situation.

February 16

Like Precious Faith

*To those who have obtained like precious faith with us by the
righteousness of our God and Savior Jesus Christ: Grace and peace
be multiplied to you in the knowledge of God and of Jesus our Lord.*
—2 Peter 1:1–2

Scripture reading: 2 Peter 1:1–11

We are often so dull of comprehension because we let the
cares of this world blind our eyes, but if we can be open to
God, we will see that He has a greater plan for us in the
future than we have ever seen or dreamed of in the past. It is God's
delight to make possible to us what seems impossible, and when we
reach a place where He alone has the right-of-way, then all the
things that have been obscured and misunderstood are clarified.

This *"like precious faith"* that Peter was writing about is a gift
that God is willing to give to all of us, and I believe God wants us to
receive it so that we may subdue kingdoms, work righteousness,
and, if need be, stop the mouths of lions (Heb. 11:33). We should be
able to triumph under all circumstances, not because we have confidence in ourselves, but because our confidence is only in God. It is
always those people who are full of faith who have a good report,
who never murmur, who are in the place of victory, who are not in
the place of human order but of divine order, since God has come to
dwell in them.

The Lord Jesus is the Divine Author and brings into our
minds the "Thus says the Lord" every time. We cannot have anything in our lives, except when we have a "Thus says the Lord" for
it. We must see to it that the Word of God is always the standard of
everything.

This *"like precious faith"* is for us all, but there may be some
hindrances in your life that God will have to deal with. At one point
in my life, it seemed as if I had had so much pressure come into my
life that I would break like a potter's vessel. There is no other way
into the deep things of God except through a broken spirit (Ps.
51:17). There is no other way into the power of God. God will do for
us exceedingly abundantly above all we ask or think (Eph. 3:20)
when He can bring us to the place where we can say with Paul, "I

live no longer" (see Galatians 2:20), and Another, even Christ, has taken the reins and the rule.

We are no better than our faith. He who believes that Jesus is the Son of God overcomes the world (1 John 5:5). How? This Jesus, upon whom your faith is placed—the power of His name, His personality, His life, His righteousness—is made yours through faith. As you believe in Him and set your hope only on Him, you are purified even as He is pure. You are strengthened because He in whom you trust is strong. You are made whole because He who is all your confidence is whole. You may receive of His fullness, all the untold fullness of Christ, as your faith rests wholly in Him.

I understand God by His Word. I cannot understand God by impressions or feelings. I cannot get to know God by sentiments. If I am going to know God, I am going to know Him by His Word. I know I will be in heaven, but I cannot determine from my feelings that I am going to heaven. I am going to heaven because God's Word says it, and I believe God's Word. And *"faith comes by hearing, and hearing by the word of God"* (Rom. 10:17).

Thought for today: Whatever your estimation is of your ability, or your righteousness, you are no better than your faith.

February 17

God's Real Working

*I myself always strive to have a conscience without offense
toward God and men.*
—Acts 24:16

Scripture reading: 1 Corinthians 2

One thing that can hinder our faith is a conscience that is seared. In contrast, there is a conscience that is so open to the presence of God that the smallest thing in the world will drive it to God. When we can come into the presence of God with clear consciences and genuine faith, our hearts not condemning us, then we have confidence toward God (1 John 3:21), *"and whatever we ask we receive from Him"* (v. 22).

Sugarcoating won't do. We must have reality, the real working of our God. We must know God. We must be able to go in and converse with God. We must also know the mind of God toward us, so that all our petitions are always in line with His will.

As this *"like precious faith"* (2 Pet. 1:1) becomes a part of you, it will make you so that you will dare to do anything. And remember, God wants daring followers: people who will risk all, who will be strong in Him and willing to do exploits. How will we reach this place of faith? Give up your own mind. Let go of your own thoughts, and take the thoughts of God, the Word of God. If you build yourself on imaginations, you will go wrong. You have the Word of God, and it is enough.

A man gave this remarkable testimony concerning the Word: "Never compare this Book with other books. Comparisons are dangerous. Never think or say that this Book contains the Word of God. It *is* the Word of God. It is supernatural in origin, eternal in duration, inexpressible in value, infinite in scope, regenerative in power, infallible in authority, universal in interest, personal in application, inspired in totality. Read it through. Write it down. Pray it in. Work it out. Then pass it on."

Thought for today: We need a conscience that does not allow one thing to come into and stay in our lives to break up our fellowship with God and shatter our faith in Him.

February 18

The Power of His Name

Therefore God also has highly exalted Him and given Him
the name which is above every name,
that at the name of Jesus every knee should bow.
—Philippians 2:9–10

Scripture reading: Philippians 2:1–13

There is power to overcome everything in the world through the name of Jesus. *"There is no other name under heaven given among men by which we must be saved"* (Acts 4:12).

Six people went into the house of a sick man to pray for him. He was a leader in the Episcopal Church, and he lay in his bed utterly helpless. He had read a little tract about healing and had heard about people praying for the sick. So he sent for these friends, who, he thought, could pray *"the prayer of faith"* (James 5:15). He was anointed according to James 5:14, but because he had no immediate manifestation of healing, he wept bitterly. The six people walked out of the room, somewhat crestfallen to see the man lying there in an unchanged condition.

When they were outside, one of the six said, "There is one thing we could have done. I wish you would all go back with me and try it." They all went back and got together in a group. This brother said, "Let us whisper the name of Jesus." At first, when they whispered this worthy name, nothing seemed to happen. But as they continued to whisper "Jesus! Jesus! Jesus!" the power began to fall. As they saw that God was beginning to work, their faith and joy increased, and they spoke the name louder and louder. As they did so, the man rose from his bed and dressed himself. The secret was just this: those six people had gotten their eyes off the sick man and were taken up with the Lord Jesus Himself. Their faith grasped the power in His name. Oh, if people would only appreciate the power in His name, there is no telling what would happen.

Thought for today: Through the name of Jesus and through the power of His name, we have access to God.

Raising Lazarus
Part One

The LORD will guide you continually.
—Isaiah 58:11

Scripture reading: Isaiah 58:1–14

One day while in Wales, I went up onto a mountain to pray. As I spent the day in the presence of the Lord, His wonderful power seemed to envelop and saturate me.

Two years before this time, two young men from Wales had come to our house. They were just ordinary lads, but they became very zealous for God. They came to our mission and saw some of the works of God. They said to me, "We would not be surprised if the Lord brings you down to Wales to raise our Lazarus." They explained that the leader of their church was a man who had spent his days working in a tin mine and his nights preaching; the result was that he had collapsed and contracted tuberculosis. For four years he had been a helpless invalid, having to be fed by others.

As I was on the mountaintop that day, the Lord said to me, "I want you to go and raise Lazarus." I told the brother who had accompanied me about this word from the Lord, and when we got down to the valley, I wrote a postcard. It read, "When I was up on the mountain praying today, God told me that I was to go and raise Lazarus." When we arrived at the place, we went to the man to whom I had addressed the postcard. He looked at me and asked, "Did you send this?" "Yes," I replied. He said, "Do you think we believe in this? Here, take it." And he threw the card at me.

The man called a servant and said, "Take this man and show him Lazarus." Then he said to me, "The moment you see him, you will be ready to go home. Nothing will keep you here." Everything he said was true from a human standpoint. The man was helpless. He was nothing but a mass of bones with skin stretched over them. There was no life to be seen. Everything in him spoke of decay.

I said to him, "Will you shout? You remember that at Jericho the people shouted while the walls were still up. God has a similar victory for you if you will only believe." But I could not get him to believe. There was not an atom of faith there.

It is a blessed thing to learn that God's Word can never fail. Never listen to human plans. God can work mightily when you persist in believing Him in spite of discouragement from the human standpoint. When I got back to the man to whom I had sent the postcard, he asked, "Are you ready to go now?" I replied, "I am not moved by what I see. I am moved only by what I believe. I know this: no man looks at the circumstances or relies on his feelings if he believes. The man who believes God has his request."

There were difficult conditions in that Welsh village, and it seemed impossible to get the people to believe. "Ready to go home?" I was asked. But a man and a woman there asked us to come and stay with them. I said to the people, "I want to know how many of you people can pray." No one wanted to pray. I asked if I could get seven people to pray for the poor man's deliverance. I said to the two people we were to stay with, "I will count on you two, and there is my friend and myself. We need three others." I told the people that I trusted that some of them would awaken to their privilege and come in the morning and join us in prayer for the raising of Lazarus.

Thought for today: It will never do to give way to human opinions. If God says a thing, you have to believe it.

February 20

Raising Lazarus
Part Two

The LORD will guide you continually.
—Isaiah 58:11

Scripture reading: Isaiah 59:1–2, 16–21

I told the people that I would not eat anything that night. When I got to bed, it seemed as if the Devil tried to place on me everything that he had placed on that poor man on the sickbed. When I awoke in the middle of the night, I had a cough and all the weakness of a man with tuberculosis. I rolled out of bed onto the floor and cried out to God to deliver me from the power of the Devil. I shouted loud enough to wake everybody in the house, but nobody was disturbed. God gave the victory, and I got back into bed again as free as I had ever been in my life. At five o'clock the Lord awakened me and said, "Don't break bread until you break it around My table." At six o'clock He gave me these words: *"And I will raise him up"* (John 6:40). I elbowed the fellow who was sleeping in the same room. He said, "Ugh!" I elbowed him again and said, "Do you hear? The Lord says that He will raise him up."

At eight o'clock they said to me, "Have a little refreshment." But I have found prayer and fasting the greatest joy, and you will always find it so when you are led by God. When we went to the house where Lazarus lived, there were eight of us altogether. No one can prove to me that God does not always answer prayer. He always does more than that. He gives *"exceedingly abundantly above all that we ask or think"* (Eph. 3:20).

I will never forget how the power of God fell on us as we went into that sick man's room. As we made a circle around the bed, I got one brother to hold the sick man's hand on one side, and I held the other, and we each held the hand of the person next to us. I said, "We are not going to pray; we are just going to use the name of Jesus." We all knelt down and whispered that one word, "Jesus! Jesus! Jesus!" The power of God fell, and then it lifted. Five times the power of God fell, and then it remained. But the man in the bed was unmoved. Two years previously, someone had come along and had tried to raise him up, and the Devil had used his lack of success as a means of discouraging Lazarus. I said, "I don't care what the Devil says. If God says He will raise you up, it must be so. Forget everything else except what God says about Jesus."

A sixth time the power fell, and the sick man's lips began moving, and the tears began to fall. I said to him, "The power of God is here; it is yours to accept." He said, "I have been bitter in my heart, and I know I have grieved the Spirit of God. Here I am, helpless. I cannot raise my hands or even lift a spoon to my mouth." I said, "Repent, and God will hear you." He repented and cried out, "O God, let this be to Your glory." As he said these words, the power of the Lord went right through him.

I have asked the Lord to let me never tell this story except the way it happened, for I realize that God can never bless exaggerations. As we again said, "Jesus! Jesus! Jesus!" the bed shook, and the man shook. I said to the people who were with me, "You can all go downstairs now. This is all God. I'm not going to assist him." I sat and watched that man get up and dress himself. We sang the doxology as he walked down the steps. I said to him, "Now tell what has happened."

It was soon told everywhere that Lazarus had been raised up. People came from all over to see him and to hear his testimony. God brought salvation to many. Right out in the open air, this man told what God had done, and as a result, many were convicted and converted. All this occurred through the name of Jesus, *"through faith in His name"* (Acts 3:16). Yes, the faith that comes by believing in Jesus gave this sick man perfect soundness in the presence of them all.

Thought for today: The living God has chosen us for His divine inheritance, and it is He who is preparing us for our ministry, so that it may be of God and not of man.

February 21

A Lame Man Healed

Silver and gold I do not have, but what I do have I give you: In the name of Jesus Christ of Nazareth, rise up and walk.
—Acts 3:6

Scripture reading: Acts 3:1–16

*P*eter and John were helpless and uneducated. They had no college education; they had only some training in fishing. But they had been with Jesus. To them had come a wonderful revelation of the power of the name of Jesus. They had handed out the bread and fish after Jesus had multiplied them. They had sat at the table with Him, and John had often gazed into His face. Jesus often had had to rebuke Peter, but He had manifested His love to him through it all. Yes, He loved Peter, the wayward one. Oh, He's a loving Savior! I have been wayward and stubborn. I had an unmanageable temper at one time, but how patient He has been. I am here to tell you that there is power in Jesus and in His wondrous name to transform anyone, to heal anyone.

If only you will see Him as God's Lamb, as God's beloved Son, upon whom was laid *"the iniquity of us all"* (Isa. 53:6). If only you will see that Jesus paid the whole price for our redemption so that we might be free. Then you can enter into your purchased inheritance of salvation, of life, and of power.

Poor Peter and John! They had no money. I don't think there are many who are as poor as Peter and John were. But they had faith; they had the power of the Holy Spirit; they had God. You can have God even though you have nothing else. Even if you have lost your character, you can have God. I have seen the worst men saved by the power of God.

Thought for today: He will lead you into nothingness, but when you are in nothingness, you will be in power. He will lead you into weakness, but when you are in weakness, God will be with you in might. Everything that seems weak from a human perspective will be under the control of divine power.

February 22

Changed by the Power of Jesus

They brought to Him many who were demon-possessed. And He cast out the spirits with a word, and healed all who were sick, that it might be fulfilled which was spoken by Isaiah the prophet, saying: "He Himself took our infirmities and bore our sicknesses."
—Matthew 8:16–17

Scripture reading: 2 Corinthians 3

I was preaching one day about the name of Jesus, and there was a man leaning against a lamppost, listening. He needed the lamppost to enable him to stay on his feet. I asked him, "Are you sick?" He showed me his hand, and I saw that inside his coat he had a silver-handled dagger. He told me that he had been on his way to kill his unfaithful wife but that he had heard me speaking about the power of the name of Jesus and could not get away. He said that he felt helpless. I said, "Kneel down." There on the square, with people passing back and forth, he got saved.

I took him to my home and clothed him with a new suit. I saw something in that man that God could use. He said to me the next morning, "God has revealed Jesus to me. I see that all has been laid upon Jesus." I lent him some money, and he soon got together a wonderful little home. His faithless wife was living with another man, but he invited her back to the home that he had prepared for her. She came. Where enmity and hatred had been before, the whole situation was transformed by love. God made that man a minister wherever he went. Everywhere there is power in the name of Jesus. God can *"save to the uttermost"* (Heb. 7:25).

Another miraculous healing took place in Stockholm. There was a home for incurables there, and one of the patients was brought to the meeting. He had palsy and was shaking all over. In front of three thousand people, he came to the platform, supported by two others. The power of God fell on him as I anointed him in the name of Jesus. The moment I touched him, he dropped his crutch and began to walk in the name of Jesus. He walked around that great building in view of all the people.

Thought for today: There is nothing that our God cannot do. He will do everything if you will dare to believe.

95

Come to Jesus

I am willing; be cleansed.
—Matthew 8:3

Scripture reading: Mark 1:28–45

*T*oday there are many needy, afflicted people, but I do not think most of them are half as bad as this first case that we read of in Matthew 8. This man was a leper. You may be suffering from tuberculosis, cancer, or other things, but God will show forth His perfect cleansing, His perfect healing, if you have a living faith in Christ. He is a wonderful Jesus.

This leper must have been told about Jesus. So much is missed because people are not constantly telling what Jesus will do in our day. Probably someone had come to that leper and said, "Jesus can heal you." So he was filled with expectation as he saw the Lord coming down the mountainside. Lepers were not allowed to come within reach of people; they were shut out as unclean. Ordinarily, it would have been very difficult for him to get near because of the crowd that surrounded Jesus. But as Jesus came down from the mountain, He met the leper; He came to the leper.

There was no help for him, humanly speaking, but nothing is too hard for Jesus. The man cried, *"Lord, if You are willing, You can make me clean"* (Matt. 8:2). Was Jesus willing? You will find that He is always more willing to work than we are to give Him an opportunity to work. The trouble is that we do not come to Him; we do not ask Him for what He is more than willing to give.

If you are definite with Him, you will never go away disappointed. Divine life will flow into you, and instantaneously you will be delivered. Jesus is just the same today, and He says to you, *"I am willing; be cleansed."* He has an overflowing cup for you, a fullness of life. He will meet you in your absolute helplessness. All things are possible if you will only believe (Mark 9:23). God has a real plan. It is very simple: come to Jesus. You will find Him just the same as He was in days of old (Heb. 13:8).

Thought for today: You will never find Jesus missing an opportunity to do good.

February 24

The Power of Jesus' Words

Only speak a word, and my servant will be healed.
—Matthew 8:8

Scripture reading: Matthew 8:5–13

A centurion came to Jesus, pleading on behalf of his servant, who was paralyzed and dreadfully tormented. This Roman officer was so earnest that he came seeking Jesus. Notice this certainty: there is no such thing as seeking without finding. *"He who seeks finds"* (Matt. 7:8). Listen to the gracious words of Jesus: *"I will come and heal him"* (Matt. 8:7).

In most places where I go, there are many people for whom I cannot pray. In some places there are two or three hundred people who would like me to visit them, but I am not able to do so. Yet I am glad that the Lord Jesus is always willing to come and heal. He longs to help the sick ones. He loves to heal them of their afflictions. The Lord is healing many people today by means of handkerchiefs, even as He did in the days of Paul. (See Acts 19:11–12.)

A woman came to me in the city of Liverpool and said, "I would like you to help me by joining me in prayer. My husband is a drunkard and every night comes into the home under the influence of alcohol. Won't you join me in prayer for him?" I asked the woman, "Do you have a handkerchief?" She took out a handkerchief, and I prayed over it and told her to lay it on the pillow of the drunken man. He came home that night and laid his head on the pillow in which this handkerchief was tucked. He laid his head on more than the pillow that night, for he laid his head on the promise of God. In Mark 11:24, we read, *"Whatever things you ask when you pray, believe that you receive them, and you will have them."*

The next morning the man got up and, going into the first saloon that he had to pass on his way to work, ordered some beer. He tasted it and said to the bartender, "You put some poison in this beer." He could not drink it and went on to the next saloon and ordered some more beer. He tasted it and said to the man behind the counter, "You put some poison in this beer. I believe you folks have plotted to poison me." The bartender was indignant at being charged with this crime. The man said, "I will go somewhere else."

97

He went to another saloon, and the same thing happened as in the two previous saloons. He made such a fuss that he was thrown out.

After he left work that evening, he went to another saloon to get some beer, and again he thought the bartender was trying to poison him. He made such a disturbance that he was thrown out. He went to his home and told his wife what had happened and said, "It seems as though all the fellows have agreed to poison me." His wife said to him, "Can't you see the hand of the Lord in this, that He is making you dislike the stuff that has been your ruin?" This word brought conviction to the man's heart, and he came to the meeting and got saved. The Lord still has power to set the captives free.

Jesus was willing to go and heal the sick servant, but the centurion said, *"Lord, I am not worthy that You should come under my roof. But only speak a word, and my servant will be healed"* (Matt. 8:8). Jesus was delighted with this expression and *"said to the centurion, 'Go your way; and as you have believed, so let it be done for you.' And his servant was healed that same hour"* (v. 13).

Jesus is equal to every occasion. He is waiting for an opportunity to bless. He is ready for every opportunity to deliver souls. When we receive Jesus, the following verse is true of us: *"Greater is he that is in* [us], *than he that is in the world"* (1 John 4:4 KJV). He is greater than all the powers of darkness. No one can meet the Devil in his own strength, but anyone filled with the knowledge of Jesus, filled with His presence, filled with His power, is more than a match for the powers of darkness. God has called us to be *"more than conquerors through Him who loved us"* (Rom. 8:37).

Thought for today: The living Word is able to destroy satanic forces. There is power in the words of Jesus.

February 25

A New Faith

Where is your faith?
—Luke 8:25

Scripture reading: Luke 8:22–39

*P*aul spoke of two classes of Christians, the obedient and the disobedient. The obedient always obey God when He first speaks. It is these people whom God will use to make the world know Him.

You cannot talk about things that you have never experienced. God has a process of training us. You cannot take people into the depths of God unless you have been broken yourself. I have been broken and broken and broken. Praise God, for *"the LORD is near to those who have a broken heart"* (Ps. 34:18). You must have a brokenness to get into the depths of God.

There is a rest of faith that rests in confidence in God. God's promises never fail. *"Faith comes by hearing, and hearing by the word of God"* (Rom. 10:17). The Word of God can create an irresistible faith, a faith that is never daunted, a faith that never gives up and never fails. We fail to realize the largeness of our Father's supply. We forget that He has a supply that cannot be exhausted. It pleases Him when we ask for much. *"If you then, being evil, know how to give good gifts to your children, how much more will your Father who is in heaven give good things to those who ask Him!"* (Matt. 7:11). It is the *"much more"* that God shows me.

There are times when a stone wall seems to be in front of us. There are times when there are no feelings, when everything seems as black as midnight, and there is nothing left but confidence in God. What you must do is have the devotion and confidence to believe that He will not fail and cannot fail. You will never get anywhere if you depend on your feelings. There is something a thousand times better than feelings, and it is the powerful Word of God. A divine revelation within you came when you were born from above, and this is real faith. To be born into the new kingdom is to be born into a new faith.

Thought for today: If God definitely tells you to do anything, do it, but be sure it is God who is telling you.

What Are You Focused On?

And the prayer of faith will save the sick,
and the Lord will raise him up.
—James 5:15

Scripture reading: James 5:13–20

Baptist minister came to me and said, "The doctor says that this is the last day that my wife has to live." I said, "Oh, Brother Clark, why don't you believe God? God can raise her up if you will only believe Him." He replied, "I have looked at you when you talked and have wept and said, 'Father, if You could give me this confidence, I would be so happy.'" I said, "Could you trust God?" I felt that the Lord would heal her.

I sent word to a certain man and asked if he would come with me to pray for a dying woman, and I believed that if two of us would go and anoint her according to James 5:14–15, she would be raised up. This man said, "Oh, why do you come to me? I could not believe, although I believe the Lord would be sure to heal her if you would go."

Then I sent word to another man and asked him to go with me. This man could pray by the hour. When he was on his knees, he could go around the world three times and come out at the same place. I told him that whatever his impression was, to be sure to go on and pray right through. We entered the house. I asked this man to pray first. He cried in his desperation and prayed that this man might be comforted after he was left with these little motherless children, and that he might be strengthened to bear his sorrow. I could hardly wait until he was finished; my whole being was moved. I thought, "What an awful thing to bring this man all this way to pray that kind of a prayer." What was the matter with him? He was looking at the dying woman instead of looking at God. The Lord wants to help us right now to learn this truth and to keep our eyes on Him.

When this man had finished, I said to Brother Clark, "Now you pray." He took up the thread where the other man had left off and went on with the same kind of prayer. He got so down beneath the burden I thought he would never rise again, and I was glad when he was through. I could not have borne it much longer. These prayers seemed to be the most out-of-place prayers that I had ever heard; the whole atmosphere was being charged with unbelief. My soul was stirred. I was eager for God to get a chance to do something and to have His way. I did not wait to pray but rushed up to the bed and tipped the oil bottle, pouring nearly the whole contents on the woman. Then I saw Jesus just above the bed with the sweetest smile on His face, and I said to her, "Woman, Jesus Christ makes you whole." The woman stood up, perfectly healed, and she is a strong woman today.

Oh, beloved, may God help us to get our eyes off the conditions and symptoms, no matter how bad they may be, and get them fastened on Him. Then we will be able to pray *the prayer of faith.*

Thought for today: You can never pray *"the prayer of faith"* if you look at the person who is needing it; there is only one place to look, and that is to Jesus.

The Purpose of the Power

*And they were all filled with the Holy Spirit and began to speak
with other tongues, as the Spirit gave them utterance.
—Acts 2:4*

Scripture reading: Acts 1:4–14; 2:1–4

*B*efore Jesus went to heaven, He told His disciples that they
would receive the power of the Holy Spirit (Acts 1:8). Thus,
through them, His gracious ministry would continue. This
power of the Holy Spirit was not only for a few apostles, but even
for those who were afar off (Acts 2:39), even for us way down in
this century. Some ask, "But wasn't this power just for the privileged few in the first century?" No. Read the Master's Great Commission as recorded in Mark 16:15–18, and you will see it is for
those who believe.

After I received the baptism in the Holy Spirit, I sought the
mind of the Lord as to why I had been baptized. One day I came
home from work and went into the house. My wife asked me,
"Which way did you come in?" I told her that I had come in the
back door. She said, "There is a woman upstairs who has brought
an eighty-year-old man to be prayed for. He is raving, and a great
crowd has gathered outside the front door, ringing the doorbell and
wanting to know what is going on in the house." The Lord quietly
whispered, "This is what I baptized you for."

I carefully opened the door of the room where the man was,
desiring to be obedient to what my Lord would say to me. The man
was crying and shouting in distress, "I am lost! I am lost! I have
committed the unpardonable sin. I am lost! I am lost!" My wife
asked, "Smith, what should we do?" The Spirit of the Lord moved
me to cry out, "Come out, you lying spirit." In a moment the evil
spirit went, and the man was free. God gives deliverance to the
captives. And the Lord said again to me, "This is what I baptized
you for." There is a place where God, through the power of the
Holy Spirit, reigns supreme in our lives. The Spirit reveals, un-
folds, and takes of the things of Christ and shows them to us (John
16:14).

Thought for today: The Holy Spirit prepares us to be more than a
match for satanic forces.

February 28

Christ's Works Continue

Your healing shall spring forth speedily.
—Isaiah 58:8

Scripture reading: Jeremiah 33:3–16

The ministry of Christ did not end at the Cross. Our blessed Lord Jesus is still alive and continues His ministry through those who are filled with His Spirit. He is still healing the brokenhearted and delivering the captives through those on whom He places His Spirit.

I was traveling on a train in Sweden. At one station, an old lady boarded with her daughter. That old lady's expression was so troubled that I asked what was the matter with her. I heard that she was going to the hospital to have her leg amputated. She began to weep as she told me that the doctors had said that there was no hope for her except through having her leg amputated. I said to my interpreter, "Tell her that Jesus can heal her." The instant these words were said to her, it was as though a veil had been taken off her face; it became so radiant. We stopped at another station, and the train filled up with people. A large group of men rushed to board the train, and the Devil said, "You're done." But I knew I had the best situation. Hard things are always opportunities to gain more glory for the Lord as He manifests His power.

Every trial is a blessing. There have been times when I have been hard-pressed through circumstances, and it seemed as if a dozen steamrollers were going over me, but we have such a lovely Jesus. He always proves Himself to be such a mighty Deliverer. He never fails to plan the best things for us.

As the train began moving, I crouched down and in the name of Jesus commanded the disease to leave. The old lady cried, "I'm healed! I know I'm healed!" She stamped her leg and said, "I'm going to prove it." So when we stopped at another station, she marched up and down and shouted, "I'm not going to the hospital." Once again our wonderful Jesus had proven Himself a Healer of the brokenhearted, a Deliverer of one who was bound.

Thought for today: The hardest circumstances are just lifting places into the grace of God.

February 29

Is Anyone Sick?

They brought to Him many who were demon-possessed. And He cast
out the spirits with a word, and healed all who were sick, that it
might be fulfilled which was spoken by Isaiah the prophet, saying:
"He Himself took our infirmities and bore our sicknesses."
—Matthew 8:16–17

Scripture reading: Matthew 25:14–46

*I*s there anyone sick in this place?" This is what I ask when I
go into a sickroom. Why? I will tell you a story that will explain.

My daughter is a missionary to Africa. I am interested in
helping to support missionaries in Africa and all over. I love missionary work.

We had a missionary out in China who by some means or
other got rheumatism. I have no word for rheumatism; rheumatism, cancer, tumors, lumbago, neuralgia—all these things I give
only one name: the power of the Devil working in humanity. All
these things can be removed.

When Jesus went into Peter's house, where his wife's mother
lay sick, what did He do? Did He cover her up with a blanket and
put a hot water bottle on her feet? If He didn't do that, why didn't
He? Because He knew that the demons had all the heat of hell in
them. He did the right thing: He rebuked the fever, and it left. (See
Luke 4:38–39.) We, too, ought to do the right thing with these diseases.

This missionary came home to Belfast from China, enraged
against the work of God, enraged against God, enraged against
everything. She was absolutely outside the plan of God.

While she was in Belfast, God allowed her to fall down some
steps and dislocate her backbone. Others had to lift her up and
carry her to her bed. God allowed it.

Be careful about getting angry at God because of something
wrong with your body. Get right with God.

On the day that I was to visit the sick, she asked me to come.
When I went to her room, I looked at her and called out, "Is there
anyone sick in this room?" No response. "Is there anyone sick in this
room?" No response. "Well," I said, "we will wait until somebody
responds."

By and by, she said, "Yes, I am sick." I said, "All right, we have found you out then. You are in the room. Now the Word of God says that when you are sick, you are to pray. When you pray, I will anoint you and pray for you, but not before."

It took her almost a quarter of an hour to yield, the Devil had such possession of her. But, thank God, she yielded. Then she cried and cried, and by the power of God her body was shaken loose, and she was set free. This happened when she repented, and not before.

Oh, what would happen if everybody would repent! Talk about blessings! The glory would fall. We need to see that God wants us to be blessed, but first of all He wants us to be ready for the blessing.

God wants you to have a living faith; He wants you to possess a vital touch, shaking the foundation of all weakness. When you were saved, you were saved the moment you believed, and you will be healed the moment you believe. If you believe, you can be healed. God means for you to believe today; God means for you to be helped today.

Thought for today: God's Word can bring things to pass today as it did in the past.

March 1

My Own Remarkable Healing

With men this is impossible, but with God all things are possible.
—Matthew 19:26

Scripture reading: Psalm 77

At one time I was so bound that no human power could help me. My wife thought that I would pass away. At that time I had just a faint glimpse of Jesus as the Healer. For six months I had been suffering from appendicitis, occasionally getting temporary relief. I went to the mission of which I was the pastor, but I fell to the floor in awful agony, and I was brought home to my bed. All night I was praying, pleading for deliverance, but none came. My wife was sure it was my call home to heaven and sent for a physician. He said that there was no possible chance for me—my body was too weak. Having had the appendicitis for six months, my whole system was drained. Because of that, he thought that it was too late for an operation. He left my wife in a state of brokenheartedness.

After he left, a young man and an old lady came to our door. I knew that the old lady was a woman of real prayer. They came upstairs to my room. This young man jumped on the bed and commanded the evil spirit to come out of me. He shouted, "Come out, you devil! I command you to come out in the name of Jesus!" There was no chance for an argument or for me to tell him that I would never believe that there was a devil inside of me. The thing had to go in the name of Jesus, and it went. I was instantly healed.

I arose, dressed, and went downstairs. I was still in the plumbing business, and I asked my wife, "Is there any work in? I'm all right now, and I am going to work." I found that there was a certain job to be done, and I picked up my tools and went off to do it. Just after I left, the doctor came in, put his hat down in the hall, and walked up to the bedroom. But the invalid was not there. "Where is Mr. Wigglesworth?" he asked. "Oh, doctor, he's gone out to work," said my wife. "You'll never see him alive again," said the doctor; "they'll bring him back a corpse."

Well, God was not ready for me to be a corpse. Since that time the Lord has given me the privilege of praying for people with appendicitis in many parts of the world, and I have seen a great many people up and dressed within a quarter of an hour from the time I prayed for them. We have a living Christ who is willing to meet people in every place.

Our God is real, and He has saving and healing power today. Our Jesus is just the same *"yesterday, today, and forever"* (Heb. 13:8). He saves and heals today just as of old, and He wants to be your Savior and your Healer.

Oh, if you would only believe God! What would happen? The greatest things. Some have never tasted the grace of God, have never had the peace of God. Unbelief robs them of these blessings. It is possible to hear and yet not to perceive the truth. It is possible to read the Word and not share in the life it brings. It is necessary for us to have the Holy Spirit to unfold the Word and bring to us the life that is Christ. We can never fully understand the wonders of this redemption until we are full of the Holy Spirit.

Thought for today: If Satan were almighty, we would all have to quake with fear. But when we know that Satan is subject to the powers of God in everything, we can be conquerors over every situation.

March 2

Remember God's Goodness

In all your ways acknowledge Him, and He shall direct your paths.
—Proverbs 3:6

Scripture reading: Proverbs 3:1–26

After Jesus had departed from the Pharisees, He said to His disciples, *"Take heed and beware of the leaven of the Pharisees and the Sadducees"* (Matt. 16:6). The disciples began to discuss this warning among themselves, and all they could think of was that they had brought no bread. What were they going to do? Then Jesus uttered these words: *"O you of little faith"* (v. 8). He had been with them for quite a while, yet they were still a great disappointment to Him because of their lack of comprehension and of faith. They could not grasp the profound spiritual truth He was bringing to them and could only think about having brought no bread. So Jesus said to them,

> *O you of little faith...Do you not yet understand, or remember the five loaves of the five thousand and how many baskets you took up? Nor the seven loaves of the four thousand and how many large baskets you took up?* (Matt. 16:8–10)

Do you keep in mind how God has been gracious in the past? God has done wonderful things for all of us. If we keep these things in mind, we will be *"strengthened in [our] faith"* (Rom. 4:20). We should be able to defy Satan in everything. Remember that the Lord has led all the way. When Joshua passed over the Jordan on dry land, he told the people to pick up twelve stones and set them up in Gilgal. These were to be a constant reminder to the children of Israel that they came over the Jordan on dry land. (See Joshua 4:20–24.) How many times had Jesus shown His disciples the mightiness of His power? Yet they failed in faith right here.

Thought for today: The difference between those who are being led by the Holy Spirit and those who are being deceived by Satan is joy, gladness, and a calm expression instead of sadness, sorrow, and depression.

March 3

Lesson from a Fish

Nevertheless, lest we offend them, go to the sea, cast in a hook, and take the fish that comes up first. And when you have opened its mouth, you will find a piece of money; take that and give it to them for Me and you.
—Matthew 17:27

Scripture reading: Matthew 17:24–27; Mark 11:22–24

*P*eter had been in the fishing business all his life, but he had never before caught a fish with silver in its mouth. However, the Master does not want us to reason things out, for carnal reasoning will always land us in a bog of unbelief. He wants us simply to obey. "This is a hard job," Peter must have said as he put the bait on his hook, "but since You told me to do it, I'll try." And he cast his line into the sea. There were millions of fish in the sea, but every fish had to stand aside and leave that bait alone and let the fish with the piece of money in its mouth come up and take the bait.

Do you not see that the words of the Master are the instruction of faith? It is impossible for anything that Jesus says to miss. All His words are spirit and life (John 6:63). If you will only have faith in Him, you will find that every word that God gives is life. You cannot be in close contact with Him and receive His Word in simple faith without feeling the effect of it in your body, as well as in your spirit and soul.

A woman came to me in Cardiff, Wales, who was filled with ulcers. She had fallen in the streets twice because of this trouble. When she came to the meeting, it seemed as if the evil power within her purposed to kill her right there. She fell, and the power of the Devil was attacking her severely. Not only was she helpless, but it seemed as if she had died. I cried, "O God, help this woman." Then I rebuked the evil power in the name of Jesus, and instantly the Lord healed her. She rose up and made a great to-do. She felt the power of God in her body and wanted to testify continually. After three days she went to another place and began to testify about the Lord's power to heal. She came to me and said, "I want to tell everyone about the Lord's healing power. Don't you have any tracts on this subject?" I handed her my Bible and said, "Matthew,

Mark, Luke, and John—they are the best tracts on healing. They are full of incidents of the healing power of Jesus. They will never fail to accomplish the work of God if people will only read and believe them."

That is where men are lacking. All lack of faith is due to not feeding on God's Word. You need it every day. How can you enter into a life of faith? Feed on the living Christ of whom this Word is full. As you are taken up with the glorious fact and the wondrous presence of the living Christ, the faith of God will spring up within you. *"Faith comes by hearing, and hearing by the word of God"* (Rom. 10:17).

"He who believes in Me" (John 14:12)—the essence of divine life is in us by faith. To the one who believes, it will come to pass. We become supernatural by the power of God. If you believe, the power of the Enemy cannot stand, for God's Word is against him. Jesus gives us His Word to make faith effective. If you can believe in your heart, you begin to speak whatever you desire, and whatever you dare to say is done. You will have whatever you say after you believe in your heart. (See Mark 11:23–24.)

Thought for today: Dare to believe, and then dare to speak, for you will have whatever you say if you do not doubt.

March 4

Demonstrations of God's Might

*On this rock I will build My church, and the gates of Hades
shall not prevail against it.*
—Matthew 16:18

Scripture reading: Matthew 16:5–26

God is pleased when we stand on the Rock and believe that He is unchangeable. If you will dare to believe God, you can defy all the powers of evil. There have been times in my life when I have dared to believe Him and have had the most remarkable experiences.

One day I was traveling in a railway coach, and there were two people in the coach who were very sick, a mother and her daughter. I said to them, "Look, I've something in this bag that will cure every case in the world. It has never been known to fail." They became very much interested, and I went on to tell them more and more about this remedy that had never failed to remove disease and sickness. At last they summoned up the courage to ask for a dose. So I opened my bag, took out my Bible, and read them the verse that says, *"I am the LORD who heals you"* (Exod. 15:26).

God's Word never fails. He will always heal you if you dare to believe Him. Men are searching everywhere today for things with which they can heal themselves, and they ignore the fact that the Balm of Gilead is within easy reach. As I talked about this wonderful Physician, the faith of both mother and daughter went out toward Him, and He healed them both right in the train.

God has made His Word so precious that if I could not get another copy of it, I would not part with my Bible for all the world. There is life in the Word. There is power in it. I find Christ in it, and He is the One I need for spirit, soul, and body. It tells me of the power of His name and the power of His blood for cleansing. *"The young lions lack and suffer hunger; but those who seek the LORD shall not lack any good thing"* (Ps. 34:10).

A man came to me one time, brought by his wife. I said, "What seems to be the problem?" She said, "He gets employment, but he fails every time. He is a slave to alcohol and nicotine. He is a bright, intelligent man in most areas, but he is in bondage to these two things." I was reminded of the words of the Master, giving us

111

power to bind and to loose (Matt. 16:19), and I told him to stick out his tongue. In the name of the Lord Jesus Christ, I cast out the evil powers that gave him the taste for these things. I said to him, "Man, you are free today." He was unsaved, but when he realized the power of the Lord in delivering him, he came to the services, publicly acknowledged that he was sinner, and was saved and baptized. A few days later I asked, "How are things with you?" He said, "I'm delivered." God has given us the power to bind and the power to loose.

Another person came and said, "What can you do for me? I have had sixteen operations and have had my eardrums taken out." I said, "God has not forgotten how to make eardrums." She was so deaf that I do not think she would have heard a cannon go off. I anointed her and prayed, asking the Lord to replace the eardrums. But afterward she remained as deaf as it was possible to be. However, she saw other people getting healed and rejoicing. Had *"God forgotten to be gracious"* (Ps. 77:9)? Wasn't His power just the same? She came the next night and said, "I have come to believe God tonight." Take care that you do not come any other way. I prayed for her again and commanded her ears to be loosed in the name of Jesus. She believed, and the moment she believed, she heard. She ran and jumped on a chair and began to preach. Later I let a pin drop, and she heard it touch the floor. *"With God all things are possible"* (Matt. 19:26). God can heal the worst case.

Discouraged one, *"cast your burden on the LORD, and He shall sustain you"* (Ps. 55:22). Look to Him and be radiant (Ps. 34:5). Look to Him now.

Thought for today: Faith is an act; faith is a leap; faith jumps in; faith claims. Faith has an author, and faith's author is Jesus.

March 5

How to Obtain Spiritual Power

*How can you believe, who receive honor from one another, and do
not seek the honor that comes from the only God?*
—John 5:44

Scripture reading: Matthew 16:13–19, 21–23

*I*n Peter's life, we see evidences of the spiritual power that he
had attained, but we see also the natural power working.
Jesus saw that He must suffer if He would reach the spiritual life that God intended Him to reach. So Jesus said, "I must go
forward. Your words, Peter, are an offense to Me" (Matt. 16:23). If
you to seek to save yourself, it is an offense to God. God has been
impressing on me more and more that if at any time I were to seek
man's favor or earthly power, I would lose favor with God and
could not have faith.

God is speaking to us, every one of us, trying to get us to leave
the shoreline. There is only one place where we can have the mind
and will of God; it is alone with God. If we look to anybody else, we
cannot get it. If we seek to save ourselves, we will never reach the
place where we will be able to bind and loose. (See Matthew 16:19.)
There is a close companionship between you and Jesus that nobody
knows about, where every day you have to choose or refuse.

It is in the narrow way that you get the power to bind and the
power to loose. I know that Jesus was separated from His own
family and friends. He was deprived of the luxuries of life. It seems
to me that God wants to get every one of us separated to Himself in
this holy war, and we are not going to have faith if we do not give
ourselves wholly to Him. Beloved, it is in these last days that I
cannot have the power I want to have unless, as a sheep, I am
willing to shear myself. The way is narrow. (See Matthew 7:13–14.)

Beloved, you will not be able to bind and loose if you have sin
in you. There is not one person who is able to deal with the sins of
others if he is not free himself. *"He breathed on them, and said to
them, 'Receive the Holy Spirit'"* (John 20:22). Jesus knew the Holy
Spirit would give them both a revelation of themselves and a revelation of God. He must reveal to you your depravity.

Do you believe that the Father in heaven would make you a
judge over a kingdom if there were anything crooked in you? Do

113

you believe you will be able to bind unless you are free yourself? But everyone who has this living Christ within him has the power that will put to death all sin.

With Jesus' last words on earth, He gave the disciples a commission. (See Mark 16:15–18.) The need for discipleship has never ceased. Some churches are weak today because Christ the Rock is not abiding in them in the manifestations of the power of God. This is not because it is a special gift—this power to bind and loose—but it is contingent on whether you have the rock foundation in you. In the name of Jesus, you will loose, and in the name of Jesus, you will bind. If He is in you, you ought to bring forth evidences of that power.

One can see that Peter had great sympathy, and he did not want Jesus to be crucified. It was perfectly natural for Peter to say what he did, but Jesus said, *"Get behind Me"* (Matt. 16:23). He knew He must not be turned aside by any human sympathy. The only way we can retain our humility is to stay on this narrow line and say, "Get behind me, Satan."

Beloved, we are now living in the experience of the fact that Jesus is the Rock. I am glad, for we are within reach of wonderful possibilities because of the Rock. Take a stand on the fact that the Rock cannot be overthrown.

Thought for today: If you try to go the easy way, you cannot be Jesus' disciple.

Triumphant in Trials

When He has tested me, I shall come forth as gold.
—Job 23:10

Scripture reading: 1 Peter 1:3–21

Temptations come to all. In every temptation that comes, the Lord allows you to be tempted to the very hilt, but He will never allow you to be defeated if you walk in obedience. Right in the midst of the temptation, He will always *"make the way of escape"* (1 Cor. 10:13). With His power, God sweeps away the refuge of lies (Isa. 28:17) and all the powers of darkness. He causes you always to triumph in Christ Jesus (2 Cor. 2:14). The Lord loves His saints and covers them with His almighty wings.

May God help us to see this truth. We cannot be *"to the praise of His glory"* (Eph. 1:12) until we are ready for trials and are able to triumph in them. We cannot get away from the fact that sin came in by human nature, but God comes into our nature and puts sin into the place of death. Why? So that the Spirit of God may come into the temple in all His power and liberty, and so that right here in this present, evil world Satan may be dethroned by the believer. You must come to see how wonderful you are in God and how helpless you are in yourself.

God declared Himself to be mightier than every opposing power when He cast out the powers of darkness from heaven. I want you to know that the same power that cast Satan out of heaven dwells in every person who is born of God. If you would only realize this, you would *"reign in life"* (Rom. 5:17). When you see people laid out under an evil power, when you see the powers of evil manifesting themselves, always ask them the question, "Did Jesus come in the flesh?" I have never heard an evil power answer this question in the affirmative. (See 1 John 4:2–3.) When you know you have an evil spirit to deal with, you have power to cast it out. Believe this fact, and act on it, for *"greater is he that is in you, than he that is in the world"* (1 John 4:4 KJV). God intends for you to overcome and has put a force within you whereby you may defeat the Devil.

Thought for today: If you are not worth tempting, you are not worth much.

The New Covenant

This cup is the new covenant in My blood, which is shed for you.
—Luke 22:20

Scripture reading: 2 Corinthians 3:3–18

The Israelites tried Moses tremendously. They were always in trouble. But as he went up onto the mountain and God unfolded to him the Ten Commandments, the glory fell. He rejoiced to bring those two tablets of stone down from the mountain, and his very face shone with the glory. He was bringing to Israel that which, if obeyed, would bring life.

I think of my Lord coming from heaven. I think all heaven was moved by the sight. The letter of the law was brought by Moses, and it was made glorious, but all its glory was dimmed before the exceeding glory that Jesus brought to us in the Spirit of life. The glory of Sinai paled before the glory of Pentecost. The Lord has brought in a new covenant, putting His law in our minds and writing it in our hearts (Jer. 31:33)—this new law of the Spirit of life. As the Holy Spirit comes in, He fills us with love and liberty, and we shout for joy. Henceforth, there is a new cry in our hearts: *"I delight to do Your will, O my God"* (Ps. 40:8). *"He takes away the first that He may establish the second"* (Heb. 10:9). In other words, He takes away *"the ministry of death, written and engraved on stones"* (2 Cor. 3:7), so that He may establish *"the ministry of righteousness"* (v. 9), this life in the Spirit.

You ask, "Does a man who is filled with the Spirit cease to keep the commandments?" I simply repeat what the Spirit of God has told us here, that this *"ministry of death, written and engraved on stones"* (and you know that the Ten Commandments were written on stones) is *"passing away"* (v. 11). However, the man who becomes a living epistle of Christ (2 Cor. 3:3), written by the Spirit of the living God, has ceased to be an adulterer or a murderer or a covetous man; the will of God is his delight. I love to do the will of God; there is no irksomeness to it. It is no trial to pray, no trouble to read the Word of God; it is not a hard thing to go to the place of worship. With the psalmist I say, *"I was glad when they said to me, 'Let us go into the house of the LORD'"* (Ps. 122:1).

How does this new life work out? It works out because God *"works in you both to will and to do for His good pleasure"* (Phil. 2:13). There is a big difference between a pump and a spring. The law is a pump; the baptism in the Holy Spirit is a spring. The old pump gets out of order; the parts wear out, and the well runs dry. *"The letter kills"* (2 Cor. 3:6). But the spring is ever bubbling up, and there is a ceaseless flow direct from the throne of God. There is life.

It is written of Christ, *"You love righteousness and hate wickedness"* (Ps. 45:7). In this new life in the Spirit, in this new covenant life, you love the things that are right and pure and holy, and you shudder at all things that are wrong. Jesus was able to say, *"The ruler of this world is coming, and he has nothing in Me"* (John 14:30). The moment we are filled with the Spirit of God, we are brought into a wonderful condition like this.

Thought for today: As we continue to be filled with the Spirit, the Enemy cannot have an inch of territory in us.

How to Bring Conviction of Sin

When He [the Holy Spirit] *has come, He will convict the world
of sin, and of righteousness, and of judgment.*
—John 16:8

Scripture reading: Ephesians 5:8–21

*D*o you believe that you can be so filled with the Spirit that a person who is not living right can be judged and convicted by your presence? As we go on in the life of the Spirit, it will be said of us that a vile person is convicted in our presence. Jesus lived in this realm and moved in it, and His life was a constant reproof to the wickedness around Him. "But He was the Son of God," you say. God, through Him, has brought us into the place of sonship, and I believe that if the Holy Spirit has a chance at us, He can make something of us and bring us to the same place.

I don't want to boast. If I glory in anything, it is only in the Lord (1 Cor. 1:31), who has been so gracious to me. But I remember a wonderful time of conviction. I stepped out of a railway coach to wash my hands. I had a season of prayer, and the Lord just filled me to overflowing with His love. I was going to a convention in Ireland, and I could not get there fast enough. As I returned to my seat, I believe that the Spirit of the Lord was so heavy upon me that my face must have shone. (When the Spirit transforms a man's very countenance, he cannot tell this on his own.) There were two ministers sitting together, and as I got into the coach again, one of them cried out, "You convict me of sin." Within three minutes everyone in the coach was crying to God for salvation. This has happened many times in my life. It is the ministry of the Spirit that Paul spoke of. This filling of the Spirit will make your life effective, so that even the people in the stores where you shop will want to leave your presence because they are brought under conviction.

We must move away from everything that pertains to the letter. All that we do must be done under the anointing of the Spirit. Our problem has been that we have been living in the letter. Believe what the Holy Spirit said through Paul—that this entire *"ministry of condemnation"* (2 Cor. 3:9) that has hindered your liberty in Christ is done away with. The law has been done away with. As far as you are concerned, that old order of things is forever done away with, and the Spirit of God has brought in a new life of purity and love. In the life in the Spirit, the old allurements have lost their power. The Devil will meet you at every turn, but the Spirit of God will always *"lift up a standard against him"* (Isa. 59:19).

If God had His way, we would be like torches, purifying the very atmosphere wherever we go, moving back the forces of wickedness.

What do I mean when I say that the law has been done away with? Do I mean that you will be disloyal? No, you will be more than loyal. Will you grumble when you are treated badly? No, you will turn the other cheek (Matt. 5:39). You will always respond this way when God lives in you. Leave yourself in God's hands. Enter into His rest. *"For he who has entered His rest has himself also ceased from his works as God did from His"* (Heb. 4:10). Oh, this is a lovely rest! The whole life is a Sabbath. This is the only life that can glorify God. It is a life of joy, and every day is a day of heaven on earth.

Thought for today: The Holy Spirit takes it for granted that you are finished with all the things of the old life when you become a new creation in Christ.

The Power of the New Creation

If anyone is in Christ, he is a new creation; old things have passed away; behold, all things have become new.
—2 Corinthians 5:17

Scripture reading: Romans 8:1–39

*P*eople have been in meetings where the glory of God has fallen, where the fingerprints of God have touched everything, and where fortifications have been made in the body. The next morning the power of Satan has attacked them. Why does this happen? The spiritual life, the Son manifested, the glory of the new creation, is already in our mortal bodies, but the flesh, being a battleground for the Enemy, is tested. But what God is forming is greater than the mortal body, for the spirit that is awakening to the glorious liberty of a child of God is greater. How can we compare this with what is to come?

"It is the Spirit who gives life; the flesh profits nothing" (John 6:63). Though *"my skin is destroyed"* (Job 19:26), I have a life greater than this life that will look upon God, that will see Him in His perfection, that will behold Him in His glory, that will be changed to be like Him. By the presence of God, a new creation will so clothe us that we will be like Him. Knowing this, should I give place to the Devil? Should I let my feelings change the experience of the Word of God? Should I trust in my fears? No! A million times, no! There has never been any good thing in the flesh (Rom. 7:18), but God has given life to the spirit until we live a divine new life and are eternally shaped for God.

"What then shall we say?" (Rom. 8:31). Are you going to let the past, in which God Himself has worked for you, bring you to a place of distress? Or are you standing during your testing, quoting God's Word—*"Now we are children of God"* (1 John 3:2)—and remembering how God has answered your prayers, brought light into your home, delivered you from carnality, and touched you when no power in the world could help? *"Who shall bring a charge against God's elect?"* (Rom. 8:33). *"I know whom I have believed"* (2 Tim. 1:12), and I am persuaded that He who chose us for God will surely bring us to the place where we will receive the crown of life (James 1:12) through the faith that God has given us. God is in you and is

mightily forming a new creation by the Spirit in order to make you ready for the glory that will be revealed in Him.

Someone said to me the other day, "I am in terrible trouble; a man is cursing me all the time." *"If God is for us, who can be against us?"* (Rom. 8:31). God has given us Jesus, the heart of His love, *"the express image of His person"* (Heb. 1:3), perfect in brilliance, purity, righteousness, and glory. I have seen Him many times, and seeing Him always changes me. Victory over your struggle is one of the *"all things"* (Rom. 8:32) that God has promised to give to you. Many needs have broken my heart, but I could say to the troubled one, "God is greater than your heart, greater than your circumstances, greater than the thing that holds you. God will deliver you if you dare to believe Him." But I have to emphasize it again and again and again before I can get people to believe God.

A dear woman was marvelously delivered and saved, but she said, "I am addicted to smoking. What shall I do?" "Oh," I said, "smoke night and day." She said, "Sometimes, I take a glass of wine, and it has a hold on me." "Oh," I said, "drink all you can." It brought some solace to her, but she was still in misery. She said, "We play cards." I said, "Play on!" But after being saved, she called her maid and said, "Wire to London and stop the shipment of those cigarettes." The new life does not want these things. It has no desire for them. The old is dethroned.

A clergyman came to me. He said, "I have a terrible craving for tobacco." I said, "Is it the old man or the new?" He broke down. "I know it's the old," he said. *"Put off the old man with his deeds"* (Col. 3:9).

Someone told me, "I have an unlawful affection for another." I said, "You need revelation. Since God has given you Jesus, He will give you all things. He will give you power over the thing, and it will be broken." And God broke it.

Allow God to touch your flesh. He has given life to your spirit. Allow Him to reign, for He will reign until all is subdued. He is King in your life and is preeminent over your affections, your will, your desires, your plans. He rules as Lord of Hosts over you, in you, and through you, to chasten you and bring you to perfection.

Thought for today: God is never tightfisted with any of His blessings.

March 10

The Benefit of the Flaming Sword

*So He drove out the man; and He placed cherubim at the east of the
garden of Eden, and a flaming sword which turned every way,
to guard the way to the tree of life.*
—Genesis 3:24

Scripture reading: Romans 5:1–6:2

When I was baptized in the Holy Spirit, God showed me a
wonderful truth. After Adam and Eve transgressed and
were driven out of the Garden, the Tree of Life was
guarded by a flaming sword—a sword of death if they entered the
Garden. But the baptism in the Holy Spirit put the Tree of Life
right inside of me and a flaming sword right outside of me to keep
the Devil from me, so that I can eat the eternal bread all the time. I
am eating this wonderful bread of life. Nothing can separate us
from this life. It is increasing tremendously, perpetually.

"[What] *shall separate us?*" (Rom. 8:35). Tribulations come,
but they only press us closer to persecution—the finest thing that
can come. All these things work together for our good (v. 28).
Nothing comes except what is helpful. Trials lift you. Distresses
give you a sigh, but God causes you to triumph. *"Greater is he that
is in you"* (1 John 4:4 KJV) than all the powers of darkness.

Whatever befalls you as you abide in Him is the good hand of
God upon you so that you won't lose your inheritance. Every trial
is a boost, every burden a place of exchanging strength. God will
work. *"Who shall bring a charge against God's elect?"* (Rom. 8:33).
People do it, but it makes no difference; *"God is for us"* (v. 31).
*"'Eye has not seen, nor ear heard, nor have entered into the heart of
man the things which God has prepared for those who love Him.'
But God has revealed them to us through His Spirit"* (1 Cor. 2:9–
10). *"No weapon formed against you shall prosper"* (Isa. 54:17).

Know the wisdom and purpose of God's great hand upon you.
Glorify God in distresses and persecution, for the Spirit of God is
made manifest in these situations. Be chastened. Be perfected.
Press on to higher heights, deeper depths, broader breadths. Faith
is the victory (1 John 5:4). The hope is within you (1 Pet. 3:15).
The joy is set before you. (See Hebrews 12:2.) God gives the peace
that passes all understanding (Phil. 4:7). We know that the flesh

March 10

has withered in the presence of the purifying of the Word. He who has brought you to this point will take you to the end (Phil. 1:6). I have mourned and wept bitterly when I needed revelation from God, but I did not need to do so.

The Lord lifts up and changes and operates. He remakes body and soul until He can say, *"There is no spot in you"* (Song 4:7). Yes, it was persecution, tribulation, and distress that drew us near to Him. These places of trial were places of uplifting, places of change, where God operated by the Spirit. Do not bypass this way, but let God have His way.

God stretched out His hand, covered us with the mantle of His love, and brought us nearer and nearer to the channel of His grace. Then our hearts moved and yielded and so turned to the Lord that every moment has seen a divine place where God has met us and stretched out His arms and said, *"Seek My face"* (Ps. 27:8); *"Look to Me"* (Isa. 45:22). Behold what great love the Master has for you, to lead you to the fountain of living water. Yield! Be led! Let God be glorified! Amen.

Thought for today: Among the persecuted you find those who are the ripest, the holiest, the purest, the most intent, those who are the most filled with divine order.

March 11

A Remarkable Catch

Let us run with endurance the race that is set before us, looking unto Jesus, the author and finisher of our faith.
—Hebrews 12:1–2

Scripture reading: Luke 5:1–11

*P*eople crowded around Jesus, so He sat in a boat and taught them in order that all might hear His words. Then Jesus said to Peter, *"Launch out into the deep and let down your nets for a catch"* (Luke 5:4). Peter answered, *"We have toiled all night and caught nothing"* (v. 5). Perhaps he was thinking, "Lord, You know nothing about fishing. Daytime is the wrong time to fish." But he said, *"Nevertheless at Your word I will let down the net"* (v. 5). I believe every fish in the lake tried to get into that net. They wanted to see Jesus. I must see Jesus.

Peter filled one ship, then another. Oh, what would happen if you lowered all the nets? Believe God! He says, *"Look to Me, and be saved"* (Isa. 45:22). He says, *"Come to Me, all you who labor and are heavy laden, and I will give you rest"* (Matt. 11:28). He says, *"He who believes in Me has everlasting life"* (John 6:47). Believe! Oh, believe! It is the Word of God.

Peter saw the ship sinking. He looked around and saw Jesus. He fell down at Jesus' feet, saying, *"Depart from me, for I am a sinful man, O Lord!"* (Luke 5:8). He and all who were with him were astonished at the number of fish that they had caught. That spotless Lamb stood there, and Jesus said to Peter, *"Do not be afraid. From now on you will catch men"* (v. 10).

To see Jesus is to see a new way, to see all things differently. It means a new life and new plans. As we gaze at Him, we are satisfied; there is none like Him. Sin moves away.

Jesus was the express image of the Father (Heb. 1:3). The Father could not be in the midst, so He clothed Jesus with a body—as well as with eternal resources. Let us gather together unto Him. Let us move toward Him. He has all we need. He will fulfill the desires of our hearts, granting all our petitions.

Thought for today: God has no use for anyone who is not hungering and thirsting for even more of Himself and His righteousness.

March 12

Energized by the Spirit

When they had prayed, the place where they were assembled together was shaken; and they were all filled with the Holy Spirit, and they spoke the word of God with boldness.
—Acts 4:31

Scripture reading: Ephesians 3:14–21

*I*t is a necessity for every one of us to be filled with God. It is not sufficient to have just a touch or to be filled with just a desire. Only one thing will meet the needs of the people, and that is for you to be immersed in the life of God. This means that God takes you and fills you with His Spirit until you live right in God. He does this so that *"whether you eat or drink, or whatever you do,* [it may be] *all to the glory of God"* (1 Cor. 10:31). In that place you will find that all your strength and all your mind and all your soul are filled with a zeal, not only for worship, but also for proclamation. This proclamation is accompanied by all the power of God, which must move satanic power and disturb the world.

The reason the world is not seeing Jesus is that Christian people are not filled with Jesus. They are satisfied with attending meetings weekly, reading the Bible occasionally, and praying sometimes. Beloved, if God lays hold of you by the Spirit, you will find that there is an end of everything and a beginning in God. Your whole body will become seasoned with a divine likeness of God. He will not only begin to use you, but also take you in hand, so that you might be *"a vessel for honor"* (2 Tim. 2:21). Our lives are not to be lived for ourselves, for if we live for ourselves we will die (Rom. 8:13); but if *"by the Spirit* [we] *put to death the deeds of the body,* [we] *will live"* (v. 13). He who lives in the Spirit is subject to the powers of God, but he who lives for himself will die. The man who lives in the Spirit lives a life of freedom, joy, blessing, and service—a life that brings blessing to others. God wants us see that we must live in the Spirit.

Thought for today: Jesus came to bring back to us what was forfeited in the Garden.

March 13

Ministering the Gifts of Healings

For to one is given...gifts of healings.
—1 Corinthians 12:8–9

Scripture reading: 1 Corinthians 12:4–11

*T*he gifts of healings are wonderful gifts. There is a difference between having a gift of healing and *"gifts of healings."* God wants us not to come short in anything (1 Cor. 1:7).

I like this term *"gifts of healings."* To have these gifts, I must bring myself into conformity with the mind and will of God. It would be impossible for you to have gifts of healings unless you possessed that blessed fruit of longsuffering. You will find that these gifts run parallel to that which will bring them into operation.

How is it possible to minister the gifts of healings considering the peculiarities there are in the churches and the many evil powers of Satan that confront us and possess bodies? The person who wants to go through with God and exercise the gifts of healings has to be a person of longsuffering, always having a word of comfort. If the one who is in distress and helpless doesn't see eye to eye with us about every matter and doesn't get all he wants, longsuffering Christians will bear and forbear. Longsuffering is a grace Jesus lived in and moved in. He was filled with compassion, and God will never be able to move us to help the needy until we reach that place.

You might think by the way I went about praying for the sick that I was sometimes unloving and rough, but oh, friends, you have no idea what I see behind the sickness and the one who is afflicted. I am not dealing with the person; I am dealing with the satanic forces that are binding the afflicted. As far as people go, my heart is full of love and compassion for all, but I fail to see how you will ever reach a place where God will be able to use you until you get angry at the Devil.

One day a pet dog followed a lady out of her house and ran all around her feet. She said to the dog, "I cannot have you with me today." The dog wagged its tail and made a great fuss. "Go home, pet," she said, but it didn't go. At last she shouted roughly, "Go home!" and off it went.

Some people play with the Devil like that. "Poor thing," they say. The Devil can stand all the comfort anybody in the world could give him. Cast him out! You are not dealing with the person; you are dealing with the Devil. If you say with authority, "Come out, you demons, in the name of the Lord!" they must come out. You will always be right when you dare to treat sickness as the Devil's work.

Gifts of healings are so varied that you will often find the gift of discernment operating in connection with them. Moreover, the manifestations of the Spirit are given to us *"for the profit of all"* (1 Cor. 12:7).

You must never treat a cancer case as anything else but a living, evil spirit that is destroying the body. It is one of the worst kind of evil spirits I know. Not that the Devil has anything good— every disease of the Devil is bad, either to a greater or lesser degree—but this form of disease is one that you must cast out. In casting out demons, we have to be careful about who gives the command. Man may say, "Come out," but unless his command is by the Spirit of God, man's words are useless.

You must be sure of your ground; you must be sure that there is a power mightier than you that is destroying the Devil. Take your position from the first epistle of John and say, *"Greater is he that is in* [me], *than he that is in the world"* (1 John 4:4 KJV). If you think the power comes from you, you make a great mistake. It comes from your being filled with Him, from His acting in the place of you—your thoughts, your words, your all being used by the Spirit of God.

Thought for today: It is no mistake to declare yourself against the Devil.

March 14

Ministering to a Lame Man

*I desire therefore that the men pray everywhere, lifting up holy
hands, without wrath and doubting.*
—1 Timothy 2:8

Scripture reading: 1 Timothy 3

I remember when I was at Antwerp and Brussels. The power
of God was very mighty upon me there. Going on to London,
I called on some friends. To show you the leading of the
Lord, these friends said, "Oh, God sent you here. How much we
need you!" There was a young man twenty-six years old who had
been in bed eighteen years. His body was much bigger than an ordinary body because of inactivity, but his legs were like a child's.
He had never been able to dress himself.

When his family received the wire saying we were coming, the
father dressed the young man. He was sitting in a chair when we
arrived. I felt it was one of the opportunities of my life. I said to
this young man, "What is the greatest desire of your heart?" "Oh,"
he said, "to be filled with the Holy Spirit!" I put my hands on him
and said, "Receive; receive the Holy Spirit." Instantly he became
drunk with the Spirit and fell off the chair like a big bag of pota-
toes. I saw what God could do with a helpless cripple. First, his
head began shaking terrifically; then his back began moving very
fast, and then his legs. Then he spoke clearly in tongues, and we
wept and praised the Lord. Looking at his legs, I saw that they
were still as they had been, by all appearances, and this is where I
missed it.

These "missings" are sometimes God's opportunities of
teaching us important lessons. He will teach us through our weaknesses what is not faith. It was not faith for me to look at that
body, but human nature. The man who wants to work the works of
God must never look at conditions but at Jesus, in whom everything is complete.

I looked at the boy, and there was absolutely no help. I turned
to the Lord and said, "Lord, tell me what to do," and He did. He
said, "Command him to walk in My name." This is where I missed
it. I looked at his condition. I got the father to help lift him up to
see if his legs had strength. We did our best, but he and I together

could not move him. Then the Lord showed me my mistake, and I said, "God, forgive me." I got right down and repented and said to the Lord, "Please tell me again." God is so good. He never leaves us to ourselves. Again He said to me, "Command him in My name to walk." So I shouted, "Arise and walk in the name of Jesus." Did he do it? No, I declare he never walked. He was lifted up by the power of God in a moment, and he *ran*. The door was wide open; he ran out across the road into a field where he ran up and down and came back. Oh, it was a miracle!

Thought for today: Faith is actively refusing the power of the Devil.

I Am the Lord Who Heals You

*Is anyone among you sick? Let him call for the elders of the church,
and let them pray over him, anointing him with oil in the name of
the Lord. And the prayer of faith will save the sick, and the Lord
will raise him up. And if he has committed sins, he will be forgiven.*
—James 5:14–15

Scripture reading: James 5:7–20

We have in this precious Word a real basis for the truth of healing. In these verses God gives very definite instructions to the sick. If you are sick, your part is to call for the elders of the church; it is their part to anoint and pray for you in faith. Then the whole situation rests with the Lord. When you have been anointed and prayed for, you can rest assured that the Lord will raise you up. It is the Word of God.

I believe that we all can see that the church cannot play with this business. If believers turn away from these clear instructions, they are in a place of tremendous danger. Those who refuse to obey do so to their unspeakable loss. Many turn away from the Lord like King Asa, who *"in his disease...did not seek the LORD"* (2 Chron. 16:12). Consequently, *"he died"* (v. 13).

Does the Lord meet those who look to Him for healing and who obey the instructions set forth in the book of James? Most assuredly. He will undertake for the most extreme case.

A woman came into one of my meetings suffering terribly. Her whole arm was filled with poison, and her blood was so diseased that it was certain to bring her to her death. We rebuked the thing, and the next day she testified that she was without pain and had slept all night, a thing she had not done for two months. To God be all the praise! You will find that He will do this kind of thing all along.

God provides the double cure, for even if sin has been the cause of the sickness, His Word declares in James 5:15, *"If he has committed sins, he will be forgiven."*

Thought for today: If you turn away from any part of God's truth, the Enemy will certainly get an advantage over you.

March 16

Kept by God's Power

While I was with them in the world, I kept them in Your name.
Those whom You gave Me I have kept.
—John 17:12

Scripture reading: John 17

There are evil powers, but Jesus is greater than all evil powers. There are tremendous diseases, but Jesus is the Healer. No case is too hard for Him. The Lion of Judah will break every chain. He came to relieve the oppressed and to set the captive free (Luke 4:18). He came to bring redemption, to make us as perfect as man was before the Fall.

People want to know how to be kept by the power of God. He will contend for your body. When you are saved, Satan will come around and say, "See, you are not saved." The Devil is a liar.

I remember the story of the man whose life was swept and put in order. The evil power had been swept out of him. But the man was not filled with the Holy Spirit. If the Lord heals you, you dare not remain unresponsive to His Spirit. The evil spirit came back to that man, found his house swept, and took seven others worse than himself and dwelt there. The last stage of that man was worse than the first. (See Matthew 12:43–45.) Be sure to get filled with God. Get an Occupier. Be filled with the Spirit.

God's power cannot come out of you unless it is within you. We must have all inward confidence and knowledge that we are God's property, bought and paid for by the precious blood of Jesus. God wants you to know how to claim the victory and shout in the face of the Devil and say, "Lord, it is done." (See Revelation 21:6.)

God has a million ways of undertaking for those who go to Him for help. He has deliverance for every captive. He loves you so much that He even says, *"Before they call, I will answer"* (Isa. 65:24). Don't turn Him away.

Thought for today: Every position of grace into which you are led—forgiveness, healing, any kind of deliverance—will be contested by Satan.

March 17

Life in the Word

As for God, His way is perfect; The word of the LORD is proven;
He is a shield to all who trust in Him.
—Psalm 18:30

Scripture reading: Psalm 119:9–28

*I*n the days when the number of disciples began to multiply, there arose a situation in which the Twelve had to make a definite decision not to occupy themselves with serving tables, but to give themselves continually to prayer and to the ministry of the Word. How important it is for all God's ministers to be continually in prayer and constantly feeding on the Scriptures of Truth. I often offer a reward to anyone who can catch me anywhere without my Bible or my New Testament.

None of you can be strong in God unless you are diligently and constantly listening to what God has to say to you through His Word. You cannot know the power and the nature of God unless you partake of His inbreathed Word. Read it in the morning, in the evening, and at every opportunity you get. After every meal, instead of indulging in unprofitable conversation around the table, read a chapter from the Word, and then have a season of prayer. I endeavor to make a point of doing this no matter where or with whom I am staying.

The psalmist said that he had hidden God's Word in his heart so that he might not sin against Him (Ps. 119:11). You will find that the more of God's Word you hide in your heart, the easier it is to live a holy life. He also testified that God's Word had given him life (v. 50). As you receive God's Word, your whole physical being will be given life, and you will be made strong. As you receive with meekness the Word (James 1:21), you will find faith springing up within. You will have life through the Word.

Thought for today: I find nothing in the Bible but holiness, and nothing in the world but worldliness. Therefore, if I live in the world, I will become worldly; on the other hand, if I live in the Bible, I will become holy.

A Better Plan for You

Be faithful until death, and I will give you the crown of life.
—Revelation 2:10

Scripture reading: Acts 6:1–7; Revelation 2:9–11

The Twelve told the rest of the disciples to find seven men to look after the business side of things. They were to be men with a good reputation and filled with the Holy Spirit. Those who were chosen were just ordinary men, but they were filled with the Holy Spirit, and this infilling always lifts a man to a plane above the ordinary. He can baptize *"with the Holy Spirit and fire"* (Matt. 3:11).

The multitude chose seven men to serve tables. Undoubtedly, they were faithful in their appointed tasks, but we see that God soon had a better plan for two of them—Philip and Stephen. Philip was so full of the Holy Spirit that he could have a revival wherever God put him down. (See Acts 8:5–8, 26–40.) Man chose him to serve tables, but God chose him to win souls.

Oh, if I could only stir you up to see that, as you are faithful in the humblest role, God can fill you with His Spirit, make you a chosen vessel for Himself, and promote you to a place of mighty ministry in the salvation of souls and in the healing of the sick. Nothing is impossible to a man filled with the Holy Spirit. The possibilities are beyond all human comprehension. When you are filled with the power of the Holy Spirit, God will wonderfully work wherever you go.

When you are filled with the Spirit, you will know the voice of God. I want to give you one illustration of this. When I was going to Australia recently, our boat stopped at Aden and Bombay. In Aden the people came around the ship selling their wares—beautiful carpets and all sorts of Oriental things. One man was selling some ostrich feathers. As I was looking over the side of the ship watching the trading, a gentleman said to me, "Would you join me in buying that bunch of feathers?" What did I want with feathers? I had no use for such things and no room for them either. But the gentleman asked me again, "Will you join me in buying that bunch?" The Spirit of God said to me, "Do it."

March 18

The feathers were sold to us for three pounds, and the gentle-man said, "I have no money on me, but if you will pay the man for them, I will send the cash down to you by the steward." I paid for the feathers and gave the gentleman his share. He was traveling first class, and I was traveling second class. I said to him, "No, please don't give that money to the steward. I want you to bring it to me personally in my cabin." I asked the Lord, "What about these feathers?" He showed me that He had a purpose in my purchasing them.

A little while later, the gentleman came to my cabin and said, "I've brought the money." I said to him, "It is not your money that I want; it is your soul that I am seeking for God." Right there he opened up the whole story of his life and began to seek God, and that morning he wept his way through to God's salvation.

You have no idea what God can do through you when you are filled with His Spirit. Every day and every hour you can have the divine leading of God. To be filled with the Holy Spirit is great in every respect.

Thought for today: It does not take a cultured or an educated man to fill a position in God's church. What God requires is a yielded, consecrated, holy life, and He can make it a flame of fire.

March 19

The Blessing of Persecution

Blessed are you when they revile and persecute you, and say all kinds of evil against you falsely for My sake.
—Matthew 5:11

Scripture reading: Psalm 119:77–93

How is it that the moment you are filled with the Holy Spirit persecution starts? It was so with the Lord Jesus Himself. We do not read of any persecution before the Holy Spirit came down upon Him like a dove. Shortly after this, we find that after He preached in His hometown, the people wanted to throw Him over the brow of a hill. (See Luke 4:16–30.) It was the same way with the twelve disciples. They had no persecution before the Day of Pentecost, but after they were filled with the Spirit, they were soon in prison. The Devil and the priests of religion will always get disturbed when a man is filled with the Spirit and does things in the power of the Spirit. Nevertheless, persecution is the greatest blessing to a church. When we have persecution, we have purity. If you desire to be filled with the Spirit, you can count on one thing, and that is persecution. The Lord came to bring division (Luke 12:51), and even in your own household you may find *"three against two"* (v. 52).

At a meeting I was holding, the Lord was working, and many were being healed. A man saw what was taking place and remarked, "I'd like to try this thing." He came up for prayer and told me that his body was broken in two places. I laid my hands on him in the name of the Lord and said to him, "Now believe God." The next night he was at the meeting, and he got up like a lion. He said, "I want to tell you people that this man here is deceiving you. He laid his hands on me last night for a rupture in two places, but I'm not a bit better." I stopped him and said, "You are healed; your trouble is that you won't believe it."

He was at the meeting the next night, and when there was opportunity for testimonies, this man arose. He said, "I'm a stonemason by trade. Today I was working with a laborer, and he had to put a big stone in place. I helped him and did not feel any pain. I said to myself, 'How did I do that?' I went to a private place where I could take off my clothes, and I found that I was healed." I told

135

the people, "Last night this man was against the Word of God, but now he believes it. It is true that *'these signs will follow those who believe...they will lay hands on the sick, and they will recover'* (Mark 16:17–18). Healing is through the power that is in the name of Christ." It is the Spirit who has come to reveal the Word of God and to make it spirit and life to us (John 6:63).

Those of you who are seeking the baptism in the Holy Spirit are entering a place where you will have persecution. Your best friends will leave you—or those you may think are your best friends. No good friend will ever leave you. But be assured that your seeking is worthwhile. You will enter into a realm of illumination, a realm of revelation by the power of the Holy Spirit. He reveals the preciousness and the power of the blood of Christ. I find by the revelation of the Spirit that there is not one thing in me that the blood does not cleanse (1 John 1:9). I find that God sanctifies me by the blood and reveals the effectiveness of His work by the Spirit.

Thought for today: The Lord Jesus gives you peace, but soon after you get peace within, you get persecution without. If you remain stationary, the Devil and his agents will not disturb you much. But when you press on and go the whole length with God, the Enemy has you as a target. But God will vindicate you in the midst of the whole thing.

March 20

Delivered from Alcohol

As many as touched [His garment] *were made perfectly well.*
—Matthew 14:36

Scripture reading: Matthew 14:23–36

Stephen was just an ordinary man, but he was clothed with the divine. He was *"full of faith and power"* (Acts 6:8), and great wonders and miracles were done by him. Oh, this life in the Holy Spirit! Oh, this life of deep inward revelation, of transformation from one state to another, of growing in grace, in all knowledge, and in the power of the Spirit! In this state, the life and the mind of Christ are renewed in you, and He gives constant revelations of the might of His power. It is only this kind of thing that will enable us to stand.

In this life, the Lord puts you in all sorts of places and then reveals His power. I had been preaching in New York, and one day I sailed for England on the *Lusitania*. As soon as I got on board, I went down to my cabin. Two men were there, and one of them said, "Well, will I do for company?" He took out a bottle and poured a glass of whiskey and drank it, and then he filled it up for me. "I never touch that stuff," I said. "How can you live without it?" he asked. "How could I live with it?" I asked. He admitted, "I have been under the influence of this stuff for months, and they say my insides are all shriveled up. I know that I am dying. I wish I could be delivered, but I just have to keep on drinking. Oh, if I could only be delivered! My father died in England and has given me his fortune, but what good will it be to me except to hasten me to my grave?"

I said to this man, "Say the word, and you will be delivered." He asked, "What do you mean?" I said, "Say the word—show that you are willing to be delivered—and God will deliver you." But it was just as if I were talking to a board for all the understanding he showed. I said to him, "Stand still," and I laid my hands on his head in the name of Jesus and cursed that alcohol demon that was taking his life. He cried out, "I'm free! I'm free! I know I'm free!" He took two bottles of whiskey and threw them overboard, and God saved, sobered, and healed him.

I continued to preach all the way across the ocean. He sat beside me at the table. Prior to this, he had not been able to eat, but now at every meal he went right through the menu.

137

Oh, the name of Jesus! We make too little use of that name. Even the children cried, *"Hosanna"* (Matt. 21:15). If we would let ourselves go and praise Him more and more, God would give us the shout of victory.

You need only a touch from Jesus to have a good time. The power of God is just the same today. To me, He's lovely. To me, He's saving health. To me, He's the Lily of the Valley. Oh, this blessed Nazarene, this King of Kings! Hallelujah! Will you let Him have your will? Will you let Him have you? If so, all His power is at your disposal.

Thought for today: There is always a place of deliverance when you let God search out what is spoiling and marring your life.

March 21

A Vision Becomes Reality

He Himself took our infirmities and bore our sicknesses.
—Matthew 8:17

Scripture reading: Isaiah 53:1–12

I want to tell you a remarkable story. One day I was standing at the bottom of Shanklin Road, Belfast, Ireland, with a piece of paper in my hand, looking at the addresses of where I had to go, when a man came over and said to me, "Are you visiting the sick?" "Yes," I said. "Go there," he said, and pointed to a house nearby.

I knocked at the door. No reply. I knocked again, and then a voice inside said, "Come in!" So I opened the door and walked in. Then a young man pointed for me to go up the stairway.

When I got up onto the landing, there was a door wide open. So I walked right through the doorway and found a woman sitting up on the bed. As soon as I looked at her, I knew she couldn't speak to me, so I began to pray. She was rocking back and forth, gasping for breath. I knew she was beyond answering me.

When I prayed, the Lord said to me—the Holy Spirit said distinctly—"Read Isaiah 53." So I opened the Book and began to read aloud,

> *Who has believed our report? And to whom has the arm of the LORD been revealed? For He shall grow up before Him as a tender plant, and as a root out of dry ground.* (Isa. 53:1–2)

When I got to the fifth verse, *"But He was wounded for our transgressions, He was bruised for our iniquities; the chastisement for our peace was upon Him, and by His stripes we are healed,"* the woman shouted, "I am healed!"

"Oh!" I said. "Tell me what happened."

"Two weeks ago I was cleaning the house," she said. "In moving some furniture, I strained my heart. The doctors examined me and said that I would die of suffocation. But last night, in the middle of the night, I saw you come into the room. When you saw me, you knew I could not speak, so you began to pray. Then you opened to Isaiah 53 and read until you came to the fifth verse, and when you read the fifth verse, I was completely healed. That was a vision; now it is a fact."

So I know the Word of God is still true. Now that is a word from the Lord. You will never get anything more distinct than that from the Lord. People miss the greatest plan of healing because of moving from one thing to another. Become grounded. God wants you to take the Word, claim the Word, and believe the Word. That is the perfect way of healing. Do not turn to the right hand or to the left (Deut. 5:32), but believe God.

God wants to sweep away all unbelief from your heart. He wants you to dare to believe His Word. It is the Word of the Spirit. If you allow anything to come between you and the Word, it will poison your whole system, and you will have no hope. It is like the Devil putting a spear into you. The Word of Life is the breath of heaven, the life-giving power by which your very self is changed. By it, you begin to bear the image of the heavenly One.

Thought for today: One bit of unbelief against the Word is poison.

March 22

The Bread of Healing

If a son asks for bread from any father among you,
will he give him a stone?
—Luke 11:11

Scripture reading: Mark 7:24–30; Luke 11:5–13

The following question arises: Are salvation and healing for all? They are for all who will press right in and claim their portion. Do you remember the case of that Syro-Phoenician woman who wanted the demon cast out of her daughter? Jesus said to her, *"Let the children be filled first, for it is not good to take the children's bread and throw it to the little dogs"* (Mark 7:27). Note that healing and deliverance are here spoken of by the Master as *"the children's bread"*; therefore, if you are a child of God, you can surely press in for your portion.

The Syro-Phoenician woman purposed to get from the Lord what she was after, and she said, *"Yes, Lord, yet even the little dogs under the table eat from the children's crumbs"* (v. 28). Jesus was stirred as He saw the faith of this woman, and He told her, *"For this saying go your way; the demon has gone out of your daughter"* (v. 29).

Today many children of God are refusing their blood-purchased portion of health in Christ and throwing it away. Meanwhile, sinners are pressing through and picking it up from under the table and are finding the cure, not only for their bodies, but also for their spirits and souls. The Syro-Phoenician woman went home and found that the demon had indeed gone out of her daughter. Today there is bread—there is life and health—for every child of God through His powerful Word.

The Word can drive every disease away from your body. Healing is your portion in Christ, who Himself is our bread, our life, our health, our all in all. Though you may be deep in sin, you can come to Him in repentance, and He will forgive and cleanse and heal you. His words are spirit and life to those who will receive them (John 6:63). There is a promise in the last verse of Joel that says, *"I will cleanse their blood that I have not cleansed"* (Joel 3:21 KJV). This essentially says that He will provide new life within. The life of Jesus Christ, God's Son, can so purify people's

141

hearts and minds that they become entirely transformed—spirit, soul, and body.

The sick people were around the pool of Bethesda, and one particular man had been there a long time. His infirmity was of thirty-eight years' standing. Now and again an opportunity to be healed would come as the angel stirred the waters, but he would be sick at heart as he saw another step in and be healed before him. Then one day Jesus was passing that way, and seeing him lying there in that sad condition, He asked, *"Do you want to be made well?"* (John 5:6). Jesus said it, and His words are *"from everlasting to everlasting"* (Ps. 90:2). These are His words today to you, tried and tested one. You may say, like this poor sick man, "I have missed every opportunity until now." Never mind that. *"Do you want to be made well?"*

Thought for today: One touch of living faith in Him is all that is required for wholeness to be your portion.

Why Did Ananias and Sapphira Die?

You have not lied to men but to God.
—Acts 5:4

Scripture reading: Acts 5:1–16

nanias and Sapphira were in the wonderful revival that God gave to the early church, yet they missed it. They thought that possibly the thing might fail. They wanted to have a reserve for themselves in case it turned out to be a failure.

Many people are like them today. Many make vows to God in times of great crisis in their lives but fail to keep their vows, and in the end they become spiritually bankrupt. Blessed is the man *"who swears to his own hurt and does not change"* (Ps. 15:4), who keeps the vow he has made to God, who is willing to lay his all at God's feet. The man who does this never becomes a lean soul. God has promised to *"strengthen [his] bones"* (Isa. 58:11). There is no dry place for such a man. He is always *"fresh and flourishing"* (Ps. 92:14), and he becomes stronger and stronger. It pays to trust God with all and to hold back nothing.

I wish I could make you see how great a God we have. Ananias and Sapphira were really doubting God and were questioning whether this work that He had begun would go on. They wanted to receive some glory for selling their property, but because of their lack of faith, they kept part of the proceeds in reserve in case the work of God were to fail.

Many are doubting whether this Pentecostal revival will go on. Do you think this Pentecostal work will stop? Never. For fifteen years I have been in constant revival, and I am sure that it will never stop. When George Stephenson built his first locomotive engine, he took his sister Mary to see it. She looked at it and said to her brother, "George, it'll never go." He said to her, "Get in, Mary." She said again, "It'll never go." He said to her, "We'll see; you get in." Mary at last got in. The whistle blew, there was a puff and a rattle, and the engine started off. Then Mary cried out, "George, it'll never stop! It'll never stop!"

People are looking at this Pentecostal revival, and they are very critical. They are saying, "It'll never go." However, when they are induced to come into the work, they one and all say, "It'll never stop." This revival of God is sweeping on and on, and there is no stopping the current of life, of love, of inspiration, and of power.

God has brought unlimited resources for everyone. Do not doubt. Hear with the ear of faith. God is in the midst. See that it is God who has set forth what you see and hear today (Acts 2:33).

I want you to see that in the early church, controlled by the power of the Holy Spirit, it was not possible for a lie to exist. The moment it came into the church, there was instant death. And as the power of the Holy Spirit increases in these days of the latter rain (see James 5:7), it will be impossible for any man to remain in our midst with a lying spirit. God will purify the church. The Word of God will be in such power in healing and other spiritual manifestations, that great fear will be upon all those who see these things.

To the natural mind, it seems a small thing for Ananias and Sapphira to have wanted to have a little to fall back on, but I want to tell you that you can please God and get things from God only through a living faith that gives Him all. God never fails. God never can fail.

Thought for today: The power of God is just the same today as it was in the past. People need to be taken back to the old paths, to the old-time faith, to believing God's Word and every "Thus says the Lord" in it.

March 24

Be on Guard

But the Lord is faithful, who will establish you
and guard you from the evil one.
—2 Thessalonians 3:3

Scripture reading: 2 Thessalonians 2

These are the last days, the days of *"the falling away"* (2 Thess. 2:3). These are days when Satan is having a great deal of power. But we must keep in mind that Satan has no power except as he is allowed.

It is a great thing to know that God is loosing you from the world, loosing you from a thousand things. You must seek to have the mind of God in all things. If you don't, you will stop His working.

The striking thing about Moses is that it took him forty years to learn human wisdom, forty years to know his helplessness, and forty years to live in the power of God. It took one hundred and twenty years to teach that man, and sometimes it seems to me that it will take that many years to bring us to the place where we can discern the voice of God, the leadings of God, and all His will concerning us.

I see that all revelation, all illumination, everything that God had in Christ was to be brought forth into perfect light so that we might be able to live the same way, produce the same things, and in every activity be children of God with power. It must be so. We must not limit the Holy One. We must clearly see that God brought us forth to make us supernatural, so that we might be changed all the time along the lines of the supernatural. He wants us every day to live in the Spirit so that all of the revelations of God are just like a canvas thrown before our eyes, on which we see clearly step by step all the divine will of God.

Thought for today: We will never know the mind of God until we learn to know the voice of God.

145

March 25

The Sweet Touch of Heaven

[Come] to Him as to a living stone, rejected indeed by men,
but chosen by God and precious.
—1 Peter 2:4

Scripture reading: 1 Peter 2:1–16

I know many of you think before you speak. Here is a great word: *"For your obedience has become known to all. Therefore I am glad on your behalf; but I want you to be wise in what is good, and simple concerning evil"* (Rom. 16:19). Innocent. No inward corruption or defilement, that is, not full of distrust, but a holy, divine likeness of Jesus that dares believe that the almighty God will surely watch over all. Hallelujah! *"No evil shall befall you, nor shall any plague come near your dwelling; for He shall give His angels charge over you, to keep you in all your ways"* (Ps. 91:10–11). The child of God who is rocked in the bosom of the Father has the sweetest touch of heaven, and the honey of the Word is always in his life.

If the saints only knew how precious they are in the sight of God (Isa. 43:4), they would scarcely be able to sleep for thinking of His watchful, loving care. Oh, He is a precious Jesus! He is a lovely Savior! He is divine in all His attitudes toward us, and He makes our hearts burn. There is nothing like it. "Oh," said the two men who had traveled to Emmaus with Jesus, "didn't our hearts burn within us as He walked with us and talked with us?" (See Luke 24:32.) Oh, beloved, it must be so today.

Always keep in mind that the Holy Spirit must bring manifestation. We must understand that the Holy Spirit is breath, the Holy Spirit is a person, and it is the most marvelous thing to know that this Holy Spirit power can be in every part of our bodies. You can feel it from the crown of your head to the soles of your feet. Oh, it is lovely to be burning all over with the Holy Spirit! And when that takes place, the tongue must give forth the glory and the praise.

You must be in the place of magnifying the Lord. The Holy Spirit is the great Magnifier of Jesus, the great Illuminator of Jesus. After the Holy Spirit comes in, it is impossible to keep your tongue still. Why, you would burst if you didn't give Him utterance! What about a silent baptized soul? Such a person is not to be found in the Scriptures. You will find that when you speak to God in the new tongue He gives you, you enter into a close communion with Him never experienced before. Talk about preaching! I would like to know how it will be possible for all the people filled with the Holy Spirit to stop preaching. Even the sons and daughters must prophesy (Joel 2:28). After the Holy Spirit comes in, a man is in a new order in God. You will find it so real that you will want to sing, talk, laugh, and shout. We are in a strange place when the Holy Spirit comes in. If the incoming of the Spirit is lovely, what must be the outflow? The incoming is only to be an outflow.

I am very interested in scenery. When I was in Switzerland, I wasn't satisfied until I went to the top of the mountain, though I like the valleys also. On the summit of the mountain, the sun beats on the snow and sends the water trickling down the mountain right through to the meadows. Go there and see if you can stop the water. It is the same way in the spiritual realm. God begins with the divine flow of His eternal power, which is the Holy Spirit, and you cannot stop it.

Thought for today: Faith is the open door through which the Lord comes in.

March 26

Spiritual Giants

Why look so intently at us, as though by our own power or godliness
we had made this man walk?
—Acts 3:12

Scripture reading: Acts 3:2–26

We must always clearly see that the baptism in the Spirit must make us ministering spirits. Peter and John had been baptized only a short time when they met the lame man at the temple. Did they know what they had? No. I challenge you to try to know what you have. No one knows what he has in the baptism in the Holy Spirit. You have no conception of it. You cannot measure it by any human standards. It is greater than any man can imagine; consequently, those two disciples had no idea what they had.

For the first time after they had been baptized in the Holy Spirit, they came down to the Gate Beautiful. There they saw the man sitting who had been lame for over forty years. What was the first thing that happened after they saw him? Ministry. What was the second? Operation. What was the third? Manifestation, of course. It could not be otherwise. You will always find that this order in the Scriptures will be carried out in everybody.

I clearly see that we ought to have spiritual giants in the earth, mighty in understanding, amazing in activity, always having a wonderful testimony because of their faith-filled works. I find instead that there are many people who perhaps have better discernment than the average believer, better knowledge of the Word than the average believer, but they have failed to put their discernment and knowledge into practice, so the gifts lie dormant. I am here to help you to begin doing mighty acts in the power of God through the gifts of the Spirit. You will find that what I am speaking about is from personal knowledge derived from wonderful experiences in many lands. The man who is filled with the Holy Spirit is always acting. The first verse of the Acts of the Apostles says, *"Jesus began both to do and teach."* Jesus had to begin to do, and so must we.

Thought for today: I would rather have the Spirit of God on me for five minutes than receive a million dollars.

March 27

Help for the Hurting

You, O Lord, are a God full of compassion, and gracious,
longsuffering and abundant in mercy and truth.
—Psalm 86:15

Scripture reading: Lamentations 3:21–41

*I*n Sydney, Australia, a man with a cane passed by a friend and me. He had to get down and then twist over, and the torture on his face made a deep impression on my soul. I asked myself, "Is it right to pass by this man?" So I said to my friend, "There is a man in awful distress, and I cannot go farther. I must speak to him." I went over to this man and said to him, "You seem to be in great trouble." "Yes," he said, "I am no good and never will be." I said, "You see that hotel? Be in front of that door in five minutes, and I will pray for you, and you will be able to stand as straight as any man here." This statement exercised my faith in Jesus.

I came back after paying a bill, and he was there. I will never forget him wondering if he was going to be trapped, or why a man would stop him on the street and tell him he would be made to stand straight. However, I had said it, so it had to be. If you say anything, you must stand with God to make it so. Never say anything for bravado, unless you have the right to say it. Always be sure of your ground, and be sure that you are honoring God. If there is anything about the situation that will make *you* anything, it will bring you sorrow. Your whole ministry has to be along the lines of grace and blessing.

We helped him up the two steps, took him to the elevator, and got him upstairs. It was difficult to get him from the elevator to my room, as though Satan was making the last attempt for his life, but we got him there. In five minutes' time this man walked out of that room with his body as straight as any man's. He walked perfectly and declared he hadn't a pain in his body.

If God will stretch out His mighty power to loose afflicted legs, what mercy will He extend to that soul of yours that must exist forever? He invites you: *"Come to Me, all you who labor and are heavy laden, and I will give you rest"* (Matt. 11:28). God is willing in His great mercy to touch limbs with His mighty power, and if He is willing to do this, how much more eager He is to deliver from the power of Satan. How much more necessary it is for us to be healed of our soul sicknesses than of our bodily ailments! God is willing to give the double cure.

Beloved, it is ministry; it is operation; it is manifestation! Those are three of the leading principles of the baptism in the Holy Spirit. We must see to it that God is producing these three through us.

The Bible is the Word of God. It has the truths, and whatever people may say of them, they stand stationary, unmovable. Not one word of all His good promises will fail (1 Kings 8:56). His Word will come forth. In heaven it is settled (Ps. 119:89). On earth the fact must be made manifest that He is the God of everlasting power.

Thought for today: Grace is God's blessing coming down to you. You open the door to God as an act of faith, and God does all you want.

March 28

Begin to Act

Be diligent to present yourself approved to God, a worker who does not need to be ashamed, rightly dividing the word of truth.
—2 Timothy 2:15

Scripture reading: 2 Timothy 2:1–15; 20–21

God wants His glory to be seen. We are going to miss a great deal if we don't begin to act. But once we begin to act according to the will of God, we will find that God establishes our faith and from that day makes His promises real to us.

I was speaking about faith and what would take place if we believed God. When I left that place, it appeared that one man who worked in the coal mine had heard me. He had trouble with a stiff knee. He said to his wife, "I cannot help but think every day that Wigglesworth's message was to stir us to do something. I cannot get away from it. All the men in the pit know how I walk with a stiff knee, and you know how you have wrapped it with yards of flannel. Well, I am going to act. You have to be the congregation." He got his wife in front of him. "I am going to act and do just as Wigglesworth did." He got hold of his leg unmercifully, saying, "Come out, you devils; come out in the name of Jesus! Now, Jesus, help me. Come out, you devils; come out." Then he said, "Wife, they are gone! They are gone!" So he went to his place of worship, and all the coal miners were there. As he told them this story, they became delighted. They said, "Jack, come over here and help me." And Jack went. As soon as he was through in one home, he was invited to another, loosing these people from the pains they had gotten in the coal mine.

We have no idea what God has for us if we will only begin! But, oh, the grace we need! If we do this work outside of Him, if we do it for ourselves, it will be a failure. We will be able to succeed only as we do the work in the name of Jesus. Oh, the love that God's Son can put into us if we are only humble enough, weak enough, and helpless enough to know that unless He does it, it will not be done!

Live and walk in the Spirit. Talk with God. Let go of what is earthly, and take hold of God's ideals. God will bring you to an end of yourself. Begin with God this moment.

Thought for today: God wants us to be blessed, but first of all He wants us to be ready for the blessing.

March 29

A Double Cure

You shall receive power when the Holy Spirit has come upon you.
—Acts 1:8

Scripture reading: Romans 5:19–6:18

My friend, you need a double cure. You first need saving and cleansing and then the baptism of the Holy Spirit, until the old man never rises anymore, until you are absolutely dead to sin and alive to God by His Spirit and know that old things have passed away. When the Holy Spirit gets possession of a person, he is a new being entirely—he becomes saturated with divine power. We become a habitation of Him who is all light, all revelation, all power, and all love. Yes, God the Holy Spirit is manifested within us in such a way that it is glorious.

A certain rich man in London had a flourishing business. He used to count his many assets, but he was still troubled inside; he didn't know what to do. Walking around his large building, he came upon a boy who was the doorkeeper; he found the boy whistling. Looking at him, he sized up the whole situation completely and went back to his office again and puzzled over the matter. Although he continued with his business, he could find no peace. His bank could not help him; his money, his success, could not help him. He had an aching void. He was helpless within. My friend, having the world without having God is like being *"whitewashed tombs"* (Matt. 23:27).

When he could get no rest, he exclaimed, "I will go and see what the boy is doing." Again he went and found him whistling. "I want you to come into my office," he said. When they entered the office, the man said, "Tell me, what makes you so happy and cheerful?" "Oh," replied the boy, "I used to be so miserable until I went to a little mission and heard about Jesus. Then I was saved and filled with the Holy Spirit. I am always whistling inside; if I am not whistling, I am singing. I am just full!"

This rich man obtained the address of the mission from the boy, went to the services, and sat near the door. But the power of God moved so strongly that when the altar call was given, he responded. God saved him and, a few days afterward, filled him with the Holy Spirit. The man found himself at his desk, shouting, "Oh, hallelujah!"

The blessed Son of God wants to fill us with such glory until our whole body is aflame with the power of the Holy Spirit. I see there is *"much more"* (Rom. 5:9). Glory to God! My daughter asked some African boys to tell her the difference between being saved and being filled with the Holy Spirit. "Ah," they said, "when we were saved, it was very good; but when we received the Holy Spirit, it was more so." Many of you have never received the "more so."

After the Holy Spirit comes upon you, you will have power. God will mightily move within your life; the power of the Holy Spirit will overshadow you, inwardly moving you until you know there is a divine plan different from anything that you have had in your life before.

Has He come? He is going to come to you. I am expecting that God will so manifest His presence and power that He will show you the necessity of receiving the Holy Spirit. Also, God will heal those who need healing. Everything is to be had now: salvation, sanctification, the fullness of the Holy Spirit, and healing. God is working mightily by the power of His Spirit, bringing to us a fullness of His perfect redemption until every soul may know that God has all power.

Thought for today: God is the essence of joy to us in a time when all seems barren, when it seems that nothing can help us but the light from heaven that is far brighter than the sun. When that touches you and changes you, you realize nothing is worthwhile but that.

March 30

Life-Giving Faith

When He had come into the house, the blind men came to Him. And Jesus said to them, "Do you believe that I am able to do this?" They said to Him, "Yes, Lord." Then He touched their eyes, saying, "According to your faith let it be to you."
—Matthew 9:28–29

Scripture reading: Romans 4:8–5:2

What it means for people to have faith! What it will mean when we all have faith! We know that as soon as faith is in perfect operation, we will be in the place where God is manifested right before our eyes. The pure in heart will see God (Matt. 5:8), and all the steps of purity are a divine appointment of more faith. The more purity, the more faith.

When Lazarus died and Jesus knew that Mary, Martha, and everyone around them had lost confidence and faith, He turned to the Father in prayer and said, *"Father...I know that You always hear Me"* (John 11:41–42). Jesus commanded Lazarus to come out of the tomb; death had to give him up, and everything had to come to pass as He said.

Fellowship, purity, unity—these things reflect a living cooperation in which we are being changed from faith to faith. May the Lord grant to you this thought today: How may I more and more abandon myself from any earthly, human fellowship, until I am absolutely so bound to God that God has the right-of-way to the throne of my heart, until the center of my emotions is blessedly purified, until there is no room for anything except the Son of God, who is the Author and Finisher of faith (Heb. 12:2)? Then Christ will be manifested in your flesh, destroying everything that is outside of Him.

Thought for today: Jesus' blood and His mighty name are an antidote to all the subtle seeds of unbelief that Satan will try to sow in your mind.

March 31

Be Satisfied

If anyone thirsts, let him come to Me and drink.
—John 7:37

Scripture reading: John 7:37–8:12

*M*ost of us have seen water baptism in action so often that we know what it means. But I want you to see that God's very great desire is for you to be covered with the baptism of the Holy Spirit. He wants you to be so immersed with the light and revelation of the Holy Spirit, the third person of the Trinity, that your whole body will be not only filled but also covered over until you walk in the presence of the power of God.

Jesus saw all the people at the Feast of Tabernacles, and He not only had a great ability to scrutinize, to unfold the inward thoughts and intents of the heart, but He also saw things at a glance; He took in a situation in just a moment's time.

We must not forget that He was filled with the Holy Spirit. He was lovely because He was full of the divine inflow of the life of God. Look at how He dealt with this situation. He saw the people who had been at Jerusalem at the feast, and they were coming back dissatisfied. My Lord could never be satisfied when anybody was dissatisfied.

Nowhere in Scripture is it recorded that you should be famished, naked, full of discord, full of evil, full of disorder, full of sensuality, or full of carnality. That was what was taking place at the feast, and they came away hungrier than they were before. Jesus saw them like that, and He said, "*'Ho! Everyone who thirsts, come to the waters'* (Isa. 55:1). Come to Me, you who are thirsty, and I will give you drink."

Oh, the Master could give! The Master had it to give. Beloved, He is here to give, and I am sure He will give.

Yes, the heavy hand of God is full of mercy. The two-edged sword is full of dividing. (See Hebrews 4:12.) His quickening Spirit puts to death everything that needs to die so that He might transform you by the resurrection of His life.

Thought for today: The death of Christ brings forth the life of Christ.

April 1

Dare to Believe God

Until now you have asked nothing in My name.
Ask, and you will receive, that your joy may be full.
—John 16:24

Scripture reading: 2 Chronicles 20:15–30

God has a plan for us that is greater than our thoughts, greater than words can say. You who have been asking great things from God for a long time would be amazed if you entered into prayer understanding that the Master, Jesus, has such knowledge of the mightiness of the Father's power and of the joint union with Him that He can say: nothing is impossible for you to ask. He alone can say, *"Until now you have asked nothing."*

If you will only dispose of yourself—for nothing but yourself will hinder you—it may be today that God will transform you so that you will be an altogether different person, as you have never been before. Move beyond your human mind, your human measure, your own strength, and all your resources—this is a big thing for me to say—and let inspiration take charge of you entirely, and bring you out of yourself into the power of God.

Believe that today is a new beginning for you. You have never passed this way before. So I bring you to another day of passing over any heights, passing through mists or darkness. Dare to believe that the cloud is upon you, and it will break with an exceeding reward of blessing. Don't be afraid of clouds—they are all earthly. Never be afraid of an earthly thing. You belong to a higher order, a divine order, a spiritual order. Believe that God wants you to soar high this day.

Thought for today: Begin to believe in extravagant asking, believing that God is pleased when you ask large things.

April 2

The Elect of God

As the elect of God, holy and beloved, put on tender mercies,
kindness, humility, meekness, longsuffering; bearing with one
another, and forgiving one another, if anyone has a complaint
against another; even as Christ forgave you, so you also must do.
—Colossians 3:12–13

Scripture reading: Colossians 3:1–17

*T*ake note of this: there is an elect of God. I know that God
has people who are the elect of God, and if you would examine yourself, you would be amazed to find that you are
one of them. People are tremendously afraid of this position because they have so often heard, "Oh, you know you are the elect of
God! You are sure to be all right." There have been great churches
in England that were founded upon these things. I thank God that
they have all withered. If you go to England, you will find that
those strong people who used to hold all these things are almost
withered out. Why? Because they went on to say that, if you were
elect, you were right in whatever you did. That is wrong.

The elect of God are those who are pressing forward. The elect
of God cannot hold still: they are always on the wing. Every person
who has a knowledge of the elect of God realizes it is important
that he press forward. He cannot endure sin or shady things. The
elect are so in earnest to be elect for God that they burn every
bridge behind them.

Know that first there will be a falling away (2 Thess. 2:3). God
will bring into His treasury the realities of the truth and put them
side by side: the false, the true; those that can be shaken, and those
that cannot be shaken.

Thought for today: God wants us to be built upon the foundation
of truth so that we cannot be shaken in our minds, no matter what
comes.

April 3

The Man of Sin

*Many deceivers have gone out into the world who do not confess
Jesus Christ as coming in the flesh. This is a deceiver
and an antichrist.*
—2 John 7

Scripture reading: 1 John 2

When I was in Sydney, they said, "Whatever you do, you must see this place that they built for the man, the new man who is coming."

Theosophy, which is based on theories of reincarnation and other falsities, has a new man. Nothing but Theosophy could have a new man. The foundation of this Theosophy has always been corruptible. The formation of Theosophy was connected to one of the greatest atheists of the day. Theosophy sprang out of atheism.

The Man of Sin, as he comes forth, will do many things. There will be many false christs, and they will be manifestations of the forthcoming of the Man of Sin, but they will all come to an end. The Man of Sin will be revealed.

These people are determined to have a man. They know someone has to come. We Christians know who He is who is coming to us. But these people begin to make a man in this manner: they find a man in India, they polish him up as much as they can; they dress him up, but we are told by the Lord that soft clothing can go onto wolves' backs (Matt. 7:15).

We find that they are going to bring this man forth in great style. When I went around the amphitheater in Sydney that was made for this man to come, I saw as clearly as anything it was the preparation for the Man of Sin. But they do not believe that.

What will make you to know it is the Man of Sin? This: every religious sect and creed that are in the world all join to it. There is not a religion known that has not joined with it.

Why, that is exactly what the Devil wants. He wants all the false religions joining together, and the Man of Sin will be received with great applause when he comes.

Who will be saved? Who will know the day? Who now knows the Man of Sin? We feel him when we touch him, when he opens his mouth, when he writes in the newspaper, when we see his actions—we know who he is.

What has the Man of Sin always said? Why, exactly what Jehovah's Witnesses say. What? That there is no hell. The Devil has always said that. What does Christian Science say? No hell, no Devil. They are ready for him. The Devil has always said no hell, no evil. And these people are preparing, though they do not know it, for the Man of Sin.

We have to see that these days have to come before the Lord can come. There has to be a *"falling away"* (2 Thess. 2:3). There has to be in this day a manifestation so clear, of such undeniable fact. I tell you, when they begin to build temples for the Man of Sin to come (though they don't know it), you know the Day is at hand.

A person said to me, "You see, the Christian Scientists must be right. Look at the beautiful buildings; look at all the people following them." Yes, everybody can belong to it. You can go to any brothel you like, you can go to any theater you like, you can go to any race course you like, you can be mixed up with the rest of the people in your life and still be a Christian Scientist. You can have the Devil right and left and anywhere and still belong to Christian Science.

When the Man of Sin comes, he will be hailed on all sides. When he is manifested, who will miss him? Why, the reverent, the holy, the separated will miss him. Why will they miss him? Because they will not be here to greet him!

Thought for today: He who has been begotten in you is the very God of power who will preserve you and bring forth light and truth so that your vision will be clear.

Freedom from Fear

There is no fear in love; but perfect love casts out fear.
—1 John 4:18

Scripture reading: 1 John 4:7–21

Never be afraid of anything. There are two things in the world: one is fear, the other faith. One belongs to the Devil, the other to God. If you believe in God, there is no fear. If you sway toward any delusion of Satan, you will be brought into fear. Fear always brings bondage. There is a place of perfect love for Christ in which you are always casting out all fear and you are living in the place of freedom. (See 1 John 4:18.) Be sure that you never allow anything to make you afraid. God is for you; who can be against you (Rom. 8:31)?

The reason why so many people have gone into Christian Science is that the church is barren; it does not have the Holy Spirit. Christian Science exists because the churches have a barren place where the Holy Spirit has not been allowed to rule. There would be no room for Christian Science if the churches were filled with the Holy Spirit. But because the churches had nothing, then the needy people went to the Devil to fill the void, and he persuaded them that they had something. Now the same people are coming out knowing they have had nothing—only a wilderness experience.

Let us save ourselves from all this trouble by letting the Holy Spirit fill our hearts. Don't depend on any past tense, any past momentum, but let the anointing be upon you, let the presence and the power be upon you. Are you thirsty, longing, desiring? Then God will pour out of His treasures all you need. God wants to satisfy us with His great, abounding, holy love, imparting love upon love and faith upon faith.

If you have fallen short, it is because you refused the Holy Spirit. Let the Holy Spirit be light in you to lighten even the light that is in you, and no darkness will befall you; you will be kept in the middle of the road.

Be careful when anybody comes to you with a sugar-coated pill or a slimy tongue. The Spirit of the Lord always deals with truth. Give the Devil the biggest chase of his life by saying these words: *"If we walk in the light as He is in the light, we have fellowship*

April 4

with one another, and the blood of Jesus Christ His Son cleanses us from all sin" (1 John 1:7).

Look to the coming of the Lord. Be at peace; live in peace; forgive, and learn how to forgive. Never bear malice; don't hold any grudge against anybody. Forgive everybody. It does not matter whether they forgive you or not, you must forgive them. Live in forgiveness; live in repentance; live wholeheartedly. Set your house in order, for God's Son is coming to take what is in the house.

Thought for today: The cause of all deterioration is refusal of the Holy Spirit.

Joy in This Life

You will show me the path of life; in Your presence is fullness of joy;
at Your right hand are pleasures forevermore.
—Psalm 16:11

Scripture reading: Psalm 16

The Word of Life is to make your joy full. We must remember that what is absent in the world is joy. The world has never had joy; the world never will have joy. Joy is not in the five senses of the world. Feelings are there, happiness is there, but joy can only be produced where there is no alloy. Now, there is no alloy in heaven. Alloy means that there is a mixture. In the world there is happiness, but it is a mixture; very often it comes very close to sorrow. Often in the midst of festivities, there is a place of happiness, and right underneath is a very heavy heart.

But what Christians have is this: it is joy without alloy, without a mixture. It is inwardly expressive. It rises higher and higher until, if it had its perfect order, we would drown everything with a shout of praise coming from this holy presence.

We want everyone to receive the Holy Spirit because the Holy Spirit has a very blessed expression of the Lord in His glory, in His purity, in His power, and in all His blessed words. All these are coming forcefully through as the Holy Spirit is able to witness to you of Him. And every time the Son is manifested in your hearts by the Holy Spirit, you get a real stream of heavenly glory on earth: joy in the Holy Spirit—not in eating and drinking, but in something higher, something better. We all enjoy eating and drinking, but this is something higher, something better, something more substantial: joy in the Holy Spirit! And the Holy Spirit can bring this joy to us.

Thought for today: No one gets his answers to his prayers—he never does—for God answers prayers abundantly above what we ask or think to pray for.

April 6

His Glory and Ours

*But we all, with unveiled face, beholding as in a mirror the glory of
the Lord, are being transformed into the same image from glory to
glory, just as by the Spirit of the Lord.*
—2 Corinthians 3:18

Scripture reading: 1 Corinthians 15:35–58

The coming of the Lord is for the life of the Lord, not for our
bodies. Our bodies will never be in heaven; they will never
reach there. They are terrestrial things, and everything terrestrial will come to an end on this earth.

What is going to be there? The life of the Son of God, the nature of the Son of God, the holiness of the Son of God, the purity.
Life will be there, as well as the likeness and everything pertaining
to it.

As we go on, we will see that He is in this life that is going to
have a new body. This life will demand a new body; it is demanding
it now. This is a law of life. You have a law of life in nature. But
now you have to have a law of a spirit of life, which is free from
everything of the natural order (Rom. 8:2). And this is the law of
life, of the life of Christ that is in you, which I am taking you
through or bringing you to, so that you may be firmly fixed on the
perfect knowledge that no matter what happens, you know you will
go. When I say "you," it is right to say you will go. You will go up,
but you, as you now know yourself, won't go in. You will be dissolved as you go. But the nature of the Son, the new life, will go in
with your new body.

We move on now to a further foundation. In the first chapter
of John, the fourteenth verse, we read, *"And the Word became flesh*
[they saw it] *and dwelt among us* [it was right in the midst of
them, and they couldn't help seeing the glory of it], *and we beheld
His glory, the glory as of the only begotten of the Father, full of
grace and truth.*

Now you have to receive that—full of grace, full of truth, the
glory of the Lord. You must remember that glory is not a halo
around your head. In some paintings of the Lord Jesus or of saints,
you will see a light patch painted just over their heads, the idea
being to exhibit glory. Glory never is that way. Glory is expressive.

April 6

Glory had two mighty powers with it: it not only had grace, which was the canopy of the mercy of the high order of God, all the time prevailing and covering and pressing Him, but it also had truth. Christ spoke so that every heart was filled with what He said.

And this glory is what we have to have. This is what will be caught up to heaven and expressed. Can expressiveness be taken up? Yes, because it is the nature of the new birth. Will truth be taken up? Yes, for truth is the very embodiment of the Son. Just as this life permeates through your body, it would be impossible for any saint ever to be free to give anything but absolute truth. The saint has to become an embodiment of truth, life, and Christ manifested. We have to be like Him, just as He was, filled with His glory, this divine order speaking out of fullness, greater than anything we have ever had. Our minds and souls must perceive the things of God so that we live, move, and act in this glory.

The glory of the Lord, the presence of the Lord, the power of the Lord, the life of the Lord is being made manifest. It is not you He is after: it is what has been created in you.

Thought for today: Glory is not an outside halo; glory is an inward conception.

April 7

The New Birth

As we have borne the image of the man of dust, we shall also bear
the image of the heavenly Man.
—1 Corinthians 15:49

Scripture reading: John 3:1–21

*J*esus spoke to Nicodemus and told him that this new birth is not flesh and blood; it is the life of God. It is a spiritual life, as real as God, as true as God. We are formed in God's very image. He has quickened us and made us to be like Him with an inward, spiritual life. Just as we have our humanity, so the new nature, the new power, is continually forming a new man in us after the order of Him. The first Adam was formed, and we are in the vision of him; the last Adam, the new creation, is going to have a vision and expression like Him.

I was once exactly where Nicodemus was; I said, *"How can these things be?"* (John 3:9). Then there came by faith a regenerating power that made me know I was born of God. It came like the wind. I could not see it, but I felt it. It had a tremendous effect upon my human nature, and I found that I was a new creation. I found I wanted to pray and to talk about the Lord. Oh, I will never forget saying "Father."

If you catch this truth, it does not matter where you are. If you are in exile somewhere—isolated from everybody, far from any human comfort—if this life gets into you, you will know that when He comes again, you will go to meet Him.

When you are born of God, God's nature comes in. I won't call it the germ of eternal life, but the seed of God, because we are conceived by the Word, we are quickened by the power, we are made after His order. What is from above has entered into what is below, and you have now become a quickened spirit. You were dead, without aspiration, and without desire. As soon as His life comes in, aspiration, desire, and prayer ascend, lifting higher and higher, and you have already moved toward heavenly things.

Thought for today: This new creation cannot live bound to the earth. It always lives, soaring higher—higher and higher, loftier and loftier, holier and holier.

April 8

The Beginning of Life

Whoever desires to save his life will lose it,
but whoever loses his life for My sake will find it.
—Matthew 16:25

Scripture reading: Matthew 16:13–26

God is pruning us, teaching us to observe that those who enter into this life have ceased from their own works (Heb. 4:10). Those who enter into this spiritual awakening have no more bondage. They have learned that *"no one engaged in warfare entangles himself with the affairs of this life"* (2 Tim. 2:4). They have a new inspiration of divine power. It is the nature of the Son of God.

But the Bible says, *"Strive to enter through the narrow gate"* (Luke 13:24). Yes, beloved, this means you will have to work for it, because your own nature will interfere with you; your friends will often stand in the way. Your position will many times almost bring you to a place where you will be doomed if you take that stand.

The apostle Peter had entered into this divine position just before Jesus made His statement, *"Whoever desires to save his life will lose it, but whoever loses his life for My sake will find it."* Peter had just received this new life; he had just entered into the place where he knew that Jesus was the Son of God, saying, *"You are the Christ, the Son of the living God"* (Matt. 16:16). Then Jesus began breaking the seal of His ministry. He said, *"The Son of Man must be delivered into the hands of sinful men, and be crucified, and the third day rise again"* (Luke 24:7).

Peter said, "This will not happen. I'll see to that! You leave that business with me. Let anybody touch you, and I will stand in your place; I will be with you." And Jesus said, *"Get behind Me, Satan! You are an offense to Me, for you are not mindful of the things of God, but the things of men"* (Matt. 16:23).

Anything that hinders me from falling into the ground, everything that interferes with my taking up my cross, dying to self, separating from the world, cleaning my life up, or entering through the narrow gate, anything that interferes with that is Satan's power. *"Unless a grain of wheat falls into the ground and dies, it remains alone"* (John 12:24).

166

April 8

Strive to enter in. Seek to be worthy to enter in. Let God be honored by your leaving behind the things that you know are taking your life, hindering your progress, blighting your prospects, and ruining your mind—for nothing will dull the mind's perceptions like touching earthly things that are not clean.

When God began dealing with me on holy lines, I was working for thirteen saloons, meaning that I was going to thirteen different bars. Of course, I was among hundreds of other customers. God dealt with me in this matter, and I cleared up the whole situation in the presence of God. That was only one thing; there were a thousand other things.

God wants us to be holy, pure, and perfect the whole way through. The inheritance is an incorruptible inheritance; it is undefiled, and it does not fade away (1 Pet. 1:4). Those who are entering in are judging themselves so that they will not be condemned with the world (1 Cor. 11:32). Many people have fallen asleep. (See verses 27–30.) Why? Because they did not listen to the correction of the Word of the Lord. Some have been ill, and God dealt with them; they would not heed, and then God put them to sleep.

Oh, that God the Holy Spirit will have a choice with us today, that we will judge ourselves so that we are not condemned with the world! *"For if we would judge ourselves, we would not be judged"* (v. 31). What is it to judge yourself? If the Lord speaks, if He says, "Let it go," no matter if it is as dear as your right eye, you must let it go. If it is as costly as your right foot, you must let it go. It is far better to let it go.

Strive to enter in.

Thought for today: Human life has an end; divine life has only a beginning.

The Bread of Life

Moses did not give you the bread from heaven, but My Father gives you the true bread from heaven. For the bread of God is He who comes down from heaven and gives life to the world.
—John 6:32–33

Scripture reading: John 6:5–11; 26–51

*B*eloved, I want God to give you a spiritual appetite so that you will have a great inward desire to eat the Word, where you will savor it with joy, where you will consume it with grace. As the Word comes to you—the Word of God, the Bread of Heaven, the very thing you need, the very nature of the life of the Son of God—and as you eat, you will be made in a new order after Him who has created you for His plan and purpose.

The process of the Word of God must kindle in us a separation from the world. It must bring death to everything except the life of the Word of Christ in our hearts. I want to save you from judging, because to the degree that you have not come into the revelation of this eternal working in you, to that degree you will not come right through believing in the true principle of the Word of Life.

The Word of God is to give you light. The Spirit of the Lord and the Word of the Lord—one is light, the other is life. We must see that God wants us to have these two divine properties, life and light, so that we are in a perfect place to judge ourselves by the Word of God. The Word of God will stand true, whatever our opinions may be. Scripture says very truly, *"For what if some did not believe? Will their unbelief make the faithfulness of God without effect?"* (Rom. 3:3). Will it change the Word?

God will sift the believer. Get away from the chaff. Chaff is judgment; chaff is unbelief; chaff is fear; chaff is failing. It is the covering of the weak, and as long as it covers the weak, it hinders them from coming for bread. So God has to deal with the chaff; He has to remove it so that you might be the pure bread, the pure life, the pure word, and so that there will be no strange thing in you, no misunderstanding.

God has to deal with His people, and if God deals with the house of God, then the world will soon be dealt with (1 Pet. 4:17). The principle is this: all the world needs and longs to be right, and so we have to be salt and light to guide them, to lead them, to operate before them so that they see our good works and glorify our Lord.

You need the Bread to feed the life to you. The Word of God is the Bread. There is no famine going on now; God is giving us the Bread of Life.

"He who comes to Me shall never hunger, and he who believes in Me shall never thirst" (John 6:35). It is a constant satisfaction, an inward joyful expression, a place of peace.

Thought for today: The Word of God will be the same whether people believe it or not.

Faith—Not Feelings

He who believes in the Son of God has the witness in himself.
—1 John 5:10

Scripture reading: 1 John 5:1–13

I find people continually deceived because they look around them, and many people have lost all because of their feelings. You did not come to Jesus. God gave you to Jesus. Where did He find you? He found you in the world, and He gave you to Jesus, and Jesus gave you eternal life. As He received everyone whom He had given His life for and given His life to, He said He would lose nothing; He would preserve them (John 17:12).

"Oh," you say, "that all depends." Yes, it does, it depends upon whether you believe God or not. I am not going to believe that all who say they are believers, believe. There was one group who came up to Jesus and said, "We are the seed of Abraham; we have Abraham for our father." (See John 8:39.) He said, "You are mistaken; you are the seed of the Devil." (See verses 39–44.)

We know that we are the sons of God because we do those things that please Him. We know we are the sons of God because we love to keep His commandments. *"His commandments are not burdensome"* (1 John 5:3). And we know we are the sons of God because we overcome the world. (See verse 4.)

That is what every son of God has to do—overcome the world. And this life we receive from Him is eternal and everlasting and will not see corruption. But God is feeding us with that wonderful Word of promise, so that we might know that we have the inheritance in the Spirit, and so that we may know that we are going on to the place of "Ready, Lord, ready!"

Are you ready to go? It is impossible for the life of God or the law of the life of the Spirit to be in you unless it is doing its work. The law of the life of the Spirit will be putting to death all the natural life and will quicken you continually with spiritual life until your earthly life is over.

When I see white hair and wrinkled faces, I say, "You have to go. It does not matter what you say, you cannot stop; you have to go. You will begin blossoming, and in a short time you will bloom and be off."

That is a natural plan, but I am talking about a supernatural plan. We know that as we have borne the image of the earthly, we are going to bear the image of the heavenly (1 Cor. 15:49). Mortality will be swallowed up in life (2 Cor. 5:4). The very nature of the Son of God is in us, creating life, immortality, and power. The power of the Word of the living Christ!

The Gospel of the grace of God has power to bring immortality and life. What is the Gospel? It is the Word, the Bread of the Son of God. Feed on it in your heart. It is immortality; it is life by the Word of quickening and by the Word of truth.

You look good, you are an inspiration, but you know there are many marks and blemishes. You know that as you pass through the weary days of toil, battling with sin on every side, there is a light in you, a life in you that is going to pass away, and you are going to be like Him. It will be the same face, but the marks, the scars, and the spots will have gone. What will do it? The Bread! Oh, Lord, ever more give us this Bread, the Bread of the Son of God!

"Most assuredly, I say to you, he who believes in Me has everlasting life. I am the bread of life" (John 6:47–48). Everlasting life means Bread. Men cannot live by earthly bread alone, but by the Word of the living God (Matt. 4:4).

Thought for today: The Bible is my heavenly bank. I find everything I want in it. It brings life, health, peace, and abundance so that we should never be poor anymore.

Tried by Fire, Enriched by Grace

His name is called The Word of God.
—Revelation 19:13

Scripture reading: 1 Peter 1:3–21

*H*is name is the Word of God, who gave His life for the world. And of His life, of His Spirit, of His grace, of His faith we have received. What does this mean? Oh, you tried ones, grace is being poured into you—grace from heaven, grace enriched, grace abundant. His grace is for your weakness, so that you might be sustained in the trial, in the fire, passing through it, coming out more like the Lord.

This inspires me. Why? Because time comes to an end. All the beautiful buildings in the world, the mountains, the heavens and all, will pass away. The heavens will be rolled up as a scroll (Isa. 34:4), and all things *"will melt with fervent heat"* (2 Pet. 3:10). But one thing cannot be burned; one thing cannot be changed; one thing can stand the fire, the water, persecution, and anything else. What is it? The same thing that went into the fire and remained untouched while the men on the outside were slain by the fire.

Shadrach, Meshach, and Abednego were in the fire, and it did not burn them. The king was amazed when he saw them walking. "Oh!" he said. *"Did we not cast three men bound into the midst of the fire?"* (Dan. 3:24).

"True, O king" (v. 24), his men replied.

"'Look!' he answered, 'I see four men loose, walking in the midst of the fire...and the form of the fourth is like the Son of God'" (v. 25).

There is no consuming. There is a life of the Son of God that cannot be burned, cannot see corruption, passes through fire, passes through clouds, passes through legions of demons and will clear them out of the way, passes through everything. Oh, that life! What is it? The life of the Son of God. He came to give life; He came to give life more abundantly (John 10:10). Oh, what a life, abounding life, resurrection life!

Do you have it? Is it yours? Are you afraid you will lose it? Do you believe He will lose you?

"What makes you say that?" you ask.

April 11

Because sometimes I hear doubters. This is a wonderful Scripture for doubters.

My sheep hear My voice, and I know them, and they follow Me. And I give them eternal life, and they shall never perish; neither shall anyone snatch them out of My hand. My Father, who has given them to Me, is greater than all; and no one is able to snatch them out of My Father's hand. (John 10:27–29)

Oh, that life—full of deity, full of assurance, full of victory, full of a shout. Will you be ready? How can you help it? Is it possible not to be ready? Why, it is not your life, it is His life. You did not seek Him; it was He who sought you. You cannot keep yourself; it is He who keeps you. You did not make the offering; it was God who made the offering. So it is all of grace. But what a wonderful grace!

What is going? The life. He gives everlasting life, and those who receive it will never perish.

Oh, where is your faith? Is your faith inspired? Are you quickened? Is there within you a truth that is saying, "I feel it, I know it. It moves me; I have it"? Yes, and you will be there in heaven—as surely as you are here, you will be there.

This thing that we are entering into is going to continue forever. Let us feed on this Bread; let us live in this holy atmosphere. This is divine nature that God is causing us to know, which will last forever.

Thought for today: Keep us, Lord, in a place of buying up opportunities, burning up bridges, paying the prices, denying ourselves so that we might be worthy of being Your own forever.

April 12

The Power of the Blood

Through death He...destroy[ed] *him who had the power of death,*
that is, the devil, and release[d] *those who through fear of death*
were all their lifetime subject to bondage.
—Hebrews 2:14–15

Scripture reading: Hebrews 2:1–18

*G*od wants you to know that He has redemption for you through the blood of Jesus, a new birth unto righteousness, a change from darkness into light, from the power of Satan unto God. This blessed salvation through the blood of Jesus will free you from all the power of Satan and make you a joint-heir with Christ. Oh, this is a glorious inheritance that we have in Jesus Christ. Glory to God! Jesus was manifested in the flesh, manifested to destroy the works of the Devil. Christ can make us overcomers, destroying the power and passion of sin and dwelling in us by His mighty power. He can so transform our lives that we will love righteousness and hate iniquity; He can make us holy, because just as God dwelt in His Son by the power of the Holy Spirit, so God can dwell in us through Christ.

I want you to see that we receive sonship because of Christ's obedience. Do not forget what the Scripture says, *"Though He was a Son, yet He learned obedience by the things which He suffered"* (Heb. 5:8). If you turn to the Scriptures, you will see how the people reviled Him and how they tried to kill Him by throwing Him over the cliff. But He passed through the midst of the whole crowd, and as soon as He got out, He saw a blind man and healed him. He was in the world but not of it.

It is lovely—it is divinely glorious—this power of the new creation, this birth unto righteousness by faith in the Atonement. It can transform you so that you can be in Jesus Christ and know that it is another power dominating, controlling, filling you, and making you understand that though you are still in the body, you are governed by the Spirit. Oh, to live in all the beauty of the glory and grandeur of the Holy Spirit!

Thought for today: Leave Doubting Street; live on Faith-Victory Street.

April 13

Changed by His Love

The sacrifices of God are a broken spirit, a broken and a contrite heart; these, O God, You will not despise.
—Psalm 51:17

Scripture reading: Psalm 51:1–17

A constraining power in Christ causes you to know that His love is different from anything else in the world. In Scripture it is called a *"sincere love"* (1 Pet. 1:22). This has a tremendously deep meaning. What is it, exactly? Beloved, Jesus will tell you what it is. It is a denunciation of yourself as the power of Christ lays hold of you. He loved you when you were yet a sinner (Rom. 5:8), and He seeks your love in return. His is an unfeigned love, a love that can stand ridicule, persecution, and slander, because it is a love brought about in you by the power of the Holy Spirit, changing you from one state of glory to another. Christ is King of Kings and Lord of Lords, and *"of His kingdom there will be no end"* (Luke 1:33). *"He shall see His seed, He shall prolong His days, and the pleasure of the LORD shall prosper in His hand"* (Isa. 53:10).

Oh, beloved, what a Christ we have! I want you to see that there is nothing like Him. If you see Him today, you needy ones, and gaze at Him, you will be changed. As you look at Him, you will find that even your natural bodies will change. His strength will come into you, and you will be transformed. He is the God of the sinner; He is the God of the helpless; He is full of mercy. I like the thought of His calling Himself the God of Jacob (Exod. 3:6). When He says He is the God of Jacob, there is room for everybody. I tell you, He is your God, and He is preparing to meet you exactly as He met Jacob.

Jacob had deceived someone in everything he had done. He had deceived Esau to get his birthright (Gen. 25:29–34) and Laban to get his cattle (Gen. 30:25–43). The Devil manipulated Jacob, but, praise God, there was one thing that Jacob knew: he knew that God had fulfilled His promise. In Bethel, God let Jacob see the ladder—a wonderful ladder, for it reached from earth to heaven—and Jacob saw angels ascending and descending upon it (Gen. 28:12). Bethel is the place of prayer. It is a place of changing conditions, of earth entering heaven. God brought Jacob right back to the same place, regardless of how he had wandered. Jacob had to let everything go, and he was left alone. The same old Jacob remained, and as long as God would let him wrestle with Him, he wrestled.

This is an example of holding on to this world—we never let go until we have to. God touched Jacob, and as soon as he was touched, he found out that he was no good. Then the Man said, *"Let Me go."* But Jacob answered, *"I will not let You go unless You bless me!"* (Gen. 32:26). Friend, God will bless you if you get to that point, but you are no good as long as you wrestle. It is marvelous how God meets us in our distresses. When the cry comes from broken hearts, then God comes.

Thought for today: When you come in helplessness and with a real cry of brokenness, then God will meet you.

April 14

What Is in Your Heart?

*A good man out of the good treasure of his heart
brings forth good things, and an evil man out of the evil treasure
brings forth evil things.*
—Matthew 12:35

Scripture reading: Matthew 12:25–45

God's mercy never fails. When Jesus came down from the Mount of Transfiguration, He set His face to go to the cross for you and me. When He came down from the mountain, there was a man there who had a son whom the Devil had taken and thrown down and bruised. The man cried out, saying, "Lord, come and help me. Here is my son; the Devil takes him and tears at him until he foams at the mouth. I brought him to Your disciples, but they could not help him." (See Mark 9:17–18.)

May God strengthen our hands and take away all our unbelief. Jesus said, *"O faithless generation, how long shall I be with you?…Bring him to Me"* (v. 19), and they brought him to Jesus, who cast out the evil spirit. But even in the presence of Jesus, those evil spirits tore the boy and left him as one dead until Christ lifted him up. (See verses 20–27.)

Just think of that satanic power. The Devil goes about to kill, *"seeking whom he may devour"* (1 Pet. 5:8), but Christ said, "I came to give life, and life more abundantly" (John 10:10). May God keep us in the place where the Devil will have no power and no victory. I pray God that the demon powers that come out of people in today's churches will never return again.

Oh, if I could only show you what it means to be delivered by the power of Jesus and what it means to lose your deliverance through your own foolishness! I know of a case like this. A man possessed by demonic power and sickness and weakness came to Jesus, and He cast the evil spirit out. The man was made whole. Then, instead of the man seeking the Holy Spirit and the light of God, he afterward went to the races. God save us! The healing power is for the glory of God, and it appears that this man was like the teaching that Jesus gave in Matthew 12. His house was *"empty, swept, and put in order"* (Matt. 12:44), but he did not receive Christ and the power of the Spirit. So the evil spirit went back and

177

found he could gain an entrance again because the man had no other inhabitant in him. He took with him other evil spirits, and the man's case was worse than before. (See verses 43-45.)

We must make sure that the power of God comes to inhabit us. Are you willing to so surrender yourself to God today that Satan will have no dominion over you?

Thought for today: If you want to be healed by the power of God, it means that your life has to be filled with God.

April 15

Filled with the Spirit

*Do not be conformed to this world, but be transformed by the
renewing of your mind, that you may prove what is that good and
acceptable and perfect will of God.*
—Romans 12:2

Scripture reading: 2 Corinthians 4

God wants to make us pillars: honorable, strong, and holy. God
will move us on. I am enamored with the possibility of this.
God wants you to know that you are saved, cleansed, delivered, and marching to victory. He has given you the faith to believe. God has a plan for you! *"Set your mind on things above"* (Col.
3:2), and get into the heavenly places with Christ.

You cannot repeat the name of Jesus too often. What a privilege it is to kneel and get right into heaven the moment we pray,
where the glory descends, the fire burns, faith is active, and the
light dispels the darkness.

Jesus is the light and the life of men; no man can have this
light and still walk in darkness. (See John 8:12.) *"When Christ who
is our life appears, then you also will appear with Him in glory"*
(Col. 3:4). Where His life is, disease cannot remain. Is not He who
dwells in us greater than all? Is He greater? Yes, when He has full
control. If one thing is permitted outside the will of God, it hinders
us in our standing against the powers of Satan. We must allow the
Word of God to judge us, lest we stand condemned with the world
(1 Cor. 11:32).

"When Christ who is our life appears" (Col. 3:4). Can I have
any life apart from Him, any joy or any fellowship apart from Him?
Jesus said, *"The ruler of this world is coming, and he has nothing
in Me"* (John 14:30). All that is contrary in us is withered by the
indwelling life of the Son of God.

Are we ready? Have we been clothed with the Holy Spirit? Has
mortality been swallowed up in life? If He who is our life came, we
should go. I know that the Lord laid His hand on me. He filled me
with the Holy Spirit.

Heaven has begun within me. I am happy now, and free, since
the Comforter has come. The Comforter is the great Revealer of
the kingdom of God. He came to give us the more abundant life.

God has designed the plan, and nothing else really matters because the Lord loves us. God sets great store in us.

The way into glory is through the flesh being torn away from the world and separated unto God. This freedom of spirit, freedom from the law of sin and death, is cause for rejoicing every day. The perfect law destroys the natural law. Spiritual activity takes in every passing ray, ushering in the days of heaven upon earth, when there is no sickness and when we do not even remember that we have bodies. The life of God changes us and brings us into the heavenly realm, where our reign over principalities and over all evil is limitless, powerful, and supernatural.

If the natural body decays, the Spirit renews. Spiritual power increases until, with one mind and one heart, the glory is brought down over all the earth, right on into divine life. When the whole life is filled, this is Pentecost come again. The life of the Lord will be manifested wherever we are, whether in a bus or on a train. We will be filled with the life of Jesus unto perfection, rejoicing in hope of the glory of God (Rom. 5:2), always looking for our translation into heaven.

I must have the overflowing life in the Spirit. God is not pleased with anything less. It is a disgrace to be part of an ordinary plan after we are filled with the Holy Spirit. We are to be salt in the earth (Matt. 5:13). We are to be hot, not lukewarm (Rev. 3:16), which means seeing God with eagerness, liberty, movement, and power. Believe! Believe!

Thought for today: The life of the Lord in us draws us as a magnet, with His life eating up all else.

April 16

The Appointed Hour

When the hour had come, He sat down,
and the twelve apostles with Him.
—Luke 22:14

Scripture reading: Luke 22:7–53

That was the most wonderful hour. There never was an hour, never will be an hour like that hour. What hour was it? It was when all of creation passed under the blood, when all that ever lived came under the glorious covering of the blood. It was an hour of destruction of demon power. It was an appointed hour of life coming out of death. It was an hour when all the world was coming into emancipation by the blood. It was an hour in the world's history when it emerged from dark chaos. It was a wonderful hour! Praise God for that hour! Was it a dark hour? It was a dark hour for Him, but a wonderful light dawned for us. It was tremendously dark for the Son of Man, but, praise God, He came through it.

There are some things in the Scriptures that move me greatly. I am glad that Paul was a human being. I am glad that Jesus became a man. I am glad that Daniel was human, and I am also glad that John was human. You ask, "Why?" Because I see that whatever God has done for other people, He can do for me. And I find that God has done such wonderful things for other people that I am always expecting that these things are possible for me. Think about this. It is a wonderful thought to me.

Jesus said in that trying hour—hear it for a moment—*"With fervent desire I have desired to eat this Passover with you before I suffer"* (Luke 22:15). Desire? What could be His desire? It was His desire because of the salvation of the world, His desire because of the dethronement of the powers of Satan, His desire because He knew He was going to conquer everything and make every man free who ever lived. It was a great desire, but what lay between Him and its fulfillment? Gethsemane lay between that and the cross!

Some people say that Jesus died on the cross. It is perfectly true, but is that the only place? Jesus also died in Gethsemane. That was the tragic moment! That was the place where He paid the debt. It was in Gethsemane, and Gethsemane was between Him and the cross. He had a desire to eat this Passover, and He knew that Gethsemane was between Him and the cross.

I want you to think about Gethsemane. There, alone and with the tremendous weight and the awful effect of all sin and disease upon that body, He cried out, *"If it is possible, let this cup pass from Me"* (Matt. 26:39). He could only save men when He was man, but here, like a giant who has been refreshed and is coming out of a great chaos of darkness, He comes forth: *"For this cause I was born"* (John 18:37). It was His purpose to die for the world.

Oh, believer, will it ever pass through your lips or your mind for a moment that you will not desire to serve Christ? Can you, under any circumstances, stoop to take up your cross fully, to be in the place of ridicule, to surrender anything for the Man who said He desired to eat the Passover with His disciples, knowing what it meant? It can only come out of the depths of love we have for Him that we can say right now, "Lord Jesus, I will follow You."

Thought for today: Only by the Spirit can we understand what is spiritual.

April 17

Spiritual Revelation

*Take, eat; this is My body which is broken for you;
do this in remembrance of Me.*
—1 Corinthians 11:24

Scripture reading: Matthew 26:20–56

*I*t is a wonderful inheritance of faith to find shelter under the blood of Jesus. He took the cup, He took the bread, and He gave thanks. The very attitude of giving thanks for His shed blood, giving thanks for His broken body, overwhelms the heart. To think that my Lord could give thanks for His own shed blood! To think that my Lord could give thanks for His own broken body! Only divinity can reveal this sublime act to the heart.

The natural man cannot receive this revelation, but the spiritual man, the man who has been created anew by faith in Christ, is open to it. The man who believes that God comes in has the eternal seed of truth and righteousness and faith born into him. From the moment that he sees the truth through faith, he is made a new creation. The flesh ceases; the spiritual man begins. One is taken off, and the other is taken on, until a man is in the presence of God. I believe that the Lord brings a child of faith into a place of rest, causes him to sit with Him in heavenly places (Eph. 2:6), gives him a language in the Spirit, and makes him know that he no longer belongs to the law of creation.

Do you see the bread that represents His broken body? The Lord knew He could not bring us any nearer to His broken body, so He took the natural elements and said, "This bread represents my broken body." (See Luke 22:19.) Now, will it ever become that body of Christ? No, never. You cannot make it so. It is foolishness to believe it, but I receive it as an emblem. When I eat it, the natural leads me into the supernatural, and instantly I begin to feed on the supernatural by faith. One leads me into the other.

Jesus said, *"Take, eat; this is My body"* (Matt. 26:26). I have a real knowledge of Christ through this emblem. We may take from the table of the riches of His promises. The riches of heaven are before us. Fear not; only believe, for God has opened the treasures of His holy Word.

As the disciples were gathered together with Jesus, He looked on them and said right into their ears, *"One of you will betray Me"* (v. 21). Jesus knew who would betray Him. They whispered to one another, "Who is it?" None of them had real confidence that it would not be he. That is the serious part about it; they had so little confidence in their ability to face the opposition that was before them, and they had no confidence that it would not be one of them.

Jesus knew. I can imagine that He had been talking to Judas many times, rebuking him and telling him that his course would surely bring him to a bad end. Jesus never had told any of His disciples, not even John who *"leaned on His breast"* (John 21:20). Now, if that same spirit of keeping things secret was in any church, it would purify the church. But I fear sometimes that Satan gets the advantage, and things are told before they are even known to be true.

There was strife among them as to who should be the greatest, but He said, *"He who is greatest among you, let him be as the younger, and he who governs as he who serves"* (Luke 22:26). Then He, the Master, said, *"I am among you as the One who serves"* (v. 27). He, the noblest, the purest, was the servant of all! Exercising lordship over another is not of God. We must learn in our hearts that fellowship, true righteousness, loving one another, and preferring one another, must come into the church. Pentecost must outreach everything that ever has been, and we know it will if we are willing.

Thought for today: I believe God wants to so sanctify us, so separate us, that we will have that perfection of love that will not speak ill of a brother, that we will not slander a fellow believer whether it is true or not.

April 18

Moving toward Perfection

I am among you as the One who serves.
—Luke 22:27

Scripture reading: Hebrews 6:1–20

We can never be filled with the Holy Spirit as long as there is any human craving for our own wills. Selfishness must be destroyed. Jesus was perfect, the end of everything, and God will bring us all there. It is giving that pays; it is helping that pays; it is loving that pays; it is putting yourself out for another person that pays.

I believe there is a day coming that will be greater than anything any of us have any conception of. This is the testing road. This is the place where your whole body has to be covered with the wings of God so that your nakedness will not be seen. This is the thing that God is getting you ready for, the most wonderful thing your heart can imagine. How can you get into it? First of all, *"You...have continued with Me in My trials"* (v. 28). Jesus had been in trials; He had been in temptation. There is not one of us who is tempted beyond what He was (Heb. 4:15).

If a young man can be so pure that he cannot be tempted, he will never be fit to be made a judge, but God intends us to be so purified during these evil days that He can make us judges in the world to come. If you can be tried, if you can be tempted on any line, Jesus said, *"You are those who have continued with Me in My trials"* (Luke 22:28). Have faith, and God will keep you pure in the temptation.

Follow Him in constant regeneration. Every day is a regeneration; every day is a day of advancement; every day is a place of choice. Every day you find yourself in need of fresh consecration. If you are in a place to yield, God moves you in the place of regeneration.

Thought for today: If you are not on fire, you are not in the place of regeneration. It is only the fire of God that burns up the entanglements of the world.

185

On the Way to Heaven

I, John, saw the holy city, New Jerusalem, coming down out of heaven from God, prepared as a bride adorned for her husband.
—Revelation 21:2

Scripture reading: Revelation 21:4, 10–27

We long for that eternal day when all are holy, all are good, all are washed in Jesus' blood. But guilty, unrenewed sinners cannot come there. There is no sickness in heaven. There is no death in heaven. They have never had a funeral in that land. They have never known what it means to ring the death toll or to have the drum muffled. Never once has anyone died there. There is no death there, no sickness, no sorrow.

Will you go there? Are you getting ready for it?

Remember this: you were created by the power of God for one purpose in particular. God had no thought in Creation but to bring forth through mortality a natural order so that you might be quickened in the Spirit, be received into glory, and worship God in a way that the angels never could. But in order for that to be, He has brought us through the flesh and quickened us by the Spirit, so that we may know the love, the grace, the power, and all the perfect will of God.

He is a wonderful God—His intelligence, His superabundance in all revelation, His power to keep everything in perfect order. The sun in all its glory, shining so majestically on the earth today, is the mighty power of our glorious God who can make a new heaven and a new earth, in which righteousness will dwell, where no sin will ever darken the place, where the glory of that celestial place will be wonderful.

This city—figurative, but not exactly figurative, for it is a luminous fact—will surely exist, and we cannot miss it. It will be a city greater than any city ever known, with millions, billions, trillions all ready for the marriage of the Lamb and His bride. It will be a great city—architecture, domes, pinnacles, cornices, foundations—and the whole city will be made up of saints coming to a marriage.

Oh, the glory of it! I'll be there. I will be one of its inhabitants. I do not know what part, but it will be glorious to be in it anyhow.

All these billions of people will have come through tribulation, distress, brokenness of spirit, hard times, strange perplexities, weariness, and all kinds of conditions in the earth. They will be quickened and made like Him, to reign with Him forever and ever.

What a thought God had when He was forming creation and making it, so that we could bring forth sons and daughters in the natural, who are quickened by the Spirit in the supernatural and received up to glory, to be made ready for a marriage! May God reveal to us our position in this Holy Spirit order, so that we may see how wonderful it is that the Lord has His mind upon us. I want you to see security, absolute security, where there will be no shaking, no trembling, no fear, absolute soundness in every way, knowing that, as sure as the Celestial City is formed, you are going to that City.

Salvation takes us to glory. New life is resurrection; new life is ascension; and this new life in God has no place for its feet anywhere between here and glory.

The Spirit of the Lord is with us, revealing the Word. He does not bring eternal life to us, for we have that already, and we believe and are in this place because of that eternal life. But He brings to us a process of this eternal life, showing us that it puts everything else to death. Eternal life came to us when we believed, but the process of eternal life can begin today, making us know that now we are sons of God.

Thought for today: God's Son became the Bread of Life, and as we eat of this Bread, we live forever!

April 20

Maintaining the Divine Life

Lord, to whom shall we go? You have the words of eternal life.
—John 6:68

Scripture reading: John 6:63–69; 14:1–28

God will give divine life only to those who seek eternal life. Do not get away from this. For every person who has eternal life, it is the purpose of the Father, it is the loyalty of God's Son, it is the assembly of the firstborn (Heb. 12:23), it is the newly begotten of God, it is the new creation, it is a race designed for heaven that is going to equip you and get you through everything. As surely as you are seeking now, you are in the glory. There is a bridge of eternal security for you if you dare to believe in the Word of God. There is not a drop between you and the glory. It is divine, it is eternal, it is holy, it is the life of God; He gives it, and no man can take from you the life that God gives to you.

I hope no one will say, "Wigglesworth is preaching eternal security." I am not. I have a thousand times better things in my mind than that. My preaching is this: I know I have what will not be taken away from me. (See Luke 10:42.)

I am dwelling upon the sovereignty, the mercy, and the boundless love of God. I am dwelling upon the wonderful power of God's order. The heavens, the earth, and everything under the earth are submissive to the Most High God. Demon power has to give place to the royal kingship of God's eternal throne. *"Every knee shall bow"* (Isa. 45:23), every devil will be submitted, and God will bring us someday right into the fullness of the blaze of eternal bliss. And the brightness of His presence will cast every unclean spirit and every power of devils into the pit forever and ever and ever. Oh, Jesus!

But if you choose to leave the Master, where will you go? Where can we go? If we need a touch in our bodies, where can we go? If we want life, where can we go? Is there anywhere? This world is a big world, but tell me if you can find life outside of Christ or anywhere but in Christ.

Could you find life if you soared the heights of the Alps of Switzerland and looked over those glassy mountains where the sun is shining? As I looked over one of those mountains one morning, I saw eleven glaciers and three lakes, like diamonds before me in the glittering sun. I wept and I wept, but I did not receive consolation. Then I dropped on my knees and looked to God—then I found consolation.

Where will we go? All the grandeur and the glories of earth are to be seen, but they do not satisfy me. They all belong to time; they will all fold up like a garment that is laid aside; they will all melt with fervent heat (2 Pet. 3:10).

Where will we go? *"You have the words of eternal life."* Jesus, You fed us with bread from heaven. Jesus, give us Your life. Oh, breathe it into us! Then we will eat and drink and breathe and think in God's Son until our own natures are consumed with divine life, until we are perpetually in the sweetness of His divine will and in the glory. In fact, we are already in it! Praise Him! You can always be holy; you can always be pure. It is the mind of the Spirit that is making you know holiness, righteousness, and rapture.

Thought for today: If our fellowship here is so sweet, if the touches of eternal glory inspire us, how wonderful heaven will be!

April 21

Changed from Glory to Glory

If the ministry of death, written and engraved on stones,
was glorious, so that the children of Israel could not look steadily
at the face of Moses because of the glory of his countenance,
which glory was passing away, how will the ministry of the Spirit
not be more glorious?
—2 Corinthians 3:7–8

Scripture reading: Matthew 17:1–13

The glory on the face of Moses had to pass away. Why was it to be done away with? So that something else that had exceeding glory could take its place.

We have no conception of the depths and heights of the liberty and blessing of the *"ministry of the Spirit."* We must reach for this position of godliness and be partakers of the divine nature (2 Pet. 1:4). The law was so glorious that Moses was filled with joy in the expectation of what it would mean. To us, there is the excellence of Christ's glory in the ministry of the Holy Spirit. It is no longer, "Thou shalt not." Rather, it is God's will, revealed to us in Christ. *"I delight to do Your will, O my God"* (Ps. 40:8). And, beloved, in our hearts there is exceeding glory. Oh, the joy of this celestial touch!

When Peter was recalling that wonderful day on the Mount of Transfiguration, he said, *"Such a voice came to Him from the Excellent Glory"* (2 Pet. 1:17). If I were to come to you right now and say, "Whatever you do, you must try to be holy," I would miss it. I would be altogether outside of God's plan. But I take the words of the epistle, which says by the Holy Spirit, *"Be holy"* (1 Pet. 1:16). It is as easy as possible to be holy, but you can never be holy by your own efforts. God wants us to be entirely eaten up by this holy zeal for Him, so that every day we will walk in the Spirit. It is lovely to walk in the Spirit, for He will cause you to dwell in safety, to rejoice inwardly, and to praise God reverently.

Thought for today: When you lose your heart and Another takes it, and you lose your desires and He takes them, then you live in that sunshine of bliss that no mortal can ever touch.

190

April 22

The Righteousness of Christ

The ministry of righteousness exceeds much more in glory.
—2 Corinthians 3:9

Scripture reading: John 2:1–21

All excellent glory is in Christ; all righteousness is in Him. Everything that pertains to holiness and godliness, everything that denounces and brings to death the natural, everything that makes you know that you have forever ceased to be, is always in an endless power in the risen Christ.

Whenever you look at Jesus, you can see so many different facts of His life. I see Him in those forty days before His ascension, with wonderful truth, infallible proofs of His ministry. What was the ministry of Christ? When you come to the very essence of His ministry, it was the righteousness of His purpose. The excellence of His ministry was the glory that covered Him. His Word was convincing, inflexible, and divine, with a personality of an eternal endurance. It never failed. He spoke, and it stood fast. It was an immovable condition with Him, and His righteousness abides.

Jesus was true, inwardly and outwardly. He is *"the way, the truth, and the life"* (John 14:6), and on this foundation we can build. When we know that our own hearts do not condemn us (1 John 3:21), we can say to the mountain, *"Be removed"* (Matt. 21:21). But when our own hearts do condemn us, there is no power in prayer, no power in preaching. We are just *"sounding brass or a clanging cymbal"* (1 Cor. 13:1). May the Holy Spirit show us that there must be a ministry of righteousness.

Christ was righteousness through and through. God wants to settle it in our hearts that we are to be like Him—like Him in character. God wants righteousness in the inward parts, so that we may be pure through and through. The Bible is the plumb line of everything, and unless we are plumbed right up with the Word of God, we will fail in righteousness. Here, we come again to the law. I see that it was truly a schoolmaster that brought us to Christ (Gal. 3:24).

Thought for today: We must be people of the Word, so that people will be able to depend upon our word.

191

April 23

Divinely Used by God

You are an epistle of Christ.
—2 Corinthians 3:3

Scripture reading: Colossians 3:16–4:6

*L*aw is beautiful when it is established in the earth. In every country and town, you will find that the law has something to do with keeping things straight, and in a measure, cities have some kind of sobriety because of their laws. But, beloved, we belong to a higher, nobler citizenship, not an earthly citizenship, for *"our citizenship is in heaven"* (Phil. 3:20). If the natural law will keep an earthly city in somewhat moderate conditions, what will the excellent glory be in divine relationship to the citizenship to which we belong? What is meant by *excellent glory* is that it out-shines. The earth is filled with broken hearts, but the excellent glory fills redeemed men and women so that they show forth the excellency of the grace of the glory of God.

The man who is going on with God will have no mix-up in his speech. He will be so plain, precise, and divine in his conversation that everything will have a lift toward the glory. He may use great clarity of speech, but he must be a person who knows his message. He must know what God has in His mind in the Spirit, not in the letter. He is there as a vessel for honor, God's mouthpiece; there-fore, he stands in the presence of God, and God speaks through him and uses him.

If your life is not in constant pitch, you will never ring the bells of heaven. We must be the mouthpiece of God, not by letter, but by the Spirit, and we must be so in the will of God that He will rejoice over us with singing (Zeph. 3:17). If we are in the Spirit, the Lord of life is the same Spirit. *"Now the Lord is the Spirit; and where the Spirit of the Lord is, there is liberty"* (2 Cor. 3:17).

There is no liberty that is going to help people so much as tes-timony. I find people who do not know how to testify in the right way. We must testify only as the Spirit gives utterance. You are not to use your liberty except for the glory of God. So many meetings are spoiled by long prayers and long testimonies. If the speaker remains in the Spirit, he will know when he should sit down. When you begin to repeat yourself, the people get wearied, and they wish you would sit down, for the anointing has then ceased.

April 23

It is lovely to pray, and it is a joy to hear you pray when you are in the Spirit; but if you keep going after the Spirit has finished, everyone gets tired of it. So God wants us to know that we are not to use liberty simply because we have it to use, but we are to let the liberty of the Spirit use us. Then we will know when to end. Our services ought to be so free in the Spirit that people can always go away with the feeling, "Oh, I wish the meeting had gone on for another hour," or "Was not that testimony meeting a revelation!"

Beloved, when we get God's Word in our hearts, it absolutely changes us in everything. And as we feast on the Word of the Lord, eat and digest the truth, and inwardly eat of Christ, we are changed every day from one state of glory to another. You will never find anything else but the Word that takes you there, so you cannot afford to put aside that Word.

I implore you, beloved, that you come short of none of these blessed teachings. These grand truths of the Word of God must be your testimony, your life, your pattern. *"You are an epistle of Christ."* God says this to you by the Spirit. When there is a standard that has not yet been reached in your life, God by His grace, by His mercy, and by your yieldedness can equip you for that place. You can never be prepared for it except by a broken heart and a contrite spirit, and by yielding to the will of God. But if you will come with a whole heart to the throne of grace, God will meet you and build you up on His spiritual plane.

Thought for today: You cannot sing a song of victory in a minor key.

April 24

Follow God's Path

The path of the just is like the shining sun, that shines
ever brighter unto the perfect day.
—Proverbs 4:18

Scripture reading: Proverbs 4:5–18

*J*acob was on his way to the land of his fathers, but he was very troubled at the thought of meeting his brother Esau. Years before, Jacob and his mother had formed a plan to secure the blessing that Isaac was going to give Esau. How inglorious was the fulfilling of this carnal plan! It resulted in Esau's hating Jacob and saying in his heart, "When my father is dead, then will I slay my brother Jacob." (See Genesis 27:41.) Our own plans frequently lead us into disaster.

Jacob had to flee from the land, but how good the Lord was to the fugitive. He gave him a vision of a ladder and angels ascending and descending it (Gen. 28:12). How gracious is our God! He refused to have His plans of grace frustrated by the carnal workings of Jacob's mind, and that night He revealed Himself to Jacob saying, *"I am with you and will keep you wherever you go, and will bring you back to this land; for I will not leave you until I have done what I have spoken to you"* (v. 15). It is the goodness of the Lord that leads to repentance. I believe that Jacob really did some repenting that night as he was made aware of his own sinfulness.

Many things may happen in our lives to show us how depraved we are by nature, but when the veil is lifted, we see how merciful and tender God is. His tender compassion is over us all the time.

From the time when Jacob had the revelation of the ladder and the angels, he had twenty-one years of testing and trial. But God had been faithful to His promise all through these years. Jacob could say to his wives, *"Your father has deceived me and changed my wages ten times, but God did not allow him to hurt me"* (Gen. 31:7). He said to his father-in-law,

> *Unless the God of my father, the God of Abraham and the Fear of Isaac, had been with me, surely now you would have sent me away empty-handed. God has seen my affliction and the labor of my hands.* (Gen. 31:42)

194

Now that Jacob was returning to the land of his birth, his heart was filled with fear. If he ever needed the Lord, it was then. And he wanted to be alone with God. His wives, his children, his sheep, his cattle, his camels, and his donkeys had gone on, and *"Jacob was left alone; and a Man wrestled with him until the breaking of day"* (Gen. 32:24). The Lord saw Jacob's need and came down to meet him. It was He who wrestled with the supplanter, breaking him, changing him, transforming him.

Jacob knew that his brother Esau had power to take away all that he had, and to execute vengeance upon him. He knew that no one could deliver him but God. And there alone, lean in soul and impoverished in spirit, he met with God. Oh, how we need to get alone with God, to be broken, to be changed, to be transformed! And when we do meet with Him, He interposes, and all care and strife are brought to an end.

Thought for today: Get alone with God, and receive the revelation of His infinite grace and of His wonderful purposes and plans for your life.

April 25

Sifted as Wheat, Tried like Gold

You have been grieved by various trials, that the genuineness of your faith...though it is tested by fire, may be found to praise, honor, and glory at the revelation of Jesus Christ.
—1 Peter 1:6–7

Scripture reading: 1 Peter 1:3–16

I believe there are people who will be put in the place where they will have to stand upon God's Word. You will be sifted as wheat (Luke 22:31). You will be tried *"as though some strange thing happened to you"* (1 Pet. 4:12). You will be put in the most difficult places, where all hell seems to surround you, but God will sustain and empower you and will bring you into an unlimited place of faith. God will not allow you to be *"tempted beyond what you are able, but with the temptation will also make the way of escape, that you may be able to bear it"* (1 Cor. 10:13).

God will surely tell you when you have been tried sufficiently in order to bring you out as pure gold. Every trial is to prepare you for a greater position for God. Who is going to live a dormant, weak, trifling, slow, indolent, prayerless, Bible-less life when he knows he must go through these things? And if you are to be *"made perfect in weakness"* (2 Cor. 12:9), you must be tried as by fire in order to know that no man is able to win a victory unless the power of God is in him. The Holy Spirit will lead us day by day. You will know that these light afflictions, which are only for a moment, are working out for us an eternal weight of glory (2 Cor. 4:17).

We must have people receive the Holy Spirit; we must have people healed in their seats; we must see God come forth. Some of you have been longing for the Holy Spirit. God can baptize you just where you are. There may be some who have not yet tasted of the grace of God. Close beside you is the water of life. Have a drink, brother, sister, for God says, *"And let him who thirsts come. Whoever desires, let him take the water of life freely"* (Rev. 22:17).

Thought for today: Your tried faith will make you know that you will have the faith of God to go through the next trial.

April 26

For the Poor in Spirit

Blessed are the poor in spirit,
for theirs is the kingdom of heaven.
—Matthew 5:3

Scripture reading: Psalm 37:3–24

This is one of the richest places into which Jesus brings us. The poor have a right to everything in heaven. *"Theirs is."* Do you dare believe it? Yes, I dare. I believe, I know, that I was very poor. When God's Spirit comes in as the ruling, controlling power of our lives, He gives us God's revelation of our inward poverty and shows us that God has come with one purpose: to bring heaven's best to earth. He also shows that with Jesus He will indeed *"freely give us all things"* (Rom. 8:32).

An old man and an old woman had lived together for seventy years. Someone said to them, "You must have seen many clouds during those days." They replied, "Where do the showers come from? You never get showers without clouds." It is only the Holy Spirit who can bring us to the place of realization of our poverty; but, every time He does it, He opens the windows of heaven, and the showers of blessing fall.

But I must recognize the difference between my own spirit and the Holy Spirit. My own spirit can do certain things on natural lines—it can even weep and pray and worship—but it is all on a human plane. We must not depend on our own human thoughts and activities or on our personalities. If the baptism means anything to you, it should bring you to the death of the ordinary, where you are no longer putting faith in your own understanding but, conscious of your own poverty, you are ever yielded to the Spirit. Then it is that your body becomes filled with heaven on earth.

How may I get nearer to God? How may I be in the place of helplessness—in my own place and dependent on God? I see a tide rising. *"Blessed are the poor in spirit, for theirs is the kingdom of heaven."* God is making us very poor, but we are rich because our hands are stretched out toward Him in this holy day of His visitation to our hearts.

Thought for today: Exercising lordship over another is not of God.

197

April 27

A Spirit of Poverty

Blessed are the poor in spirit,
for theirs is the kingdom of heaven.
—Matthew 5:3

Scripture reading: Psalm 37:25–40

When we grasp this idea of being poor in spirit and identify ourselves with the Lord Jesus Christ, we have come to a place where we now see that all things are possible with God. We recognize that God has an unlimited supply, and in our poverty of spirit, we are entitled to all that God has, *"for [ours] is the kingdom of heaven."*

When Jesus came to Sychar, a city of Samaria, *"being wearied from His journey"* (John 4:6), He sat down by a well. His disciples were not with Him because they had gone to buy food in a nearby city (v. 8). When they returned, they saw Him at peace. He was not looking for food but was quite relaxed. When Jesus was not interested in eating the food they had bought, *"the disciples said to one another, 'Has anyone brought Him anything to eat?'"* (v. 33). This shows us the possibility for man to live in God, to be absorbed in God, with no consciousness of the world under any circumstances, except as we bring help to it. And He said to them, *"Behold, I say to you, lift up your eyes and look at the fields, for they are already white for harvest!"* (v. 35). That is His food, the spiritual life in God, which is joy in the Holy Spirit.

He comes to enrapture our souls, to break every bond of mere human affection and replace in us the divine instead of the earthly, the pure instead of the unholy, the eyes of faith that see God instead of human feelings. The divine Son of God is to be in us, mightily moving through us, as we cease to be. This poverty of spirit spoken of in this Beatitude helps us.

Thought for today: In spite of my meekness, humility, and helplessness, all that God has is mine.

April 28

For Those Who Mourn

Blessed are those who mourn,
for they shall be comforted.
—Matthew 5:4

Scripture reading: 1 Corinthians 15:51–57; 1 Thessalonians 4:13–18

*P*eople get a wrong idea of mourning. In Switzerland, they have a day set apart to take wreaths to graves. I questioned the people's ignorance and said, "Why are you spending time around the graves? The people you love are not there. All that taking of flowers to the graves is not faith at all. Those who died in Christ are gone to be with Him, *'which,'* Paul said, *'is far better'* (Phil. 1:23)."

My wife once said to me, "Watch me when I'm preaching. I get so near to heaven when I'm preaching that some day I'll be off." One night she was preaching, and when she had finished, off she went. I was going to Glasgow and had said goodbye to her before she went to the meeting. As I was leaving the house, the doctor and policeman met me at the door and told me that she had fallen dead at the church door. I knew she had gotten what she wanted. I could not weep, but I was in tongues, praising the Lord. Humanly, she was everything to me; but I could not mourn on natural lines, and I just laughed in the Spirit. The house was soon filled with people. The doctor said, "She is dead, and we can do no more for her." I went up to her lifeless corpse and commanded death to give her up, and she came back to me for a moment. Then God said to me, "She is Mine; her work is done." I knew what He meant.

They laid her in the coffin, and I brought my sons and my daughter into the room and said, "Is she there?" They said, "No, Father." I said, "We will cover her up." If you go mourning the loss of loved ones who have gone to be with Christ—I say this to you out of love—you have never had the revelation of what Paul spoke of when he showed us that it is better to go than to stay. (See 2 Corinthians 5:8.) We read this in Scripture, but the trouble is that people will not believe it. When you believe God, you will say, "Whatever it is, it is all right. If You want to take the one I love, it is all right, Lord."

April 28

But the mourning that Jesus spoke of in Matthew 5 is a mourning in the Spirit. God will bring you to a place where things must be changed, and there is a mourning, an unutterable groaning until God comes. Jesus mourned over Jerusalem. He saw the conditions; He saw the unbelief; He saw the end of those who closed their ears to the Gospel. But God gave a promise that He would see *"the labor of His soul, and be satisfied"* (Isa. 53:11) and that He would *"see His seed"* (v. 10).

What happened on the Day of Pentecost in Jerusalem was a promise of what would be the results of His travail, to be multiplied a billionfold all down the ages in all the world. And as we enter in the Spirit into travail over conditions that are wrong, such mourning will always bring results for God, and our joy will be complete in the satisfaction that is thereby brought to Christ.

Thought for today: Faith removes all tears of self-pity.

April 29

A Spirit of Mourning

Blessed are those who mourn,
for they shall be comforted.
—Matthew 5:4

Scripture reading: Psalm 23

We must live in such a pure atmosphere that God will shine in and through our souls. Oh, this uttermost salvation (Heb. 7:25)! I am satisfied that as we get to know the Son of God, we will never be weak anymore. The tide will turn. Let us look at Matthew 5:4, *"Blessed are those who mourn, for they shall be comforted."*

Did Jesus mean mourning over death? No, He meant mourning over our sons and daughters who have not yet reached heaven, who know nothing about the things of the Spirit of Life. When God places within us a mourning cry to move the powers of God, then He will send a revival in every home.

It is impossible to get this spiritual mourning over lost souls without having the very next thing that God says, "[You] *shall be comforted."* As though God could give you a spirit of mourning over a needy soul, then not give you victory! Beloved, it is the mighty power of God in us. And when the Spirit brings us to this mourning attitude over lost souls and over all the failures that we see in professing Christians, until we can go into the presence of God with that mourning spirit, nothing will happen. But when that happens, rejoice; God will bring you through.

Revival is coming. God's heart is in the place of intense passion. Let us bend or break, for God is determined to bless us. Oh, the joy of service and the joy of suffering! Oh, to be utterly cast upon Jesus! God is coming forth with power. There must be no coming down from the cross but a going on from faith to faith and from glory to glory with an increasing diligence so that we may be found in Him *"without spot and blameless"* (2 Pet. 3:14). The spirit of mourning will turn into rejoicing as we are faithful before Him.

Thought for today: The end of all real faith always is rejoicing.

April 30

For the Meek

Blessed are the meek,
for they shall inherit the earth.
—Matthew 5:5

Scripture reading: Isaiah 11:1–10

*M*oses was headstrong in his zeal for his own people, and it resulted in his killing a man. (See Exodus 2:11–12.) His heart was right in his desire to correct things, but he was relying on human wisdom, and when we work on natural lines we always fail. Moses had a mighty passion, and that is one of the best things in the world when God has control and it becomes a passion for souls to be born again. But apart from God it is one of the worst things.

Paul was tremendously zealous, and, breathing out threats, he was sending men and women to prison. (See Acts 8:3.) But God changed him, and later he said he could wish himself accursed from Christ for the sake of his fellowmen, his kinsmen according to the flesh (Rom. 9:3–4).

God took the headstrong Moses and molded him into the meekest of men. He took the fiery Saul of Tarsus and made him the foremost exponent of grace. Oh, brothers and sisters, God can transform you in the same manner, and plant in you a divine meekness and every other thing that you lack.

In our Sunday school, we had a boy with hair as red as fire, and so was his temper. He was such a trial. He kicked his teachers and the superintendent. He was simply uncontrollable. The teachers had a meeting in which they discussed the matter of expelling him. But they thought that God might somehow work in that boy, and so they decided to give him another chance. One day he had to be kicked out, and he broke all the windows of the church. He was worse outside than in. Sometime later, we had a ten-day revival meeting. There was nothing much going on in that meeting, and people thought it was a waste of time, but there was one result—the redheaded lad got saved.

After he was saved, the difficulty was to get rid of him at our house. He would be there until midnight, crying to God to make him pliable and use him for His glory. God delivered the lad from his temper and made him one of the meekest, most beautiful boys you ever saw. For twenty years he has been a mighty missionary in China.

I can remember the time when I used to go white with rage and shake all over with temper. I could hardly hold myself together. But one time I waited on God for ten days. In those ten days, I was being emptied out, and the life of the Lord Jesus was being worked into me. My wife testified of the transformation that took place in my life. She said, "I never saw such a change. I have never been able to cook anything since that time that has not pleased him. Nothing is too hot or too cold; everything is just right." God must come and reign supreme in your life. Will you let Him do it? He can do it, and He will if you will let Him.

It is no use trying to tame the *"old man"* (Eph. 4:22). But God can deal with him. The carnal mind will never be subjected to God, but God will bring it to the Cross where it belongs and will put in its place. With God's transforming power, we can become pure and holy, having the meek mind of the Master.

Thought for today: God takes us just as we are and transforms us by His power.

May 1

A Spirit of Meekness

Blessed are the meek,
for they shall inherit the earth.
—Matthew 5:5

Scripture reading: Isaiah 11:1–9

God wants us to rejoice today. He has brought us into this blessed place so that we may mourn and then rejoice. Let us look at the next verse in Matthew 5: *"Blessed are the meek, for they shall inherit the earth."*

You say, "Don't talk to me about being meek; I will never be able to be like that." Take the case of Moses. He surely was not meek when he killed the Egyptian. But when God got Moses into His hand in the land of Midian, He molded him so that he became the meekest man in all the earth. I do not care what your temper is like. If you get only a little touch of heaven, God can mold you so that you can become meek.

I used to have such a bad temper that it made me tremble all over. It would make me furious with its evil power. I saw that this temper had to be destroyed; it could not simply be patched up. One day the power of God fell upon me. I came to the meeting and fell down before the Lord. The people began asking, "What sin has Wigglesworth been committing?" This went on for two weeks. Every time I came to the altar, God used to sweep through me with such a manifestation of my helplessness that I would go down before God and weep right through. Then the preacher or the leader was broken up and came beside me. God started a revival that way. God had broken me up, and revival began through His revival in me. Oh, it was lovely!

Only God can make people right. Only melted gold is minted. Only moistened clay accepts the mold. Only softened wax receives the seal. Only broken, contrite hearts receive the mark as the Potter turns us on His wheel. Oh, Lord, give us that blessed state where we are perfectly and wholly made meek.

Thought for today: Perfect love will never want the preeminence in everything; it will never want to take the place of another; it will always be willing to take the back seat.

May 2

Those Who Hunger and Thirst

Blessed are those who hunger and thirst for righteousness,
for they shall be filled.
—Matthew 5:6

Scripture reading: Psalm 42

Meet the conditions, and God will fulfill His Word to you. Note that the verse says, *"shall be filled."* The Spirit of God is crying, *"Everyone who thirsts, come to the waters; and you who have no money, come, buy and eat"* (Isa. 55:1). The Spirit of God will take the things of Christ and show them to you so that you may have a longing for Christ in His fullness, and when there is that longing, God will not fail to fill you.

See the crowd of worshippers who have come up to the feast. They are going away utterly dissatisfied, but on the last day, that great day of the feast, Jesus will stand and cry out, saying, *"If anyone thirsts, let him come to Me and drink. He who believes in Me, as the Scripture has said, out of his heart will flow rivers of living water"* (John 7:37–38).

Jesus knew that they were going away without the living water, and so He directed them to the true source of supply. Are you thirsty today? The living Christ still invites you to Himself, and I want to testify that He still satisfies the thirsty soul and fills the hungry with good things.

In Switzerland, I learned of a man who met with a particular congregation. He attended their various meetings, and one morning at their Communion service, he arose and said, "Brothers, we have the Word, and I feel that we are living very much in the letter of it, but there is a hunger and thirst in my soul for something deeper, something more real than we have, and I cannot rest until I enter into it." The next Sunday this brother rose again and said, "We are all so poor here, there is no life in this assembly, and my heart is hungry for reality." He did this for several weeks until it got on the nerves of these people, and they protested, "Sands, you are making us all miserable; you are spoiling our meetings. There is only one thing for you to do, and that is to clear out."

He went out of the meeting in a very sad condition. As he stood outside, one of his children asked him what was the matter, and he said, "To think that they should turn me out from their midst for being hungry and thirsty for more of God!" I did not know anything more of this situation until afterward.

Days later, someone rushed up to Sands and said, "There is a man over here from England, and he is speaking about tongues and healing." Sands said, "I'll fix him. I'll go to the meeting and sit right up in the front and challenge him with the Scriptures. I'll dare him to preach these things in Switzerland. I'll publicly denounce him." So he came to the meetings. There he sat. He was so hungry and thirsty that he drank in every word that was said. His opposition soon petered out. The first morning he said to a friend, "This is what I want." He drank and drank of the Spirit. After three weeks he said, "God will have to do something new or I'll burst." He breathed in God, and the Lord filled him to such an extent that he spoke in other tongues as the Spirit gave utterance. Sands is now preaching and is in charge of a new Pentecostal assembly.

God is making people hungry and thirsty after His best. And everywhere He is filling the hungry and giving them what the disciples received at the very beginning. Are you hungry? If you are, God promises that you will be filled.

Thought for today: If you ever see a *"shall"* in the Bible, make it yours.

A Spirit of Hunger and Thirst

Blessed are those who hunger and thirst for righteousness,
for they shall be filled.
—Matthew 5:6

Scripture reading: Hebrews 1:8–9; 2:1–18

The Beatitudes of the Spirit are truly lovely. We must emphasize that God will not fail to fill us. No man can *"hunger and thirst after righteousness"* unless God has put the desire in him. This righteousness is the righteousness of Jesus.

In 1 John 5:4–5, we find these verses: *"This is the victory that has overcome the world; our faith. Who is he who overcomes the world, but he who believes that Jesus is the Son of God?"* Righteousness is more than paying our way. We hear someone say, "Oh, I never do anything wrong to anybody. I always pay my way." This is simply life in the flesh, but there is a higher *"law of the Spirit of life in Christ Jesus"* (Rom. 8:2). I must see that Jesus is my perfect righteousness. He came by the power of God:

> *For what the law could not do in that it was weak through the flesh, God did by sending His own Son in the likeness of sinful flesh, on account of sin: He condemned sin in the flesh.*
> (Rom. 8:3)

But the divine touches of heaven never leave you stationary but rather increase your thirst and appetite for greater things. Something within makes you press on until you are empty of everything else so that you may be filled with what God is pressing in. This righteousness is a walk with God and a divine inheritance. It is seeking the face of Jesus until you cannot be satisfied without drinking of His Spirit and being overflowed continually with His blessings. I cannot be satisfied without Christ's righteousness. He gives us thirst for the immensity of God's power. It is a divine problem that is solved in only one way: having Him.

Thought for today: Having Him, we have all things.

May 4

A Spirit of Mercy

Blessed are the merciful, for they shall obtain mercy.
—Matthew 5:7

Scripture reading: Hosea 6:1–6; Psalm 85:4–13

I pray that God will bring you to a death of self and a life of righteousness, which will please God in the Spirit. Thus we understand in some measure what God has for us in the seventh verse of Matthew 5: *"Blessed are the merciful, for they shall obtain mercy."*

I believe this is truly a spiritual condition, which is higher than the natural law. Sometimes when we talk about mercy, we think of being kind, amiable, or philanthropic toward others. We think those are respected positions. So they are, but the world has that. Beloved, we should have all that, but we should have much more. We will never understand the meaning of the mercy of Jesus until He fills us with Himself. My blessed Lord! Can there ever be one like Him? Can you think of such rarity, such beauty, such self-sacrifice? *"Blessed are the merciful."* You cannot be filled with the Lord and not be merciful. You cannot have the baptism with power without this supernatural mercy, this divine touch of heaven that stops satanic forces, frees the oppressed, and strengthens the helpless. This is the spirit that God wants to give us. Oh, for heaven to bend down upon us with this deep inward cry for a touch of Him, His majesty, His glory, His might, His power!

It is a very remarkable thing that the merciful always obtain mercy. Look at the measure of this spiritual life: first full, then pressed down, then shaken together, and then running over (Luke 6:38). This divine touch of heaven is lovely. It is the most charming thing on earth, sweeter than all. God wants you to have this new wine. It thrills the human heart. How it mightily sweeps you right into heaven!

I ask you all, needy souls, whatever you want, to *"come boldly to the throne of grace"* (Heb. 4:16). Come, and the Lord will bless you.

Thought for today: We must have heaven's riches to give to souls in poverty.

Elected by God

*To the pilgrims of the Dispersion…elect according to the
foreknowledge of God the Father, in sanctification of the Spirit.*
—1 Peter 1:1–2

Scripture reading: 1 Thessalonians 1:2–7; 4:3–12

*H*umanity, flesh, and natural things are all against divine things. Evil powers work upon this position of the human life, especially when the will is unyielded to God. Then, the powers of darkness rise up against the powers of divine order, but they never defeat them. Divine order is very often in the minority, but always in the majority. Did I say that right? Yes, and I meant it, too. Though it is in the minority, it always triumphs.

I want you to notice the text verse because it says *"Dispersion."* This was meant to say that these people did not have much liberty to meet together, so they were driven from place to place. Even in the days of the Scottish religious reformer John Knox, the people who served God had to meet in very close quarters because the Roman church set out to destroy them, nailed them to judgment seats, and destroyed them in all sorts of ways. They were in the minority, but they swept through in victory, and the Roman power was crushed and defeated. Take care that such a thing does not rise again. May God bring us into such perfect order that we may understand these days, that we may be in the minority, but we will always obtain the victory through God.

The Holy Spirit wants us to understand our privileges: we are *"elect according to the foreknowledge of God…in sanctification of the Spirit."* Now this sanctification of the Spirit is not on the lines of being cleansed from sin. It is a higher order than the work of redemption. The blood of Jesus is rich unto all powerful cleansing, and it takes away other powers and transforms us by the mighty power of God. But when sin is gone, yes, when we are clean and when we know we have the Word of God right in us and the power of the Spirit is bringing everything to a place where we triumph, then comes revelation by the power of the Spirit, lifting us onto higher ground, into all the fullness of God, which unveils Christ in such a way.

May 5

This is what is called sanctification of the Spirit: sanctified by the Spirit, elected by God. I don't want you to stumble at the word *elect*—it is a most blessed word. You might say you are all elect. God has designed that all men should be saved. This is the election, but whether you accept and come into your election, whether you prove yourself worthy of your election, whether you have so allowed the Spirit to fortify you, whether you have done this I don't know, but your election, your sanctification, is to be seated at the right hand of God.

This word *election* is very precious to me. Foreordained, predestined—these are words that God designed before the world existed, to bring us into triumph and victory in Christ. Some people play around with it and make it a goal. They say, "Oh, well, you see, we are elected; we are all right." I know many of them who believe in that condition of election, and they say they are quite all right because they are elected to be saved. I believe these people are so diplomatic that they believe others can be elected to be damned. It is not true! Everybody is elected to be saved, but whether they come into it, that is another thing.

Many don't experience salvation because the god of this world has blinded their eyes *"lest the light of the gospel of the glory...should shine on them"* (2 Cor. 4:4). What does that mean? It means that Satan has mastery over their minds, and they have an ear to listen to corrupt things. Be careful of things that do not have Jesus in them. I sometimes shout for all I am worth about Jesus, because I know there is no Jesus inside some things.

Beloved, I want you to see this election I am speaking about, to catch a glimpse of heaven, with your heart always on the wing, where you grasp everything spiritual, when everything divine makes you hungry for it.

It is through the sanctification of the Spirit unto obedience and the sprinkling of the blood of Jesus Christ. There is no sanctification if it is not sanctification unto obedience.

Thought for today: Wickedness may increase and abound, but when the Lord raises His flag over the saint, it is victory.

May 6

The Spirit Moves upon You

God so loved the world that He gave His only begotten Son, that whoever believes in Him should not perish but have everlasting life.
—John 3:16

Scripture reading: John 3:5–21

*I*t does not matter what age you are. If I were to say to you, "Do you ever remember a time when the Spirit did not strive with you," it would be marvelous how many people would answer, "No." What do you call it? God bringing you in, His grace drawing you to Himself.

When I think of my own case, I recall that on my mother's and father's sides of the families there was no desire for God, yet in my very infancy I was strangely moved upon by the Spirit. At the age of eight, I was definitely saved, and when I was nine years old, I felt the Spirit come upon me, just as when I spoke in tongues. I was *"elect according to the foreknowledge of God"* (1 Pet. 1:2), and many have had the same experience.

It is a most blessed thought that we have a God of love, compassion, and grace, who does not will the death of even one sinner. God has made it possible for all men to be saved by causing Jesus, His well-beloved Son, to die for the sins of all people. It is true that He took our sins; it is true that He paid the price for the whole world; it is true that He gave Himself as a ransom for many (Matt. 20:28). And you say, "For whom?" *"Whoever desires, let him take the water of life freely"* (Rev. 22:17).

"What about those who do not receive His gift of salvation?" you ask. It takes their direct refusal of the blood of Jesus; they have to refuse to have Christ reign over them. It is *"whoever desires"* on this side and whoever does not on the other side. There are people living in the world who do not desire God's gift. Why do they respond this way? Because *"the god of this age has blinded* [them], *who do not believe, lest the light of the gospel of the glory of Christ, who is the image of God, should shine on them"* (2 Cor. 4:4).

Thought for today: Jesus is bigger than any assembly, yet He is small enough to fill every heart.

May 7

Peace and Hope

May the God of hope fill you with all joy and peace in believing,
that you may abound in hope by the power of the Holy Spirit.
—Romans 15:13

Scripture reading: Ephesians 1:2–21

*T*hrough sanctification of the Spirit, you will come to a place of rest. There is a peace in sanctification because it is a place of revelation, taking you into heavenly realms. God comes, speaks, and makes Himself known to you, and when you are face-to-face with God, you receive a peace *"which surpasses all understanding"* (Phil. 4:7), lifting you to a state of inexpressible wonderment.

> Oh, this is like heaven to me,
> This is like heaven to me,
> I've crossed over Jordan to Canaan's fair land;
> And this is like heaven to me.

This sanctification of the Spirit brings us into definite alignment with the wonderful hope of the glory of God. Lively hope is movement. It presses forward. Lively hope leaves everything behind. It keeps the vision. Lively hope sees Him coming! And you live in it—this lively hope. You are not trying to make yourself feel that you are believing, but the lively hope fills you with joy and expectation of the King's coming. Praise the Lord! I want you to know that God has this experience in His mind for you.

I pray God the Holy Spirit that He will move you this way. I trust that you will be so reconciled to God that there is not one thing that would interfere with your possessing this lively hope.

How He loves us, hovers over us, rejoices in us! How the Lord by the Holy Spirit fills our cup full and running over (Ps. 23:5)! *"The joy of the LORD is your strength"* (Neh. 8:10). I hope you won't forget the lively hope. It is the purpose of God for your soul. It is wonderful. Hallelujah!

Thought for today: A lively hope is the opposite of a dead hope.

May 8

Rejoice in Being Purified

*That the genuineness of your faith, being much more precious than
gold that perishes, though it is tested by fire, may be found to praise,
honor, and glory at the revelation of Jesus Christ.*
—1 Peter 1:7

Scripture reading: 2 Corinthians 4:7–5:9

*Y*ou have no idea what God will mean to you in trials and temptations—it is purification of the Spirit. Gold perishes, but faith
never perishes; it is more precious than gold, though it may
be tried with fire. I went into a place one day, and a gentleman said
to me, "Would you like to see purification of gold this morning?" I
replied, "Yes." He got some gold and put it in a crucible and put a
blast of heat on it. First, it became bloodred, and then it changed
and changed. Then this man took an instrument and passed it over
the gold, drawing something off that was foreign to the gold. He did
this several times until every part was taken away. "Look," he said,
and there we both saw our faces in the gold. It was wonderful.

Dear believer, the trial of your faith is much more precious
than gold that perishes. When God purifies you through trials,
misunderstandings, persecution, and suffering because you are
wrongfully judged, Jesus has given you the keynote: rejoice in that
day. He is cleaning away all the dross from your life, and every evil
power, until He sees His face right in the life, until He sees His face
right in your life.

"*Always carrying about in the body the dying of the Lord Jesus, that the life of Jesus also may be manifested in our body*" (2
Cor. 4:10). This process may not seem to any of us to be very joy-
ous, because it is not acceptable to the flesh, but I have told you
already that your flesh is against the Spirit. Your flesh and all your
human powers have to be perfectly submitted to the mighty power
of God inwardly, to express and manifest His glory outwardly. But
you must be willing for the process and say "Amen" to God. It may
be very hard, but God will help you.

It is lovely to know that in the chastening times, in the times
of misunderstanding and hard tests when you are in the right and
are treated as though you were in the wrong, God is meeting you
and blessing you. People say it is the Devil. Never mind, let the fire

burn; it will do you good. Don't begin complaining, but endure the situation joyfully. It is so sweet to understand that *"love suffers long and is kind"* (1 Cor. 13:4). How lovely to get to a place where you think no evil, you are not easily provoked, and you can bear all things and endure all things! Praise the Lord. Oh, the glory of it, the joy of it!

I understand what it means to jump for joy. I could jump for joy because of the Lord.

> I know the Lord, I know the Lord,
> I know the Lord has laid His hand on me.

"Whom having not seen you love. Though now you do not see Him, yet believing, you rejoice with joy inexpressible and full of glory" (1 Pet. 1:8). We love our Lord Jesus Christ, whom we have not seen. There is no voice so gentle, so soft, so full of tenderness to me. There is no voice like His, and there is no touch like His. Is it possible to love the One we have not seen? God will make it possible to all. *"Though now you do not see Him, yet believing, you rejoice with joy inexpressible and full of glory."*

Thought for today: Beloved, as you are tested in the fire, the Master is purifying everything that cannot bring out His image in you.

May 9

Spiritual Drunkenness

For if we are beside ourselves, it is for God;
or if we are of sound mind, it is for you.
—2 Corinthians 5:13

Scripture reading: Psalm 96

There is a place to reach in the Holy Spirit that is mystifying to the world and to many people who are not going on with God. Here is a most remarkable lesson. We can be so filled with the Spirit, so clothed upon by Him, so purified within, so made ready for the Rapture, that all the time it is as if we are drunk.

When I come in contact with people who would criticize my drunkenness, I am sober. I can be sober one minute; I can be drunk in the Spirit the next. I tell you, to be drunk with the presence of God is wonderful! *"And do not be drunk with wine, in which is dissipation; but be filled with the Spirit"* (Eph. 5:18). In this there is a lively hope, filled with indiscreetness in regard to what anyone else thinks.

Consider a man who is drunk. He stops at a lamppost, and he has a lot to say to it. He says the most foolish things possible, and the people say, "He's lost his senses."

Oh, Lord, that I may be so drunk with You that it makes no difference what people think! I am speaking to the Lord in hymns and spiritual songs, making my boast in the Lord. The Lord of Hosts is around me, and I am so free in the Holy Spirit that I am ready to be taken to heaven. But He does not take me. Why not? I am ready, and it is better for me to go, but for the church's sake it is preferable that I stay. (See Philippians 1:23–25.)

It is best that I am clothed with the Spirit, living in the midst of the people, showing no nakedness. I need to be full of purity, full of power, full of revelation for the church's sake. It is far better to go to heaven now, but for the church's sake I must stay, so that I may be helpful, telling others how they can have their nakedness covered, how their minds can be clothed, how all their inward impurities can be made pure in the presence of God. It is better that I am living, walking, and acting in the Holy Spirit. This may seem impossible, yet this is the height that God wants us to reach.

May 9

Here is another verse to help you: *"And if Christ is in you, the body is dead because of sin, but the Spirit is life because of righteousness"* (Rom. 8:10). There is no such thing as having liberty in your body if there is any sin there. When righteousness is there, righteousness abounds. When Christ is in your heart, enthroning your life, and sin is dethroned, then righteousness abounds and the Holy Spirit has great liberty.

"And if children, then heirs; heirs of God and joint heirs with Christ" (v. 17). My, what triumphs of height, of length, of depth, and of breadth there are in this holy place! Where is it? Right inside. Freedom, purity, power, separateness are ours, and we are ready for the Great Trumpet!

Thought for today: Holiness is the habitation of God.

May 10

The Riches of His Glory

May the God of peace Himself sanctify you completely.
—1 Thessalonians 5:23

Scripture reading: 1 Thessalonians 5:8–24

*M*ay the Lord of Hosts so surround us with revelation and blessing that our bodies get to the place where they can scarcely contain the joys of the Lord. He will bring us to so rich a place that forever we will know we are only the Lord's. What a blessed state of grace to be brought into, where we know that the body, the soul, and the spirit are preserved blameless until the coming of the Lord (1 Thess. 5:23)!

God is greatly desirous for us to have more of His presence. We have only one purpose in mind: to strengthen you, to build you up in the most holy faith, and to present you for every good work so that you should be faultless in Him, quickened by the might of the Spirit, so that you might be prepared for everything that God has for you in the future. Our human nature may be brought to a place where it is so superabundantly attended to by God that in the body we will know nothing but the Lord of Hosts.

To this end, I invite you to the banquet that cannot be exhausted, a supply beyond all human thought, an abundance beyond all human extravagances.

Are you ready to be brought by the power of God into His new plan of righteousness? Are you ready to be able as never before to leave the things of the world behind and press on toward the prize of the high calling (Phil. 3:13–14)?

Are you ready to be so in God's plan that you will feel God's hand upon you? You will know that He has chosen you, so that you might be a firstfruit unto God.

Are you ready for the Lord to have His choice, so that His will and purpose will be yours, so that the "Amen" of His character may sweep through your very nature, and so that you may know as you have never known before that this is the day of the visitation between you and Him?

Thought for today: No matter how you come into great faith and believing in God, God says, "Much more abundantly, much more."

May 11

From Human to Divine

The Gentiles should be fellow heirs, of the same body,
and partakers of His promise in Christ through the gospel.
—Ephesians 3:6

Scripture reading: 1 Corinthians 15:41–55

I thank God for the glorious transformation He makes in us, taking us from fallen humanity into divine life. The God of all grace sees us; He knows us; He is acquainted with us. He is bending over us so that His infinite, glorious, exhaustless pleasure may move us today. What can please Him more than to see His sons and daughters clothed, in their right minds (see Luke 8:35), listening to His voice, their eyes and ears awake, coming into the treasury of the Most High?

If only we could comprehend today more than ever before why the Gentiles have been brought into the glories of His treasury, to feed on the finest of the wheat, to drink at the riches of His pleasure, to be filled with the God of love that has no measure.

Without doubt, the greatest mystery of all time from the commencement of creation to now is Christ made manifest in human flesh. What can be greater than eternal life working mightily through eternal death? What can be greater than the nature and appearance of Adam being changed by a new nature that is the fullness of the expression of the Father in heaven?

Everybody recognizes the Adamic race, but may God today let us understand fullness, the divine reflection. May He put us in the glorious position so that we may be changed—the living manifestation of the power of God changing our appearance. May He allow us to see the very expression of the Father, until the terrestrial will pass away, the celestial will come, and the rightness of His glory will press through all our humanity. Heaven will have an exhibition in us that it never before could have, and all the saints will be gathered. The very expression of the Master's face and the very glory of the Father will be in us. Oh, that the breath of heaven would move us today until we would feel, whatever happened, that we must move on to get ready for exit!

Thought for today: To be conformed to this world is all loss, but to be transformed from this world is all gain.

May 12

Our Joint Inheritance

This grace was given, that I should preach among the Gentiles the unsearchable riches of Christ.
—Ephesians 3:8

Scripture reading: Galatians 3:7–29

The fullness of the expression of the Holy Spirit today is giving us a glimpse into what has been provided by the Father. We know that in the old Israel, from Abraham right down, God had a special relationship with His chosen people.

But the Gentiles had no right to it. The Master said to the Syro-Phoenician woman, "Shall I take the bread of the children and give it to dogs?" (See Mark 7:27.) Did Jesus mean that the Gentiles were dogs? No, He meant that the whole race of the Gentiles knew that they were far below the standard and the order of those people who belonged to the royal stock of Israel. The Samaritans all felt it.

"But isn't it possible for the dogs to have some crumbs?" was the woman's question. (See verse 28.) God has something better than crumbs. He has made the Gentiles of the same body, the same heirs as His chosen people. He has put no difference between them and us, but He has included us in the promises for all who are forgiven by the blood of Christ. Paul spoke about it, knowing that *"if you are Christ's, then you are Abraham's seed, and heirs according to the promise"* (Gal. 3:29).

Thank God! God so manifests His power that He has brought us into oneness, and we know we are sharing in the glory. We are sharing in the knowledge that we belong to the aristocracy of the church of God.

It is wonderful to know that I am in the body. It is wonderful to know that the apostles and prophets and all those who have passed down the years, holding aloft the torch, going on from victory to victory, all will be in the body. But how wonderful if we may be in the body so that we might be chosen out of the body to be the bride! It will be according as you are yielded to the *"effective working of His power"* (Eph. 3:7).

Thought for today: God has met the needs of all nations, of all ranks, of all conditions.

May 13

Your Part in the Body

The Gentiles should be fellow heirs, of the same body, and partakers of His promise in Christ through the gospel.
—Ephesians 3:6

Scripture reading: 1 Corinthians 12:12–27

I want you to see your place in the body of Christ. There is no greater language than this about the Lord, that all fullness dwells in Him. (See Colossians 1:19.) Christ is to be manifested fully in humanity.

Do not be afraid of claiming your right. It is not a measure that you have to reach. Remember, John saw Him, and he said that he had a measure that could not be measured. Christ is coming to us in a measureless measure. Human calculation cannot fathom it.

The church is rising in all her vision and destroying the powers of darkness, ruling among the powers of wickedness, and transforming darkness to light by the power of the new creation in us. The church is doing all this so that we might know the power that is working in us by the resurrection of the life of Christ.

So we are enriched with all enrichment; we are endued with all beatitudes; we are covered with all graces; and now we are coming into all the mysteries so that the gifts of the Spirit may be manifested in us.

The revelation of Paul, which never from the foundation of the world had been revealed, is that the Son of God, the very embodiment of the nature of the Most High, the very incarnation of His presence and power, could fill a human vessel to its utmost capacity, until His very nature will sweep through by the power of God.

You cannot enter into this life without being enlarged, abounding, and superabundant. Everything in God is enlargement. God never wants a child of His in the world to be measured. All the riches of God are infinite and boundless. There is no such thing as measuring them. If ever you measure God, you will be thin and little and dwarfed. You cannot measure. You have an exhaustless place.

God's Son is in you with all the power of development, until you are so enriched by this divine grace that you live in the world knowing that God is transforming you from grace to grace, from victory to victory.

The Spirit in you has no other foundation than from glory unto glory. Paul was so enlarged in the Spirit in this third chapter of Ephesians that his language failed to express the glory of Christ Jesus. And then, when he failed to go on in his language, he bowed his knees unto the Father. Oh, this is supreme! This is beyond all that could be! When language failed, when prophecy had no more room, it seems that he came to a place where he got down on his knees. Then we hear by the power of the Spirit language beyond all Paul could ever say: *"For this reason I bow my knees to the Father of our Lord Jesus Christ, from whom the whole family in heaven and earth is named"* (Eph. 3:14–15).

Paul realized that he was joining earth and heaven together. They are one, thank God! There is nothing between us and heaven. Gravity may hold us, but all in heaven and in earth are joined under one blood, with no division or separation. *"To be absent from the body* [is] *to be present with the Lord"* (2 Cor. 5:8).

Thought for today: You might measure your land, you might measure your harvest, but you cannot measure the purposes of the Spirit life: they are boundless; they are infinite.

May 14

Persecution after Baptism

They were filled with indignation, and laid their hands on the
apostles and put them in the common prison.
—Acts 5:17–18

Scripture reading: Acts 5:12–42

*P*eople were scattered, and persecution had come. God
knows—I say it reverently—that we never make progress
when life is easy. You may settle down in your ease and
miss the great plan of God.

A man may be saved for many years without knowing much
about persecution. A man may be sanctified for many years without knowing much about persecution. But it is impossible to be
baptized with the Holy Spirit without entering into persecution.

The disciples had a wonderful time when they were with Jesus. They had no persecution, but there was One in the midst of
them whom the people of Nazareth tried to throw over the brow of
the hill. (See Luke 4:16–30.)

Let us see that whatever happens there is no harsh judgment
in us, no bitterness. We have been quickened, brought into,
changed by a new authority, incorruptible in the corruptible. We
must see that we have divine life where death was, love where hatred was, the power of God reigning in the human, the Lord shining the light of His countenance on us right in the midst of death,
and life breaking forth like rivers in the desert.

The days will come when your ministry and your own life will
be tested on all lines. If you can get beyond your nature, beyond
your natural line of thought, and beyond yourself into a plane of
almighty provision for you in the flesh, quickened by the Spirit, you
will survive. It will be as the Word of God says, *"Having done*
all...stand" (Eph. 6:13).

Thought for today: When the trial is on, when everything comes to
a point where it seems it is the last strand in the rope, then the
Lord will very mightily bring you into a land of plenty.

May 15

Satan Cannot Be Made Holy

For this purpose the Son of God was manifested,
that He might destroy the works of the devil.
—1 John 3:8

Scripture reading: 1 John 3:1–17

There is no such thing as purifying the impure. Evil things never get purer, but more vile. All impurity, all evil must be cast out. You can never make Satan holy. He will be hellish and fiendish forever, and when the brightness of God comes, the Devil will be glad to get in the pit and stay there forever and ever.

Some foolish people say that the Devil will be saved, and that they will go arm in arm with him. It is because they do not rightly understand the Word of God. You will never purify sin. *"The carnal mind...is not subject to the law of God, nor indeed can be"* (Rom. 8:7). Carnality has to be destroyed. Evil propensities must be rooted out. God's plan is, "I will give you a pure heart and a right spirit." And this is the order of the new creation in God.

It does not matter what you say; if your human spirit does not get wholly sanctified, you will always be in danger. It is that position where the Devil has a chance to work upon you. Therefore, we are taught to come into sanctification where uncleanness and corruption pass away, and where all kinds of lusts lose their power.

Only in the pursuit of sanctification does God bless us in our purifying state so that we ascend with Him in the glory. The saints of God, as they go on into perfection and holiness and understand the mind of the Spirit and the law of the spirit of life, are brought into a very blessed place.

It is the place of holiness, the place of entire sanctification, the place where God reigns on the throne of the heart. It is the place where the mind is so concentrated in the power of God that a person thinks about the things that are pure and lives in holy ascendancy. The Spirit can sanctify your spirit until you will never vaunt yourself and will never say "I, I, I," but it will be "Christ, Christ, Christ." Then Christ will be glorified.

Thought for today: Holiness is power; sin is defeat. Sin is weakness; holiness is strength.

223

May 16

Supernatural Fullness

*The thief does not come except to steal, and to kill, and to destroy.
I have come that they may have life, and that they may
have it more abundantly.*
—John 10:10

Scripture reading: Romans 8:1–17

*I*f I cannot make a person who is suffering from disease righteously indignant against that condition, I cannot help him. If I can make every sufferer know that suffering, disease, and all these things are the workings of the Devil, I can help him.

If you can see that the Devil is after you, to kill you for all he is worth, believe that Christ is enthroned in your heart to destroy the very principles of the Devil in every way. Have the reality of this; build upon it by perfect soundness until you are in the place of perfect bliss, for to know Christ is perfect bliss. Be so built in Him that you are not afraid of evil. You must have a fullness that presses out beyond; you must have a life that is full of divine power; you must have a mind that is perfectly in Christ; you must cease to be natural and begin to be supernatural.

Are you ready to be so changed by God that you will never have this human fear anymore? Remember that *"perfect love casts out fear"* (1 John 4:18).

Step into the full tide of the life of the manifestation of God. Your new nature has no corruption in it. Eternal life is not just during your lifetime; it is forever. You are regenerated by the power of the Word of God, and it is in you as an incorruptible force, taking you on from victory to victory until death itself can be overcome, until sin has no authority, until disease could not be in the body. This is a living fact by the Word of God.

Right in this present moment, there is *"no condemnation"* (Rom. 8:1). This law of the Spirit of life is a law in the body; it is a law of eternity; it is a law of God, a new law. It is not the law of the Ten Commandments, but a law of life in the body, changing you until there is no sin power, no disease power, and no death power.

You who desire to go a thousand miles through faith, beyond what you have ever gone before, leap into it. Believe that the blood of Christ makes you clean; believe that you have come into resurrection life. Believe it!

Trying is an effort, whereas believing is a fact. Don't join the Endeavor Society, but come into the Faith Society, and you will leap into the promises of God, which are *"Yes"* and *"Amen"* (2 Cor. 1:20) to all who believe.

Don't look down your nose and murmur anymore. Have a rejoicing spirit; get the praise of God in your heart; go forth from victory to victory; rise in faith, and believe it. You must not live in yourself; you must live in Christ. *"Set your mind on things above"* (Col. 3:2), and keep your whole spirit alive in God. Let your inheritance be so full of divine life that you live above the world and all its thoughts and cares.

Thought for today: God is on His throne and can take you a thousand miles in a moment. Have faith to jump into His supernatural plan.

May 17

Room for Jesus

She...laid Him in a manger,
because there was no room for them in the inn.
—Luke 2:7

Scripture reading: 1 Thessalonians 4:1–12

*J*esus said, *"Foxes have holes and birds of the air have nests, but the Son of Man has nowhere to lay His head"* (Matt. 8:20). Is this true? Yes, but at the same time, it is not true. He could have had a dozen beds. Then why did He not use them? For the simple reason that the people loved Jesus and wanted Him, yet they dared not have Him in their homes. If He would go to their homes, such convicting truths would fall from His lips that they could not stand in His presence. They wanted this holy, lovely Jesus, this beautiful Nazarene, and yet they did not want Him. Thus the Son of Man did not have any place to lay His head, so He spent His nights on the Mount of Olives.

The centurion said, *"Lord, I am not worthy that You should come under my roof. But only speak a word, and my servant will be healed"* (v. 8). The centurion knew that Jesus did not have to be physically present to heal the sick servant. He believed that just a word from Jesus would be sufficient. Jesus was amazed at this man's faith, and He told the centurion, *"Go your way; and as you have believed, so let it be done for you"* (v. 13). The servant was healed as Jesus spoke.

But some do not want Jesus to come to their homes, and it is not because they have such great faith. They do not want Him to come because of the changes they would have to make in their lives. They know that if Jesus were to live in their hearts, their lives would be totally transformed. Many refuse salvation because they know they cannot continue to live in the same old ways; therefore, they do not invite Christ to their homes. Beloved, let us not be afraid to ask Him to come in to stay. Ask Him to give you grace to come to Him. He is not looking at our unworthiness, but at His worthiness. My whole heart cries out to God that I might touch Him afresh.

Thought for today: It is only a step to Jesus.

Our Living Hope

Blessed be the God and Father of our Lord Jesus Christ,
who according to His abundant mercy has begotten us again to a
living hope through the resurrection of Jesus Christ from the dead.
—1 Peter 1:3

Scripture reading: 1 Corinthians 15:1–34

A farmer surveys his land, eagerly scanning the first ears of corn poking through the soil. He knows that first beginnings often indicate the outcome of the harvest. In the same manner, we can be assured of resurrection because Jesus Christ has risen from the dead. And *"as He is, so are we in this world"* (1 John 4:17). Christ is now getting the church ready for translation. In Peter, we read that we are *"begotten...again to a living hope through the resurrection of Jesus Christ from the dead."* Oh, to be changed. What a living hope He gives!

Although Paul and Peter were together very little, they both were inspired to bring before the church the vision of this wonderful truth that the living are being changed. If Christ did not rise, our faith is in vain, and we are still in our sins (1 Cor. 15:17). But Christ has risen and become the firstfruits (v. 23), and we now have the glorious hope that we will also be changed. We who were *"not a people...are now the people of God"* (1 Pet. 2:10). We have been lifted from the mire to be among princes. Beloved, God wants us to see the preciousness of it. It will drive away the dullness of life. Jesus gave all for this treasure. He purchased the field because of the pearl, *"the pearl of great price"* (Matt. 13:46). Jesus purchased it, and we are the pearl of great price for all time. Our inheritance is in heaven, and in 1 Thessalonians 4:18, we are told to *"comfort one another with these words."*

What could be better than the hope that in a little while, the change will come? It seems like such a short time ago that I was a boy. Soon, I will be changed by His grace and be more than a conqueror with *"an inheritance incorruptible and undefiled and that does not fade away"* (1 Pet. 1:4). The inheritance is in you. It is something that is accomplished by God for you. When my daughter was in Africa, she often wrote of things corroding. Our nature is corruptible, but as the natural decays, the spiritual is at work. As the corruptible is doing its work, we are changing.

When will it be seen? When Jesus comes. Most beautiful of all, we will be like Him. What is the process? Grace! What can work it out? Love! It cannot be translated into human phrases. God so loved that He gave Jesus (John 3:16).

There is something very wonderful about being undefiled in the presence of my King, never to change, only to be more beautiful. Unless we know something about grace and the omnipotence of His love, we will never be able to grasp it. But believers can say:

> Love, fathomless as the sea.
> Grace flowing for you and for me.

Thought for today: Just as in the flesh Jesus triumphed by the Spirit, we can be like Him in His victory.

May 19

Our Place Is Reserved

In My Father's house are many mansions; if it were not so,
I would have told you. I go to prepare a place for you.
—John 14:2

Scripture reading: John 14:1–24

*J*esus has prepared a beautiful place for us, and we will have no fear of anyone else taking it; it is reserved. When I went to certain meetings, I would have a reserved seat. I could walk in at any time, and my seat would be unoccupied. What is good about having a reservation? You have a place where you can see Him; it is the very seat you would have chosen. He knows just what you want! He has designed the place for you. Because of His love, you will have joy instead of discord throughout eternity. Will you be there? Is it possible to miss it? We *"are kept by the power of God through faith for salvation ready to be revealed in the last time"* (1 Pet. 1:5).

What is distinctive about it? It will be the fullness of perfection, the ideal of love. The poor in spirit, the mourners, the meek, the hungry and thirsty, the merciful, the pure—all will be ready to be revealed at the appearing of Jesus Christ. You could not remain there unless you had experienced His purifying, perfecting, and establishing. You will be ready when His perfect will has been worked out in you. When you are refined enough, you will go.

But there is something to be done yet to establish you, to make you purer. A great price has been paid: *"The genuineness of your faith...*[is] *much more precious than gold that perishes"* (v. 7). And we must give all and yield all as our Great Refiner puts us in the melting pot again and again. He does this so that we will lose the chaff (Matt. 3:12), so that the pure gold of His presence will be clearly seen, and His glorious image will be reflected.

Thought for today: We must be steadfast and immovable, until all His purposes are worked out.

May 20

Standing Firm through Trials

*But who can endure the day of His coming? And who can stand
when He appears? For He is like a refiner's fire
and like launderer's soap.*
—Malachi 3:2

Scripture reading: Malachi 3

*P*raising God in a meeting is a different thing than thanking Him for the trials you face in your life. There must be no perishing though we are tried by fire. What is going to appear at the appearing of Jesus? Faith! Your heart will be established by the grace of the Spirit, which doesn't crush, but refines; doesn't destroy, but enlarges. Oh, beloved, the Enemy is a defeated foe, and Jesus not only conquers but also displays the spoils of His conquest. The pure in heart will see God (Matt. 5:8). *"If therefore your eye is good, your whole body will be full of light"* (Matt. 6:22).

What is it? It is loyalty to the Word by the power of the blood. You know your inheritance within you is more powerful than all that is without. How many have gone to the stake and through fiery persecution? Did they desire it? Faith tried by fire had power to stand all ridicule, all slander. We need to have the faith of the Son of God, *"who for the joy that was set before Him endured the cross"* (Heb. 12:2). Oh, the joy of pleasing Him!

No trial, no darkness, nothing is too hard for me. If only I may see the image of my Lord again and again. In the melting pot, He removes the skimmings until His face is seen. When the metal reflects Him, it is pure. Who is looking into our hearts? Who is the Refiner? My Lord. He will remove only what will hinder. Oh, I know the love of God is working in my heart.

Thought for today: You will do more in one year if you are really filled with the Holy Spirit than you could do in fifty years apart from Him.

May 21

Getting Ready for Review

Who is able to stand before this holy LORD God?
—1 Samuel 6:20

Scripture reading: Romans 2:1–16

I remember going to the Crystal Palace when General Booth had a review of representatives of the Salvation Army from all nations. It was a grand sight as company after company with all their distinctive characteristics passed a certain place where he could view them. It was a wonderful scene. Similarly, we are going to be presented to God. We are to be a joy to look at, to be to His praise and glory. No one will be there but those who have been tried by fire. Is it worth it? Yes, a thousand times. Oh, the ecstasy of exalted pleasure! God reveals Himself to our hearts.

Peter speaks of *"sincere love"* (1 Pet. 1:22). What does it mean to have *"sincere love"*? It means that even when you are misused or shamed, it never alters; this love is only more refined, making you more like Him. *"Sincere love"* is full of appreciation for those who do not see eye to eye with you. Jesus illustrated it on the cross when He said, *"Father, forgive them"* (Luke 23:34). And Stephen demonstrated it as he was being stoned. He said, *"Lord, do not charge them with this sin"* (Acts 7:60). *"Sincere love"* is the greatest thing God can give to my heart.

We are saved by an incorruptible power—a process always refining, a grace always enlarging, a glory always increasing. We are neither barren nor unfruitful in the knowledge of our Lord Jesus Christ. *"The spirits of just men made perfect"* (Heb. 12:23) are stored in the treasury of the Most High. We are purified as sons and are to be as holy and blameless as He is. Through all eternity, we will gaze at Him with pure, genuine love. God will be glorified as the song is continuously sung: *"Holy, holy, holy, Lord God Almighty"* (Rev. 4:8).

How can we be sad, or hang our heads, or be distressed? If we only knew how rich we are! May God's name be blessed.

Thought for today: Our trials are getting us ready for the procession and the presentation before the Lord.

May 22

What Is Inside Will Come Out

As in water face reflects face, so a man's heart reveals the man.
—Proverbs 27:19

Scripture reading: Matthew 15:1–20

We praise God that our glorious Jesus is the risen Christ. Those of us who have tasted the power of the indwelling Spirit know something about how the hearts of those two disciples burned as they walked to Emmaus with the risen Lord as their companion. (See Luke 24:13–32.)

Note the words of Acts 4:31: *"And when they had prayed, the place where they were assembled together was shaken."* There are many churches where they never pray the kind of prayer that you read of here. A church that does not know how to pray and to shout will never be shaken. If you live in a place like that, you might as well write over the threshold: "Ichabod"—*"The glory has departed from Israel!"* (1 Sam. 4:21). It is only when men have learned the secret of prayer, power, and praise that God comes forth. Some people say, "Well, I praise God inwardly," but if your heart is full of praise, you will have to let the praise come out.

The inner working of the power of God must come first. It is He who changes the heart and transforms the life. Before there is any real outward evidence, there must be the inflow of divine life. Sometimes I say to people, "You weren't at the meeting the other night." They reply, "Oh, yes, I was there in spirit." I say to them, "Well, next time come with your body also. We don't want a lot of spirits here and no bodies. We want you to come and get filled with God." When all the people come and pray and praise as did these early disciples, there will be something happening. People who come will catch fire, and they will want to come again. But they will have no use for a place where everything has become formal, dry, and dead.

The power of Pentecost came in order to loose men. God wants us to be free. Men and women are tired of imitations; they want reality; they want to see people who have the living Christ within, who are filled with Holy Spirit power.

Thought for today: The shout cannot come out unless it is within.

May 23

God Is with You

*No temptation has overtaken you except such as is common to man;
but God is faithful, who will not allow you to be tempted beyond
what you are able, but with the temptation will also make the way of
escape, that you may be able to bear it.*
—1 Corinthians 10:13

Scripture reading: Romans 8:31–39

*D*are you take your inheritance from God? Dare you believe God? Dare you stand on the record of His Word? What is the record? If you will believe, you will see the glory of God. You will be sifted as wheat. You will be tested as though some strange thing tried you. You will be put in places where you will have to put your whole trust in God.

Every trial is to bring you to a greater position in God. The trial that tries your faith will take you on to the place where you will know that the faith of God will be forthcoming in the next test. No man is able to win any victory except through the power of the risen Christ within him. You will never be able to say, "I did this or that." You will desire to give God the glory for everything.

If you are sure of your ground, if you are counting on the presence of the living Christ within, you can laugh when you see things getting worse. God wants you to be settled and grounded in Christ and to become steadfast and unmoveable in Him. The Lord Jesus said, *"I have a baptism to be baptized with, and how distressed I am till it is accomplished!"* (Luke 12:50). Assuredly, He was obedient to the will of His Father in Gethsemane, in the judgment hall, and, after that, on the cross, where He, *"through the eternal Spirit offered Himself without spot to God"* (Heb. 9:14). God will take us right on in like manner, and the Holy Spirit will lead every step of the way. God led Him right through to the empty tomb, to the glory of the Ascension, to a place on the throne.

Thought for today: The Son of God will never be satisfied until He has us with Himself, sharing His glory and sharing His throne.

May 24

Pressing Through

We never saw anything like this!
—Mark 2:12

Scripture reading: Mark 2:1–17

*I*f anything stirs me in my life, it is words such as these: *"We never saw anything like this!"* These words were spoken following the healing of a paralyzed man. His four friends removed a portion of the roof in order to *"let down the bed on which the paralytic was lying"* (Mark 2:4). Jesus healed the man, and *"immediately he arose, took up the bed, and went out in the presence of them all"* (v. 12).

It is an ideal thing to get people to believe that when they ask, they will receive (Matt. 21:22). But how could it be otherwise? It must be so when God says it. Now we have a beautiful word brought before us in the case of this paralyzed man, helpless and so weak that he could not help himself get to Jesus. Four men, whose hearts were full of compassion, carried the man to the house, but the house was full. Oh, I can see that house today as it was filled, jammed, and crammed. There was no room, even by the door. It was crowded inside and out.

Something should happen all the time to cause people to say, "We never saw anything like that." God is dissatisfied with stationary conditions. He opens the storehouse of the Most High, *"the unsearchable riches of Christ"* (Eph. 3:8), to us. God wants to move us into this divine position so that we are completely new creations (2 Cor. 5:17). You know that *"the flesh profits nothing"* (John 6:63). Paul says in Romans that *"the carnal mind is enmity against God; for it is not subject to the law of God, nor indeed can be"* (Rom. 8:7). As we cease to live in the old life and come to know the resurrection power of the Lord, we enter a place of rest, faith, joy, peace, blessing, and life everlasting. Glory to God!

May the Lord give us a new vision of Himself and fresh touches of divine life. May His presence shake off all that remains of the old life and bring us fully into His newness of life. May He reveal to us the greatness of His will concerning us, for there is no one who loves us like He does. Yes, beloved, there is no love like

His, no compassion like His. He is filled with compassion and never fails to take those who will fully obey Him into the Promised Land.

Thought for today: So many people stop at the doorway when God in His great plan is inviting them into His treasury.

May 25

The Way to Jesus

Come to Me, all you who labor and are heavy laden,
and I will give you rest.
—Matthew 11:28

Scripture reading: Matthew 7:13–27; 11:25–30

*I*n God's Word, there is always more to follow, always more to know. If only we could be like children in taking in the mind of God, what wonderful things would happen. Do you apply the whole Bible to your life? It is grand. Never mind those who take only a part. You take it all. When we get such a thirst that nothing can satisfy us but God, we will have a royal time.

The child of God must have reality all the time. After the child of God comes into the sweetness of the perfume of the presence of God, he will have the hidden treasures of God. He will always be feeding on that blessed truth that will make life full of glory. Are you dry? There is no dry place in God, but all good things come out of hard times. The harder the place you are in, the more blessing can come out of it as you yield to His plan. Oh, if only I had known God's plan in its fullness, I might never have had a tear in my life. God is so abundant, so full of love and mercy; there is no lack to those who trust in Him. I pray that God will give us a touch of reality, so that we may be able to trust Him all the way.

What an example of faith we have in the story of the paralytic's healing told in Mark 2. When the sick man's four friends found that the house where Jesus was staying was too crowded to enter, the men asked among themselves, "What will we do?" But there is always a way. I have never found faith to fail, never once. May the Holy Spirit give us a new touch of faith in God's unlimited power. May we have a living faith that will dare to trust Him and say, "Lord, I do believe."

There was no room, *"not even near the door"* (Mark 2:2), but these men said, "Let's go up on the roof." Unbelieving people would say, "Oh, that is silly, ridiculous, foolish!" But men of faith say, "We must get our friend help at all costs. It is nothing to move the roof. Let's go up and go through."

Lord, take us today, and let us go through; let us drop right into the arms of Jesus. It is a lovely place to drop into, out of your self-righteousness, out of your self-consciousness, out of your un-belief. Some people have been in a strange place of deadness for years, but God can shake them out of it. Thank God, some of the molds have been broken. It is a blessed thing when the old mold gets broken, for God has a new mold.

Thought for today: God can perfect the imperfect by His own loving touch.

May 26

Paid in Full

The Son of Man has come to seek and to save that which was lost.
—Luke 19:10

Scripture reading: Mark 2:1–12

I tell you, friends, that since the day that Christ's blood was shed, since the day of His atonement, He has paid the price to meet all the world's needs and its cries of sorrow. Truly Jesus has met the needs of broken hearts and sorrowful spirits, withered limbs and broken bodies. God's dear Son paid the debt for all, for He *"took our infirmities and bore our sicknesses"* (Matt. 8:17). He was *"in all points tempted as we are, yet without sin"* (Heb. 4:15). I rejoice to bring Him to you today, even though it is in my crooked Yorkshire speech, and say to you that He is the only Jesus; He is the only plan; He is the only life; He is the only help; but thank God, He has triumphed to the utmost. He heals all who come to Him.

As the paralyzed man was lowered through the roof, there was a great commotion, and all the people gazed up at this strange sight. We read, *"When Jesus saw their faith, He said to the paralytic, 'Son, your sins are forgiven you'"* (Mark 2:5). What had the forgiveness of sins to do with the healing of this man? It had everything to do with it. Sin is at the root of disease. May the Lord cleanse us from outward sin and from inbred sin and take away all that hinders the power of God to work through us.

"Some of the scribes were sitting there and reasoning in their hearts" (v. 6). They asked, *"Who can forgive sins but God alone?"* (v. 7). But the Lord answered the thoughts of their hearts by saying,

> Which is easier, to say to the paralytic, *"Your sins are forgiven you,"* or to say, *"Arise, take up your bed and walk"*? But that you may know that the Son of Man has power on earth to forgive sins; He said to the paralytic, *"I say to you, arise, take up your bed, and go to your house."*   (Mark 2:9–11)

Jesus healed that man. He saw also the faith of the four men. There is something in this for us today. Many people will not be saved unless some of you are used to stir them up. Remember that you are your *"brother's keeper"* (Gen. 4:9). When these men carried the paralyzed man, they pressed through until he could hear the voice of the Son of God, and liberty came to the captive. The man became strong by the power of God, arose, took up his bed, and went forth before them all.

I have seen wonderful things like this accomplished by the power of God. We must never think about our God in small ways. He spoke the word one day and made the world. That is the kind of God we have, and He is just the same today. There is no change in Him. He is lovely and precious above all thought and comparison. There is none like Him.

Thought for today: We must take our brother to Jesus.

Faith like Abraham

To those who have obtained like precious faith with us by the righteousness of our God and Savior Jesus Christ.
—2 Peter 1:1

Scripture reading: John 6:22–51

*A*s we are filled with the Holy Spirit, God purposes that like our Lord, we should love righteousness and hate lawlessness. There is a place for us in Christ Jesus where we are no longer under condemnation but where the heavens are always open to us. God has a realm of divine life opening up to us where there are boundless possibilities, limitless power, and untold resources. We have victory over all the power of the Devil. As we are filled with the desire to press on into this life of true holiness, desiring only the glory of God, nothing can hinder our true advancement.

Through faith, we realize that we have a blessed and glorious union with our risen Lord. When He was on earth, Jesus told us, *"I am in the Father and the Father in Me"* (John 14:11). *"The Father who dwells in Me does the works"* (v. 10). And He prayed to His Father, not only for His disciples, but also for those who would believe on Him through their testimonies: *"That they all may be one, as You, Father, are in Me, and I in You; that they also may be one in Us, that the world may believe that You sent me"* (John 17:21). What an inheritance is ours when the very nature, the very righteousness, the very power of the Father and the Son are made real in us. This is God's purpose, and as, we take hold of the purpose by faith, we will always be conscious that *"He who is in* [us] *is greater than he who is in the world"* (1 John 4:4). The purpose of all Scripture is to move us to this wonderful and blessed elevation of faith where our constant experience is the manifestation of God's life and power through us.

Peter went on writing to those who had obtained *"like precious faith,"* saying, *"Grace and peace be multiplied to you in the knowledge of God and of Jesus our Lord"* (2 Pet. 1:2). We can have the multiplication of this grace and peace only as we live in the realm of faith. Abraham reached the place where he became a *"friend of*

God" because he *"believed God"* (James 2:23). He *"believed God, and it was accounted to him for righteousness"* (v. 23). Righteousness was credited to him on no other ground than that he *"believed God."* Can this be true of anybody else? Yes, it can be true for every person in the whole wide world who is saved and is blessed along with faithful Abraham.

Some people are anxious because, when they are prayed for, the thing that they are expecting does not happen right then. They say they believe, but you can see that they are really in turmoil from their unbelief. Abraham believed God. You can hear him saying to Sarah, "Sarah, there is no life in you, and there is nothing in me; but God has promised us a son, and I believe God." That kind of faith is a joy to our Father in heaven.

Thought for today: When we believe God, there is no telling where the blessings of our faith will end.

May 28

Eyes of Faith

Jesus went about...teaching...preaching...and healing.
—Matthew 4:23

Scripture reading: Isaiah 58:8–12

One day, a young woman from a place called Ramsbottom came to be healed of an enlargement of her thyroid gland. Before she came she said, "I am going to be healed of this goiter, Mother." After one meeting she came forward and was prayed for. The next meeting she got up and testified that she had been wonderfully healed. She said, "I will be so happy to go and tell Mother about my healing."

She went to her home and testified to her wonderful healing. The next year when we were having the convention, she came again. From a human perspective, it looked as though the goiter was just as big as ever, but that young woman was believing God. Soon she was on her feet giving her testimony, saying, "I was here last year, and the Lord wonderfully healed me. I want to tell you that this has been the best year of my life." She seemed to be greatly blessed in that meeting, and she went home to testify more strongly than ever that the Lord had healed her.

She believed God. The third year, she was at the meeting again, and some people who looked at her said, "How big that goiter has become!" But when the time came for testimonies, she was on her feet and testified, "Two years ago, the Lord gloriously healed me of a goiter. I had a most wonderful healing. It is grand to be healed by the power of God." That day someone questioned her and said, "People will think there is something the matter with you. Why don't you look in the mirror? You will see that your goiter is bigger than ever." The young woman went to the Lord about it and said, "Lord, You so wonderfully healed me two years ago. Won't You show all the people that You healed me?" She went to sleep peacefully that night still believing God. When she came down the next day, there was not a trace or a mark of that goiter.

Thought for today: A faint heart can never have a gift. Two things are essential: first, love; second, determination—a boldness of faith that will cause God to fulfill His Word.

The Mirror of Faith

But he who looks into the perfect law of liberty and continues in it,
and is not a forgetful hearer but a doer of the work,
this one will be blessed in what he does.
—James 1:25

Scripture reading: Daniel 3:10–30

God's Word is *"from everlasting to everlasting"* (Ps. 90:2). His Word cannot fail. God's Word is true, and when we rest in its truth, what mighty results we can get. Faith never looks in the mirror. The mirror of faith is the perfect law of liberty.

To the man who looks into this perfect law of God, all darkness is removed. He sees his completeness in Christ. There is no darkness in faith. Darkness is only in nature. Darkness exists when the natural replaces the divine.

Grace and peace are multiplied to us through a knowledge of God and of Jesus Christ. As we really know our God and Savior, we will have peace multiplied to us like the multiplied fires of ten thousand Nebuchadnezzars. Our faith will increase even though we are put into a den of lions, and we will live with joy in the middle of the whole thing.

What was the difference between Daniel and the king that night when Daniel was put into the den of lions? Daniel's faith was certain, but the king's was experimental. The king came around the next morning and cried, *"Daniel, servant of the living God, has your God, whom you serve continually, been able to deliver you from the lions?"* (Dan. 6:20). Daniel answered, *"My God sent His angel and shut the lions' mouths"* (v. 22). The thing was done. It was done when Daniel prayed with his windows open toward heaven. Prayer links us to our lovely God, our abounding God, our multiplying God. Oh, I love Him. He is so wonderful!

Thought for today: All our victories are won before we go into the fight.

Holiness Opens the Door

Grace and peace be multiplied to you in the knowledge of God
and of Jesus our Lord.
—2 Peter 1:2

Scripture reading: 2 Peter 1:1–11

Note that grace and peace are multiplied through the knowledge of God, but first our faith comes through the righteousness of God. Righteousness comes first and knowledge afterwards. It cannot be otherwise. If you expect any revelation of God apart from holiness, you will have only a mixture. Holiness opens the door to all the treasures of God.

He must first bring us to the place where we, like our Lord, "[love] *righteousness and* [hate] *lawlessness*" (Heb. 1:9), before He opens up to us these good treasures. When we "*regard iniquity in* [our hearts], *the Lord will not hear*" us (Ps. 66:18), and it is only as we are made righteous, pure, and holy through the precious blood of God's Son that we can enter into this life of holiness and righteousness in the Son. It is the righteousness of our Lord Himself made real in us as our faith remains in Him.

After I was baptized with the Holy Spirit, the Lord gave me a blessed revelation. I saw Adam and Eve turned out of the Garden for their disobedience. They were unable to partake of the Tree of Life, for the cherubim with flaming sword kept them away from this tree. When I was baptized, I saw that I had begun to eat of this Tree of Life, and I saw that the flaming sword surrounded it. It was there to keep the Devil away. How marvelously He keeps us so that the Wicked One cannot touch us. I see a place in God where Satan cannot come. We are "*hidden with Christ in God*" (Col. 3:3). He invites us all to come and share this wonderful hidden place. We dwell "*in the secret place of the Most High*" and "*abide under the shadow of the Almighty*" (Ps. 91:1). God has this place for you in this blessed realm of grace.

Thought for today: Oh, what privileges are ours when we are born of God!

May 31

Faith Claims the Victory

[Through the] *exceedingly great and precious promises...you may be partakers of the divine nature.*
—2 Peter 1:4

Scripture reading: Philippians 3:1–15

*T*he Lord has called us to share in His glory and power. As our faith claims His promises, we will see this truth evidenced. I remember one day I was holding a meeting. My uncle came to that meeting and said, "Aunt Mary would like to see you before she dies." I went to see her, and she was assuredly dying. I said, "Lord, can't You do something?" All I did was stretch out my hands and lay them on her. It seemed as though there was an immediate touch of the glory and power of the Lord. Aunt Mary cried, "It is going all over my body." That day she was made perfectly whole.

One day I was preaching, and a man brought a boy who was wrapped up in bandages. It was impossible for him to walk, so it was difficult for them to get him to the platform. They passed him over about six seats. The power of the Lord was present to heal, and it entered right into the child as I placed my hands on him. The child cried, "Daddy, it is going all over me." They took off the boy's bandages and found nothing wrong with him.

The Lord wants us to be walking letters of His Word. Jesus is the Word and is the power in us. It is His desire to work in and through us *"for His good pleasure"* (Phil. 2:13). We must believe that He is in us. There are boundless possibilities for us if we dare to act in God and dare to believe that the wonderful power of our living Christ will be made clear through us as we lay our hands on the sick in His name (Mark 16:18).

I feel the Holy Spirit is grieved with us when we know these things but do not do greater deeds for God. Does not the Holy Spirit show us wide-open doors of opportunity? Will we not let God lead us to greater things? Will we not believe God to take us on to greater demonstrations of His power?

Thought for today: Keep men's eyes off you, but get their eyes on the Lord.

June 1

God Is for You

If God is for us, who can be against us?
—Romans 8:31

Scripture reading: 1 John 4:16–5:5

*I*t does not matter where you are if God is with you. He who is for you is a million times greater than all who can be against you. Oh, if by the grace of God we could only see that the blessings of God's divine power come to us with such sweetness, whispering to us, "Be still, My child. All is well." Be still and see the salvation of the Lord.

What would happen if we learned the secret to asking once and then believing? What an advantage it would be if we could come to a place where we know that everything is within reach of us. God wants us to see that every obstacle can be removed. God brings us into a place where the difficulties are, where the pressure is, where the hard corner is, where everything is so difficult that you know there are no possibilities on the human side. God must do it. All these places are in God's plan. God allows trials, difficulties, temptations, and perplexities to come along our path, but there is not a temptation or trial that can come to us without God providing a way out (1 Cor. 10:13). You do not have the way out; it is God who can bring you through.

Many believers come to me and want me to pray for their nervous systems. I guarantee there is not a person in the whole world who could be nervous if he or she understood 1 John 4. Believe that God loves you!

Every expression of love is in the heart. When you begin to pour out your heart to God in love, your very being, your whole self, desires Him. Perfect love cannot fear (1 John 4:18).

Thought for today: Perfect love means that Jesus has taken hold of your intentions, desires, and thoughts and has purified everything.

June 2

God Will Deliver You

Our God whom we serve is able to deliver us from the burning fiery furnace, and He will deliver us from your hand, O king.
—Daniel 3:17

Scripture reading: John 21:15–25

God wants is to saturate us with His Word. His Word is a living truth. I pity one who has gone a whole week without temptation because God tries only the people who are worthy. If you are passing through difficulties, trials are rising, darkness is appearing, and everything becomes so dense you cannot see through, hallelujah! God will see you through. He is a God of deliverance, a God of power. He is near to you if you will only believe. He can anoint you with fresh oil and make your cup run over (Ps. 23:5). Jesus is the *"balm in Gilead"* (Jer. 8:22), the *"rose of Sharon"* (Song 2:1).

I believe that God wants to align us with such perfection of blessing and beauty that we will say, *"Though He slay me, yet will I trust Him"* (Job 13:15). When the hand of God is on you, and the clay is fresh in the Potter's hands, the vessel will be made perfect as you are pliable in God's hands. He can put His stamp on you today. He can mold you anew and change your vision. He can remove the difficulty.

The Lord of Hosts is here, waiting for your affection. Remember Jesus' question, *"Simon, son of Jonah, do you love Me more than these?"* (John 21:15). If there is anything in you that is not yielded and bent to the plan of the Almighty, you cannot preserve what is spiritual only in part. When the Spirit of the Lord gets perfect control, then we begin to be changed by the expression of God's light in our human frame. The whole body begins to have the fullness of His life manifested until God so has us that we believe all things.

Thought for today: God never lets the chastening rod fall upon anything except what is marring the vessel.

247

June 3

Experience His Joy

Count it all joy when you fall into various trials.
—James 1:2

Scripture reading: James 1:2–18

*P*erhaps you have been counting it all sadness when trials come. Never mind. Tell it to Jesus now. Express your deepest feelings to Him:

> He knows it all, He knows it all,
> My Father knows, He knows it all,
> The bitter tears, how fast they fall,
> He knows, my Father knows it all.

Sorrow may come at night, but *"joy comes in the morning"* (Ps. 30:5). So many believers never look up. When Jesus raised Lazarus from the dead, He lifted His eyes and said, *"Father, I thank You that You have heard Me"* (John 11:41). God wants us to have a resurrection touch about us. Never use your human plan when God speaks His Word. You have your cue from an almighty Source whose resources never fade away. His treasury is past measuring, abounding with extravagances of abundance, waiting to be poured out upon us.

Hear what the Scripture says, *"God...gives to all liberally and without reproach"* (James 1:5). The almighty hand of God comes to our weakness and says, "If you will dare to trust Me and not doubt, I will abundantly satisfy you from the treasure house of the Most High." He forgives, He supplies, He opens the door into His fullness and makes us know that He has done it all. When you come to Him, He gives you an overflow without measure, an expression of a Father's love.

He can satisfy every need. He satisfies the hungry with good things (Luke 1:53). Will you cast *"all your care upon Him, for He cares for you"* (1 Pet. 5:7)? God will help us. Glory to God. How He meets the needs of the hungry!

Thought for today: We may enter into things that will bring us sorrow and trouble, but through them, God will bring us to a deeper knowledge of Himself.

June 4

True Worship

God is Spirit, and those who worship Him
must worship in spirit and truth.
—John 4:24

Scripture reading: John 4:1–30

We appreciate cathedrals and churches, but God does not dwell in temples made by hands but in the sanctuary of the heart. (See Acts 7:48.) The Father seeks *"true worshipers"* (John 4:23) who will worship Him *"in spirit and truth."* The church is the body of Christ. Its worship is a heart worship, a longing to come into the presence of God. God sees our hearts and will open our understanding. The Lord delights in His people. He wants us to come to a place of undisturbed rest and peace that is found only in God. Only simplicity will bring us there.

As Jesus placed a little child in the middle of the disciples, He said, *"Unless you are converted and become as little children, you will by no means enter the kingdom of heaven"* (Matt. 18:3). He did not mean that we should seek to have a child's mind, but a child's meek and gentle spirit. It is the only place to meet God. He will give us that place of worship.

How my heart cries out for a living faith and a deep vision of God. The world cannot produce it. It is a place where we see the Lord, a place where we pray and know that God hears. We can ask God and believe Him for the answer, having no fear but a living faith to come into the presence of God. *"In [His] presence is fullness of joy; at [His] right hand are pleasures forevermore"* (Ps. 16:11).

Thought for today: Everyone who is born of God is kept alive by a power that he cannot see but can feel, a power that is generated in glory, comes down into earthen vessels, and returns to the throne of God.

Changed by God

Let us not love in word or in tongue, but in deed and in truth.
—1 John 3:18

Scripture reading: 1 John 3:1–17

God is looking for people in whom He can reveal Himself. I used to have a tremendous temper, going white with passion. My whole nature was outside of God in that way. God knew I could never be of service to the world unless I was wholly sanctified. I was difficult to please. My wife was a good cook, but I could always find something wrong with the meal. I heard her testify in a meeting that after God sanctified me, I was pleased with everything she served.

I had men working for me, and I wanted to be a good testimony to them. One day, they waited after work was over and said, "We would like that spirit you have." There is a place of death and life where Christ reigns in the body. Then all is well. This Word is full of stimulation. It is by faith that we come into a place of grace. Then all can see that we have been made new. The Holy Spirit arouses our attention. He has something special to say: if you will believe, you can be sons of God, like Him in character, spirit, longings, and actions until all know that you are His child.

The Spirit of God can change our nature. God is the Creator. His Word is creative, and if you believe, His creative power can change your whole nature. You can become *"children of God"* (John 1:12). You cannot reach this altitude of faith alone. No man can keep himself. The all-powerful God spreads His covering over you, saying, *"If you can believe, all things are possible to him who believes"* (Mark 9:23). The old nature is so difficult to manage. You have been ashamed of it many times, but the Lord Himself offers the answer. He says, "Come, and I will give you peace and strength. I will change you. I will operate on you by My power, making you a *'new creation'* (2 Cor. 5:17) if you will believe."

Jesus says, *"Learn from Me, for I am gentle and lowly in heart, and you will find rest for your souls"* (Matt. 11:29). The world has no rest. It is full of troubles, but in Christ, you can move and act in the power of God with a peace that *"surpasses all understanding"* (Phil. 4:7). An inward flow of divine power will change your nature.

June 5

"Therefore the world does not know us, because it did not know Him" (1 John 3:1).

What does this mean? I have lived in one house for fifty years. I have preached from my own doorstep; all around, people know me. They know me when they need someone to pray, when there is trouble, when they need a word of wisdom. But at Christmas time when they call their friends to celebrate, would they invite me? No. Why? They would say, "He is sure to want a prayer meeting, but we want a party."

Wherever Jesus came, sin was revealed, and men don't like sin to be revealed. Sin separates us from God forever. You are in a good place when you weep before God, repenting over the least thing. If you have spoken unkindly, you realized it was not like the Lord. Your keen conscience has taken you to prayer. It is a wonderful thing to have a sensitive conscience. When everything is wrong, you cry to the Lord. It is when we are close to God that our hearts are revealed. God intends for us to live in purity, seeing Him all the time.

Thought for today: Our human spirit has to be controlled by the Holy Spirit.

June 6

Equipped for Service

Blessed are those who are persecuted for righteousness' sake,
for theirs is the kingdom of heaven.
—Matthew 5:10

Scripture reading: Romans 12:1–13

We can be equipped with the power of God. I want you to keep your minds fixed on this fact, for it will help to establish you. It will strengthen you if you think about Paul, who was *"one born out of due time"* (1 Cor. 15:8).

Paul was *"a brand plucked from the fire"* (Zech. 3:2), chosen by God to be an apostle to the Gentiles (Eph. 3:1). I want you to see him, first as a persecutor, furious to destroy those who were bringing glad tidings to the people. See how madly he rushed them into prison, urging them to blaspheme the holy name of Christ. Then see this man changed by the power of Christ and the Gospel of God. See him divinely transformed by God, filled with the Holy Spirit. As you read the ninth chapter of Acts, you see how special his calling was. In order for Paul to understand how he might be able to minister to the needy, God's Son said to Ananias, *"I will show him how many things he must suffer for My name's sake"* (Acts 9:16).

I don't want you to think I mean suffering with diseases. I mean suffering in persecution, with slander, strife, bitterness, abusive scoldings, and with many other evil ways of suffering; but none of these things will hurt you. Instead, they will kindle a fire of holy ambition within you.

To be persecuted for Christ's sake is to be united with a blessed people, with those chosen to cry under the altar, *"How long?"* (Rev. 6:10). Oh, to know that we may cooperate with Jesus. If we suffer persecution, rejoice in that day. Beloved, God wants witnesses, witnesses of truth, witnesses to the full truth, witnesses to the fullness of redemption, witnesses to the deliverance from the power of sin and disease, witnesses who can claim their territory, because of the eternal power working in them, eternal life beautifully, gloriously filling the body, until the body is filled with the life of the Spirit. God wants us to believe that we may be ministers of that kind.

June 6

Paul was lost in the zeal of his ministry. Those first disciples gathered together on the first day of the week to break bread (Acts 20:7). See their need for breaking bread. As they were gathered together, they were caught up with the ministry. In Switzerland, the people said to me, "How long can you preach to us?" I said, "When the Holy Spirit is upon me, I can preach forever!"

If it were only man's ability or college training, we might be crazy before we began, but if it is the Holy Spirit's ministry, we will be as sound as a bell that has no flaw in it. It will be the Holy Spirit at the first, in the middle, and at the end. I do not want to think of anything during the preaching so that the preaching will reflect nothing except, "Thus says the Lord." The preaching of Jesus is that blessed incarnation, that glorious freedom from bondage, that blessed power that liberates from sin and the powers of darkness, that glorious salvation that saves you from death to life, and from the power of Satan to God.

Thought for today: The cup of suffering from heaven is united with a baptism of fire.

June 7

Take Each Opportunity

[Paul] is a chosen vessel of Mine to bear My name before Gentiles, kings, and the children of Israel. For I will show him how many things he must suffer for My name's sake.
—Acts 9:15–16

Scripture reading: Acts 20:7–12, 17–38

*P*aul preached from evening to midnight, and in the middle of the night, something startling happened. If you turn to Philippians, you will see a wonderful truth there where Paul says, *"I may attain to the resurrection"* (Phil. 3:11). Hear the words spoken to Martha, that wonderful saying when Jesus said to her, *"I am the resurrection and the life. He who believes in Me, though he may die, he shall live"* (John 11:25). Paul desired to attain resurrection life, and it is remarkable evidence to me that you never attain anything until opportunity comes. On the activity of faith, you will find that God will bring so many things before your notice that you will have no time to think over them. You will jump into them and bring authority by the power of the Spirit. If you took time to think, you would miss the opportunity.

I was in San Francisco riding down the main street one day. I came across a group in the street, so the driver stopped, and I jumped out of the car. Rushing across to where the commotion was, I found, as I broke through the crowd, a body laid on the ground apparently in a tremendous seizure of death. I got down and asked, "What is wrong?" He replied in a whisper, "Cramp." I put my hand underneath his back and said, "Come out in the name of Jesus," and the boy jumped up and ran away. He never even said, "Thank you."

Likewise, you will find out that with the baptism of the Holy Spirit, you will be in a position where you must act because you have no time to think. The Holy Spirit works on the power of divine origin. It is the supernatural, God filling until it becomes a freeing power by the authority of the Almighty. It sees things come to pass that could not come to pass in any other way.

Let me say more about Paul's position: it is midnight, and death comes to a young man as a result of a fall from a window. The first thing Paul does is the most absurd thing to do, yet it is the most practical thing to do in the Holy Spirit: he fell on the young man. Yes, fell on him, embraced him, and left him alive. Some would say he fell on him, crushed life into him, and brought him back. It is the activity of the Almighty. We must see that in any meeting, the Holy Spirit can demonstrate His divine power until we realize that we are in the presence of God. All can be healed, where the power of the resurrection of Jesus Christ is clearly in evidence, where we see nothing but Jesus. This same Jesus is present today.

Thought for Today: God's Son is placed in power over the power of the Enemy; anybody who deals falsely with the Word of God nullifies the position of authority that Christ has given him over Satan.

The Need for Humility

Serving the Lord with all humility.
—Acts 20:19

Scripture reading: James 4

None of us will be able to be ministers of the new covenant of promise in the power of the Holy Spirit without humility. It is clear to me that in the measure the death of the Lord is in me, the life of the Lord will abound in me. To me, the baptism of the Holy Spirit is not a goal; it is an infilling that allows us to reach the highest level, the holiest position that it is possible for human nature to reach. The baptism of the Holy Spirit comes to reveal Him who is filled fully with God.

To be baptized with the Holy Spirit is to be baptized into death, into life, into power, into fellowship with the Trinity, where we cease to be and God takes us forever. Paul said, *"I have been crucified with Christ; it is no longer I who live, but Christ lives in me"* (Gal. 2:20). I believe that God wants to put His hand upon us so that we may reach ideal definitions of humility, of human helplessness, of human insufficiency, until we will rest no more upon human plans, but have God's thoughts, God's voice, and God the Holy Spirit to speak to us. Now here is a word for us: *"And see, now I go bound in the spirit"* (Acts 20:22). There is the Word. Is that a possibility? Is there a possibility for a person to align himself so completely with the divine will of God?

Jesus was a man, flesh and blood like us, while at the same time, He was the incarnation of divine authority, power, and majesty of the glory of heaven. He bore in His body the weaknesses of human flesh. He was tempted *"in all points...as we are, yet without sin"* (Heb. 4:15). He is so lovely, such a perfect Savior. Oh, that I could shout "Jesus" in such a way that the world would hear. There is salvation, life, power, and deliverance through His name. But, beloved, I see that *"the Spirit drove Him"* (Mark 1:12), that He was *"led by the Spirit"* (Luke 4:1), and here comes Paul *"bound in the spirit"* (Acts 20:22).

What an ideal condescension of heaven that God should lay hold of humanity and possess it with His holiness, His righteousness, His truth, and His faith so that Paul could say, *"'I go bound'*

(v. 22); I have no choice. The only choice is for God. The only desire or ambition is God's. I am bound with God." Is it possible, beloved?

If you look at the first chapter of Galatians, you will see how wonderfully Paul rose to this state of bliss. If you look at the third chapter of Ephesians, you see how he became *"less than the least of all saints"* (v. 8). In Acts 26, you will hear him say, *"King Agrippa, I was not disobedient to the heavenly vision"* (v. 19). In order to keep the vision, he yielded not to flesh and blood. God laid hold of him; God bound him; God preserved him. I ought to say, however, that it is a wonderful position to be preserved by the Almighty. We ought to see to it in our Christian experience that when we commit ourselves to God, the consequences will be all right. He who *"seeks to save his life will lose it, and whoever loses his life will preserve it"* (Luke 17:33).

What is it to be bound by the Almighty, preserved by the Infinite? There is no end to God's resources. They reach right into glory. They never finish on the earth. God takes control of a man in the baptism of the Holy Spirit as he yields himself to God. There is the possibility of being taken and yet left—taken charge of by God and left in the world to carry out His commands. That is one of God's possibilities for humanity: to be taken over by the power of God while being left in the world to be salt as the Scripture describes (Matt. 5:13).

Thought for today: The way to get up is to get down.

A Fresh Vision for Each Day

His compassions fail not. They are new every morning.
—Lamentations 3:22–23

Scripture reading: Psalm 62

I am out to win souls. It is my business to seek the lost. It is my business to make everybody hungry, dissatisfied, mad, or glad. I want to see every person filled with the Holy Spirit. I must have a message from heaven that will not leave people as I found them. Something must happen if we are filled with the Holy Spirit. Something must happen at every place. Men must know that a man filled with the Holy Spirit is no longer a man. A man can be swept by the power of God in his first stage of revelation of Christ, and from that moment on, he has to be an extraordinary man. In order to be filled with the Holy Spirit, he has to become a free body for God to dwell in.

I appeal to you who have been filled with the Holy Spirit: whatever the cost, let God have His way. I appeal to you who have to move on, who cannot rest until God does something for you. God has been revealing to me that anyone who does not sin yet remains in the same place spiritually for a week is a backslider. You say, "How is it possible?" Because God's revelation is available to anyone who will wholeheartedly be committed to following God.

Staying the same for two days would almost indicate that you had lost the vision. The child of God must have a fresh vision every day. The child of God must be more active by the Holy Spirit every day. The child of God must come into line with the power of heaven, where he knows that God has put His hand upon him.

Jesus went about doing good, for God was with Him. God anointed Him. Beloved, is that not the ministry to which God would have us become heirs? Why? Because the Holy Spirit has to bring us a revelation of Jesus, and the purpose of being filled with the Holy Spirit is to give us a revelation of Jesus. He will make the Word of God just the same life as was given by the Son, as new, as fresh, as effective as if the Lord Himself were speaking.

I wonder how many of you are a part of the bride of Christ? The bride loves to hear the Bridegroom's voice (John 3:29). Here it is, the blessed Word of God, the whole Word, not just part of it. No, we believe in the whole thing. Day by day, we find out that the Word itself gives life. The Spirit of the Lord breathes through us. He makes the Word come alive in our hearts and minds. So I have within my hands, within my heart, within my mind, this blessed reservoir of promises that is able to do so many marvelous things.

God has indeed been manifesting Himself. I must tell you one of those cases. In Oakland, California, I held meetings at a theater. Only to glorify God, I tell you that Oakland was in a very serious state. There was very little Pentecostal work there, and so a large theater was rented. God worked especially in filling the place until we had to have overflow meetings. In these meetings, we had a rising flood of people getting saved by standing up voluntarily, all over that place, getting saved the moment they stood. Then we had a large number of people who needed help in their bodies, rising up in faith and being healed.

One of them was an old man who was ninety-five years of age. He had been suffering for three years until he gradually got to the place that for three weeks he was consuming only liquids. He was in a terrible state, but this man was different from the others. I got him to stand while I prayed for him, and he came back and told us with such a radiant face that new life had come into his body. He said, "I am ninety-five years old. When I came into the meeting, I was full of pain with cancer in the stomach. I have been healed so that I have been eating perfectly, and I have no pain." Similarly, many people were healed.

I hope you are expecting big things.

Thought for today: No man can have the Trinity abiding in him and be the same as he was before.

Free from Sin

There is therefore now no condemnation to those who are in Christ Jesus, who do not walk according to the flesh, but according to the Spirit. For the law of the Spirit of life in Christ Jesus has made me free from the law of sin and death.
—Romans 8:1–2

Scripture reading: Romans 8:1–17

*T*he Spirit of the Lord wants to bring you into revelation. He wants you without condemnation. What will that mean? It will mean a great deal in every way, because God wants all His people to be clear witnesses so that the world will know we belong to Him. More than that, He wants us to be *"the salt of the earth"* (Matt. 5:13); to be *"the light of the world"* (v. 14); to be like cities built on a hill so that they cannot be hidden (v. 14). He wants us to be so *"in God"* (1 John 4:15) that the world will see God in us. Then they can look to Him for redemption. That is the law of the Spirit. What will it do? *"The law of the Spirit of life in Christ Jesus"* will make you *"free from the law of sin and death."* Sin will have no dominion over you (Rom. 6:14). You will have no desire to sin, and it will be as true of you as it was of Jesus when He said, *"The ruler of this world is coming, and he has nothing in Me"* (John 14:30). Satan cannot influence; he has no power. His power is destroyed: *"The body is dead because of sin, but the Spirit is life because of righteousness"* (Rom. 8:10).

To be filled with God means that you are free. You are filled with joy, peace, blessing, and strength of character. You are transformed by God's mighty power.

Notice there are two laws. *"The law of the Spirit of life in Christ Jesus"* makes you *"free from the law of sin and death."* *"The law of sin and death"* is in you as it was before, but it is dead. You still have your same flesh, but its power over you is gone. You are the same person, but you have been awakened into spiritual life. You are a *"new creation"* (2 Cor. 5:17), created in God afresh after the image of Christ. Now, beloved, some people who conform to this truth do not understand their inheritance, and they go down. Instead of becoming weak, you have to rise triumphantly over *"the law of sin and death."* In Romans, we read, *"I thank God; through*

260

Jesus Christ our Lord! So then, with the mind I myself serve the law of God, but with the flesh the law of sin" (Rom. 7:25).

God wants to show you that there is a place where we can live in the Spirit and not be subject to the flesh. We can live in the Spirit until sin has no dominion over us. We reign in life and see the covering of God over us in the Spirit. Sin reigned unto death, but Christ reigned over sin and death, and so we reign with Him in life. Through the agony He suffered, He purchased our blessed redemption.

Thought for today: In the Garden of Gethsemane, Jesus restored to you everything that was lost in the Garden of Eden.

June 11

Filled with God

You may be filled with all the fullness of God.
—Ephesians 3:19

Scripture reading: Ephesians 3

Some people come with very small expectations concerning God's fullness, and a lot of people are satisfied with a thimbleful. You can just imagine God saying, "Oh, if they only knew how much they could take away!" Other people come with a larger container, and they go away satisfied. God is longing for us to have such a desire for more, a desire that only He can satisfy.

You women would have a good idea of what I mean from the illustration of a screaming child being passed from one person to another. The child is never satisfied until he gets to the arms of his mother. You will find that no peace, no help, no source of strength, no power, no life, nothing can satisfy the cry of the child of God but the Word of God. God has a special way of satisfying the cries of His children. He is waiting to open the windows of heaven until He has moved in the depths of our hearts so that everything unlike Himself has been destroyed.

What a wonderful, divine position God intends us all to have, to be filled with the Holy Spirit. It is something so remarkable, so divine; it is, as it were, a great open door into all the treasury of the Most High. As the Spirit comes like *"rain upon the mown grass"* (Ps. 72:6 KJV), He turns the barrenness into greenness, freshness, and life. Your dryness becomes springs, your barrenness becomes floods, your whole life is vitalized by heaven, and you begin to live as a new creation.

No one needs to go away empty. God wants you to be filled. My brother, my sister, God wants you today to be like a watered garden, filled with the fragrance of His own heavenly joy, until you know at last that you have touched the immense fullness of God. The Son of God came for no other purpose than to lift, to mold, and to remold, until *"we have the mind of Christ"* (1 Cor. 2:16).

Thought for today: The Spirit of the living God sweeps through all weaknesses.

Ask Largely of God

He who believes in Me, as the Scripture has said,
out of his heart will flow rivers of living water.
—John 7:38

Scripture reading: John 7:37–8:12

I know that dry ground can be flooded (Isa. 44:3). May God prevent me from ever wanting anything less than a flood. Through the blood of Christ's atonement, we may have riches and riches. We need the warming atmosphere of the Spirit's power to bring us closer and closer until nothing but God can satisfy. Then we may have some idea of what God has left after we have taken all that we can. It is like a sparrow taking a drink of the ocean and then looking around and saying, "What a vast ocean! I could have taken a lot more if only I had room."

Sometimes you have things you can use, and you don't know it. You could be dying of thirst right in a river of plenty. There was once a boat in the mouth of the Amazon River. The people on board thought they were still in the ocean. They were dying of thirst, some of them nearly mad. They saw a ship and asked if they would give them some water. Someone on the ship replied, "Dip your bucket right over; you are in the mouth of the river." There are a number of people today in the middle of the great river of life, but they are dying of thirst because they do not dip down and take from the river. Dear friend, you may have the Word, but you need an awakened spirit. The Word is not alive until it is moved upon by the Spirit of God, and in the right sense, it becomes Spirit and Life when it is touched by His hand alone.

Beloved, *"there is a river whose streams shall make glad the city of God, the holy place of the tabernacle of the Most High"* (Ps. 46:4). There is a stream of life that makes everything move. There is a touch of divine life and likeness through the Word of God that comes from nowhere else. We think of death as the absence of life, but there is a death-likeness in Christ, who is full of life.

There is no such thing as an end to God's beginnings. We must be in Christ; we must know Him. Life in Christ is not a touch; it is not a breath; it is the almighty God; it is a Person; it is the Holy One dwelling in the temple *"not made with hands"* (Heb. 9:11). Oh, beloved, He touches, and it is done. He is the same God over all, *"rich to all who call upon Him"* (Rom. 10:12). Pentecost is the last thing that God has to touch the earth with. If you do not receive the baptism of the Holy Spirit, you are living in a weak and impoverished condition, which is no good to you or anybody else. May God move us on to a place where there is no measure to this fullness that He wants to give us. God exalted Jesus and gave Him a name above every name. You notice that everything has been put under Him.

The tide is rolling in. Let us see to it today that we get right into the tide, for it will hold us. God's heart of love is the center of all things. Get your eyes off yourself; lift them up high, and see the Lord, for in Him, there *"is everlasting strength"* (Isa. 26:4).

If you went to see a doctor, the more you told him about yourself, the more he would know. But when you come to Doctor Jesus, He knows all from the beginning, and He never prescribes the wrong medicine. Jesus sends His healing power and brings His restoring grace, so there is nothing to fear. The only thing that is wrong is your wrong conception of His redemption.

Thought for today: I will not settle for small things when I have such a big God.

June 13

Take Authority over Satan

Get behind Me, Satan!
—Luke 4:8

Scripture reading: Luke 4:1–13

*J*esus was wounded so that He might be able to identify with your weaknesses (Heb. 4:15). He took your flesh and laid it upon the cross so that *"He might destroy him who had the power of death, that is, the devil, and release those who through fear of death were all their lifetime subject to bondage"* (Heb. 2:14–15).

You will find that almost all the ailments that you experience come as a result of Satan, and they must be dealt with as satanic; they must be cast out. Do not listen to what Satan says to you, for the Devil is a liar from the beginning (John 8:44). If people would only listen to the truth of God, they would realize that every evil spirit is subject to them. They would find out that they are always in the place of triumph, and they would *"reign in life through the One, Jesus Christ"* (Rom. 5:17).

Never live in a place other than where God has called you, and He has called you from on high to live with Him. God has designed that everything will be subject to man. Through Christ, He has given you authority over all the power of the Enemy. He has worked out your eternal redemption.

I was finishing a meeting one day in Switzerland. When the meeting ended and we had ministered to all the sick, we went out to see some people. Two boys came to us and said that there was a blind man present at the meeting that afternoon. He had heard all the words of the preacher and said he was surprised that he had not been prayed for. They went on to say that this blind man had heard so much that he would not leave until he could see. I said, "This is positively unique. God will do something today for that man."

We got to the place. The blind man said he had never seen. He was born blind, but because of the Word preached in the afternoon, he was not going home until he could see. If ever I have joy, it is when I have a lot of people who will not be satisfied until they get all that they have come for. With great joy, I anointed him and laid hands on his eyes. Immediately, God restored his vision. It was very strange how the man reacted. There were some electric lights. First he counted them; then he counted us. Oh, the ecstatic pleasure that this man experienced every moment because of his sight! It made us all feel like weeping and dancing and shouting. Then he pulled out his watch and said that for years he had been feeling the raised figures on the watch in order to tell the time. But now, he could look at it and tell us the time. Then, looking as if he had just awakened from some deep sleep, or some long, strange dream, he realized that he had never seen the faces of his father and mother. He went to the door and rushed out. That night, he was the first person to arrive for the meeting. All the people knew him as the blind man, and I had to give him a long time to talk about his new sight.

I wonder how much you want to take with you today. You could not carry it if it were substance, but there is something about the grace, the power, and the blessings of God that can be carried, no matter how big they are. Oh, what a Savior! What a place we are in, by grace, that He may come in to commune with us. He is willing to say to every heart, *"Peace, be still"* (Mark 4:39), and to every weak body, *"Be strong"* (Deut. 31:6). Are you going halfway, or are you going all the way to the end?

Thought for today: Do not be deceived by Satan, but believe God.

June 14

What Is Your Response?

*Let us therefore come boldly to the throne of grace, that we may
obtain mercy and find grace to help in time of need.*
—Hebrews 4:16

Scripture reading: Hebrews 4

*F*riends, it is the purpose of God that you should rise into the place of sonship. Don't miss the purpose God has in His heart for you. Realize that God wants to make of you the firstfruits (James 1:18) and separate you unto Himself. God has lifted some of you up again and again. It is amazing how God in His mercy has restored and restored, and *"whom He called, these He also justified; and whom He justified, these He also glorified"* (Rom. 8:30). The glorification is still going on and is going to exceed what it is now.

Within your heart there surely must be a response to this call. It does not matter who is against us: *"What then shall we say to these things? If God is for us, who can be against us?"* (v. 31). If there are millions against you, God has purposed it and will bring you right through to glory. Human wisdom has to stand still. It is *"with the heart one believes unto righteousness"* (Rom. 10:10).

Brothers and sisters, what do you want God to do for you? That is the question. What have you come here for? We have seen God work in horribly diseased bodies. Our God is able to heal and to meet all of our needs. The Scripture says, *"He who did not spare His own Son, but delivered Him up for us all, how shall He not with Him also freely give us all things?"* (Rom. 8:32).

Do you need to be healed of a critical spirit? The Scripture warns: *"Who shall bring a charge against God's elect?"* (v. 33). I tell you, it is bad business for the man who harms God's anointed (1 Chron. 16:21–22). *"Who is he who condemns?"* (Rom. 8:34). How much of that there is today: brother condemning brother, everybody condemning one another. You also go about condemning yourself. The Devil is the *"accuser of* [the] *brethren"* (Rev. 12:10). But there is power in the blood of Christ to free us, to keep us, and to bring us healing.

Do not let the Enemy cripple you and bind you. Why don't you believe God's Word? There is a blessed place for you in the Holy

June 14

Spirit. Instead of condemning you, Christ is interceding for you. Rest in this promise:

> *For I am persuaded that neither death nor life, nor angels nor principalities nor powers, nor things present nor things to come, nor height nor depth, nor any other created thing, shall be able to separate us from the love of God which is in Christ Jesus our Lord.* (Rom. 8:38–39)

Beloved, you are in a wonderful place. Because you are sons and joint heirs, you have a right to healing for your bodies and to be delivered from all the power of the Enemy.

Thought for today: Because God has called and chosen you, He wants you to know that you have power with Him.

June 15

Follow God's Command

*I press toward the goal for the prize
of the upward call of God in Christ Jesus.*
—Philippians 3:14

Scripture reading: Philippians 3:1–21

God's Word is our food. If we do not edify ourselves with it, our needs will not be met. Let us preach by our lives, actions, presence, and praise, always being living letters of Christ. We should strive to be examples to all men of the truth contained in the Word of God.

Follow the truth, and do not abandon it. Always be watchful for divine inspiration. If we were to go all the way with God, what would happen? Seek the honor that comes from God alone. Paul spoke about the desire to attain. He said that he reached for *"the goal for the prize of the upward call of God in Christ Jesus"* (Phil. 3:14). There is no standing still. We are renewed by the Spirit.

Abraham left his home and followed God to a new land (Gen. 12:1–4). We never get into a new place until we come out of the old one. We must model God's personality. We can never be satisfied to stay where we are spiritually, for the truth continues to enlighten us. We must move on, or we will perish. We must be obedient to the Holy Spirit who guides us.

Paul was a man who had kept the law blamelessly. He had tried in his humanity to follow an ideal standard. Then Paul saw a light from heaven, and he was made new. Are you new? He was not with the other apostles, but he had been told of *"the Word of life"* (1 John 1:1). He had not yet attained to these ideal principles, but he had zeal. Before him was a challenge. He was to *"go into the city"* (Acts 9:6) where he would be told what to do. The present was nothing to him; he was motivated to follow God's command. Everything that had been important to him before, he now counted *"loss for the excellence of the knowledge of Christ Jesus* [his] *Lord"* (Phil. 3:8). His chief goal was to *"gain Christ"* (v. 8).

When Judas and the soldiers came after Jesus in the Garden, Jesus spoke, and the men fell backward (John 18:6). He, the Creator, submitted Himself to these men. Yet He said, *"Let these go their way"* (v. 8), referring to the disciples. When they abused Him,

June 15

He did not retaliate. Paul understood these Christlike principles. He recognized the power of Christ, which is able to lift our humanity.

Jesus' followers sought to make Him a King, but Jesus retired to pray. Paul desired to *"gain Christ and be found in Him"* (Phil. 3:8–9). Oh, can I gain Him? Is it possible to change and change, having His compassion, His love?

In an effort to prevent Jesus from being taken, Peter cut off Malchus's ear (John 18:10). Jesus put it on again. See the dignity of Christ, who comes to create a new order of life. May we *"gain Christ and be found in Him"* so that we might have the *"righteousness which is from God by faith"* (Phil. 3:8–9).

Jesus identified Himself with us. He came to be a firstfruit (1 Cor. 15:23). How zealous is the farmer as he watches his crops to see the first shoots and blades of the harvest! Jesus was a firstfruit, and God will have a harvest. What a lovely position to be children of God, perfectly adjusted in the presence of God and *"found in Him"* (Phil. 3:9)! You say, "It is a trying morning," or "I am in a needy place." He knows and understands your needs. When Jesus saw a great crowd coming toward Him, He said to Philip, *"Where shall we buy bread, that these may eat?"* (John 6:5). Jesus knew where the food would come from. He was testing Philip's faith. From a little boy's lunch, Jesus fed over five thousand. They were all filled, and twelve baskets of bread were left over (v. 13).

Thought for today: Although we are always striving for more of God, we have a sense of contentment in Him.

Experience Resurrection Power

That I may know Him and the power of His resurrection, and the
fellowship of His sufferings.
—Philippians 3:10

Scripture reading: Philippians 3

*J*esus had what Paul desired. Paul knew Jesus by revelation as
we do. He did not know Him from being with Him in His human ministry as the other apostles did. Paul saw that Jesus
lived in resurrection power. Paul wanted to gain the rest of faith,
so he refused all hindrances and pressed on. He wanted to remove
any interference that stood in the way of his knowing Christ. Before facing the Cross, Jesus told His disciples to *"stay here and
watch"* (Mark 14:34) while He went further in the garden to pray.

One day Jesus came upon a funeral procession. A widow's only
son had died, and Jesus' great heart had compassion for her. He
touched her son in his coffin and said, *"Young man, I say to you,
arise"* (Luke 7:14). Death had no power; it could not hold him: *"He
who was dead sat up and began to speak"* (v. 15). Oh, compassion is
greater than death, greater than suffering. Oh, God, give it to us.

One day, I saw a woman with tumors. In the condition she was
in, she could not live out that day. I said, "Do you want to live?"
She could not speak, but she was able to move her finger. In the
name of Jesus, I anointed her with oil. Mr. Fisher, who was with
me, said, "She's gone!"

It had been a little blind girl who had led me to this dying
mother's bedside. Compassion broke my heart for that child. I had
said to the mother, "Lift your finger." Carrying the mother across
the room, I put her against the wardrobe. I held her there. I said,
"In the name of Jesus, death, come out." Like a fallen tree, leaf after leaf, her body began moving. Upright instead of lifeless, her feet
touched the floor. "In Jesus' name, walk," I said. She did, back to
her bed.

I told this story in the service. There was a doctor there who
said, "I'll prove that." He saw her and confirmed that the story was
true. She told the doctor: "It is all true. I was in heaven, and I saw
countless numbers all like Jesus. He pointed, and I knew I had to
go. Then I heard a voice saying, 'Walk, in the name of Jesus.'"

June 16

There is power in His resurrection. There is a *"righteousness which is from God by faith"* (Phil. 3:9). Are we able to comprehend it? Can we have it? It is His love. It is His life in us. It is His compassion.

See that you understand and possess the righteousness of God. Do not miss it. Oh, do not miss knowing Christ! It is the *"righteousness which is from God by faith"*—the rest of faith.

Thought for today: We are here on probation to slay the Enemy and destroy the kingdoms of darkness, to move among satanic forces and subdue them in the name of Jesus.

Sonship

Behold what manner of love the Father has bestowed on us, that we should be called children of God!
—1 John 3:1

Scripture reading: John 1:1–13

God has done something marvelous for the believer. He has taken him out of the world. It is a remarkable word that Jesus said: *"I do not pray that You should take them out of the world....They are not of the world"* (John 17:15–16). It is a great truth for us to understand. In this glorious position of God's own, we come to a place where we know with confidence, we say it without fear of contradiction from our own hearts or even outside voices, *"Beloved, now we are children of God"* (1 John 3:2).

I want us to examine ourselves in the light of the Word. God has definitely purposed that we should inherit all of the Scriptures, but we must meet the requirements necessary to claim them. Remember this, there are any number of things you may quote without possessing the essential reality of them. I want us to have something more than the literal word. Words are of no importance unless the believer has the assurance of the abiding of those words. You can quote the words of Scripture without being in the place of victory.

Any person who has come to the place of this word, *"He who is in you is greater than he who is in the world"* (1 John 4:4), is mightier than all the powers of darkness, mightier than the power of disease, mightier than his own self. There is something reigning supremely great in him more than in the world when he is in that place. But we must come to the place of knowledge. It is not sufficient for you to quote the Word of God. You never come to a place of righteousness and truth until you are in possession of the promises contained in the Word.

Beloved, God wants us to be something more than ordinary people. Remember this: if you are ordinary, you have not reached the ideal principles of God. The only thing that God has for a man is to be extraordinary. God has no room for an ordinary man. There are millions of ordinary people in the world. But when God takes hold of a man, He makes him extraordinary in personality, power, thought, and activity.

"Beloved, now we are children of God" (1 John 3:2). It is a divine plan fashioned by His divine will. God has not given anything that He does not mean for us to attain. God means for us to possess all these things. *"Beloved, now we are children of God."* God has such purposes to perform in us that He has a great desire to utter these words in our hearts so that we may rise, that we may claim, that we may be ambitious, that we may be covetous for these purposes, that there may be something in us that nothing can satisfy unless we not only tow the line but also live in the line and claim the whole thing as ours.

You will never reach ideal purposes in any way unless you become the living epistle of the Word by the power of the Holy Spirit. You become the living force of the revelation of God, the incarnation of the personality of His presence in the human soul. Then you know that you are His children. Look at Christ. He is the most beautiful of all. He is utterly glorious, passionate for God, filled with all the fullness of God. He came to earth in the glory of the majesty of His Father, and He stood in the earth in human form.

I like to think about the manifestation of the power of God. God came and resided in flesh, in weakness, under the law—for you. He came in human form, worshipped in it, lived in it, and moved in it. Some even recognized Him as the Son of God.

Beloved, there is the principle. The remarkable position of every soul is to be so inhabited by Jesus as to become a living personality of God's ideal Son. It is very remarkable and beautiful. God has these divine plans for us. So many people believe that because they are in the flesh, they are always to be in the place of weakness. Friends, your weaknesses have to be swallowed up with the ideal of Him who never failed.

Every time He was tried, He came out victorious. He *"was in all points tempted as we are, yet without sin"* (Heb. 4:15). The purpose for His temptations was so that He might be able to help all who are tempted and tried and oppressed in any way. He was the great embodiment of God to human life. He came to expose our weaknesses so that we might behold His mightiness. Through Him, we can be strong in the Lord. Praise the Lord!

Thought for today: It is always all right when He is Almighty.

Divinely Adjusted

For with the heart one believes unto righteousness.
—Romans 10:10

Scripture reading: Psalm 57

May God show us that the only thing that is ever going to help us is the heart. It is the heart where we believe in faith. It is the heart that is inhabited by the Spirit. It is the heart that is moved by God. The mind is always secondary.

The heart conceives, the mind reflects, and the mouth is operated. But you must not try to reverse the order. Some people are all tongue, neither head nor heart. But when He comes, there is perfect order. It is as right as rain. Look how it comes! The heart believes and then like a ventilator, it flows through and quickens the mind. Then the tongue speaks of the glory of the Lord.

The Scriptures are perfect, the sacrifice is perfect, the revelation is perfect. Everything is so divinely adjusted by God Almighty that every person who comes into infinite revelation touched by God sees that the whole canon of Scripture is perfect from the beginning to the end. Not a single thing in the Scriptures clashes with or contradicts the Spirit and makes trouble.

When the power of God surges through the whole life, the Word becomes the personality of the subject. We become the subjects of the Spirit of the living God, and we are moved by the power of God until *"we live and move and have our being"* (Acts 17:28) within this flow of God's integrity. What a wonderful adjustment for weaknesses! God is able to shake us thoroughly, to send a wind and blow the chaff away until it will never be seen anymore. God is able to refine us in a way that everyone would desire to proclaim His praises:

> It is better to shout than to doubt,
> It is better to rise than to fail,
> It is better to let the glory out,
> Than to have no glory at all.

I am the last man to say anything about fasting, praying, or anything that has been a source of blessing to others. But I have learned by personal experience that I can get more out of one moment's faith than I can get out of a month's yelling. I can get more by believing God in a moment than I can get by screaming for a month. Also, I am positive that blessing comes out of fasting when the fasting is done in the right way. But I find so many people who make up their minds to fast, and they finish with a thick head, troubled bones, and sleepy conditions. I am satisfied that that is no way to fast. A way to fast is described in many Scriptures.

Praying and fasting go together. The Spirit leads you to pray. The Spirit holds on to you until you forget even the hour or the day, and you are so caught up by the power of the Spirit that you want nothing, not even food or drink. Then God gets His plan through because He has you through and through. So the Lord of Hosts, I trust, will *"surround* [us] *with songs of deliverance"* (Ps. 32:7) and give us inward revelations until our whole beings will be uplifted.

Who dares to believe God? Who dares to claim his rights? What are your rights? *"Now we are children of God"* (1 John 3:2). This is a position of absolute rest, a position of faith. It is a place of perfect trust and perfect habitation where there are no disturbances. You experience peace like a river. Look at the face of God. Hallelujah! The very Word that comes to judge comes to help.

The law came as a judgment, but when the Spirit comes and breathes through the law, He comes to lift us higher and higher. Hallelujah! We must go a little further. God comes to us and says, "I will make it all right if you dare believe."

All the great things of God come to us as we realize our sinfulness before Him. Instead of hiding as Adam and Eve did when they realized they were naked (Gen. 3:7–10), we should come to God to be clothed. We cannot associate with the evil of this world. If you can be attracted by anything earthly, you have missed the greatest association that God has for you. If your property, your money, your friends, or any human thing can attract you from God, you are not His child in this respect. Come into line with God's Word. Let us encounter the Word; let us face God and see if this thing really is so.

Thought for today: Many people have lost out because their minds prevent them from letting God reach their hearts.

Sanctified by God

*If anyone hears My voice and opens the door, I will come in to him
and dine with him, and he with Me.*
—Revelation 3:20

Scripture reading: Colossians 1:9–23

*L*ook at the tremendous power of God behind our inheritance. First, we are adopted; then we receive an inheritance; then we are made coheirs with Jesus. God touches our souls, making our whole bodies cry out for the living God.

Do you want God? Do you want fellowship in the Spirit? Do you want to walk with Him? Do you desire communion with Him? Everything else is no good. You want the association with God, and God says, *"I will come in to* [you] *and dine with* [you]*, and* [you] *with Me."* Hallelujah! We can attain spiritual maturity, fullness of Christ, a place where God becomes the perfect Father and the Holy Spirit has a rightful place now as never before.

The Holy Spirit breathes through us, enabling us to say, "You are my Father." Because you have been adopted, *"God has sent forth the Spirit of His Son into your hearts, crying out, 'Abba, Father!'"* (Gal. 4:6). May God the Holy Spirit grant to us that richness of His pleasure, that unfolding of His will, that consciousness of His smile upon us. There is *"no condemnation"* (Rom. 8:1). We find that *"the law of the Spirit of life"* makes us *"free from the law of sin and death"* (v. 2). Glory!

If we see the truth as clearly as God intends for us to see it, we will all be made so much richer, looking forward to the Blessed One who is coming again. Here we are, face-to-face with the facts. God has shown us different aspects of the Spirit. He has shown us the pavilion of splendor. He has revealed to us the power of the relationship of sonship. He has shown us that those who are God's children bear His image. They actively claim the rights of their adoption. They speak, and it is done. They bind the things that are loose, and loose the things that are bound (Matt. 16:19). And the perfection of sonship is so evident that more and more people are becoming children of God.

Do you believe it? Let us see you act it. Beloved, God the Holy Spirit has a perfect plan to make us a movement. There is a difference between a movement and a monument. A movement is something that is always active. A monument is something that is erected on a corner and neither speaks nor moves, but there is a tremendous lot of humbug and nonsense to get it in place. It is silent and does nothing. A movement is where God comes into the very being of a person, making him active for God. He is God's property, God's mouthpiece, God's eyes, and God's hands. God will *"sanctify you completely"* (1 Thess. 5:23).

The sanctification of the eyes, the hands, the mouth, the ears—to be so controlled by the Spirit who lives within us—is a wonderful place for God to bring us to. *"Beloved, now we are children of God; and it has not yet been revealed what we shall be"* (1 John 3:1–2). What a great thought: to be heirs, *"joint heirs with Christ"* (Rom. 8:17); to receive revelations and kindnesses from God; to have God dwell within man. The believer is filled, moved, and intensified until he takes wing. It would not take a trumpet to rouse him, for he is already on the wing, and he will land very soon. He would hear God's voice no matter how much noise surrounded him.

Everything that is going to help you, you have to make yours. He has stored it up already. You don't need a stepladder to get to it. It is ready to be handed to you when you become joined with Him. Beloved, it is impossible in our finite condition to estimate the lovingkindness or the measureless mind of God. When we come into like-mindedness with the Word, instead of looking at the Word, we begin to see what God has for us in the Word. Our prayer will be,

> Me with a quenchless thirst inspire,
> A longing, infinite desire
> Fill my craving heart.
> Less than Thyself You do not give,
> Thy might within me now to live.
> Come, all Thou hast.

God, please come and make it impossible for me to ever be satisfied but to always have an unquenchable desire for You, the living God. Then I will not be overtaken. Then I will be ready. Then I will have shining eyes, filled with delight as they look at the Master.

Thought for today: Will you shiver like someone hesitating on the edge of a pool? Or will you take a plunge into omnipotence and find the waters are not as cold as people told you?

June 20

The Son of God Revealed

Love has been perfected among us in this: that we may have boldness in the day of judgment; because as He is, so are we in this world.
—1 John 4:17

Scripture reading: Hebrews 2

*Y*ou ask, "Can we see the Master?" Here, look at Him. His Word is Spirit and life-giving. This is the breath, the Word of Jesus. Through the Holy Spirit, men have written and spoken. Here is the life. Here is the witness. Here is the truth. Here is the Son of God *"revealed from faith to faith"* (Rom. 1:17), from heart to heart, from vision to vision, until we all come into perfect unity of fellowship into the fullness of Christ.

There it is, beloved. Look! *"Now we are children of God"* (1 John 3:2). If you are there, we can take a step further. But if you are not there, you may hear but not cross over. There is something about the Word of God that benefits the hearer who has faith, but if the hearer does not have faith, it will not profit him.

The future is what you are today, not what you are going to be tomorrow. This is the day when God makes the future possible. When God reveals something to you today, tomorrow is filled with a further illumination of God's possibility for you.

Do you dare to come into the place of omnipotence, of wonderment? Do you dare to say to God, "I am ready for all that You have for me"? It will mean living a pure and holy life. It will mean living a sanctified, separate life. It will mean your heart is so perfect and your prospects are so divinely separated that you say to the world, "Goodbye."

The second chapter of Hebrews describes the mighty, glorified position for the children of God. God wants me to announce it to every heart, like a great trumpet call. The plan is to bring you to glory as a child clothed with the power of the gifts, graces, ministries, and operations. You are to be clothed with the majesty of heaven. This is like heaven to me. My very body is filled with thoughts of heaven.

Seeing that these things are so, what kind of people should we be (2 Pet. 3:11)? We should be keeping our eyes upon Him so that we may be ready for the Rapture. Oh, brothers and sisters, what immense pleasure God has for us! There is no limit to the sober-mindedness God is bringing us to so that we may be able to understand all that God has planned for us. Oh, that we may look not on the things that are, but with eyes of purity see only the invisible Son. Having our whole bodies illuminated by the power of the Holy Spirit, we grow in grace, in faith, and in Christlikeness until there is no difference between us and Him.

Are you prepared to go all the way? Are you willing for your heart to have only one attraction? Are you willing to have only one Love? Are you willing for Him to become your perfect Bridegroom?

The more bridelike we are, the more we love to hear the Bridegroom's voice; the less bridelike we are, the less we long for His Word. If you cannot rest without it, if it becomes your food day and night, if you eat and drink of it, His life will be in you, and when He appears, you will go with Him. Help us, Jesus!

How many of you are prepared to reveal yourselves before the King? Are you prepared to yield to His call, yield to His will, yield to His desires? How many are going to say, "At all costs I will go through!" Who says so? Who means it? Are you determined? Is your soul on the wing? Make a full consecration to God right now. It is between you and God. You are going now to enter the presence of God.

Thought for today: Come clean with everything in the presence of God!

Brokenness Precedes Blessing

Then Jesus said to His disciples, "If anyone desires to come after
Me, let him deny himself, and take up his cross, and follow Me."
—Matthew 16:24

Scripture reading: Matthew 10:16–42

We must acknowledge our helplessness and nothingness. Although laboring in the Spirit is painful, God can lift the burden from us. I have had those days when I feel burdened. I have had it this morning, but now God is lifting the heaviness. And I say, brother and sister, unless God brings us into a place of brokenness of spirit, unless God remolds us in the great plan of His will for us, the best of us will utterly fail. But when we are absolutely taken in hand by the almighty God, God turns even our weakness into strength. He makes even that barren, helpless, groaning cry come forth, so that men and women are reborn in the travail. There is a place where our helplessness is touched by the power of God and where we come out shining as *"gold refined in the fire"* (Rev. 3:18).

It was on the cross that our Lord died with a broken heart. Pentecost came out of jeering and sneering. It included being mocked and beaten and an offer of sour wine. Jesus received an unfair judgment and a cross that He had to bear. But, glory to God, Pentecost rings out today for you through the words, *"It is finished!"* (John 19:30). And now because it is finished, we can take the same place that He took and rise out of that death in majestic glory with the resurrection touch of heaven. People will know that God has done something for us.

Thought for today: There is no hope for Pentecost unless we come to God in our brokenness.

June 22

Be Made New

But what things were gain to me, these I have counted loss for Christ. Yet indeed I also count all things loss for the excellence of the knowledge of Christ Jesus my Lord.
—Philippians 3:7–8

Scripture reading: 2 Corinthians 5

*D*aily, there must be a revival touch in our hearts. God must change us after His fashion. We are to be made new all the time. There is no such thing as having all grace and knowledge. God wants us to begin with these words of power found in Philippians 3 and never stop, but go on to perfection. I am positive that no man can attain like-mindedness except by the illumination of the Spirit.

God has been speaking to me over and over that I must urge people to receive the baptism of the Holy Spirit. In the baptism of the Holy Spirit, there is unlimited grace and endurance as the Spirit reveals Himself to us. The excellency of Christ can never be understood apart from illumination. I must witness about Christ. Jesus said to Thomas, *"Thomas, because you have seen Me, you have believed. Blessed are those who have not seen and yet have believed"* (John 20:29).

There is a revelation that brings us into touch with Him where we get all and see right into the fullness of Christ. As Paul saw the depths and heights of the grandeur, he longed that he might gain Him. Before his conversion, in his passion and zeal, Paul would do anything to bring Christians to death. His passion raged like a mighty lion. As he was going to Damascus, he heard the voice of Jesus saying, *"Saul, Saul, why are you persecuting Me?"* (Acts 9:4). What touched him was the tenderness of God.

Friends, it is always God's tenderness that reaches us. He comes to us in spite of our weakness and depravity. If somebody came to oppose us, we would stand our ground, but when He comes to forgive us, we do not know what to do. Oh, to gain Christ! A thousand things in the nucleus of a human heart need softening a thousand times a day. There are things in us that unless God shows us *"the excellence of the knowledge of Christ Jesus,"* we will never be broken and brought to ashes. But God will do it. We will not merely be saved, but we will be saved a thousand times over! Oh, this transforming regeneration by the power of the Spirit of the living God makes me see there is a place to *"gain Christ"* (Phil. 3:8), so that I may stand complete there. As He was, so am I to be.

We cannot depend upon our works, but upon the faithfulness of God, being able under all circumstances to be hidden in Him, covered by the almighty presence of God. The Scriptures tell us that we are in Christ and Christ is in God (1 Cor. 3:23). What is able to move you from this place of omnipotent power? *"Shall tribulation, or distress, or persecution, or famine, or nakedness, or peril, or sword?"* (Rom. 8:35). Oh, no! Will life, or death, or principalities, or powers? (v. 38). No, *"we are more than conquerors through Him who loved us"* (v. 37).

Thought for today: The Holy Spirit is the great Illuminator who makes me understand all the depths of Him.

June 23

Found in Him

I have suffered the loss of all things, and count them as rubbish,
that I may gain Christ and be found in Him.
—Philippians 3:8–9

Scripture reading: 2 Peter 3:9–18

here is a place of seclusion, a place of rest and faith in Jesus. Nothing else is like it. Jesus came to His disciples on the water, and they were terrified. But He said, *"It is I; do not be afraid"* (Matt. 14:27). My friend, He is always there. He is there in the storm as well as in the peace; He is there in adversity. When will we know He is there? When we are *"found in Him,"* not having our own work, our own plan, but resting in the omnipotent plan of God. Oh, is it possible for the child of God to fail? It is not possible, for *"He who keeps Israel shall neither slumber nor sleep"* (Ps. 121:4). He will watch over us continually, but we must be *"found in Him."*

I know there is a secret place in Jesus that is available to us today. My brother, my sister, you have been nearly weighed down with troubles. They have almost crushed you. Sometimes you thought you would never get out of this place of difficulty, but you have no idea that behind the whole thing, God has been working a plan greater than all.

Today is a resurrection day. We must know the resurrection of His power in brokenness of spirit: *"That I may know Him and the power of His resurrection"* (Phil. 3:10). Jesus said to Martha, *"I am the resurrection and the life"* (John 11:25). Oh, to know the resurrection power, to know the rest of faith. Any one of us, without exception, can reach this happiness in the Spirit. There is something different between saying you have faith and then being pressed into a tight corner and proving that you have faith. If you dare to believe, it will be done according to your faith: *"Whatever things you ask when you pray, believe that you receive them, and you will have them"* (Mark 11:24). Jesus is *"the resurrection and the life"* (John 11:25). With God's help, we must gain this life. We can reach it with the knowledge that He will make us as white as snow, as pure and holy as He, that we may go with boldness to His *"throne of grace"* (Heb. 4:16). Boldness is in His holiness. Boldness is in His righteousness. Boldness is in His truth. You cannot have the boldness of faith if you are not pure. What blessed words follow: *"the fellowship of His sufferings"* (Phil. 3:10). Remember, unless that fellowship touches us, we will never have much power.

Jesus came forth in the glory of the Father, filled with all the fullness of God. It was God's plan before *"the foundation of the world"* (Matt. 25:34). God loved the fearful, helpless human race, with all its blackness and hideousness of sin, and He provided the way for redemption. May God give us such *"fellowship of His sufferings"* (Phil. 3:10) that when we see a person afflicted with cancer, we will pray right through until the disease is struck dead. When we see a bent and helpless woman or a man who is weak and sick, may God give us compassion and a fellowship with them that will lighten their heavy burdens and set them free. How often we have missed the victory because we did not have compassion at the needed moment. We failed to pray with a broken heart.

Is there anything more? Oh, yes, we must see the next thing. We must be *"conformed to His death"* (Phil. 3:10). *"Unless a grain of wheat falls into the ground and dies, it remains alone; but if it dies, it produces much grain"* (John 12:24). God wants you to see that unless you are dead indeed, unless you come to a perfect crucifixion, unless you die with Him, you are not in the *"fellowship of His sufferings"* (Phil. 3:10). May God move upon us in this life to bring us into an absolute death, not merely to talk about it. In this way, Christ's life may be made manifest.

The Lord wants us to understand that we must come to a place where our natural life ceases, and by the power of God, we rise into a life where God rules and reigns. Do you long to know Him? Do you long to be *"found in Him"*? Your longing will be satisfied today. I ask you to fall in the presence of God. If you want to know God, yield to His mighty power, and obey the Spirit.

Thought for today: When the Spirit of the Lord moves within you, you will be broken down and then built up.

June 24

Receive the Holy Spirit

*That the blessing of Abraham might come upon
the Gentiles in Christ Jesus.*
—Galatians 3:14

Scripture reading: John 16:7–22

*W*hen we have the right attitude, faith becomes remarkably active. But it can never be remarkably active in a dead life. When sin is out, when the body is clean, and when the life is made right, then the Holy Spirit comes, and faith brings the evidence.

Why should we tarry, or wait, for the Holy Spirit? Why should we wrestle and pray with a living faith to be made ready? Because we need the Holy Spirit to convict the world of sin, righteousness, and judgment—that is why the Holy Spirit is to come into your body. First of all, your sin is gone, and you can see clearly to speak to others. But Jesus does not want you to point out the speck in somebody else's eye while the plank is in your own. (See Matthew 7:3–5.)

The place of being filled with the Holy Spirit is the only place of operation where the believer binds the power of Satan. Satan thinks that he has a right, and he will have a short time to exhibit that right as the Prince of the World; but he can't be Prince as long as there is one person filled with the Holy Spirit. That is why the church will go before the Tribulation.

Now, how dare you resist coming into the place of being filled with the life and power of the Holy Spirit? What is the attitude of your life? Are you thirsty? Are you longing? Are you willing to pay the price? Are you willing to forfeit in order to have? Are you willing to allow yourself to die so that He may live? Are you willing for Him to have the right-of-way in your heart, your conscience, and all you are? Are you ready to have God's deluge of blessing upon your soul? Are you ready to be changed forever, to receive the Holy Spirit, to be filled with divine power forever?

Thought for today: There are two sides to the baptism of the Holy Spirit: the first condition is that you possess the baptism; the second is that the baptism possesses you.

286

June 25

Ask in Faith

Ask, and it will be given to you; seek, and you will find;
knock, and it will be opened to you.
—Matthew 7:7

Scripture reading: Hebrews 11:1–40

Many people do not receive the Holy Spirit because they are continually asking and never believing. *"Everyone who asks receives"* (Matt. 7:8). He who is asking is receiving; he who is seeking is finding. The door is being opened right now; that is God's present Word. The Bible does not say, "Ask and you will not receive." Believe that asking is receiving, seeking is finding, and to him who is knocking, the door is being opened.

When will we see people filled with the Holy Spirit and things done as they were in the Acts of the Apostles? It will be when people say, "Lord, You are God." I want you to come into a place of such relationship with God that you will know your prayers are answered because He has promised.

Faith has its request. Faith claims it because it has it. *"Faith is the substance of things hoped for"* (Heb. 11:1). As sure as you have faith, God will give you the overflowing, and when He comes in, you will speak as the Spirit gives utterance (Acts 2:4).

You must come to a place of ashes, a place of helplessness, a place of wholehearted surrender where you do not refer to yourself. You have no justification of your own in regard to anything. You are prepared to be slandered, to be despised by everybody. But because of His personality in you, He reserves you for Himself because you are godly, and He sets you on high because you have known His name (Ps. 91:14). He causes you to be the fruit of His loins and to bring forth His glory so that you will no longer rest in yourself. Your confidence will be in God. Ah, it is lovely. *"The Lord is the Spirit; and where the Spirit of the Lord is, there is liberty"* (2 Cor. 3:17).

Thought for today: If you would believe half as much as you ask, you would receive.

June 26

A Life of Perfect Activity

My God shall supply all your need according to His riches
in glory by Christ Jesus.
—Philippians 4:19

Scripture reading: Acts 5:14–42

Only believe! God will not fail you, beloved. It is impossible for God to fail. Believe God; rest in Him. The Bible is the most important book in the world. But some people have to be pressed in before they can be pressed on. Oh, this glorious inheritance of holy joy and faith, this glorious baptism in the Holy Spirit—it is a perfected place. *"All things have become new"* (2 Cor. 5:17), because *"you are Christ's, and Christ is God's"* (1 Cor. 3:23).

God means for us to walk in this royal way. When God opens a door, no man can shut it (Rev. 3:8). John made a royal way, and Jesus walked in it. Jesus left us the responsibility of allowing Him to bring forth through us the greater works (John 14:12). Jesus left His disciples with much and with much more to be added until God receives us in that Day.

When we receive power, we must stir ourselves up with the truth that we are responsible for the need around us. God will supply all our need so that the need of the needy may be met through us. God has given us a great indwelling force of power. If we do not step into our privileges, it is a tragedy.

There is no standing still. *"As He is, so are we in this world"* (1 John 4:17). *"We are the offspring of God"* (Acts 17:29), and we have divine impulses. After we have received, we will have power. We have been focusing too much on feeling the power. God is waiting for us to act. Jesus lived a life of perfect activity. He lived in the realm of divine appointment.

We must dare to press on until God comes forth in mighty power. May God give us the hearing of faith so that the power may come down like a cloud. Press on until Jesus is glorified and multitudes are gathered in.

Thought for today: God's rest is an undisturbed place where heaven bends to meet you.

June 27

Called to Serve

Walk worthy of the calling with which you were called.
—Ephesians 4:1

Scripture reading: Galatians 6:1–10

We are privileged to be able to gather together to worship the Lord. The very thought of Jesus will confirm truth and righteousness and power in your mortal body. There is something very remarkable about Him. When John saw Him, the impression that he had was that He was the *"lamb without blemish and without spot"* (1 Pet. 1:19). When revelation comes, it says, *"In Him dwells all the fullness"* (Col. 2:9).

His character is beautiful. His display of meekness is lovely. His compassion is greater than that of anyone in all of humanity. He felt infirmities. He helps those who pass through trials. And it is to be said about Him what is not said about anyone else: "[He] *was in all points tempted as we are, yet without sin"* (Heb. 4:15).

I want you, as the author of Hebrews wonderfully said, to *"consider Him who endured such hostility from sinners against Himself, lest you become weary and discouraged in your souls"* (Heb. 12:3). When you are weary and tempted and tried and all men are against you, consider Him who has passed through it all, so that He might be able to help you in the trial as you are passing through it. He will sustain you in the strife. When all things seem to indicate that you have failed, the Lord of Hosts, the God of Jacob, the salvation of our Christ will so reinforce you that you will be stronger than any concrete building that was ever made.

Paul was an example for the church. He was filled with the loveliness of the character of the Master through the Spirit's power. He was zealous that we may walk worthy. This is the day of calling that he spoke about; this is the opportunity of our lifetime. This is the place where God increases strength or opens the door of a new way of ministry.

Thought for today: If there is anything in your life that in any way resists the power of the Holy Spirit and the entrance of His Word into your heart and life, drop on your knees and cry aloud for mercy.

June 28

Lowliness and Meekness

I am among you as the One who serves.
—Luke 22:27

Scripture reading: John 15:9–27

*J*esus emphasized this new commandment when He left us: "A new commandment I give to you, that you love one another; as I have loved you, that you also love one another" (John 13:34). To the extent that we miss this instruction, we miss all the Master's instruction. If we miss that commandment, we miss everything. All the future summits of glory are yours in that you have been recreated in a deeper order by this commandment to love.

When we reach this attitude of love, then we make no mistake about lowliness. We will submit ourselves in the future in order that we may be useful to one another. And when we come to a place where we serve for pure love's sake, because it is the divine hand of the Master upon us, we will find out that we will never fail. Love never fails when it is divinely appointed in us. However, the so-called love in our human nature does fail and has failed from the beginning.

Suppose a man corresponds with me, seeking to learn more about me and to establish a relationship. The only thing I would have to say in answering his letters is, "Brother, all that I know about Wigglesworth is bad." There is no good thing in human nature. However, all that I know about the new creation in Wigglesworth is good. The important thing is whether we are living in the old creation or the new creation.

So I implore you to see that there is a lowliness, a humbleness, that leads you to meekness, that leads you to separate yourself from the world, that puts you so in touch with the Master that you know you are touching God. The blood of Jesus cleanses you from sin and all pollution (1 John 1:7). There is something in this holy position that makes you know you are free from the power of the Enemy.

Thought for today: The greatest plan that Jesus ever presented in His ministry was the ministry of service.

To Be Like Jesus

The word of God is living and powerful, and sharper than any
two-edged sword, piercing even to the division of soul and
spirit...and is a discerner of the thoughts and intents of the heart.
—Hebrews 4:12

Scripture reading: Philippians 2:1–22

We have yet to see the forcefulness of the Word of God. The Word, the life, the presence, the power is in your body, in the very marrow of your bones, and absolutely everything else must be discharged. Sometimes we do not fully reflect on this wonderful truth: the Word, the life, the Christ who is the Word divides you from soul affection, from human weakness, from all depravity. The blood of Jesus can cleanse you until your soul is purified and your nature is destroyed by the nature of the living Christ.

In Christ, we have encountered divine resurrection touches. In the greatest work God ever did on the face of the earth, Christ was raised from the dead by the operation of the power of God. As the resurrection of Christ operates in our hearts, it will dethrone wrong things and will build right things. Callousness will have to change; hardness will have to disappear; all evil thoughts will have to go. In the place of these will be lowliness of mind.

What beautiful cooperation with God in thought and power and holiness! The Master *"made Himself of no reputation"* (Phil. 2:7). He absolutely left the glory of heaven, with all its wonder. He left it and submitted Himself to humiliation. He went down, down, down into death for one purpose only: that He might destroy the power of death, even the Devil, and deliver those people who all their lifetime have been subject to fear—deliver them from the fear of death and the Devil (Heb. 2:14–15).

How will this wonderful plan come to pass? By transformation, resurrection, thoughts of holiness, intense zeal, desire for all of God, until we live and move in the atmosphere of holiness.

Thought for today: If you will let go, God will take hold and keep you up.

June 30

Resurrection Life

Let this mind be in you which was also in Christ Jesus.
—Philippians 2:5

Scripture reading: Romans 6:1–14

Have you been to the place of illumination? Illumination means that your very mind, which was depraved, is now the mind of Christ; the very nature that was bound now has a resurrection touch; your very body has come in contact with the life of God until you who were lost are found, and you who were dead are alive again by the resurrection power of the Word of the life of Christ. What a glorious inheritance in the Spirit!

Believer, if you have not reached all this, the ladder extends from heaven to earth to take you from earth to heaven. Do not be afraid of taking the steps. You will not slip back. Have faith in God. Experience divine resurrection life—more divine in thought, more wonderful in revelation. Resurrection life means living in the Spirit, wakened into all likeness, made alive by the same Spirit!

Are you lowly and meek in your mind? It is the divine plan of the Savior. You must be like Him. Do you desire to be like Him? There is nothing but yourself that can hinder you in this. You are the one who stops the current. You are the one who stops the life.

While ministering in one place, we had a banquet for people who were distressed—people who were lame and weary, blind and diseased in every way. A dear man got hold of a boy who was encased in iron from top to bottom, lifted him up, and placed him onto the platform. Hands were laid on him in the name of Jesus.

"Papa! Papa! Papa!" the boy said. "It's going all over me! Oh, Papa, come and take these irons off!" I do like to hear children speak; they say such wonderful things. The father took the irons off, and the life of God had gone all over the boy!

Don't you know this is the resurrection touch? This is the divine life; this is what God has brought us into. Let it go over us, Lord—the power of the Holy Spirit, the resurrection of heaven, the sweetness of Your blessing, the joy of the Lord!

Thought for today: God rejoices when we manifest a faith that holds Him to His Word.

July 1

Unity of the Spirit

Endeavoring to keep the unity of the Spirit in the bond of peace.
—Ephesians 4:3

Scripture reading: Psalm 133

*Y*ou are bound forever out of loyalty to God to see that no division comes into the church body, to see that nothing comes into the assembly, as it came into David's flock, to tear and rend the body. You have to be careful. If a person comes along with a prophecy and you find that it is tearing down and bringing trouble, denounce it accordingly; judge it by the Word. You will find that all true prophecy will be perfectly full of hopefulness. It will have compassion; it will have comfort; it will have edification. So if anything comes into the church that you know is hurting the flock and disturbing the assembly, you must see to it that you begin to pray so that this thing is put to death.

Bring unity in the bonds of perfection so that the church of God will receive edification. Then the church will begin to be built up in the faith and the establishing of truth, and believers will be one. There is one body. Recognize that fact. When schism comes into the body, believers always act as though there were more than one body.

Do not forget that God means for us to be very faithful to the church so that we do not allow anything to come into the church to break up the body. You cannot find anything in the body in its relation to Christ that has schism in it. Christ's life in the body—there is no schism in that. When Christ's life comes into the church, there will be no discord; there will be a perfect blending of heart and hand, and it will be lovely. Endeavor *"to keep the unity of the Spirit in the bond of peace."*

Thought for today: When we think that the church is poor and needy, we forget that the spirit of intercession can unlock every safe in the world.

293

July 2

The God Who Is over All

One God and Father of all, who is above all,
and through all, and in you all.
—Ephesians 4:6

Scripture reading: Psalm 95

*T*hink of it! It does not matter what the Enemy brings to you, or tries to bring; the Father, who is above all, is over you. The God of power, majesty, and glory can bring you to a place of dethroning everything else! Do you dare to believe it?

Remember, God our Father is so intensely desirous to have all the fullness of the manifestation of His power that we do not have to have one thing that His Son did not come to bring. We have to have perfect redemption; we have to know all the powers of righteousness; we have to understand perfectly that we are brought to the place where He is with us in all power, dethroning the power of the Enemy.

God over you—that is real. The God who is over you is more than a million times greater than the Devil, than the powers of evil, than the powers of darkness. How do I know? Hear what the Devil said to God about Job: *"Have You not made a hedge around him?"* (Job 1:10). The Devil was unable to get near Job because there was a hedge. What was the hedge? It was the almighty power of God. It was not a thorny hedge; it was not a hedge of thistles. It was the presence of the Lord all around Job. And the presence of the Lord Almighty is so around us that the Devil cannot break through that wonderful covering.

The Devil is against the living Christ and wants to destroy Him; if you are filled with the living Christ, the Devil is eager to get you out of the way in order to destroy Christ's power. Say this to the Lord: "Now, Lord, look after this property of yours." Then the Devil cannot get near you. When does he get near? When you dethrone Christ, ignoring His rightful position over you, in you, and through you.

Thought for today: You will be strong if you believe this truth: faith is the victory—always. Glory to Jesus!

July 3

The Gifts of Christ

*To each one of us grace was given according to
the measure of Christ's gift.*
—Ephesians 4:7

Scripture reading: Ephesians 4:1–16

The apostle Paul spoke about the grace and the gifts of Christ—not the gifts of the Holy Spirit, but the gifts of Christ. You are joined to Christ's body the moment you believe. For instance, some of you may have children, and they have different names, but the moment they appeared in the world, they were in your family. The moment they were born, they became a part of your family.

The moment you are born of God, you are in the family, and you are in the body, as He is in the body, and you are in the body collectively and particularly. After you come into the body, then the body has to receive the sealing of the promise, or the fulfillment of promise, that Christ will be in you, reigning in you mightily. The Holy Spirit will come to unveil the King in all His glory so that He might reign as King there, the Holy Spirit serving in every way to make Him King.

You are in the body. The Holy Spirit gives gifts in the body. Living in this holy order, you may find that revelation comes to you and makes you a prophet. Some of you may have a clear understanding that you have been called into apostleship. Some of you may have perfect knowledge that you are to be pastors. When you come to be sealed with the Spirit of promise, then you find out that Jesus is pleased and gives gifts in order that the church might come into a perfect position of being so blended together that there could be no division. Jesus wants His church to be a perfect body— perfect in stature, perfect in oneness in Him.

I have been speaking to this end: that you may see the calling that Paul was speaking about—humility of mind, meekness of spirit, knowing that God is in you and through you, knowing that the power of the Spirit is mightily bringing you to the place where not only the gifts of the Spirit but also the gifts of Christ have been given to you, making you eligible for the great work you have to do.

July 3

My purpose is not to tell what God has for you in the future. Press in now, and claim your rights. Let the Lord Jesus be so glorified that He will make you fruit-bearers—strong in power, giving glory to God, having *"no confidence in the flesh"* (Phil. 3:3) but being separated from natural things, now in the Spirit, living fully in the will of God.

Thought for today: Let your whole soul reach out unto God; dare to breathe in heaven; dare to be awakened to all God's mind; listen to the language of the Holy Spirit.

July 4

The Cry of the Spirit

Behold the Lamb of God!
—John 1:36

Scripture reading: John 1:6–36

*J*ohn the Baptist's clothing was camel's hair, his belt leather, his food locusts and wild honey (Matt. 3:4). No angels, shepherds, wise men, or stars heralded John's birth. But the heavenly messenger Gabriel, who had spoken to Daniel and to Mary, also spoke to John's father, Zacharias.

In the wilderness, John was without the food and clothing of his earthly father's priestly home. He had only a groan, a cry—the cry of the Spirit. Yet from John's place in the wilderness, he moved the whole land. God cried through him. It was the cry of the Spirit—oh, that awful cry. All the land was moved by that piercing cry.

God spoke to John and told him about a new thing—water baptism. It was a clean cut; it was a new way. He had been with those of the circumcision; now he was an outcast. It was the breaking down of the old plan.

The people heard his cry—oh, that cry, the awful cry of the Spirit—and the message that he gave: "*'Repent, for the kingdom of heaven is at hand!'* (v. 2). Make straight paths—no treading down of others or exacting undue rights. *'Make straight paths for your feet'* (Heb. 12:13)." All were startled! All were awakened! They thought the Messiah had come. The searching was tremendous! Is this He? Who can it be? John said, "I am a voice, crying, crying, making a way for the Messiah to come" (John 1:23).

Individuals were purged; they found purpose. God pressed life through John. Through him, God moved multitudes and changed the situation. The banks of the Jordan were covered with people. The conviction was tremendous. They cried out. The prophet Isaiah had predicted, *"The rough ways* [will be made] *smooth; and all flesh shall see the salvation of God"* (Luke 3:5–6). The people, the multitude, cried out and were baptized by John in the Jordan, confessing their sins.

Oh, to be alone with God. God's Word came to John when he was alone: *"The word of God came to John the son of Zacharias in the wilderness. And he went into all the region around the Jordan, preaching a baptism of repentance for the remission of sins"* (Luke 3:2–3).

> Alone! Alone!
> Jesus bore it all alone!
> He gave Himself to save His own.
> He suffered—bled and died alone—alone.

Oh, to be alone with God, to get His mind, His thoughts, and His impression and revelation of the need of the people.

There was nothing ordinary about John—all was extraordinary. Herod was reproved by him because of Herodias, his brother Philip's wife, and for all the evils that Herod had done. Herodias's daughter danced before Herod, who promised her up to half his kingdom. She asked for John the Baptist's head. (See Matthew 14:3–11.)

This holy man was alone. God had John in such a way that he could express that cry—the burden for the whole land. He could cry for the sins of the people. God is holy. We are the children of Abraham—the children of faith. Awful judgment is coming. Cry! Cry!

John could not help but cry because of the people's sin. John had been filled with the Holy Spirit from his mother's womb (Luke 1:15). He had the burden. He was stern, but through his work, the land was open to Jesus. Jesus walked in the way; He came a new way.

"John came neither eating nor drinking" (Matt. 11:18)—John came crying. John's father and mother were left behind. His heart bled at the altar. He bore the burden, the cry, the need of the people. The only place he could breathe and be free was in the wilderness—the atmosphere of heaven—until he turned with a message to declare the preparation needed. Before Jesus came, repentance came to open up the place of redemption.

Like John, there must be a working of the Spirit in you; then God will work through you for others.

Thought for today: God is with a person who has only a cry.

July 5

Knowing Our Need

If only I may touch His clothes, I shall be made well.
—Mark 5:28

Scripture reading: Mark 5:25–6:6

What a privilege to care for the flock of God, to be used by God to encourage the people, to help stand against the many trials that affect the needy. What a holy calling! We each have our own work, and we must do it, so that boldness may be ours in the day of the Master's appearing, and so that no man can take our crowns (Rev. 3:11). Since the Lord is always encouraging us, we have encouragement for others. We must have a willingness, a ready mind, a yielding to the mind of the Spirit. There is no place for the child of God in God's great plan except in humility.

God can never do all He wants to do, all that He came to do through the Word, until He gets us to the place where He can trust us, and where we are in abiding fellowship with Him in His great plan for the world's redemption. We have this truth illustrated in the life of Jacob. It took God twenty-one years to bring Jacob to the place of humility, contrition of heart, and brokenness of spirit. God even gave him power to wrestle with strength, and Jacob said, "I think I can manage after all," until God touched his thigh, making him know that he was mortal and that he was dealing with immortality. As long as we think we can save ourselves, we will try to do it.

In Mark 5:25–34, we have the story of the woman who had suffered many things from many physicians and had spent all that she had. She was no better but rather grew worse. She said, *"If only I may touch His clothes, I shall be made well."* She came to know her need. It is when we are empty and undone, when we come to God in our nothingness and helplessness, that He picks us up.

Thought for today: Our full cupboard is often our greatest hindrance.

Peter's Words of Wisdom

Humble yourselves under the mighty hand of God,
that He may exalt you in due time.
—1 Peter 5:6

Scripture reading: 1 Peter 5:1–11

*L*et's take a look at the fifth chapter of 1 Peter. *"Humble yourselves"* (v. 6). Look at the Master at the Jordan River, submitting Himself to the baptism of John, then again submitting Himself to the cruel Cross. Truly, angels desire to look into these things (1 Pet. 1:12), and all heaven is waiting for the man who will burn all the bridges behind him and allow God to begin a plan in righteousness, so full, so sublime, beyond all human thought, but according to the revelation of the Spirit.

"Casting all your care upon Him, for He cares for you" (1 Pet. 5:7). He cares! We sometimes forget this. If we descend into the natural, all goes wrong, but when we trust Him and abide beneath His shadow, how blessed it is. Oh, many times I have experienced my helplessness and nothingness, and casting my care upon Him has proved that He cares.

Verse eight tells us to *"be sober, be vigilant."* What does it mean to be sober? It means to have a clear knowledge that we are powerless to manage, but also to have a rest of faith. The Adversary's opportunity is when we think that we are something and try to open our own door. Our thoughts, words, and deeds must all be in the power of the Holy Spirit. Oh yes, we need to be sober—not only sober, but also vigilant. We need not only to be filled with the Spirit but also to have a "go forth" in us, a knowledge that God's holy presence is with us. To be sober and vigilant, to have an ability to judge, discern, and balance things that differ—this is what we need.

"Your adversary the devil walks about like a roaring lion, seeking whom he may devour. Resist him, steadfast in the faith" (vv. 8–9). We must resist in the hour when Satan's schemes may bewilder us, when we are almost swept off our feet, and when darkness is upon us to such a degree that it seems as if some evil thing had overtaken us. *"Resist him, steadfast in the faith."* *"He who keeps*

July 6

Israel shall neither slumber nor sleep" (Ps. 121:4). God covers us, for no human can stand against the powers of hell.

"After you have suffered a while" (1 Pet. 5:10). Then there is some suffering? Yes! But it is *"not worthy to be compared with the glory which shall be revealed in us"* (Rom. 8:18). The difference is so great that our suffering is not even worthy of mention. Ours is an eternal glory, from glory to glory, until we are swallowed up, until we are swallowed up in Him, the Lord of glory.

Thought for today: God is close at hand to deliver all the time.

Four Helps for the Heart

May the God of all grace, who called us to His eternal glory by
Christ Jesus, after you have suffered a while, perfect, establish,
strengthen, and settle you.
—1 Peter 5:10

Scripture reading: 1 Peter 5

The God of all grace wants to do the following in us: first, *"perfect"*; second, *"establish"*; third, *"strengthen"*; and fourth, *"settle."*

First is *"perfect."* In the book of Hebrews, we read, *"May the God of peace...make you complete* ["perfect," KJV] *in every good work to do His will, working in you what is well pleasing in His sight, through Jesus Christ"* (Heb. 13:20–21). Keep in mind that when perfection is spoken of in the Word, it is always through a joining up with eternal things. Perfection is a working in us of the will of God.

Some of us would be fainthearted if we thought we had to be perfect in order to receive the blessing of God. We would ask ourselves, "How is it going to happen?" However, we find as we continue to follow God that the purpose of eternal life is an advancement, for we are saved by the blood. Our actions, our minds, are covered by the blood of Jesus, and as we yield and yield, we find ourselves in possession of another mind, even the mind of Christ (1 Cor. 2:16), which causes us to understand the perfection of His will.

Someone may be saying, "I can never be perfect! It is beyond my greatest thought." You're right; it is! But as we press on, the Holy Spirit enlightens, and we enter in, as Paul said, according to the revelation of the Spirit (Eph. 1:17–18). I am perfected as I launch out into God by faith, His blood covering my sin, His righteousness covering my unrighteousness, His perfection covering my imperfection. This is a very important fact: I am holy and perfect in Him.

Second is *"establish."* You must be established in the fact that it is His life, not yours. You must have faith in His Word, faith in His life. You are supplanted by Another. You are disconnected from the earth. You are insulated by faith.

July 7

Third is *"strengthen."* You are strengthened by the fact that God is doing the business, not you. You are in the plan that God is working out.

Fourth is *"settle."* What does it mean to be settled? It means knowing that I am in union with His will, that I am established in the knowledge of it, that day by day, I am strengthened. It is an eternal work of righteousness, until by the Spirit we are perfected. First is an enduring, then an establishing, a strengthening, and a settling. This happens according to our faith. It happens as we believe.

Now a closing word: *"To Him be the glory and the dominion forever and ever"* (1 Pet. 5:11). How can this verse be realized in my case? By living for His glory. There must be no withdrawal, no relinquishing, no looking back, but going on, on, on, for His glory now and forever. We must go on until, like Enoch, we walk with God and are not, for God has taken us (Gen. 5:24).

Thought for today: Unbelief is the great dethroning place; faith is the great rising place.

July 8

The Flood Tide of Revival

Will You not revive us again,
that Your people may rejoice in You?
—Psalm 85:6

Scripture reading: Psalm 85:7–86:13

Wherever Jesus went, multitudes followed Him, because He lived, moved, breathed, was swallowed up, clothed, and filled by God. He was God; and as the Son of Man, the Spirit of God—the Spirit of creative holiness—rested upon Him. It is lovely to be holy. Jesus came to impart to us the Spirit of holiness.

We are only at the edge of things; the almighty plan for the future is marvelous. God must do something to increase. We need a revival to revive all we touch within us and outside of us. We need a flood tide with a deluge behind it. Jesus left 120 men to turn the world upside down. The Spirit is upon us to change our situation. We must move on; we must let God increase in us for the deliverance of multitudes; and we must travail until souls are born and quickened into a new relationship with heaven. Jesus had divine authority with power, and He left it for us. We must preach truth, holiness, and purity *"in the inward parts"* (Ps. 51:6). Thirst for more of God.

Jesus treaded the winepress alone (Isa. 63:3), despising the cross and the shame. He bore it all alone so that we might be *"partakers of the divine nature"* (2 Pet. 1:4), sharers in the divine plan of holiness. That's revival—Jesus manifesting divine authority. He was without sin. People saw the Lamb of God in a new way. Hallelujah! Let us live in holiness, and revival will come down, and God will enable us to do the work to which we are appointed. All Jesus said came to pass: signs, wonders, mighty deeds. Only believe, and yield and yield, until all the vision is fulfilled.

Thought for today: Jesus was not only holy, but He also loved holiness.

A Mighty Faith

Increase our faith.
—Luke 17:5

Scripture reading: Romans 4

God has a design, a purpose, a rest of faith. We are saved by faith and kept by faith. Faith is substance; it is also evidence (Heb. 11:1). God is! He is! And *"He is a rewarder of those who diligently seek Him"* (v. 6). We are to testify, to bear witness to what we know. To know that we know is a wonderful position to be in. We are to be living words, epistles of Christ (2 Cor. 3:3), known and read by all men.

We are living in the inheritance of faith because of the grace of God. We are saved for eternity by the operation of the Spirit, who brings forth life unto God. Heaven is brought to earth until God quickens all things into beauty, manifesting His power in living witnesses. God is in us for the world, so that the world may be blessed. We need power to lay hold of Omnipotence and to impart to others the Word of Life. This is a new epoch with new vision and new power. Christ in us is greater than we know. All things are possible if you dare to believe. The treasure is in earthen vessels so that Jesus may be glorified (2 Cor. 4:7).

Let us go forth bringing glory to God. Faith is substance, a mightiness of reality, a deposit of divine nature, and the creative God abiding with us. The moment you believe, you are clothed with a new power to lay hold of possibility and make it reality. The people said to Jesus, *"Lord, give us this bread always"* (John 6:34). Jesus said, *"He who feeds on Me will live because of Me"* (v. 57).

Have the faith of God. The man who comes into great association with God needs a heavenly measure. Faith is the greatest of all. We are saved by a new life, the Word of God, an association with the living Christ. A new creation continually takes us into new revelation.

Thought for today: There is what seems to be faith, an appearance of faith, but real faith believes God right to the end.

July 10

The Life of God within Us

All things were made through Him.
—John 1:3

Scripture reading: Galatians 3:1–14

All was made by the Word. I am begotten by His Word. There is a substance within me that has almighty power in it if I dare to believe. Faith goes on to be an act, a reality, a deposit of God, an almighty flame moving me to act, so that signs and wonders are manifested.

Are you begotten? Is faith an act within you? Some need a touch; some are captives and need liberty. As many as Jesus touched were made perfectly whole. Faith takes you to the place where God reigns, and you drink from God's bountiful store. Unbelief is sin, for Jesus went to death to bring us the light of life.

His life is manifested power overflowing. We must decrease if the life of God is to be manifested. (See John 3:30.) There is not room for two kinds of life in one body. Death for life—that is the price to pay for the manifested power of God through you. As you die to human desire, there comes a fellowship within, perfected cooperation, you ceasing, God increasing. God in you is a living substance, a spiritual nature. You live by another life, the *"faith in the Son of God"* (Gal. 2:20).

As the Holy Spirit reveals Jesus, He is real—the living Word, effective, acting, speaking, thinking, praying, singing. Oh, it is a wonderful life, this substance of the Word of God, which includes possibility and opportunity, which confronts you, bringing you to a place undaunted. Jesus has given us power over all the power of the Enemy (Luke 10:19). He won it for us at Calvary. All must be subject to His power. What should we do to *"work the works of God?"* (John 6:28). *"This is the work of God, that you believe"* (v. 29). Whatsoever He says will come to pass. That is God's Word.

We must remain in a strong, resolute resting on the authority of God's Word. We must have one great desire and purpose: to do what He says. We must live in this holy Word, rejoicing in the manifestation of the life of God on behalf of the sick and perishing multitudes. Amen.

Thought for today: I have a living faith within my earthly body.

July 11

The Holy Spirit—Our Comforter

[God] comforts us in all our tribulation, that we may be able to comfort those who are in any trouble, with the comfort with which we ourselves are comforted by God.
2 Corinthians 1:4

Scripture reading: 2 Corinthians 1:3–11

We need a revelation of a greater power, an abiding presence sustaining and comforting us in the hour of trial, ready at a moment's notice, an inbreathing of God in the human life. What more do we need in these last days when perilous times are upon us than to be filled, saturated, baptized with the Holy Spirit? Baptized. Baptized into Him, never to come out. How comforting! Exhilarating! Joyful! May it please the Lord to establish us in this state of grace. May we know nothing among men except Jesus Christ and Him crucified (1 Cor. 2:2). May we be clothed with His Spirit—nothing outside of the blessed Holy Spirit. This, beloved, is God's ideal for us. Are we here in this experience?

> Where He may lead me I will go,
> For I have learned to trust Him so,
> And I remember it was for me,
> That He was slain on Calvary.

God has chosen me to go through certain experiences to profit others. In all ages, God has had His witnesses, and He is teaching, chastening, correcting, and moving me just up to the point that I am able to bear it, in order to meet a needy soul who would otherwise go down without such comfort. All the chastening and the hardship is because we are able to bear it. No, we are not able, but we yield to Another—even the Holy Spirit. We are strengthened so that we may endure and so that we may comfort others *"with the comfort with which we ourselves are comforted by God."*

Why do we need brokenness and travail? The reason can be found in the book of Psalms: *"Before I was afflicted I went astray, but now I keep Your word"* (Ps. 119:67).

Thought for today: The God in you will not fail if you believe the Word of God.

July 12

Yielding to God's Plan

For as the sufferings of Christ abound in us, so our consolation also abounds through Christ.
—2 Corinthians 1:5

Scripture reading: 1 Corinthians 12:12–27

Chastening provokes or bestows upon us fruits unto holiness. It is in the hard places where we see no help that we cry out to God. He delivers us so that we can help the tempted. It was said of Jesus that He was *"in all points tempted as we are"* (Heb. 4:15). Where did He receive strength to comfort us? It was at the end of *"vehement cries and tears"* (Heb. 5:7), when the angel came just in time and ministered and saved Him from death. Now He can send angels to us. When? Just when we are about to go straight down. At such times in the past, did He not stretch out to us a helping hand?

God takes us to a place of need, and before we are barely aware of it, we are full of consolation toward the needy. How? The sufferings of Christ abound! The ministry of the Spirit abounds so often. It is a great blessing. We do not know our calling in the Spirit. It is so much greater than our appreciation of it. Then we speak a word in season (Isa. 50:4); here and there we minister, sowing beside all waters as the Holy Spirit directs our paths.

Paul and the people he ministered to cooperated with one another. Here is the value of testing: it results in a great flow of life from one to another. John Wesley woke up one day and became conscious of the need of one establishing another. In this way, he bore witness to the ministry of the Spirit, and multitudes were born again in his meetings when they heard the wonderful works of God. They heard stories and had consolation poured out to them by the revelation of the Spirit.

We are members of one another. When God's breath is upon us and we are quickened by the Holy Spirit, we can pour into each other wonderful ministries of grace and helpfulness.

Thought for today: We need a strong ministry of consolation, not deterioration or living below our privileges.

July 13

Consolation out of Affliction

If we are afflicted, it is for your consolation and salvation....Or if we are comforted, it is for your consolation and salvation.
—2 Corinthians 1:6

Scripture reading: Isaiah 51:9–16

These consolations come out of deprivation, affliction, and endurance. *"Yes, we had the sentence of death in ourselves, that we should not trust in ourselves but in God who raises the dead"* (2 Cor. 1:9).

Have we gone as far as Paul? Very few of us have. Can you see how Paul could help and comfort and sustain because he yielded to God all his trust as Jesus did? Because he was yielded to the Holy Spirit to work out the sentence of death, he could help others.

I pray to God that He may never find us *"kick*[ing] *against the goads"* (Acts 9:5). We may have to go through the testing; divine healing, purity of heart, baptism in the Holy Spirit and in fire—we are tested for these truths. We cannot get out of this testing. But in every meeting, the glory rises. We descend down into trials also to be sustained and brought out for the glory of God. *"If God is for us, who can be against us?"* (Rom. 8:31). *"For our light affliction, which is but for a moment, is working for us a far more exceeding and eternal weight of glory"* (2 Cor. 4:17). Oh, the joy of being worthy of suffering! How will I stand the glory that will be after?

Many of God's people are victorious in suffering but fail or back out when things are going fine. Deprivation is often easier than success. We need a sound mind all the time to balance us so that we do not trade our liberty for something less.

We get glimpses of the glory all the time. To Paul in the glory, the presence of the Lord was so wonderful. But he said, *"Lest I should be exalted...a thorn in the flesh was given to me"* (2 Cor. 12:7). That was the mercy of God. *"The Lord knows how to deliver the godly out of temptations"* (2 Pet. 2:9) and *"saves such as have a contrite spirit"* (Ps. 34:18). What a revelation for the time to come! If Satan had his way, we would be devoured.

Thought for today: The truths you stand for, you are tried for.

309

July 14

The Spirit Is upon Me

The Spirit of the LORD is upon Me.
—Luke 4:18

Scripture reading: Luke 4:1–21

I believe God is bringing us to a place where we know that the Spirit of the Lord is upon us. If we have not gotten to that place, God wants to bring us to the fact of what Jesus said in John 14: *"I will pray the Father, and He will give you another Helper* ['*Comforter,*' KJV], *that He may abide with you forever"* (v. 16). Because the Spirit of the Lord came upon Him who is our Head, we must see to it that we receive the same anointing, and that the same Spirit is upon us. The Devil will cause us to lose the victory if we allow ourselves to be defeated by him. But it is a fact that the Spirit of the Lord is upon us, and as for me, I have no message apart from the message He will give, and I believe that the signs He speaks of will follow.

I believe that Jesus was the One sent forth from God, and the propitiation for the sins of the whole world (1 John 2:2). We see the manifestation of the Spirit resting upon Him so that His ministry was with power. May God awaken us to the fact that this is the only place where there is any ministry of power.

The Comforter has come. He has come, and He has come to abide forever. Are you going to be defeated by the Devil? No, for the Comforter has come so that we may receive and give forth the signs that must follow, so that we may not by any means be deceived by the schemes of the Devil. There is no limit to what we may become if we dwell and live in the Spirit. In the Spirit of prayer, we are taken right away from earth into heaven. In the Spirit, the Word of God seems to unfold in a wonderful way, and it is only in the Spirit that the love of God is poured out in us (Rom. 5:5).

Thought for today: Who is the man who is willing to lay down everything so that he may have God's all?

July 15

Hearts Aflame

Surely I will cause breath to enter into you, and you shall live.
—Ezekiel 37:5

Scripture reading: Ezekiel 37

As we speak in the Spirit, we feel that the fire that burned in the hearts of the two men on their way to Emmaus, when Jesus walked with them, is burning in our hearts. (See Luke 24:13–32.) It is sure to come to pass that when we walk with Him, our hearts will burn; the same power of the Spirit is present today to make it happen. The two men on their way to Emmaus could not understand what was happening on the road, but a few hours later, they saw Jesus break the bread, and their eyes were opened.

But, beloved, our hearts always ought to burn. There is a place where we can live in the anointing and the clothing of the Spirit, where our words will be clothed with power. *"Do not be drunk with wine...but be filled with the Spirit"* (Eph. 5:18). Being filled with the Spirit is a wonderful privilege.

It was necessary for John to be in the Spirit on the Isle of Patmos so that the revelation could be made clear to him (Rev. 1:9–10). What does it mean to this generation for us to be kept in the Spirit? All human reasoning and all human knowledge cannot be compared with the power of the life that is lived in the Spirit. In the Spirit, we have power to loose and power to bind (Matt. 16:19). There is a place where the Holy Spirit can put us where we cannot be anywhere else but in the Spirit. But it is only in the Spirit.

Now, I read in Matthew 16:19 that Jesus says, in essence, "I will give you power to bind, and I will give you power to loose." This is a power that many of us have not yet claimed, and we will not be able to claim this manifestation of the Spirit unless we live in the Spirit. When are you able to bind and loose? It is only in the Spirit. You cannot bind things in human strength or with the natural mind. This power was never lacking in Jesus, but I feel that there is a great lack of it in most of us. God help us!

"The Spirit of the LORD is upon Me" (Luke 4:18). Beloved, there was a great purpose in this Spirit being on Jesus, and there is a special purpose in your being baptized in the Spirit. We must not

forget that we are members of His body, and by this wonderful baptismal power, we are partakers of His divine nature (2 Pet. 1:4).

The revelation came this way: I saw Adam and Eve driven out of the Garden and a flaming sword at every side to keep them from entering into the Garden. But I saw that all around me was a flaming sword keeping me from evil, and it seemed this would be true if I would claim it, so I said, "Lord, I will." The flaming sword was around me, delivering me from the power of hell. In this way, we are preserved from evil. God is like a wall of fire around us (Zech. 2:5); why should we fear? What a wonderful salvation! What a wonderful Deliverer!

Notice Ezekiel 37. The only need of Ezekiel was to be in the Spirit, and while he was in the Spirit, it came to him to prophesy to the dry bones and say, *"O dry bones, hear the word of the LORD"* (v. 4). And as he prophesied according to the Lord's command, he saw an *"exceedingly great army"* (v. 10) rising up about him. The prophet obeyed God's command, and all we have to do is exactly this: obey God. What is impossible with man is possible with God (Luke 18:27).

I pray to God that your spirit, soul, and body may be preserved holy (1 Thess. 5:23), and that you may be always on fire, always ready with the anointing on you. If this is not so, we are out of divine order, and we ought to cry to Him until the glory comes back upon us.

Thought for today: If we breathe the Holy Spirit's thoughts into our thoughts, and live in the anointing of the Holy Spirit as Jesus lived, then there will be evidences that we are in the Holy Spirit, and we will do His works.

July 16

A Door of Utterance

[Pray] *that utterance may be given to me, that I may open my mouth boldly to make known the mystery of the gospel, for which I am an ambassador in chains; that in it I may speak boldly, as I ought to speak.*
—Ephesians 6:19–20

Scripture reading: Acts 26:1–29

*P*aul felt, as we do, the need for utterance. He had plenty of language, but he wanted utterance. We can have inspiration, operation, tongue, mind, heart—we need all these. God works through these in this divine order to give forth the truth most needed for the time. But the supreme need of the hour is prayer for utterance.

Paul and his helpers were men sent forth by the power of the Holy Spirit. But without anointing, they could not open the door or give forth the right word for the hour. Paul and his helpers were unequal to the need. Was this an indication that something was out of order? No! We are all dependent on the Holy Spirit to breathe through us.

How can we live in this place, reliant on omnipotent power? It is by the Spirit of the Lord giving vent, speaking through us. It is not an easy thing. God said to David, "It is good that the desire is in your heart." (See 2 Chronicles 6:8.) But that will not do for us who live in the latter days when God is pouring forth His Spirit, and rivers of power are available are at our word. We need to live by Mark 11:22–23: *"Have faith in God....Whoever...believes...will have whatever he says."* Let God arise. Let God breathe His Holy Spirit through your nature, through your eyes and tongue—the supernatural in the natural for the glory of God. God raised Paul for this ministry. What was the means? Jesus said, *"By faith in Me"* (Acts 26:18). The faith of God.

Thought for today: Apart from this living breath of the Spirit, the message is ordinary and not extraordinary.

July 17

Speech Inspired by the Spirit

My tongue is the pen of a ready writer.
—Psalm 45:1

Scripture reading: Isaiah 50:4; Psalm 15:1–16:1

Oh, for more people to believe God that *"the tongue of the dumb* [might] *sing"* (Isa. 35:6). When will they? When they believe and fulfill the conditions. Oh, beloved, it is not easy. But Jesus died and rose again for the possibility. *"Have faith in God"* (Mark 11:22). The whole man needs to be immersed in God so that the Holy Spirit may operate and the dying world may have the ministry of life for which it is famished.

> *But if the Spirit of Him who raised Jesus from the dead dwells in you, He who raised Christ from the dead will also give life to your mortal bodies through His Spirit who dwells in you.* (Rom. 8:11)

As the dead body of Christ was given life and brought out by the Holy Spirit, may we be given eyes to see and ears to hear and a tongue to speak as the oracles of God. *"If anyone speaks, let him speak as the oracles of God"* (1 Pet. 4:11). Those are our orders: speaking what no one knows except the Holy Spirit, as the Spirit gives divine utterance—a language that would never come at all unless the Holy Spirit gave utterance and took the things of Christ and revealed them. Did God answer Paul's prayer to be able *"to speak the mystery of Christ"* (Col. 4:3)? Yes! *"In mighty signs and wonders, by the power of the Spirit of God...from Jerusalem and round about to Illyricum I have fully preached the gospel of Christ"* (Rom. 15:19).

It was the grace of our Lord Jesus Christ, that great Shepherd of the sheep, that brought to us redemption. It was by the grace of God—His favor and mercy, a lavished love and an undeserved favor—that God brought salvation. We did not deserve it.

Thought for today: The greatest gift to mankind is to be able to say, "Christ lives in me!"

Seasoned with Salt

Let your speech always be with grace, seasoned with salt.
—Colossians 4:6

Scripture reading: James 3

*S*alt has three properties: first, it stings; second, it heals; and third, it preserves. In the same way, your words by the Spirit are filled with grace, yet they cut to the heart, and they bring preservation. We must be very careful to be salty. God's Word will not return void; it will accomplish, and it will prosper (Isa. 55:11)—but our mouths must be clean and our desire wholly for God.

Jesus' words were straightforward. To the elite of the holiness movement of His day, He said, *"Woe to you...hypocrites! For you are like whitewashed tombs"* (Matt. 23:27). To others He said, "You are deceived; you have the idea that you are the children of Abraham, but you are the children of the Devil, and you do his works." (See John 8:39, 44.) His mouth was full of meekness and gentleness and yet was so salty because of their corruption. Unless you know the charm of Christ, you might think you are out of the working of His eternal power. However, see what the prophet Isaiah said: *"A bruised reed He will not break"* (Isa. 42:3).

"Know how you ought to answer each one" (Col. 4:6). This is not easy to learn. It is only learned in the place of being absorbed by God. When we are in that place, we seek to glorify God and can give a chastening word full of power to awaken and to save. Use the salt, beloved! Use conviction; use the healing for their preservation.

How true we have to be! You are seasoned with salt. I love it! It is inspiring! It is conviction! Thus the Holy Spirit writes on the fleshly tablets of the temple of the Spirit (2 Cor. 3:3). O Lord, enlarge our sense of Your presence in the temple so that we may discern the Lord's body in our midst.

Thought for today: None are so deaf as those who won't hear the Word of God; none so blind as those who won't see its truth.

Full of Life

Be filled with all the fullness of God.
—Ephesians 3:19

Scripture reading: Ephesians 3:14–21

We want our whole being to be so full of the life of our Lord that the Holy Spirit can speak and act through us. We want to live always in Him. Oh, the charm of His divine plan! We cry out for the inspiration of the God of power. We want to act in the Holy Spirit. We want to breathe out divine life. We want the glory, miracles, and wonders that work out the plan of the Most High God. We want to be absorbed by God, and we want to know nothing among men except Jesus and Him crucified (1 Cor. 2:2). Unto You, O God, be the glory and the honor and the power (Rev. 5:13)!

> Yes, filled with God,
> Yes, filled with God,
> Emptied of self and filled with God.
>
> For He is so precious to me,
> For He is so precious to me;
> It's heaven below
> My Redeemer to know,
> For He is so precious to me.

Can you wonder why I love Him so? May there be a cry until we witness Acts 11:15: *"And as I began to speak, the Holy Spirit fell upon them."*

> Oh, be on fire, oh, be on fire,
> Oh, be on fire for God.
> Oh, be on fire, be all on fire,
> Be all on fire for God.

Thought for today: To live two days in succession on the same spiritual plane is a tragedy.

The Ministry of the Spirit

Nor do I count my life dear to myself, so that I may finish my race with joy, and the ministry which I received from the Lord Jesus.
—Acts 20:24

Scripture reading: Romans 13:14–14:19

The ministry of the Spirit has been entrusted to us. We must be in the place of edifying the church. Law is not liberty, but if there is a move of God within you, God has written His laws in your heart so that you may delight in Him. God desires to set forth in us a perfect blending of His life and our lives so that we may have abounding inward joy—a place of reigning over all things, not a place of endeavor. There is a great difference between an endeavor and a delight.

God says to us, *"Be holy, for I am holy"* (1 Pet. 1:16). Trying will never cause us to reach a place of holiness, but there is a place, or an attitude, where God gives us faith to rest on His Word, and we delight inwardly over everything. *"I delight to do Your will, O my God"* (Ps. 40:8). There is a place of great joy. Do we want condemnation?

We know there is something within that has been accomplished by the power of God, something greater than there could be in the natural order of the flesh. We are the representatives of Jesus. He was eaten up with zeal. (See John 2:17.) This intense zeal changes us by the operation of the Word; we do not rest in the letter, but we allow the blessed Holy Spirit to lift us by His power.

The disciples were with Jesus three years. He spoke out of the abundance of His heart toward them. John said, "We have touched Him; our eyes have gazed into His eyes." (See 1 John 1:1). Did Jesus know about Judas? Yes. Did He ever tell? No. When Jesus told the disciples that one of them would betray Him, they said, *"Lord, is it I?"* (Matt. 26:22). The essence of divine order is to bring the church together, so that there is no schism in the body, but a perfect blending of heart to heart.

"The letter kills, but the Spirit gives life" (2 Cor. 3:6). The sword cut off Malchus's ear, but the Spirit healed it again. (See Luke 22:50–51.) Our ministry has to be in the Spirit, *"free from the law of sin and death"* (Rom. 8:2). When we live in the ministry of

July 20

the Spirit, we are free; in the letter we are bound. If it is *"an eye for an eye"* (Matt. 5:38), we have lost the principle. If we are to come to a place of great liberty, the law must be at an end. Yet we love the law of God; we love to do it and not put one thing aside.

"Clearly you are an epistle of Christ, ministered...by the Spirit of the living God...on tablets of flesh, that is, of the heart" (2 Cor. 3:3). It's heart worship when God has made the incision; the Spirit has come to blend with humanity.

Thought for today: Ours is not an endeavor society, but a delight to live in the will of God.

July 21

Peace in Our Hearts

You will keep him in perfect peace, whose mind is stayed on You,
because he trusts in You.
—Isaiah 26:3

Scripture reading: Isaiah 54:5–55:9

We must keep in the spiritual tide—God supreme, the altar within the body. Faith is the evidence, the power, the principle, keeping us in rest. We must have the Spirit in anointing, intercession, revelation, and great power of ministry. To be baptized in the Holy Spirit is to be in God's plan—the Spirit preeminent, revealing the Christ of God, making the Word of God alive—something divine. *"Our sufficiency is from God, who also made us sufficient as ministers of the...Spirit; for the...Spirit gives life"* (2 Cor. 3:5–6).

I knew a believer whose job was to carry bags of coal. He had been in bed three weeks away from his work. I showed him Romans 7:25: *"I thank God; through Jesus Christ our Lord! So then, with the mind I myself serve the law of God, but with the flesh the law of sin."* I said, "Keep your mind on God and go to work, shouting victory." He did, and the first day he was able to carry a hundred bags, his mind stayed on God and kept in peace. *"Great peace have those who love Your law, and nothing causes them to stumble"* (Ps. 119:165).

If your peace is disturbed, there is something wrong. Apply the blood of Jesus, and keep your mind stayed upon Jehovah, where "hearts are fully blessed, finding as He promised, perfect peace and rest." Keep your mind on God, gaining strength in Him day by day.

"The law was given through Moses, but grace and truth came through Jesus Christ" (John 1:17). This is a new dispensation, this divine place: Christ in you, the hope and evidence of glory (Col. 1:27).

May God gird you with truth (Eph. 6:14). I commend you to Him in the name of Jesus.

Thought for today: If you are not free in the Spirit, your mind is in the wrong place.

July 22

At the Lord's Service

Lord, what do You want me to do?
—Acts 9:6

Scripture reading: Acts 9:1–22

*I*n the midst of persecuting the Lord's disciples, Saul was confronted with a bright light from heaven (Acts 9:3). A voice spoke to him saying, *"Saul, Saul, why are you persecuting Me?"* (v. 4). Saul asked who was speaking, and when Jesus identified Himself, Saul's response was, *"Lord, what do You want me to do?"* As soon as Saul was willing to yield, he was in a condition where God could meet his need, where God could display His power, where God could have the man.

Friend, are you saying today, *"What do You want me to do?"* The place of yieldedness is just where God wants us. People are saying, "I want the baptism of the Holy Spirit. I want to be healed. I would like to know for certain that I am a child of God," and I see nothing, absolutely nothing, in the way, except that they have not yielded to the plan of God.

In Acts 19:6, the condition was met that Paul demanded, and when he laid his hands on the Ephesian disciples, they were instantly filled with the Spirit and spoke in other tongues and prophesied. The only thing they needed was just to be in the condition where God could come in.

The main thing today that God wants is obedience. When you begin yielding and yielding to God, He has a plan for your life, and you come in to that wonderful place where all you have to do is eat the fruits of Canaan.

It is the call of God that counts. Paul answered the call of God. I believe God wants to stir our heart today to obedience. Our response should be, *"Lord, what do You want me to do?"*

Thought for today: God is looking for obedience.

July 23

Are You Willing?

Now God worked unusual miracles by the hands of Paul.
—Acts 19:11

Scripture reading: Matthew 16:24–27; Luke 14:27–35

*P*aul had been putting many believers in prison, but God brought him to such a place of yieldedness and brokenness that he cried out, *"What do You want me to do?"* (Acts 9:6). Paul's choice was to be a bondservant for Jesus Christ.

Beloved, are you willing for God to have His way today? God said about Paul, *"I will show him how many things he must suffer for My name's sake"* (Acts 9:16). But Paul saw that these things were working out *"a far more exceeding and eternal weight of glory"* (2 Cor. 4:17). Do you need a touch from God? Are you willing to follow Him? Will you obey Him?

When the Prodigal Son had returned and the father had killed the fatted calf and made a feast for him, the elder brother was angry and said, *"You never gave me a young goat, that I might make merry with my friends"* (Luke 15:29). But the father said to him, *"All that I have is yours"* (v. 31). He could kill a fatted calf at any time. When God can trust us, we will not come short in anything.

"God worked unusual miracles by the hands of Paul." Let us notice the handkerchiefs that went from his body. This passage indicates that when Paul touched handkerchiefs and sent them forth, God worked special miracles through them: diseases departed from the sick, and evil spirits went out of them. Isn't this lovely? I believe that after we lay hands on these handkerchiefs and pray over them, they should be handled very sacredly. Even as we carry them, they will bring life, if we carry them in faith to the suffering ones. The very effect, if you would only believe, would be to change your own body as you carry the handkerchief.

God wants to change our faith today. He wants us to see that it is not obtained by struggling and working and longing. *"The Father Himself loves you"* (John 16:27). *"He Himself took our infirmities and bore our sicknesses"* (Matt. 8:17). *"Come to Me, all you who labor and are heavy laden, and I will give you rest"* (Matt. 11:28). Who is the man who will take the place of Paul and yield and yield and yield until God possesses him in such a way that power will flow from his body to the sick and suffering? It will have to be the power of Christ that flows. Don't think there is some magic power in the handkerchief, or you will miss the power. It is the living faith within the man who lays the handkerchief on his body, and the power of God through that faith. Praise God, we may lay hold of this living faith today. The blood has never lost its power. As we get in touch with Jesus, wonderful things will take place. And what else? We will get nearer and nearer to Him.

Thought for today: Ministry always begins as soon as a person yields.

July 24

The Secret of Power

Jesus I know, and Paul I know; but who are you?
—Acts 19:15

Scripture reading: Acts 19:13–20

I implore you in the name of Jesus, especially those of you who are baptized, to wake up to the fact that you have power if God is with you. But there must be a resemblance between you and Jesus. The evil spirit said, *"Jesus I know, and Paul I know; but who are you?"* Paul had the resemblance. You are not going to get this resemblance without having His presence; His presence changes you. You are not going to be able to get the results without the marks of the Lord Jesus. You must have the divine power within yourself; devils will take no notice of any power if they do not see Christ. *"Jesus I know, and Paul I know; but who are you?"* The difference in these exorcists was that they did not have the marks of Christ, so the manifestation of the power of Christ was not seen.

If you want power, don't make any mistake about it. If you speak in tongues, don't mistake that for the power. If God has given you revelations along certain lines, don't mistake that for the power. Or if you have even laid hands on the sick and they have been healed, don't mistake that for the power. *"The Spirit of the LORD is upon Me"* (Luke 4:18)—that alone is the power. Don't be deceived. There is a place to be reached where you know the Spirit is upon you so that you will be able to do the works that are accomplished by this blessed Spirit of God in you. Then the manifestation of His power will be seen, and people will believe in the Lord.

God wants you to be ministering spirits, and this means being clothed with another power. You know when this divine power is there, and you know when it goes forth. Beloved, we can reach it; it is a high mark, but we can get to it. Do you ask how? Say to God, *"What do You want me to do?"* (Acts 9:6). That is the plan. It means a perfect surrender to the call of God, and perfect obedience.

Thought for today: The baptism of Jesus must bring us to the place of having our focus centered on the glory of God; everything else is wasted time and wasted energy.

323

July 25

Yield and Obey

Yield yourselves to the LORD.
—2 Chronicles 30:8

Scripture reading: John 15:1–14

A dear young Russian came to England. He did not know the language but learned it quickly and was mightily used and blessed by God. As the wonderful manifestations of the power of God were seen, people asked him the secret of his power, but he felt it was so sacred between him and God that he should not tell it. But they pressed him so much that he finally said to them, "First, God called me, and His presence was so precious that I said to God at every call that I would obey Him. I yielded and yielded and yielded until I realized that I was simply clothed with another power altogether, and I realized that God had taken me—tongue, thoughts, and everything—and I was not myself, but it was Christ working through me."

Do you know that God has called you over and over and has put His hand upon you, but you have not yielded? Have you had the breathing of His power within you, calling you to prayer, and you have to confess that you have failed?

I went to a house one afternoon where I had been called, and I met a man at the door. He said, "My wife has not been out of bed for eight months; she is paralyzed. She has been looking forward so much to your coming. She is hoping God will raise her up." I went in and rebuked the Devil's power. She said, "I know I am healed; if you leave, I will get up." I left the house and went away, not hearing anything more about her. I went to a meeting that night, and a man jumped up and said he had something he wanted to say; he had to go to catch a train but wanted to talk first. He said, "I come to this city once a week, and I visit the sick all over the city. There is a woman I have been visiting, and I was very much distressed about her. She was paralyzed and lay on her bed many months. However, when I went there today, she was up doing her work." I tell this story because I want you to see Jesus. Yield to Him today.

Thought for today: If there are any *but*s in your attitude toward the Word of truth, there is something unyielded to the Spirit.

July 26

God's Wonder-Working Power

Who can utter the mighty acts of the LORD?
Who can declare all His praise?
—Psalm 106:2

Scripture reading: Psalm 106

A letter came to our house saying that a young man was very ill. He had been to our mission a few years before with a very bad foot; he had worn no shoe but had fastened a piece of leather around his foot. God had healed him that day. Three years afterward, something else came upon him. What it was I don't know, but his heart failed, and he was helpless. He could not get up or dress or do anything for himself. In that condition, he called his sister and told her to write to me and see if I would pray. My wife said to go, and she believed that God would give me that life. I went, and when I arrived at this place, I found that the whole country was expecting me. They had said that when I came, this man would be healed.

I said to the woman when I arrived, "I have come." "Yes," she said, "but it is too late." "Is he alive?" I asked. "Yes, barely alive," she said. I went in and put my hands on him and said, "Martin." He just breathed slightly and whispered, "The doctor said that if I move from this position, I will never move again." I said, "Do you know that the Scripture says, *'God is the strength of my heart and my portion forever'* (Ps. 73:26)"? He said, "Should I get up?" I said, "No."

That day was spent in prayer and ministering the Word. I found a great state of unbelief in that house, but I saw that Martin had faith to be healed. His sister was home from an asylum. God kept me there to pray for that place. I said to the family, "Get Martin's clothes ready; I believe he is to be raised up." I felt the unbelief.

I went to the chapel and had prayer with a number of people around there, and before noon they, too, believed that Martin would be healed. When I returned, I said, "Are his clothes ready?" They said, "No." I said, "Oh, will you hinder God's work in this house?" I went into Martin's room all alone. I said, "I believe God will do a new thing today. I believe that when I lay hands on you, the glory of heaven will fill this place." I laid my hands on him in the name of the Father, Son, and Holy Spirit, and immediately the glory of the Lord filled the room, and I fell at once to the floor. I did not see what took place on the bed or in the room, but this young man began to shout, "Glory, glory!" and I heard him say, "For Your glory, Lord," and he stood before me perfectly healed. He went to the door and opened it, and his father stood there. He said, "Father, the Lord has raised me up," and the father fell to the floor and cried for salvation. The young woman brought out of the asylum was perfectly healed at that moment by the power of God in that house.

God wants us to see that the power of God coming upon people has something more in it than we have yet known. The power to heal and to baptize is available, but you must say, *"Lord, what do You want me to do?"* (Acts 9:6). You say it is four months before the harvest. If you had the eyes of Jesus, you would see that the harvest is already here (John 4:35). The Holy Spirit wants you for the purpose of manifesting Jesus through you. Oh, may you never be the same again! The Holy Spirit moving upon us will make us to be like Him, and we will truly say, *"Lord, what do You want me to do?"*

Thought for today: The Devil will say you can't have faith. Tell him he is a liar.

July 27

Higher Ground

Believe in the LORD your God, and you shall be established.
—2 Chronicles 20:20

Scripture reading: Mark 9:19–29

*A*re you ready? "Why?" you ask. Because God wants to give us higher ground, holier thoughts, and a more concentrated, clearer ministry. God wants us to be in a rising tide every day. This rising tide is a changing of faith; it is an attitude of the spirit where God rises higher and higher. He wants us to come to the place where we will never look back. God has no room for the person who looks back. (See Genesis 19:15–26.)

The Holy Spirit wants to get you ready to stretch yourself out to God and to believe that *"He is a rewarder of those who diligently seek Him"* (Heb. 11:6). You do not need to use vain repetitions when you pray (Matt. 6:7). Simply ask and believe.

People come with their needs, they ask, and then they leave with their needs because they do not faithfully wait to receive what God has promised them. If they ask for it, they will get it.

Many people are missing the highest order. I went to a person who was full of the Spirit but was constantly saying, "Glory! Glory! Glory!" I said, "You are full of the Holy Spirit, but the Spirit cannot speak because you continually speak." He kept still then, and the Spirit began to speak through him. This story illustrates the fact that often we are altogether in God's way.

I want to so change your operation in God that you will know that God is operating through you for this time and forevermore. May the Spirit awaken us to deep things today.

Are you ready to move and be moved by the mighty power of God that cannot be moved, and to be so chastened and built up that you are in the place where it doesn't matter where the wind blows or what difficulty comes because you are fixed in God?

Are you ready to come into the plan of the Most High God, believing what the Scriptures say and holding fast to what is good, believing so that no one will take your crown (Rev. 3:11)?

Thought for today: Do more believing and less begging.

July 28

Changed by the Word

How can a young man cleanse his way? By taking heed
according to Your word.
—Psalm 119:9

Scripture reading: Psalm 119:17–40

God can so change us by His Word day by day that we are altogether different. David knew this. He said, *"Your word has given me life"* (Ps. 119:50). *"He sent His word and healed them"* (Ps. 107:20). How beautiful that God can make His Word abound! *"Your word I have hidden in my heart, that I might not sin against You!"* (Ps. 119:11).

It is absolute disloyalty and unbelief to pray about anything in the Word of God. Believe and receive the Word of God, and you will always be on sure ground. If you pray about the Word of God, the Devil will be behind the whole thing. Never pray about anything concerning which it can be said, "Thus says the Lord." You need to receive God's words so that they will build you on a new foundation of truth.

In Romans 12:1, we see that Paul had been operated on:

I beseech you therefore, brethren, by the mercies of God, that you present your bodies a living sacrifice, holy, acceptable to God, which is your reasonable service.

He had undergone a mighty operation on more than just a surgical table. He had been cut to the very depths of his being, until he had absolutely reached a place on the altar of full surrender. When he came to this place, out of the depths of this experience, he gave his whole life, as it were, in a nutshell.

Thought for today: The Word of God does not need to be prayed about: the Word of God needs to be received.

Receive God's Grace

*We then, as workers together with Him also plead with you
not to receive the grace of God in vain.*
—2 Corinthians 6:1

Scripture reading: Psalm 51

*P*eople are getting blessed all the time and are receiving revelation. They go from one point to another, but they do not establish themselves in the thing that God has brought to them. If you do not let your heart be examined when the Lord comes with blessing or with correction, if you do not make the blessing or the correction a stepping-stone, or if you do not make it a rising place, then you are receiving the grace of God in vain. People could be built up much more in the Lord and be more wonderfully established if they would step out sometimes and think over the graces of the Lord.

Grace will be multiplied on certain conditions. How? In the first chapter of 2 Timothy, we have these words: *"The genuine faith that is in you"* (v. 5). Everyone in the entire church of God has the same precious faith within him. If you allow this same precious faith to be foremost, utmost in everything, you will find that grace and peace are multiplied. The Lord comes to us with His mercy, and if we do not see that the God of grace and mercy is opening to us the door of mercy and utterances, we are receiving His grace in vain.

When you are in prayer, remember how near you are to the Lord. Prayer is a time during which God wants you to be strengthened, and He wants you to remember that He is with you.

When you open the sacred pages of Scripture and the light comes right through and you say, "Oh, isn't that wonderful!" thank God, for it is the grace of God that has opened your understanding. When you go to a church meeting and the revelation comes forth and you feel that it is what you needed, receive it as the grace of the Lord. God has brought you to a place where He might make you a greater blessing.

Thought for today: If we want strength in building our spiritual character, we should never forget our blessings.

July 30

Constant Salvation

Behold, now is the accepted time;
behold, now is the day of salvation.
—2 Corinthians 6:2

Scripture reading: 1 John 1

There are two processes of salvation. First, God helped you when the Spirit was moving you and when the Adversary was against you, when your neighbors and friends did not want you to be saved, and when everybody rose up in accusation against you. When you knew there was fighting on the outside and fighting within, He helped you; He covered you until you came into salvation. Second, He keeps you in the plan of His salvation.

This is the day of salvation. The fact that you are being saved does not mean that you were not saved, but it means that you are being continually changed. In the process of regeneration, you are being made like God; you are being brought into the operation of the Spirit's power; you are being made like Him.

This is the day of salvation. God has helped you in a time when Satan would destroy you, and He is with you now. If we remain stationary, God has nothing for us. We must see that we must progress. Yesterday will not do for today. I must thank God for yesterday; however, tomorrow is affected by what I am today.

Today is a day of inspiration and divine intuition, a day in which God is enrapturing the heart, breaking all shorelines, getting my heart to the place where it is responsive only to His cry, where I live and move honoring and glorifying God in the Spirit. This is the day of the visitation of the Lord. This is the great day of salvation, a day of moving on for God.

We will praise and magnify the Lord, for He is worthy to be praised! He has helped us, and now He is building us; now He is changing us; now we are in the operation of the Holy Spirit. Every day you must climb to higher ground. You must refuse everything that is not pure and holy and separate. God wants you to be pure in heart. He wants your intense desire after holiness.

Thought for today: You must deny yourself in order to go forward with God.

July 31

In Perfect Harmony

Give no offense in anything, that our ministry may not be blamed.
—2 Corinthians 6:3

Scripture reading: 2 Corinthians 13:4–12

*I*f you, being a member of a certain church, are in a place where you would rather see one person saved at your church than two people saved at another church, then you are altogether wrong, and you need to be saved. You are still out of the order of the Spirit of God, and you are a stranger to true, holy life with God.

God wants to show us that we must so live in the Spirit that the ministry is not blamed. If your ministry is not to be blamed, how can you help to prevent it from being blamed? You have to live in love. See to it that you never say or do anything that would interfere with the work of the Lord; rather, live in the place where you are helping everybody, lifting everybody, and causing everybody to come into perfect harmony. Remember, there is always a blessing where there is harmony. "One accord" is the keynote of the victory that is going to come to us all the time.

There are thousands and thousands of different churches, but they are all one in the Spirit to the extent that they receive the life of Christ. If there is any division, it is always outside of the Spirit. The spiritual life in the believer never has known dissension, because where the Spirit has perfect liberty, there is total agreement, and there is no schism in the body.

"The letter kills, but the Spirit gives life" (2 Cor. 3:6). When there is division, it is only because people choose the letter instead of the Spirit. If we are in the Spirit, we will have life. If we are in the Spirit, we will love everybody. If we are in the Spirit, there will be no division; there will be perfect harmony.

Thought for today: More grace means more death to self; more life means more submission; more revelation means more humility.

August 1

A Life Ministry

Do not let your good be spoken of as evil.
—Romans 14:16

Scripture reading: Romans 14

*W*e recognize the Holy Spirit, but we recognize first the Spirit giving us life, saving us from every form of evil power, transforming our human nature until it is in divine order. Then, in that divine order, we see that the Lord of Hosts can very beautifully arrange the life until we live in the Spirit and are not fulfilling the lusts of the flesh (Gal. 5:16). When the Holy Spirit is perfectly in charge, He lifts and lightens and unveils the truth in a new way until we grasp it.

Oh, how wonderful it would be if every one of us would possess this word in our hearts: *"Do not let your good be spoken of as evil."* I know we all want to be good. It is not a wrong thing to desire that our goodness be appreciated. But we must watch ourselves because it is an evil day (although it is the day of salvation), and we must understand these days that the Lord wants to chasten and bring a people right into a full-tide position.

I believe that it is just as possible for God to sweep a group of believers right into glory before the Rapture as during the Rapture. It is possible for you to be taken even if others are left. May God give us a very keen inward discerning of our hearts' purity. We want to go to heaven—it is far better for us to go—but it is far better for the church that we stay (Phil. 1:23–24).

Paul realized the following truth: *"To depart* [to] *be with Christ...is far better"* (v. 23). Then there is another side to it. Believing that God made us for the proclamation of the Gospel, for the building of the church, we would say, "Lord, for the purpose of being a further blessing for Your sake and for the sake of the church, just keep us full of life to stay." We do not want to be full of disease, but we want to be full of life.

May the Lord grant to us right now a living faith to believe.

Thought for today: We will have to be utterly slain if we want to know the resurrection power of Jesus.

In Affliction for the Church

In all things we commend ourselves as ministers of God: in much patience, in tribulations, in needs, in distresses.
—2 Corinthians 6:4

Scripture reading: 2 Corinthians 6:3–7:1

The tribulations of which Paul spoke are not the tribulations of various diseases. Paul was very definite about this fact. He suffered tribulations with the people as Jesus did. There can be many tribulations within our human frame as we feel that our spiritual influence is not bearing fruit in the lives of others. You are very sorry and deeply distressed because the church is not capturing the vision, and there is tribulation in your sorrow.

God wants us to be so spiritual that we have perfect discernment of the spirit of the people. However, if I can in a moment discern the spirit in a meeting, whether it is life-giving, whether the whole church is receiving it, whether my heart is moved by this power, then I can also see faith waning, and that will bring tribulation and trouble to my life.

May God give us the realization that we are so joined to the church that we may labor to bring the church up. Paul said that he labored in birth in order that Christ might be formed in the people again (Gal. 4:19). He was not laboring so that they could be saved again. No, but they had lacked perception; they had missed divine fellowship; so he labored again so that they might be brought into this deep fellowship in the Spirit.

May God help us to see that we can labor for the church. Blessed is the person who can weep between the church door and the altar. Blessed are the people of God who can take someone else's church on their hearts and weep and cry through until the church is formed again, until she rises in glory, until the power of heaven is over her, until the spiritual acquaintance rises higher and higher, until a song lifts her to the heights.

Thought for today: You have to so live in the Spirit that when you see the church not rising into its glory, you suffer tribulation for the church.

333

August 3

Possess Your Soul in Peace

May the Lord direct your hearts into the love of God
and into the patience of Christ.
—2 Thessalonians 3:5

Scripture reading: 2 Thessalonians 1:3–12

I know I am writing to people who have many responsibilities in their churches. If the people see that you have lost your groundwork of peace, they know that you have gotten outside of the position of victory. You have to possess your soul in peace.

Strange things will happen in the church. All circumstances will appear to be against the church, and you will feel that the Enemy is busy. At that time, possess your soul in peace. Let the people know that you are acquainted with One *"who, when He was reviled, did not revile in return"* (1 Pet. 2:23).

Possess patience to such an extent that you can suffer anything for the church, for your friends, for your neighbors, or for anyone. Remember this: we build character in others as our character is built. As we are pure in our thoughts, are tender and gracious to other people, and possess our souls in patience (Luke 21:19), then people have a great desire for our fellowship in the Holy Spirit.

Now, Jesus is an example to us along these lines. The people saw Him undisturbed. I love to think about Him. He helps me so much because He is the very essence of help. I pray to God that we may learn the lesson of how to keep ourselves so that the Spirit will blend us, making the harmony beautiful.

Get ready for that. Claim your rights to God's promises. Believe the Scriptures are for you. Believe that love covers you, that His life flows through you, that His life-giving Spirit lifts you. Let the peace that passes understanding (Phil. 4:7) be yours today.

Thought for today: Remember this: you never lose as much as when you lose your peace.

August 4

Do Not Give Offense

I myself always strive to have a conscience without offense
toward God and men.
—Acts 24:16

Scripture reading: Matthew 18:3–18

*I*f ten people could have saved Sodom and Gomorrah, ten holy people in a church can hold the power of the Spirit until light reigns. We do not want to seek to save ourselves; on the contrary, we want to lose ourselves so that we may save the church (Matt. 16:25). You cannot stop distresses from coming; they will come, and offenses will come. But woe to those who cause offenses (Matt. 18:7). See that you do not cause offense. Live on a higher plane. See that your tongue does not speak evil of others.

Have you ever fully seen the picture presented in the twenty-sixth chapter of Matthew? Jesus said, *"One of you will betray Me"* (v. 21). The disciples asked, *"Lord, is it I?"* (v. 22). Every one of them was so conscious of his human weaknesses that not a single one of them could say that it would not be he.

How long do you think Jesus had known who would betray Him? Jesus had been with them, feeding them, walking up and down with them, and He had never told any of them that Judas would be His betrayer. Those who follow Jesus should be so sober and sensitive that they would not speak against someone else, whether the words are true or not.

If Jesus had told the disciples that Judas would one day betray Him, what would have been the result? Everyone would have been bitter against Judas. So He saved all His disciples from being bitter against Judas for three years.

What love! Can't you see that holy, divine Savior? If we saw Him clearly, every one of us would throw ourselves at His feet. If we had a crown worth millions of dollars, we would cast it at His feet and say, "You alone are worthy." O God, give us such a holy, intense, divine acquaintance with You that we would rather die than grieve You! O Jesus, we worship You! You are worthy!

Thought for today: Oh, for inward character that will make us say, "A thousand deaths rather than sinning once."

Filled with Life

Let no one despise your youth, but be an example to the believers in
word, in conduct, in love, in spirit, in faith, in purity.
—1 Timothy 4:12

Scripture reading: Psalm 148

The Holy Spirit fell upon a young man outside a church. He went into the church, where they were all very sedate. If anything were to move in that church out of the ordinary, it would have been extraordinary! This young man, with his fullness of life and zeal for the Master, started shouting and praising the Lord, manifesting the joy of the Lord; he disturbed the old saints.

In this church, an old man was reading the Psalms quietly one day. It touched the young Spirit-filled man who was sitting behind him. And the young man shouted, "Glory!" Said the old man, "Do you call that religion?"

The father of the young man was one of the deacons of the church. The other deacons gathered around him and said, "You must talk to your boy and make him understand that he has to wait until he is established before he manifests those things." So the father had a long talk with the boy and told him what the deacons had said. "You know," he said, "I must respect the deacons, and they have told me they won't put up with your enthusiasm. You have to wait until you are established."

As they neared their home, their horse made a sudden and complete stop. The father tried to make it go forward or backward, but the horse would not move for anything.

"What is up with the horse?" asked the father of the boy. "Father," replied the boy, "this horse has gotten established."

I pray that we will not get established in that way. God, loose us from these critical, long-faced, poisoned countenances, which haven't seen daylight for many days. Deliver us from acting in such a terrible way. We must have the reality of supernatural quickening until we are sane and active and not in any way dormant, but filled with life, God working in us mightily by His Spirit.

Thought for today: May the Lord save Pentecost from going to dry rot.

August 6

Love That Bears with Others

Bearing with one another in love.
—Ephesians 4:2

Scripture reading: Galatians 6:1–10

*W*e need to bear *"with one another in love."* How contrary this is to the hardness of men's hearts, contrary to the evil powers, contrary to the natural mind. It is God's love toward you that gives you tender, compassionate love toward one another.

Only the broken, contrite heart has received the mark of God. It is in that secluded place where He speaks to you alone and encourages you when you are down and out. When no hand is stretched out to you, He stretches out His hand with mercy and brings you into a place of compassion. Then you cannot think evil; then you cannot in any way act harshly. God has brought you into longsuffering, with tenderness and with love.

In the church of God, where a soul is on fire, kindled with the love of God, there is a deeper love between me and that brother than there is between me and my earthly brother. Oh, this love that I am speaking about is divine love; it is not human love. It is higher than human love; it is more devoted to God. It will not betray. It is true in everything. You can depend on it. It won't change its character. In divine love, you will act exactly as Jesus would act, for you will act with the same spirit. *"As He is, so are we in this world"* (1 John 4:17).

As your intimacy with Christ in the Spirit deepens, as you walk with Him *"in the light as He is in the light"* (1 John 1:7), then the fellowship becomes unique in all its plan. I pray that God will help us to understand it so that we will be able to be clothed upon (2 Cor. 5:2) as we have never been, with another majestic touch, with another ideal of heaven.

No one can love like God. And when He takes us into this divine love, we will precisely understand this word, this verse, for it is full of entreaty; it is full of passion and compassion; it has every touch of Jesus right in it. It is so lovely: *"With all lowliness and gentleness, with longsuffering, bearing with one another in love"* (Eph. 4:2).

Isn't it glorious? You cannot find it anywhere else. You cannot get these pictures in any place you go. I challenge you to go into any library in the world and find words coined or brought forth like these words, unless they are copied from this Word. They aren't in nature's garden; they are in God's. It is the Spirit explaining, for He alone can explain this ideal of beatitudes. These words are marvelous; they are beautiful; they are full of grandeur; they are God's. Hallelujah!

Thought for today: You cannot bear with others until you know how God has borne with you.

Pass It On

*Go therefore and make disciples of all the nations, baptizing them
in the name of the Father and of the Son and of the Holy Spirit,
teaching them to observe all things that I have commanded you;
and lo, I am with you always, even to the end of the age.*
—Matthew 28:19

Scripture reading: Acts 22:1–16

As it was only out of the brokenness of Paul's life that
blessing came forth, so it is out of the emptiness, brokenness, and yieldedness of our lives that God can bring forth
all His glories through us to others. As someone once said, "Unless
we pass on what we receive, we will lose it." If we didn't lose it, it
would become stagnant.

Virtue is always manifested through blessings that you have
passed on. Nothing will be of any importance to you except what
you pass on to others. God wants us to be so in the order of the
Spirit that when He breaks upon us the alabaster box of ointments,
which represents the precious anointing that He has for every child
of His, we will be filled with perfumes of holy incense for the sake
of others. Then we may be poured out for others, others may receive the graces of the Spirit, and the entire church may be edified.
The church will never know one dry day, but there will always be
freshness and life that make all of our hearts burn together as we
know that the Lord has talked with us once more.

We must have this inward burning desire for more of God. We
must not be at any stationary point. We must always have the most
powerful telescopes, looking at and hurrying toward what God has
called us to, so that He may perfect that forever.

In these days, God has for us a blessed inheritance, so that we
should no longer be barren or unfruitful, but rather be filled with
all fullness, increasing with all increasings, having a measureless
measure of the might of the Spirit in the inner man, so that we are
always like a great river that presses on and heals everything that
it touches. Oh, let it be so today!

Thought for today: We must be hungry, always ready for every
touch of God.

August 8

Being a Peacemaker

Endeavoring to keep the unity of the Spirit in the bond of peace.
—Ephesians 4:3

Scripture reading: Matthew 5:9, 17–24

Of all the things God intends for us to be, He intends for us to be peacemakers. I won't find a Scripture to help me make this point any better than Matthew 5:23–24:

> *Therefore if you bring your gift to the altar, and there remember that your brother has something against you, leave your gift there before the altar, and go your way. First be reconciled to your brother, and then come and offer your gift.*

Most Christians are satisfied with the first meaning of this passage, but the second meaning is deeper. Most people believe it is perfectly right, if you have offended another, to go to that person and say, "Please forgive me," and you win your brother when you take that part. But this is the deeper sense: *"If you...remember that your brother has something against you,"* go and forgive him his transgressions. It is so much deeper than getting your own side right to go and get his side right by forgiving him of all that he has done.

That will be a stepping-stone to very rich grace in the area of keeping *"the unity of the Spirit in the bond of peace."* Someone may say, "I cannot forgive them because she did that and he said that. You know, he didn't recognize me at all. And he hasn't smiled at me for at least six months." Poor thing! May God help you through evil report and good report (2 Cor. 6:4, 8). God can take us right through if we get to the right side of grace.

Friends, when you get to the place of forgiving your brother who has something against you, you will find that that is the greatest ideal of going on to perfection, and the Lord will help us *"to keep the unity of the Spirit in the bond of peace."* The *"bond of peace"* is an inward bond between you and another child of God. Oh, glory to God!

Thought for today: God wants us to have a pure love, a love that always helps someone else at its own expense.

One Body

There is one body and one Spirit.
—Ephesians 4:4

Scripture reading: James 4:17; 5:1–12

We must recognize that there is only one body. The longsuffering of God reaches out to believers who have the idea that only those in their church are right. That way of thinking is foolishness. It is foolishness for people to come to their Communion table and think that their table is the only table. What about the hundreds of people who are sitting around their tables partaking of the bread and the wine? Friend, the body of Christ consists of all who are in Christ.

The Scriptures definitely say that all who are Christ's at His coming will be changed. It seems that we cannot be all Christ's unless something is done, and God will sweep away so many attitudes that are spoiling our unity. We must reach the place of perfect love.

Oh, the body appearing as one body! Oh, the entire body possessing the same joy, the same peace, the same hope! No division, all one in Christ! Who can make a body like that? This body is made deep in the Cross. The blood takes away all impurities and everything that will mar the vessel. God is making a vessel for honor, fit for the Master's use (2 Tim. 2:21), joined with that body—one body.

Let us be careful that we do not in any way defile the body, because God is chastening the body and fitting it together. There is something deeper down in the spirit of the regenerated person when the impurities of life and of the flesh fall off. Oh, there is a resemblance, a likeness, a perfection of holiness, of love! O God, take away the weaknesses and all the depravities.

"Now you are the body of Christ, and members individually [*'in particular,'* KJV]*"* (1 Cor. 12:27). I like the word *"particular"*; it tells us that there is just the right place for us. God is making us fit in that place so that for all time we will have a wonderful place in that body.

Thought for today: You will never advance in the kingdom unless you see that in every church there is a nucleus that has as real a God as you have.

August 10

The Calling

You were called in one hope of your calling.
—Ephesians 4:4

Scripture reading: John 3:1–21

Many people who are called miss the call because they are dull of hearing. There is something in the call, beloved. *"Many are called, but few are chosen"* (Matt. 22:14). And how will the choice be made? The choice is always your choice first. You will find that gifts are your choice first. You will find that salvation is your choice. God has made it all, but you have to choose. God wants you to make an inward call, to be in a great intercessory condition of imploring the Holy One to prepare you for that wonderful spiritual body.

Called! Beloved, I know that some people have the idea (and it is a great mistake) that because they are not successful in everything they touch, because they have failed in so many things that they desire to go forward in, because they don't seem to aspire in prayer as some do and perhaps don't enter into the fullness of tongues, there is no hope for them in this calling. Satan comes and says, "Look at that black list of your weaknesses and infirmities! You can never expect to be in that calling!"

Yes, you can, beloved! God says it in the Scriptures. Oh, beloved, it is weakness that is made strong (2 Cor. 12:9). It is the last who can be made first (Matt. 19:30). What will make the whole situation different? Confessing our helplessness. God says that He feeds the hungry with good things, but the satisfied He sends away empty (Luke 1:53). If you want to grow in grace and in the knowledge of the grace of God, get hungry enough to be fed; get thirsty enough to cry out; be broken enough that you do not want anything in the world unless He comes Himself.

Let God comfort your heart. Let Him strengthen your weakness. Let Him cause you to come into the place of profit. Let Him help you into the place He has chosen for you, for *"many are called, but few are chosen"* (Matt. 22:14). But God has a big choice.

Thought for today: I am glad I cannot measure Jesus, but I am glad I can touch Him all the same.

The Measure of Christ's Gift

*To each one of us grace was given according to
the measure of Christ's gift.*
—Ephesians 4:7

Scripture reading: Romans 12

Grace and gifts are equally abounding in Jesus. As you place your strength on Jesus, as you allow the Holy Spirit to penetrate every thought, always bringing on the canvas of the mind a perfect picture of holiness, purity, and righteousness, you enter into Him and become entitled to all the riches of God.

How do you measure up today? God gives a measure. *"To each one of us grace was given according to the measure of Christ's gift."*

I know that salvation, while it is a perfect work, is an insulation that may have any number of volts behind it. In the days when bare wires were laid, when electric power was obtained from Niagara, I am told that there was a city whose lights suddenly went out. Following the wires, the repairmen came to a place where a cat had gotten on the wires, and the lights had been stopped.

I find that the dynamo of heaven can be stopped with a smaller thing than a cat. An impure thought stops the circulation. An act can stop the growth of the believer.

So I find that if I am going to have all the revelations of Jesus brought to me, I must strive for all that God has for me through a pure and clean heart, right thoughts, and an inward affection toward Him. Then heaven bursts through my human frame, and all the rays of heaven flow through my body. Hallelujah! It is lovely!

The measure of the gift of Christ remains with you. I cannot go on with inspiration unless I am going on with God in perfection. I cannot know the mind of the natural and the mysteries of the hidden things with God unless I have power to penetrate everything between me and heaven. And there is nothing that goes through but a pure heart, for the pure in heart will see God (Matt. 5:8).

Thought for today: We must let Him be enthroned, and then He will lift us to the throne.

God Perfects His People

When He ascended on high, He led captivity captive,
and gave gifts to men.
—Ephesians 4:8

Scripture reading: 1 Thessalonians 4:1–12

God has gifts for men. You ask, "What kind of men?" Even for rebels. Did they desire to be rebels? No. Sometimes there are transgressions that break our hearts and make us groan and travail. Was it our desire to sin? No. God looks right at the very canvas of our whole life histories, and He has set His mind upon us.

Your weakness has to be sifted like the chaff before the wind, and every seed will bring forth pure grain after God's mind. The fire will burn like an oven to burn up the stubble (Mal. 4:1), but the wheat will be gathered into the granary, the treasury of the Most High God, and He Himself will lay hold of us.

What is this process for? The perfecting of the saints. (See Ephesians 4:11–12.) Oh, just think—that brokenness of yours is to be made whole like Him; that weakness of yours is to be made strong like Him! You have to bear the image of the Lord in every detail. You have to have the mind of Christ (Phil. 2:5) in perfection, in beauty.

Beloved, don't fail and shrivel up because of the hand of God upon you, but realize that God must purify you for the perfecting of the saints. Oh, Jesus will help you. Friend, what are you going to do with this golden opportunity, with this inward pressure of a cry of God in your soul? Are you going to let others be crowned while you lose the crown? Are you willing to be brought into captivity today for God?

You must decide some things. If you are not baptized, you must seek the baptism of the Spirit of God. And if there is anything that has marred the fruit or interfered with all of His plan, I implore you to let the blood so cover, let the anointing of Christ so come, let the vision of Christ be so seen, that you will have a measure that will take all that God has for you.

Thought for today: There are no *but*s in the sanctification of the Spirit. *But* and *if* are gone, replaced with *shall* and *will*.

August 13

The Word of God in Us

Clearly you are an epistle of Christ.
—2 Corinthians 3:3

Scripture reading: Colossians 3:12–25

Think about these words: *"Clearly you are an epistle of Christ."* What an ideal position that now the sons of God are being manifested; now the glory is being seen; now the Word of God is becoming an expressed purpose in life until the Word has begun to live in God's children.

This position was truly evident in the life of Paul when he came to a climax and said, *"I have been crucified with Christ; it is no longer I who live, but Christ lives in me; and the life which I now live in the flesh I live by faith in the Son of God"* (Gal. 2:20).

How can Christ live in you? There is no way for Christ to live in you except by the manifested Word in you, declaring every day that you are a living epistle of the Word of God.

It is the living Christ; it is the divine likeness to God; it is the express image of Him. The Word is the only factor that works out and brings forth in you these glories of identification between you and Christ. It is the Word richly dwelling in your hearts by faith (Col. 3:16).

We may begin at Genesis and go right through the Scriptures and be able to recite them, but unless they are a living power within us, they will be a dead letter. Everything that comes to us must be quickened by the Spirit. *"The letter kills, but the Spirit gives life"* (2 Cor. 3:6).

We must have life in everything. Who knows how to pray except as the Spirit prays (Rom. 8:26)? What kind of prayer does the Spirit pray? The Spirit always brings to your remembrance the Scriptures, and He brings forth all your cries and your needs better than your words. The Spirit always takes the Word of God and brings your heart, mind, soul, cry, and need into the presence of God.

So we are not able to pray except as the Spirit prays, and the Spirit only prays according to the will of God (v. 27), and the will of God is all in the Word of God. No man is able to speak according to the mind of God and bring forth the deep things of God by his own mind.

345

God, help us to understand this, for it is out of the heart that all things proceed (Matt. 12:34). When we have entered in with God into the mind of the Spirit, we will find that God enraptures our hearts.

"Or do you think that the Scripture says in vain, 'The Spirit who dwells in us yearns jealously'?" (James 4:5). I have been pondering over that verse for years, but now I can see that the Holy Spirit very graciously, very extravagantly, puts everything to one side so that He may enrapture our hearts with a great inward cry for Jesus. The Holy Spirit *"yearns jealously"* for us to have all the divine will of God in Christ Jesus right in our hearts.

When I speak about the *"tablets of flesh, that is, of the heart"* (2 Cor. 3:3), I mean the inward love. Nothing is as sweet to me as to know that the heart yearns with compassion. Eyes may see, ears may hear, but you may be immovable on those two lines unless you have an inward cry where *"deep calls unto deep"* (Ps. 42:7).

When God gets into the depths of our hearts, He purifies every intention of the thoughts and the joys. We are told in the Word that it is *"joy inexpressible and full of glory"* (1 Pet. 1:8).

Beloved, it is true that the commandments were written on tablets of stone. Moses, like a great big loving father over Israel, had a heart full of joy because God had shown him a plan by which Israel could partake of great things through these commandments. But God says that now the epistle of Christ is *"not on tablets of stone"* (2 Cor. 3:3), which made the face of Moses shine with great joy. It is deeper than that, more wonderful than that: the commandments are in our hearts; the deep love of God is in our hearts; the deep movings of eternity are rolling in and bringing God in. Hallelujah!

Oh, beloved, let God the Holy Spirit have His way today in unfolding to us all the grandeur of His glory. Yes, He is mine! Beloved, He is mine!

Thought for today: No one is perfected or equipped in any area except as the living Word abides in him.

August 14

Our Trust Must Be in God

We have such trust through Christ toward God.
—2 Corinthians 3:4

Scripture reading: Psalm 37

We need to get to a place where we are beyond trusting in ourselves. It is not bad to have self-confidence, but we must never rest upon anything in the human. The only sure place to rest is where you are trusting fully in God.

In His name we go. In Him we trust. And God brings us the victory. When we do not trust in ourselves, but when our whole trust rests upon the authority of the mighty God, He has promised to be with us at all times, to make the path straight, and to make a way through all the mountains. Then we understand how it was that David could say, *"Your gentleness has made me great"* (2 Sam. 22:36).

Ah, God is the lover of souls! We have no confidence in the flesh. Our confidence can only be placed in and rest upon the One who never fails, the One who knows the end from the beginning, the One who is able to come in at the midnight hour as easily as at midday. In fact, God makes the night and the day alike to the person who rests completely in His will with the knowledge that *"all things work together for good to those who love God"* (Rom. 8:28) and trust in Him. And we have such trust in Him.

This is the worthy position; this is where God wants all souls to be. We would find that we would not run His errands and make mistakes; we would not be settling down in the wrong place. We would know that our lives were as surely in agreement with the thoughts of God as the leading of the children of Israel through the wilderness. And we would be able to say, "Not one good thing has the Lord withheld from me" (Ps. 84:11), and *"All the promises of God in Him are Yes, and in Him Amen, to the glory of God through us"* (2 Cor. 1:20).

May the Lord help you to have less confidence in yourself, and to trust wholly in Him. Bless His name!

Thought for today: There is so much failure in self-assurance.

Living in the Spirit

The letter kills, but the Spirit gives life.
—2 Corinthians 3:6

Scripture reading: John 6:53–71

As I go on with God, He wants me to understand all His deep things. We cannot define, separate, or deeply investigate and unfold this holy plan of God unless we have the life of God, the thought of God, the Spirit of God, and the revelation of God. The Word of Truth is pure, spiritual, and divine. If you try to discern it without the help of the Spirit, you will end up with a limited, human understanding.

People who are spiritual can only be fed with spiritual food. We must see that we not only need the baptism of the Spirit, but we also need to come to a place where there is only the baptism of the Spirit left. In John's gospel, Jesus says He does not speak or act of Himself: *"The words that I speak to you I do not speak on My own authority; but the Father who dwells in Me does the works"* (John 14:10).

We must know that the baptism of the Spirit immerses us into an intensity of zeal, into a likeness to Jesus; it makes us into pure, liquid metal so hot for God that it travels like oil from vessel to vessel. This divine life of the Spirit will let us see that we have ceased, yet we have begun. We are at the end for a beginning.

God, help us to see that we may be filled with the letter without being filled with the Spirit. We may be filled with knowledge without having divine knowledge. And we may be filled with wonderful natural things and still remain natural men. But we cannot remain natural men in this truth that I am dealing with here. No one is able to walk this way unless he is in the Spirit. He must live in the Spirit, and he must realize all the time that he is growing in that same ideal of his Master, *"in season and out of season"* (2 Tim. 4:2), always beholding the face of the Master, Jesus (Matt. 18:10).

Thought for today: We can understand the Word of God only by the Spirit of God.

Delight to Do God's Will

How will the ministry of the Spirit not be more glorious?
—2 Corinthians 3:8

Scripture reading: 1 Peter 1:13–25

May the Lord help us to understand His word. I see the truth as it was brought to the Israelites in the law. Paul had something to glory in when he kept the law and was blameless, but he said he threw that to one side to win Him who is even greater than that (Phil. 3:8).

Now we come to the question: what is in the law that isn't glorious? Nothing. It was so glorious that Moses was filled with joy in the expectation of what it was. But what is ours in the excellence of glory? It is this: we live, we move, we reign over all things. It is not "Do, do, do"; it is "Will, will, will." I rejoice to do. It is no longer "Thou shalt not"; it is "I will." *"I delight to do Your will, O my God"* (Ps. 40:8). So the glory is far exceeding. And, beloved, in our hearts there is exceeding glory. Oh, the joy of this celestial touch!

Oh yes, the glory is exceeding. The glory is excellent. When Peter was describing that wonderful day on the Mount of Transfiguration, he said, *"Such a voice came to Him* [Christ] *from the Excellent Glory"* (2 Pet. 1:17). And so we are hearing from the Excellent Glory. It is so lovely.

If I were to say to you, "Whatever you do, you must try to exercise self-control in order to be holy," I would miss it. I would be altogether outside of His plan. But by the Holy Spirit, I take the words of the epistle that says, *"Be holy"* (1 Pet. 1:16). For when you lose your heart and Another takes your heart, and you lose your desires and He takes the desires, then you live in that sunshine of bliss that no mortal can ever touch.

Divine immortality swallows up all natural mortality. It is lovely to walk in the Spirit; then we will not fulfill any part of the law without the Spirit causing us to dwell in safety, rejoice inwardly, praise God reverently, and know that we are an increasing force of immortality swallowing up life. Hallelujah!

Thought for today: It is as easy as possible to be holy, but you can never be holy by trying to be.

August 17

Beautiful Righteousness

For if the ministry of condemnation had glory, the ministry of righteousness exceeds much more in glory.
—2 Corinthians 3:9

Scripture reading: Psalm 11

Nothing is as beautiful as righteousness. All the excellent glory is in Him. All righteousness is in Him. Everything that pertains to holiness and godliness, everything that denounces and brings to death the carnal, everything that makes you know you have ceased to be forever, is found in the knowledge of the endless power in the risen Christ. As Paul wrote, *"If anyone is in Christ, he is a new creation; old things have passed away; behold, all things have become new"* (2 Cor. 5:17).

When you come to the very essence of Christ's ministry, you see the righteousness of His purpose. The excellence of His ministry was the glory that covered Him. His Word was convincing, inflexible, divine, and eternal. It never failed.

Oh, the righteousness of God. If Christ said it, it was there. He said it, and it stood fast (Ps. 33:9). It was an unchangeable condition with Him. When God spoke, it was done (v. 9). And His righteousness abides. God must have us in this place of righteousness. We must be people of our word. People ought to be able to depend on our word. God is establishing righteousness in our hearts so that we will not exaggerate about anything.

Jesus was true inwardly and outwardly. He is *"the way, the truth, and the life"* (John 14:6), and on these things we can build; on these things we can pray; on these things we can live. When we know that our own hearts do not condemn us (1 John 3:21), we can say to the mountain, *"Be removed"* (Matt. 21:21). But when our own hearts condemn us, there is no power in prayer, no power in preaching, no power in anything. We are just sounding brass and clanging cymbals (1 Cor. 13:1).

May God the Holy Spirit show us there must be a ministry of righteousness. We ought to stand by our word and abide by it. If we were cut in two, our persecutors should find pure gold right through us. That is what I call righteousness. Jesus was righteousness through and through. He is lovely! Oh, truly, He is beautiful!

August 17

One thing God wants to establish in our hearts is the importance of being like Him. Be like Him in character. Don't be troubled so much about your outward appearance, but be more concerned about your heart. Makeup won't change the heart. All the adorning of silks and satins won't create purity. Beloved, if I was going down a road and I saw a foxtail sticking out of a hole, I wouldn't ask anybody what was inside. And if there is anything hanging outside of us, we know what is inside. God wants righteousness in the inward parts, purity through and through.

The Bible is the plumb line of everything. And so, may God the Holy Spirit bring us into that blessed ministry of righteousness. Amen! Glory to God!

Thought for today: Unless we are lined right up with the Word of God, we will fail in the measure in which we are not righteous.

A Heavenly Citizenship

For our citizenship is in heaven.
—Philippians 3:20

Scripture reading: Philippians 3

*T*he law is truly *"our tutor to bring us to Christ, that we might be justified by faith"* (Gal. 3:24). I am glad that laws are established on the earth. Law is good when it helps to keep things in order in society.

But, beloved, we belong to a higher, nobler citizenship, and it isn't an earthly citizenship, for *"our citizenship is in heaven"* (Phil. 3:20). So we must see that there is an excellent glory about this position we are holding in Christ. For if the natural law will keep an earthly city in somewhat moderate conditions, what will the excellent glory be in the divine relationship of the citizenship to which we belong?

All those who are getting ready for this glorious eternity have a consciousness of God within. God is working to change their very natures, preparing them for greater things. There is only perfect purification in looking upward to God. All the saints of God who get the real vision of this wonderful transformation are seeing every day that the world is getting worse and worse. It is ripening for Judgment. God is bringing us to a place where we who are spiritual are have a clear vision that we must, at any cost, put off the works of darkness; we must be getting ourselves ready for the glorious Day—the excellent glory.

I call it an excellent glory because it outshines everything else. It makes all the people feel a longing to go to heaven. What there is about the excellent glory is this: the earth is filled with broken hearts, but the excellent glory is filled with redeemed men and women, filled with the excellency of the graces of the glory of God. Oh, the excellent glory is marvelous! Ah, praise the Lord, O my soul! Hallelujah!

Thought for today: There is no gravity to the spirit. There is no gravity to thought. There is no gravity to inspiration. There is no gravity to divine union with Christ. It is above all; it rises higher; it sits on the throne; it claims it purposes.

August 19

The Proper Use of Liberty

Where the Spirit of the Lord is, there is liberty.
—2 Corinthians 3:17

Scripture reading: Galatians 5:1–15

We must never abuse liberty; we must be in the place where liberty can use us. If we misuse liberty, we will be as dead as possible, and our efforts will all end with a fizzle. But if we are in the Spirit, the Lord of Life is the same Spirit. I believe it is right to jump for joy, but don't jump until the joy makes you jump, because if you do, you will jump flat. If you jump as the joy makes you jump, you will bounce up again.

In the Spirit, there is a divine plan. If Pentecostal people come into this plan in meekness and in the true knowledge of God, every heart in each meeting will be moved by the Spirit.

Liberty has many aspects to it, but no liberty is going to help people as much as testimony. I find people who don't know how to testify properly. We must testify only as the Spirit gives utterance. We find in the book of Revelation that *"the testimony of Jesus is the spirit of prophecy"* (Rev. 19:10).

Sometimes our flesh keeps us down, but our hearts are so full that they lift us up. Have you ever been like that? The flesh is fastening you to your seat, but your heart is bubbling over. At last the heart has more power, and you stand up. Then in that heart affection for Jesus, in the Spirit of love and in the knowledge of truth, you begin to testify, and when you are done, you sit down. Liberty used wrongly goes on after you have finished saying what God wants you to say, and it spoils the meeting. Do not use your liberty except for the glory of God.

So many churches are spoiled by long prayers and long testimonies. If he stays in the Spirit, the speaker can tell when he should sit down. When you begin to speak your own words, people get tired and wish that you would sit down. The anointing ceases, and you sit down worse than when you rose up.

It is nice for a person to begin cold and warm up as he goes on. When he catches fire and sits down in the midst of it, he will keep the fire afterward. Look! It is lovely to pray, and it is a joy to hear

353

you pray, but when you go on and on after you are truly done, all the people get tired of it.

This excellent glory should go on to a liberality to everybody, and this would prove that all the church is in liberty. The church ought to be free so that the people always go away feeling, "Oh, I wish the meeting had gone on for another hour," or "What a glorious time we had at that prayer meeting!" or "Wasn't that testimony meeting a revelation!" That is the way to finish up. Never finish up with something too long; finish up with something too short. Then everybody comes again eager to pick up where they left off.

Thought for today: We are not to use liberty because we have it to use, but we are to let the liberty use us.

August 20

From Glory to Glory

*But we all, with unveiled face, beholding as in a mirror the glory of
the Lord, are being transformed into the same image from glory to
glory, just as by the Spirit of the Lord.*
—2 Corinthians 3:18

Scripture reading: Psalm 34

There are glories upon glories, and joys upon joys, exceeding
joys and an abundance of joys, and a measureless measure.
Beloved, when we get the Word so wonderfully into our
hearts, it absolutely changes us in everything. As we feast on the
Word of the Lord, eat and digest the truth, inwardly eat of Him, we
are absolutely changed every day from one state of grace to another.

Look into the perfect mirror of the face of the Lord, and you
will be changed *"from glory to glory."* You will never find anything
else except the Word of God to take you there. So you cannot afford
to put aside the Word.

I implore you, beloved, that you do not come short in your own
lives of any of these blessed teachings we have been sharing. These
grand truths of the Word of God must be your testimony, must be
your life, must be your pattern. You must be in the Word; in fact,
you are of the Word. God says to you by the Spirit that *"you are an
epistle of Christ"* (2 Cor. 3:3). Let us see to it that we put off everything so that by the grace of God we may put on everything.

Where there is a standard that hasn't been reached in your
life, God, in His grace, by His mercy and your yieldedness, can
equip you for that place. He can prepare you for that place that you
can never be prepared for except by a broken heart and a contrite
spirit, except by yielding to the will of God. If you will come with a
whole heart to the throne of grace, God will meet you and build you
on His spiritual plane. Amen. Praise the Lord!

Thought for today: Give Him all; let Him have all: your heart's
joy, your very life. Let Him have it. He is worthy. He is King of
Kings. He is Lord of Lords. He is my Savior. He died to deliver me.
He should have the crown.

August 21

The Hope of Glory

We have access by faith into this grace in which we stand,
and rejoice in hope of the glory of God.
—Romans 5:2

Scripture reading: John 7

*Y*ou must know where you are going. The great, mighty master-piece of all is the great plan of the Rapture. It is the hope of glory, divine life, the peace of God, and the enrichment of the soul. It is *"poured out in our hearts by the Holy Spirit"* (Rom. 5:5).

The Holy Spirit is the manifestation of God's Son. He is so uniquely divine that He has the power to overcome. His power is pure. His power must not cease to develop. The Holy Spirit is there to create development and to help us progress in our faith as the Lord would have us to.

We are saved by His life. Now that we have received salvation, He wants to open our eyes to understand what Christ really did for us. *"In due time"* (v. 6), when there was no other to save us, when there was no hope, when the law had failed, Christ took our place, delivered us from all the powers of human weaknesses and failure, and so came to us in our sins. He reached out to us in love *"while we were still sinners"* (v. 8). At just the right moment, He died for us and delivered us from the power of the Devil, delivered us from death, delivered us from sin, delivered us from the grave, and gave us a hope of immortality through His life. We are saved by His life.

Jesus is eternal. He has the power to impart eternal gifts. He has delivered us from the curse of the law and set us free. Who loves the Gospel as much as those who have been saved? What is the Gospel? It is *"the power of God to salvation"* (Rom. 1:16). It has the power to bring immortality and life. Through His life in us, we are delivered from all things and are being prepared for the glorious hope of the coming of the Lord. That is why we sing, "He arose! He arose! Hallelujah, Christ arose!

Thought for today: Everything in the Father's house is ours, but it will come only through obedience.

August 22

Greater Works

He who believes in Me, the works that I do he will do also; and
greater works than these he will do, because I go to My Father.
—John 14:12

Scripture reading: John 14:1–14

Why was Jesus' perspective so full? Because Jesus saw great potential in the disciples. He knew He had the material that would bring out what would prove to be a real satisfaction to the world—to heaven and to the world. The glorified, trained, wonderfully modified, and then again glorified positions of these fishermen were surely ideal places in which to be.

What were the disciples? For one thing, they were unlearned. However, God taught them. It is far better to have the learning of the Spirit than anything else. They were ignorant; He enlarged them. They were beside themselves because they had been touched with the divine life. If the Most High God touches you, you will be beside yourself. As long as you hold your own, the natural and the spiritual will be mixed; but if you ever jump over the lines by the power of the new creation, you will find He has gotten a hold of you.

Divine wisdom will never make you foolish. Divine wisdom will give you a sound mind; divine wisdom will give you a touch of divine nature. Divine life is full of divine appointment and equipping, and you cannot be filled with the power of God without a manifestation. It is my prayer that we would understand that to be filled with the Holy Spirit is to be filled with manifestation, the glory of the Lord being in the midst of us, manifesting His divine power.

Jesus knew that these people He had before Him were going to do greater things than He had done. How could they do them? None of us is able; none of us is capable. But as we believe in Him, we can do greater works because He is in heaven interceding for us.

Thought for today: Our incapability has to be clothed with His divine ability, and our helplessness has to be filled with His power of helpfulness.

August 23

The Comfort of the Holy Spirit

I will pray the Father, and he shall give you another Comforter,
that he may abide with you for ever.
—John 14:16 KJV

Scripture reading: John 14:15–31

*J*esus knew that He was going away and that, if He went away, it was expedient, it was necessary, it was important that Another come in His place and continue guiding and teaching them as He had been (John 16:7, 14 KJV). *"You in Me, and I in you"* (John 14:20). There was a plan of divine order. So the Holy Spirit was to come.

I want you to see what has to take place when the Holy Spirit comes:

> *And I will pray the Father, and he shall give you another Comforter, that he may abide with you for ever; even the Spirit of truth; whom the world cannot receive, because it seeth him not, neither knoweth him: but ye know him; for he dwelleth with you, and shall be in you. I will not leave you comfortless: I will come to you.* (John 14:16–18 KJV)

I don't know a word that could be as fitting at this time as this word *"Comforter."* I want to take you with me into the coming of this Holy Spirit.

After Jesus ascended to heaven, He asked the Father to send the Comforter. It was a needy moment, a needy hour, a necessity. Why? Because the disciples would need comforting.

How could they be comforted? The Holy Spirit would take the word of Christ and reveal it to them (John 16:14). What could help them as much as a word by the Spirit? For the Spirit is breath, is life, is person, is power. He gives the breath of Himself to us, the nature of Him. How beautiful that, when the Spirit came, He should be called the *"Spirit of truth"* (John 14:17). Oh, if we would only let that truth sink deep into our hearts!

Some people have wondered that if they were to ask for the baptism of the Holy Spirit, if an evil power could come instead or if an evil power could possess them while they were waiting for the

358

Holy Spirit. No! When you receive the Holy Spirit, you receive the Spirit of Truth, the Spirit who gives revelation, the Spirit who takes the words of Jesus and makes them life to you. In your moment of need, He is the Comforter.

Thought for today: When the Holy Spirit comes into your body, He comes to unveil the King, to assure you of His presence.

The Work of the Holy Spirit

He will take of Mine and declare it to you.
—John 16:15

Scripture reading: John 16:5–15

What will the Holy Spirit do? The Holy Spirit is prophetic. He says, *"Be of good cheer"* (John 16:33); *"Take My yoke upon you and learn from Me"* (Matt. 11:29); *"Have peace with one another"* (Mark 9:50). You say, "But that is what Jesus said." It is what the Holy Spirit is taking and revealing to us. The Holy Spirit is the spokesman in these days, and He speaks the Word. The Holy Spirit takes the words of Jesus, and He is so full of truth that He never adds anything to them. He gives you the unadulterated Word of Truth, the Word of Life.

What are His words? Truths like these: *"I am the light of the world"* (John 8:12); *"For God did not send His Son into the world to condemn the world, but that the world through Him might be saved"* (John 3:17); and *"Come to Me, all you who labor and are heavy laden, and I will give you rest"* (Matt. 11:28). The Holy Spirit takes these words and gives them to you.

The Holy Spirit, the Spirit of Truth, is bringing forth the Word of Life. *"I will give you rest."* Rest? Oh, there is no rest like it! It can come in your moment of greatest trial.

When my dear wife was lying dead, the doctors could do nothing, and they said to me, "She is done; we cannot help you." My heart was so moved, and I said, "O God, I can't spare her!"

I went up to her and I said, "Oh, come back, come back and speak to me. Come back, come back!"

And the Spirit of the Lord moved, and she came back and smiled again.

Then the Holy Spirit said to me, "She is mine. Her work is done; she is mine."

Oh, the comforting word! No one else could have done it, but the Comforter came. At that moment, my dear wife passed away.

Thought for today: The Comforter has a word for us this day. There is only one Comforter, and He has been with the Father from the beginning. He comes only to give light.

Be Specific in What You Ask

One thing I have desired of the LORD, that will I seek.
—Psalm 27:4

Scripture reading: Psalm 27

*T*he person who says "I am ready for anything" will never get it. "What are you seeking, my brother?" "Oh, I am ready for anything." You will never get *anything*.

When the Lord reveals to you that you must be filled with the Holy Spirit, seek only that one thing, and God will give you that one thing. It is necessary for you to seek one thing first.

Never forget, the baptism will always be as it was in the beginning. It has not changed. And if you want a real baptism, expect it to be just the same as the early believers had it at the beginning.

"What did they have at the beginning?" you ask.

Well, they knew when others had the same experience they had had at the beginning, for they heard them speak in tongues. That is the only way they did know, because they heard the others saying the same things in the Spirit that they had said at the beginning. As it was in the beginning, so it will be forever.

I do not say anything against ordination; I think that is very good. However, there is an ordination that is better, and it is the ordination with the King. This is the only ordination that is going to equip you for the future.

The person who has passed through that ordination goes forth with fresh feet—the preparation of the Gospel (Eph. 6:15); he goes forth with a fresh voice, speaking as the Spirit gives utterance (Acts 2:4); he goes forth with a fresh mind, his mind being illuminated by the power of God (see Hebrews 8:10); he goes forth with a fresh vision and sees all things new. (See 2 Corinthians 5:17.)

When the Holy Spirit comes, He will reveal things to you. Has He revealed them yet? He is going to do it. Just expect Him to do so. The best thing for you is to expect Him to do it now.

Thought for today: The King is already on His throne, but He needs crowning; when the Holy Spirit comes, He crowns the King inside of us.

August 26

Overcoming Hindrances

*They were all filled with the Holy Spirit and began
to speak with other tongues.*
—Acts 2:4

Scripture reading: Acts 2:1–41

xpect any manifestation of the Spirit when you are coming through into the baptism. As far as I am concerned, you can have the biggest time on earth; you can scream as much as you like. Yet some people are wary of how they will react.

A woman in Switzerland came to me after I had helped her and asked to speak to me further. "Now that I feel I am healed," she said, "and that terrible carnal passion that has bound and hindered me is gone, I feel that I have a new mind. I believe I would like to receive the Holy Spirit, but when I hear these people screaming, I feel like running away."

After that, we were at another meeting in Switzerland where a large hotel was joined to the building. At the close of one of the morning services, the power of God fell—that is the only way I can describe it, the power of God *fell*. This poor, timid creature who couldn't bear to hear anybody scream, screamed so loud that all the waiters in this big hotel came out with their aprons on and with their trays to see what was up. Nothing was especially up. Something had come down, and it had so altered the situation that this woman could stand anything after that.

When God begins dealing with you on the baptism, He begins on this line: He starts with the things that are the most difficult. He starts with your fear; He starts with your human nature. He puts the fear away; He gets the human nature out of the way. And just as you dissolve, just as the power of the Spirit brings a dissolving to your human nature, in the same act the Holy Spirit flows into the place where you are being dissolved, and you are quickened just where you come into death.

Thought for today: As you die—naturally, humanly, carnally, selfishly—to every evil thing, the new life, the Holy Spirit, floods the whole condition until you become transformed.

August 27

Controlled by the Holy Spirit

No man can tame the tongue.
—James 3:8

Scripture reading: Psalm 19

When the Holy Spirit begins, He tames the whole body until the tongue, moved by the power of the Spirit, says things exactly as the Lord would be delighted for them to be said.

The Holy Spirit is the Comforter; the Holy Spirit takes the necessary words at the right time and gives them to you. After the Holy Spirit takes charge of you, He is the Comforter who brings thoughts and language to your life, and it is amazing.

If we get to the place where we take no thought for ourselves, then God takes thought for us; but as long as we are taking thought for ourselves, we are somewhat hindered in this divine order with God. Taking no thought for yourself, no desire for your human self, not seeking anything for your human condition but that God will be glorified in your body and spirit and that He will be the chief Worker on every line—this is divine appointment. This is holy order.

There is a holy order. There are sects today that call themselves "holy orders," but the only holy order is where God has so permeated your nature that the Trinity comes and blends perfectly with your human nature. Where the human nature could not help itself, God turned the captivity of the wheels of nature and poured in His divine power until the nature itself became divine property.

Thought for today: I must never, under any circumstances, as long as I live, take advantage of God or Jesus or the Holy Spirit. I have to be subservient to the power of God.

August 28

You Have an Anointing

But you have an anointing from the Holy One.
—1 John 2:20

Scripture reading: 1 John 2:15–29

A nother of the roles of the Holy Spirit that is necessary for today we find in John 14:26:

But the Comforter, which is the Holy [Spirit], *whom the Father will send in my name, he shall teach you all things, and bring all things to your remembrance, whatsoever I have said unto you.* (KJV)

Jesus said something very similar in a later chapter: *"He will take of what is Mine and declare* [reveal] *it to you"* (John 16:14). Everything that has been revealed to you was first taken. So, first, the Holy Spirit takes of what is Christ's and reveals it to you. Then you come to the place where you need another touch. What is it? In the necessity of your ministry, He will bring to your remembrance everything that you need in your ministry. That is an important thing for preachers. God will give us His Word, and if there is anything special we need, He will bring that to our memories, too. The Holy Spirit comes to bring the Word to our remembrance.

I will throw this word out to you as a help for future reflection: *"You shall receive power"* (Acts 1:8). Oh, may God grant that we will not forget it!

What do I mean by that? Many people, instead of standing on the rock-solid word of faith and believing that they have received the baptism with its anointing and power, say, "Oh, if I could only feel that I have received it!"

Very often, your feelings are a place of discouragement. You have to get away from relying on human feelings or desires. Earthly desires are not God's desires. All thoughts of holiness, all thoughts of purity, all thoughts of power from the Holy Spirit are from above. Human thoughts are like clouds that belong to the earth. *"[God's] thoughts are not* [our] *thoughts"* (Isa. 55:8).

Thought for today: Your feelings rob you of your greatest place of anointing.

August 29

A Powerful Anointing

God anointed Jesus...with the Holy Spirit and with power.
—Acts 10:38

Scripture reading: Acts 10:24–48

*S*uppose that all around me are people with needs: a woman is dying; a man has lost all the powers of his faculties; another person is apparently dying. Here they are. I see the great need, and I drop down on my knees and cry. Yet in doing so, I miss it all.

God does not want me to cry. God does not want me to labor. God does not want me to anguish and to be filled with anxiety and a sorrowful spirit. What does He want me to do? Only believe. After you have received, only believe. Come to the authority of it; dare to believe. Say, "I will do it!"

So the baptism of the Holy Spirit says to me, *"You have an anointing"* (1 John 2:20). The anointing has come; the anointing remains; the anointing is with us. But what if you have not lived in the place in which the unction, the anointing, can be increased? Then the Spirit is grieved; then you are not moved. You are like one who is dead. You feel that all the joy is gone.

What is the matter? There is something between you and the Holy One; you are not clean, not pure, not desirous of Him alone. Something else has come in the way. Then the Spirit is grieved, and you have lost the unction.

Is the Unctioner still there? Yes. When He comes in, He comes to remain. He will either be grieved, full of groaning and travail, or He will be there to lift you above the powers of darkness, transform you by His power, and take you to a place where you may be fully equipped.

Many people lose all potential positions of attainment because they fail to understand this:

> But the anointing which you have received from Him abides in you, and you do not need that anyone teach you; but as the same anointing teaches you concerning all things, and is true, and is not a lie, and just as it has taught you, you will abide in Him. (1 John 2:27)

365

What *"anointing"* is referred to here? The same anointing from God that anointed Jesus is with you, *"and you do not need that anyone teach you."* The same anointing will teach you all things.

O lovely Jesus! Blessed Incarnation of holy display! Thank God for the Trinity displayed in our hearts today. Thank God for this glorious open way. Thank God for life all along the way. Praise God for hope that we may all be changed today. Hallelujah!

> Peace, peace, sweet peace,
> Coming down from the Father above,
> Peace, peace, wonderful peace,
> Sweet peace, the gift of God's love.

This is the very position and presence that will bring everybody into a fullness.

Thought for today: Thank God for darkness that is turning into day.

A Good Foundation

Being rooted and grounded in love.
—Ephesians 2:11–22

Scripture reading: Ephesians 2:11–22

*I*t is quite easy to construct a building if the foundation is secure. On the other hand, a building will be unstable if it does not have a solid understructure. Likewise, it is not very easy to rise spiritually unless we have a real spiritual power working within us. It will never do for us to be top-heavy—the base must always be very firmly set. Many of us have not gone on in the Lord because we have not had a secure foundation in Him, and we will have to consider *"the pit from which* [we] *were dug"* (Isa. 51:1). Unless we correctly understand the spiritual leadings, according to the mind of God, we will never be able to stand when the winds blow, when the trials come, and when Satan appears as *"an angel of light"* (2 Cor. 11:14).

There must be three things in our lives if we wish to go all the way with God in the fullness of Pentecost. First, we must be grounded and settled in love; we must have a real knowledge of what love is. Second, we must have a clear understanding of the Word, for love must manifest the Word. Third, we must clearly understand our own ground, because it is our own ground that needs to be looked after the most.

The Lord speaks at least twice of the good ground into which seed was sown, which also bore fruit and brought forth some hundredfold, some sixty, and some thirty (Matt. 13:8; Mark 4:8). Even in the good ground, the seed yielded different portions of fruit. I maintain truly that there is no limitation to the abundance of a harvest when the ground is perfectly in the hands of the Lord. So we must clearly understand that the Word of God can never come forth with all its primary purposes unless our ground is right. But God will help us, I believe, to see that He can put the ground in perfect order as it is left in His hands.

Thought for today: We will never be able to stand unless we are firmly fixed in the Word of God.

August 31

The More Excellent Way

Pursue love.
—1 Corinthians 14:1

Scripture reading: 1 Corinthians 13

*W*hen love is in perfect operation, all other things will work in harmony, for prophetic utterances are of no value unless they are perfectly covered with divine love. Our Lord Jesus would never have accomplished His great plan in this world except that He was so full of love for His Father, and love for us, that His love never failed to accomplish its purpose.

I believe that His love will have to come into our lives. Christ must be the summit, the desire, the plan of all things. All our sayings, doings, and workings must be well pleasing in and to Him, and then our prophetic utterances will be a blessing through God; they will never be side issues. There is no imitation in a man filled with the Holy Spirit. Imitation is lost as the great plan of Christ becomes the ideal of his life.

God wants you to be balanced in spiritual anointing so that you will always do what pleases Him, and not what will please other people or yourself. The ideal must be that all you do will be edifying, and your primary purpose will be to please the Lord.

When someone came to Moses and said that there were two others in the camp prophesying, Moses said, *"Oh, that all the Lord's people were prophets"* (Num. 11:29). This is a clear revelation along these lines that God wants us to be in such a spiritual, holy place that He could take our words and so fill them with divine power that we would speak only as the Spirit leads in prophetic utterances.

Beloved, there is spiritual language, and there is also human language, which always stays on the human plane. The divine comes into the same language so that it is changed by spiritual power and brings life to those who hear you speak. But this divine touch of prophecy will never come in any way except through the infilling of the Spirit.

Thought for today: If you wish to be anything for God, do not miss His plan.

September 1

Speech That Edifies

And it shall come to pass afterward that I will pour out My Spirit on all flesh; your sons and your daughters shall prophesy, your old men shall dream dreams, your young men shall see visions. And also on My menservants and on My maidservants I will pour out My Spirit in those days.
—Joel 2:28–29

Scripture reading: 1 Corinthians 14:1–25

We know that the prophecy spoken by Joel was fulfilled on the Day of Pentecost. This was the first outpouring of the Spirit, but what would it be like now if we would only wake up to the words of our Master, *"Greater works than these [you] will do, because I go to My Father"* (John 14:12)?

Hear what the Scripture says to us: *"However, when He, the Spirit of truth, has come, He will guide you into all truth; for He will not speak on His own authority, but whatever He hears He will speak"* (John 16:13). The Holy Spirit is inspiration; the Holy Spirit is revelation; the Holy Spirit is manifestation; the Holy Spirit is operation. When a man comes into the fullness of the Holy Spirit, he is in perfect order, built up on scriptural foundations.

I have failed to see anyone understand 1 Corinthians 12–14 unless he has been baptized with the Holy Spirit. He may talk about the Holy Spirit and the gifts, but his understanding is only a superficial one. However, when he gets baptized with the Holy Spirit, he speaks about a deep inward conviction by the power of the Spirit working in him, a revelation of that Scripture. On the other hand, there is so much that a man receives when he is born again. He receives the first love and has a revelation of Jesus. *"But if we walk in the light as He is in the light, we have fellowship with one another, and the blood of Jesus Christ His Son cleanses us from all sin"* (1 John 1:7).

But God wants a man to be on fire so that he will always speak as an oracle of God. He wants to so build that man on the foundations of God that everyone who sees and hears him will say he is a new man after the order of the Spirit. *"Old things have passed away; behold, all things have become new"* (2 Cor. 5:17). New things have come, and he is now in the divine order. When a man is filled with the Holy Spirit, he has a vital power that makes people know he has seen God. He ought to be in such a place spiritually that when he goes into a neighbor's house, or out among people, they will feel that God has come into their midst.

"*He who prophesies speaks edification and exhortation and comfort to men. He who speaks in a tongue edifies himself, but he who prophesies edifies the church*" (1 Cor. 14:3–4). There are two edifications spoken of here. Which is the first? To edify yourself. After you have been edified by the Spirit, you are able to edify the church through the Spirit. What we need is more of the Holy Spirit. Oh, beloved, it is not merely a measure of the Spirit, it is a pressed-down measure. It is not merely a pressed-down measure, it is "*shaken together, and running over*" (Luke 6:38). Praise the Lord!

Thought for today: Anybody can hold a full cup, but you cannot hold an overflowing cup, and the baptism of the Holy Spirit is an overflowing cup.

Biblical Evidence of the Baptism
Part One

Did you receive the Holy Spirit when you believed?
—Acts 19:2

Scripture reading: Acts 19:1–20

*L*et me tell you about my own experience of being baptized with the Holy Spirit. It had to be something that was based on solid facts in order to move me. I was certain that I had received the Holy Spirit and absolutely rigid in this conviction. Many years ago, a man came to me and said, "Wigglesworth, do you know what is happening in Sunderland, England? People are being baptized in the Holy Spirit exactly the same way that the disciples were on the Day of Pentecost." I said, "I would like to go."

Immediately, I took a train, went to Sunderland, and met with the people who had assembled for the purpose of receiving the Holy Spirit. Continuously, I caused disturbances, until the people wished I had never come. They said that I was disrupting the conditions for people to receive the baptism. But I was hungry and thirsty for God, and had gone to Sunderland because I had heard that God was pouring out His Spirit in a new way. I had heard that God had now visited His people and manifested His power, and that people were speaking in tongues as on the Day of Pentecost.

Therefore, when I first got to Sunderland, I said to the people, "I cannot understand this meeting. I have left a meeting in Bradford all on fire for God. The fire fell last night, and we were all laid out under the power of God. I have come here for tongues, and I don't hear them—I don't hear anything."

"Oh!" they said. "When you get baptized with the Holy Spirit, you will speak in tongues."

"Oh, is that it?" I said. "When the presence of God came upon me, my tongue was loosened, and when I went in the open air to preach, I really felt that I had a new tongue."

"Ah, no," they said, "that is not it."

"What is it, then?" I asked.

"When you get baptized in the Holy Spirit—"

"I am baptized," I interjected, "and there is no one here who can persuade me that I am not baptized." So I was up against them, and they were up against me.

371

September 2

I remember a man getting up and saying, "You know, brothers and sisters, I was here three weeks and then the Lord baptized me with the Holy Spirit, and I began to speak with tongues."

I said, "Let us hear it. That's what I'm here for."

But he could not speak in tongues at will; he could only speak as the Spirit gave him the ability, and so my curiosity was not satisfied. I was doing what others are doing today, confusing the twelfth chapter of 1 Corinthians with the second chapter of Acts. These two chapters deal with different things; one deals with the gifts of the Spirit, and the other deals with the baptism of the Spirit with the accompanying sign of tongues.

I saw that these people were very earnest, and I became quite hungry for tongues. I was eager to see this new manifestation of the Spirit, and, as I said, I would be questioning all the time and spoiling a lot of the meetings. One man said to me, "I am a missionary, and I have come here to seek the baptism in the Holy Spirit. I am waiting on the Lord, but you have come in and are spoiling everything with your questions." I began to argue with him; the argument became so heated that when we walked home, he walked on one side of the road, and I walked on the other.

That night, there was to be another meeting, and I purposed to go. I changed my clothes and left my key in the clothes I had taken off. As we came from the meeting in the middle of the night, I found that I did not have my key with me, and this missionary brother said, "You will have to come and stay with me." But do you think we went to sleep that night? Oh, no, we spent the night in prayer. We received a precious shower from above. The breakfast bell rang, but that was nothing to me. For four days, I wanted nothing but God.

Thought for today: If you only knew the unspeakably wonderful blessing of being filled with the third person of the Trinity, you would set aside everything else to wait for this infilling.

September 3

Biblical Evidence of the Baptism
Part Two

Did you receive the Holy Spirit when you believed?
—Acts 19:2

Scripture reading: Mark 1:1–12

As the days passed, I became more and more hungry for God. I had opposed the meetings so much, but the Lord was gracious, and I will always remember that last day— the day I was to leave. God was with me so much. They were to have a meeting, and I went, but I could not rest. This revival was taking place at an Episcopal church. I went to the rectory to say goodbye, and I said to Sister Boddy, the rector's wife, "I cannot rest any longer; I must have these tongues."

She replied, "Brother Wigglesworth, it is not the tongues you need but the baptism. If you will allow God to baptize you, the other will be all right."

I answered, "My dear sister, I know I am baptized. You know that I have to leave here at four o'clock. Please lay hands on me so that I may receive the tongues."

She stood up and laid her hands on me, and the fire fell.

There came a persistent knock at the door, and she had to go out. That was the best thing that could have happened, for I was alone with God. Then He gave me a revelation. Oh, it was wonderful! He showed me an empty cross and Jesus glorified. I do thank God that the cross is empty, that Christ is no longer on the cross.

Then I saw that God had purified me. I was conscious of the cleansing power of the precious blood of Jesus, and I cried out, "Clean! Clean! Clean!" I was filled with the joy of knowing that I had been cleansed. As I was extolling, glorifying, and praising Him, I was speaking in tongues *"as the Spirit gave* [me] *utterance"* (Acts 2:4). I knew then that I had received the real baptism in the Holy Spirit.

It was all as beautiful and peaceful as when Jesus said, *"Peace, be still!"* (Mark 4:39). The tranquillity and the joy of that moment surpassed anything I had ever known up to that time. But hallelujah! These days have grown with greater, mightier, more wonderful divine manifestations and power. That was only the beginning.

There is no end to this kind of beginning. You will never come to the end of the Holy Spirit until you have arrived in glory—until you are right in the presence of God forever. And even then we will always be conscious of His presence.

What had I received? I had received the biblical evidence. This biblical evidence is wonderful to me. I knew I had received the very evidence of the Spirit's incoming that the apostles had received on the Day of Pentecost. I knew that everything I had had up to that time was in the nature of an anointing, bringing me in line with God in preparation. However, now I knew I had the biblical baptism in the Spirit. It had the backing of the Scriptures.

Thought for today: You are never right if you do not have a foundation for your testimony in the Word of God.

September 4

Biblical Evidence of the Baptism
Part Three

Did you receive the Holy Spirit when you believed?
—Acts 19:2

Scripture reading: Isaiah 61

When I returned home from Sunderland, my wife said to me, "So you think you have received the baptism of the Holy Spirit? Why, I am as much baptized in the Holy Spirit as you are." We had sat on the platform together for twenty years, but that night she said, "Tonight you will go by yourself." I said, "All right." My wife went back to one of the furthermost seats in the hall, and she said to herself, "I will watch him."

I preached that night on the text the Lord had given me from Isaiah 61. I told what the Lord had done for me. I told the people that I was going to have God in my life and that I would gladly suffer a thousand deaths rather than forfeit this wonderful infilling that had come to me.

My wife was very restless, just as if she were sitting on a red-hot poker. She was moved in a new way and said, "That is not my Smith that is preaching. Lord, You have done something for him."

As soon as I finished, the secretary of the mission got up and said, "I want what the leader of our mission has got." He tried to sit down but missed his seat and fell on the floor. There were soon fourteen of them on the floor, my own wife included. We did not know what to do, but the Holy Spirit got hold of the situation, and the fire fell. A revival started and the crowds came. It was only the beginning of the flood tide of blessing. We had touched the reservoir of the Lord's life and power. Since that time, the Lord has taken me to many different lands, and I have witnessed many blessed outpourings of God's Holy Spirit.

Thought for today: It is when you get out of the will of God that you have a hard time.

Three Witnesses to the Baptism

And now why are you waiting? Arise and be baptized, and wash
away your sins, calling on the name of the Lord.
—Acts 22:16

Scripture reading: Galatians 3:1–14

I want to take you to the Scriptures to prove my position that
tongues are the evidence of the baptism in the Holy Spirit.
Businessmen know that in cases of law where there are two
clear witnesses, they could win a case before any judge. On the
clear evidence of two witnesses, any judge will give a verdict. What
has God given us? He has given us three clear witnesses on the
baptism in the Holy Spirit—more than are necessary in law courts.

The first is in Acts 2:4, on the Day of Pentecost: *"They were all
filled with the Holy Spirit and began to speak with other tongues, as
the Spirit gave them utterance."*

Here we have the original pattern. And God gave to Peter an
eternal word that couples this experience with the promise that
came before it: *"This is what was spoken by the prophet Joel"* (v.
16). God wants you to have this—nothing less than this. He wants
you to receive the baptism in the Holy Spirit according to this
original Pentecostal pattern.

In Acts 10, we have another witness. Cornelius had had a vision of a holy angel and had sent for Peter. When Peter arrived and
proclaimed the Gospel message, the Holy Spirit fell on all those
who heard his words.

> *And those of the circumcision who believed were astonished,*
> *as many as came with Peter, because the gift of the Holy Spirit*
> *had been poured out on the Gentiles also.* (Acts 10:45)

What convinced these prejudiced Jews that the Holy Spirit had
come? *"For they heard them speak with tongues and magnify God"*
(v. 46). There was no other way for them to know. This evidence
could not be contradicted. It is the biblical evidence.

If some people were to have an angel come and talk to them as
Cornelius did, they would say that they knew they were baptized.
Do not be fooled by anything.

September 5

We have heard two witnesses. Now let us look at Acts 19:6, which records Paul ministering to certain disciples in Ephesus: *"And when Paul had laid hands on them, the Holy Spirit came upon them, and they spoke with tongues and prophesied."*

These Ephesians received the identical biblical evidence that the apostles had received at the beginning, and they prophesied in addition. Three times the Scriptures show us this evidence of the baptism in the Spirit. I do not glorify tongues. No, by God's grace, I glorify the Giver of tongues. And above all, I glorify Him whom the Holy Spirit has come to reveal to us, the Lord Jesus Christ. It is He who sends the Holy Spirit, and I glorify Him because He makes no distinction between us and those who believed at the beginning.

But what are tongues for? Look at the second verse of 1 Corinthians 14, and you will see a very blessed truth: *"For he who speaks in a tongue does not speak to men but to God, for no one understands him; however, in the spirit he speaks mysteries."* Oh, hallelujah! Have you been there, beloved? I tell you, God wants to take you there. The passage goes on to say, *"He who speaks in a tongue edifies himself"* (v. 4).

Enter into the promises of God. It is your inheritance. I pray that you may be so filled with Him that it will not be possible for you to move without a revival of some kind resulting.

Thought for today: Be sure that what you receive is according to the Word of God.

September 6

Paul's Conversion and Baptism
Part One

"Brother Saul, the Lord Jesus, who appeared to you on the road as you came, has sent me that you may receive your sight and be filled with the Holy Spirit." Immediately there fell from his eyes something like scales, and he received his sight at once; and he arose and was baptized.
—Acts 9:17–18

Scripture reading: Acts 8:1–13

*S*aul was probably the greatest persecutor that the early church had. Saul hated the Christians: *"He made havoc of the church, entering every house, and dragging off men and women, committing them to prison"* (Acts 8:3). In Acts 9, we read that he was breathing out threats and slaughter against the disciples of the Lord. He was on his way to Damascus for the purpose of destroying the church there (vv. 1–2).

How did God deal with such a person? We would have dealt with him in judgment. God dealt with him in mercy. Oh, the wondrous love of God! He loved the believers at Damascus, and the way He preserved them was through the salvation of the man who intended to scatter and destroy them. He shows mercy to all. If we would just realize that we are alive today only through the grace of our God!

More and more, I see that it is through the grace of God that I am preserved every day. It is when we realize the goodness of God that we are brought to repentance. Here was Saul, with letters from the high priest, hurrying to Damascus. He was struck down, and he saw a light, a light that was brighter than the sun. As he fell speechless to the ground, he heard a voice saying to him, *"Saul, Saul, why are you persecuting Me?"* He asked, *"Who are You, Lord?"* And the answer came back, *"I am Jesus, whom you are persecuting."* And Saul cried, *"Lord, what do You want me to do?"* (Acts 9:4–6).

I do not want to bring any word of condemnation to anyone, but I know that many have felt very much the same way toward the children of God as Paul did, especially toward those who have received the Pentecostal baptism. I know that many people tell us,

September 6

"You are mad," but the truth is that the children of God are the only people who are really glad. We are glad inside and outside. Our gladness flows from the inside. God has filled us with *"joy inexpressible and full of glory"* (1 Pet. 1:8). We are so happy about what we have received that, if it were not for the desire to keep a little decorum, we might be doing strange things. This is probably how the apostle Paul felt when, referring to himself and his co-workers, he said, *"we are beside ourselves"* (2 Cor. 5:13) in the Lord. This joy in the Holy Spirit is beyond anything else. And this joy of the Lord is our strength (Neh. 8:10).

Thought for today: Our God delights to be merciful, and His grace is granted daily to both sinner and saint.

Paul's Conversion and Baptism
Part Two

He received his sight at once; and he arose and was baptized.
—Acts 9:18

Scripture reading: Acts 8:14–40

When Saul went down to Damascus, he thought he would do wonderful things with that bunch of letters he had from the high priest. But I think he dropped them all on the road. If he ever wanted to pick them up, he was not able to, for he lost his sight. The men who were with him lost their speech, but they led him to Damascus.

Some people have an idea that it is only preachers who can know the will of God. However, this account of Saul shows us that the Lord had a disciple in Damascus, named Ananias, a man behind the scenes, who lived in a place where God could talk to him. His ears were open. He was one who listened in to the things from heaven. Oh, they are so much more marvelous than anything you can hear on earth! It was to this man that the Lord appeared in a vision. He told him to go down to the street called Straight and to inquire for Saul. And He told him that Saul had seen in a vision a man named Ananias coming in and putting his hand on him so that he might receive his sight. Ananias protested,

> *Lord, I have heard from many about this man, how much harm he has done to Your saints in Jerusalem. And here he has authority from the chief priests to bind all who call on Your name.* (Acts 9:13–14)

But the Lord reassured Ananias that Saul was a chosen vessel, and Ananias, doubting nothing, went on his errand of mercy.

The Lord had told Ananias concerning Saul, *"Behold, he is praying"* (v. 11). The Lord never despises a broken and contrite heart (Ps. 51:17). Saul was given a vision that was soon to be a reality, the vision of Ananias coming to pray for him so that he would receive his sight.

Thought for today: Repentant prayer is always heard in heaven.

Paul's Conversion and Baptism
Part Three

He received his sight at once; and he arose and was baptized.
—Acts 9:18

Scripture reading: Acts 9:1–9

nanias went down to the house on Straight Street, and he laid his hands on the one who had before been a blasphemer and a persecutor. He said to him, *"Brother Saul, the Lord Jesus, who appeared to you on the road as you came, has sent me that you may receive your sight and be filled with the Holy Spirit"* (Acts 9:17). He recognized him as a brother whose soul had already been saved and who had come into relationship with the Father and with all the family of God, but there was something necessary beyond this. Yes, the Lord had not forgotten his physical condition, and there was healing for him. But there was something beyond this. It was the filling with the Holy Spirit.

Oh, it always seems to me that the Gospel is robbed of its divine glory when we overlook this marvelous truth of the baptism of the Holy Spirit. To be saved is wonderful; to be a new creature, to have passed from death to life, to have the witness of the Spirit that you are born of God—all this is unspeakably precious. But whereas we have the well of salvation bubbling up inside us, we need to go on to a place where from within us will flow *"rivers of living water"* (John 7:38). The Lord Jesus showed us very plainly that, if we believe in Him, from within us will flow these *"rivers of living water."* And this He spoke by the Spirit. The Lord wants us to be filled with the Spirit, to have the manifestation of the presence of His Spirit, the manifestation that is indeed given *"for the profit of all"* (1 Cor. 12:7).

Thought for today: The Lord wants us to be His mouthpieces and to speak as the very oracles of God.

September 9

Paul's Conversion and Baptism
Part Four

He received his sight at once; and he arose and was baptized.
—Acts 9:18

Scripture reading: Acts 9:10–22

God chose Saul. What was he? A blasphemer. A persecutor. That is grace. Our God is gracious, and He loves to show His mercy to the vilest and worst of men.

There was a notable character in the town in which I lived who was known as the worst man in town. He was so vile, and his language was so horrible, that even wicked men could not stand it. In England, they have what is known as the public hangman who has to perform all the executions. This man held that appointment, and he told me later that he believed that when he performed the execution of men who had committed murder, the demon power that was in them would come upon him, and that, in consequence, he had been possessed by a legion of demons.

His life was so miserable that he decided to kill himself. He went down to a certain train depot and purchased a ticket. English trains are much different from American trains. In every coach there are a number of small compartments, and it is easy for anyone who wants to commit suicide to open the door of his compartment and throw himself out of the train. This man purposed to throw himself out of the train in a certain tunnel just as the train coming from the opposite direction would be about to dash past; he thought this would make a quick end to his life.

There was a young man at the depot that night who had been saved the night before. He was all on fire to get others saved, and he purposed in his heart that every day of his life, he would get someone saved. He saw this dejected hangman and began to speak to him about his soul. He brought him down to our mission, and there he came under a mighty conviction of sin. For two-and-a-half hours he was literally sweating under conviction, and you could see a vapor rising up from him. At the end of two-and-a-half hours, he was graciously saved.

I said, "Lord, tell me what to do." The Lord said, "Don't leave him. Go home with him." I went to his house. When he saw his

382

wife, he said, "God has saved me." The wife broke down, and she, too, was graciously saved. I tell you, there was a difference in that home. Even the cat knew the difference. Previous to this, the cat would always run away when that hangman came through the door. But the night that he was saved, the cat jumped onto his knee and went to sleep.

There were two sons in that house, and one of them said to his mother, "Mother, what is up in our house? It was never like this before. It is so peaceful. What is it?" She told him, "Father has gotten saved." The other son was also struck by the change.

I took this man to many special services, and the power of God was on him for many days. He would give his testimony, and as he grew in grace, he desired to preach the Gospel. He became an evangelist, and hundreds and hundreds were brought to a saving knowledge of the Lord Jesus Christ through his ministry. God saved Saul of Tarsus at the very time he was breathing out threats and slaughter against the disciples of the Lord, and He redeemed Berry the hangman. He will do it for hundreds more in response to our cries.

Thought for today: The grace of God is sufficient for the vilest, and He can take the most wicked men and make them monuments of His grace.

Paul's Conversion and Baptism
Part Five

He received his sight at once; and he arose and was baptized.
—Acts 9:18

Scripture reading: Acts 16:16–34

otice that when Ananias came into that house, he called the onetime enemy of the Gospel *"Brother Saul"* (Acts 9:17). He recognized that, in those three days, a blessed work had been accomplished and that Saul had been brought into relationship with the Father and with the Lord Jesus Christ. Was this not enough? No, there was something further, and for this purpose the Lord had sent Ananias to that house to put his hands upon this newly saved brother so that Saul might receive his sight and be filled with the Holy Spirit.

You say, "But it does not say that he spoke in tongues." We know that Paul did speak in tongues, that he spoke in tongues more than all the Corinthians (1 Cor. 14:18). In those early days, it was so soon after the time of that first Pentecostal outpouring that they would never have been satisfied with anyone receiving the baptism unless he received it according to the original pattern given on the Day of Pentecost.

When Peter was relating what had taken place in the house of Cornelius at Caesarea, he said, *"As I began to speak, the Holy Spirit fell upon them, as upon us at the beginning"* (Acts 11:15). Later, speaking of this incident, he said, *"God, who knows the heart, acknowledged them by giving them the Holy Spirit, just as He did to us, and made no distinction between us and them, purifying their hearts by faith"* (Acts 15:8–9). We know from the account of what took place at Cornelius's household that when the Holy Spirit fell, *"they heard them speak with tongues and magnify God"* (Acts 10:46).

Many people think that God makes a distinction between us and those who lived at the beginning of the church. But they have no Scripture for this. When anyone receives the gift of the Holy Spirit, there will assuredly be no difference between his experience today and what was given on the Day of Pentecost. And I cannot believe that, when Saul was filled with the Holy Spirit, the Lord made any difference in the experience that He gave him than the experience that He had given to Peter and the rest a short while before.

And so Saul was filled with the Holy Spirit, and in the later chapters of the Acts of the Apostles we see the result of this infilling. Oh, what a difference it makes!

The grace of God that was given to the persecuting Saul is available for you. The same infilling of the Holy Spirit that he received is likewise available. Move on to a life of continuous receiving of more and more of the blessed Spirit of God.

Thought for today: Do not rest satisfied with any lesser experience than the baptism that the disciples received on the Day of Pentecost.

Receiving the Baptism

You shall receive power when the Holy Spirit has come upon you.
—Acts 1:8

Scripture reading: Acts 1:1–11

I believe God wants us to know more about the baptism of the Holy Spirit. And I believe that God wants us to know the truth in such a way that we may all have a clear understanding of what He means when He desires all His people to receive the Holy Spirit.

Jesus, our Mediator and Advocate, was filled with the Holy Spirit. He commanded His followers concerning these days we are in and gave instructions about the time through the Holy Spirit. I can see that if we are going to accomplish anything, we are going to accomplish it because we are under the power of the Holy Spirit.

During my lifetime, I have seen lots of satanic forces, Spiritualists, and all other "ists." I tell you that there is a power that is satanic, and there is a power that is the Holy Spirit. I remember that after we received the Holy Spirit and when people were speaking in tongues as the Spirit gave utterance—we don't know the Holy Spirit in any other way—the Spiritualists heard about it and came to the meeting in good time to fill two rows of seats.

When the power of God fell upon us, these imitators began their shaking and moving, with utterances from the satanic forces. The Spirit of the Lord was mighty upon me. I went to them and said, "Now, you demons, clear out of here!" And out they went. I followed them right out into the street, and then they turned around and cursed me. It made no difference; they were out.

I implore you to hear that the baptism in the Holy Spirit is to possess us so that we are, and may be continually, so full of the Holy Spirit that utterances and revelations and eyesight and everything else may be so remarkably controlled by the Spirit of God that we live and move in this glorious sphere of usefulness for the glory of God.

Thought for today: There is a fullness of God where all other powers must cease to be.

God's Gift for Everyone

He who believes in Me, as the Scripture has said, out of his heart
will flow rivers of living water.
—John 7:38

Scripture reading: John 4:1–14

God wants to help us to see that every child of God ought to receive the Holy Spirit. Beloved, God wants us to understand that this is not difficult when we are in the right order. I want you to see what it means to seek the Holy Spirit.

If we were to examine John's gospel, we would see that Jesus predicted all that we are getting today with the coming of the Holy Spirit. Our Lord said that the Holy Spirit would take of the things of His Word and reveal them to us. (See John 14:26; 16:14.) He would live out in us all of the life of Jesus.

If we could only think of what this really means! It is one of the ideals. Talk about graduation! Come into the graduation of the Holy Spirit, and you will simply outstrip everything they have in any college there ever was. You will leave them all behind, just as I have seen the sun leave the mist behind in San Francisco. You will leave what is as cold as ice and go into the sunshine.

God the Holy Spirit wants us to know the reality of this fullness of the Spirit so that we will neither be ignorant nor have mystic conceptions but will have a clear, unmistakable revelation of the entire mind of God for these days.

I implore you, beloved, in the name of Jesus, that you should see that you come right into all the mind of God. Jesus truly said, *"But you shall receive power when the Holy Spirit has come upon you"* (Acts 1:8).

Thought for today: Jesus is all the time unfolding to every one of us the power of resurrection.

Entering a New Realm

He who believes in the Son of God has the witness in himself.
—1 John 5:10

Scripture reading: 1 John 5

*I*f you are a businessman, you need to be baptized in the Holy Spirit. For any kind of business, you need to know the power of the Holy Spirit, because if you are not baptized with the Holy Spirit, Satan has a tremendous power to interfere with the progress of your life. If you come into the baptism of the Holy Spirit, there is a new realm for your business.

I remember one day being in London at a meeting. About eleven o'clock, they said to me, "We will have to close the meeting. We are not allowed to have this place any later than eleven o'clock." There were several who were under the power of the Spirit. A man rose up and looked at me, saying, "Oh, don't leave me, please. I feel that I do not dare be left. I must receive the Holy Spirit. Will you go home with us?" "Yes," I said, "I will go." His wife was there as well. They were two hungry people just being awakened by the power of the Spirit to know that they were lacking in their lives and that they needed the power of God.

In about an hour's time, we arrived at their big, beautiful house in the country. It was wintertime. He began stirring the fire up and putting coal on, and he said, "We will soon have a tremendous fire, so we will get warmed. Then we will have a big supper." And I suppose the next thing would have been going to bed.

"No, thank you," I said. "I have not come here for your supper or for your bed. I thought you wanted me to come with you so that you might receive the Holy Spirit."

"Oh," he replied. "Will you pray with us?"

"I have come for nothing else." I knew I could keep myself warm in a prayer meeting without a fire.

About half past three in the morning, his wife was as full as could be, speaking in tongues. God was doing wonderful things that night. I went to the end of the table. There he was, groaning terribly. So I said, "Your wife has received the Holy Spirit." "Oh," he said, "this is going to be a big night for me." I tell you, you also will have big nights like this man had, whether you receive the baptism or not, if you will seek God with all your heart.

I often say there is more done in the seeking than in any other way. We have to get to a place where we know that unless we meet face-to-face with God and get all the crooked places out of our lives, there will be no room for the Holy Spirit, for the indwelling presence of God. But when God gets a chance at us, and by the vision of the blood of Jesus we see ourselves as God sees us, then we have a revelation. Without this, we are undone and helpless.

At five o'clock in the morning, this man stood up and said, "I am through." He was not baptized. "I am settled," he continued. "God has settled me. Now I must have a few hours' rest before I go to my business at eight o'clock."

My word! That was quite a day at his business. In many years, he had never lived a day like that. He went about his business among all his men, and they said, "What is up with the man? What is up with the boss? What has taken place? Oh, what a change!"

The whole place was electrified. Formerly he had been like a great big lion prowling about, but God had touched him. The touch of Omnipotence had broken this man down until right there in his business the men were broken up in his presence. Oh, I tell you, there is something in pursuing; there is something in waiting. What is it? It is this: God slays a man so that he may begin on a new plane in his life.

That night, at about ten o'clock, he was baptized in the Holy Spirit in a meeting. A short time afterward, when I was passing through the grounds toward this man's house, his two sons rushed out to where I was, threw their arms around me, and kissed me, saying, "You have sent us a new father."

Thought for today: God turns lions into lambs.

September 14

The Baptism Is Resurrection

That I may know Him and the power of His resurrection.
—Philippians 3:10

Scripture reading: Philippians 3

The power of the Holy Spirit creates new men and new women. The Holy Spirit takes away stony hearts and gives hearts of flesh (Ezek. 36:26–27). And when God gets His way like that, there is a tremendous shaking among the dry bones. (See Ezekiel 37:4–10.)

We must see that we are no good unless God takes charge of us. But when He has real control of us, our future takes on a new outlook. What a wonderful open door of opportunities for God to use us!

Beloved, we must seek this ideal by the Spirit. What should we do? We do not dare to do anything but go through and receive the baptism. Submit to the power of God. If you yield, other people are saved. You will die unless you have a power of resurrection, a touch for others. But if you live only for God, then other people will be raised out of death and all kinds of evil into a blessed life through the Spirit.

We must see that this baptism of the Spirit is greater than everything. You can say what you like, do as you like, but until you have the Holy Spirit, you won't know what the resurrection touch is. Resurrection is by the power of the Spirit. And remember, when I talk about resurrection, I am talking about one of the greatest things in the Scriptures. Resurrection is evidence that we have awakened with a new line of truth that cannot cease to be, but will always go on with a greater force and increasing power with God.

Remember that the baptism of the Holy Spirit is resurrection. If you can touch this ideal of God with its resurrection power, you will see that nothing earthly can remain; you will see that all disease will clear out. If you get filled with the Holy Spirit, all satanic forces that cause fits, all these lame legs, all these foot afflictions, all these kidney troubles, and all these nervous, fearful things will go. *Resurrection* is the word for it. Resurrection shakes away death and breathes life in you; it lets you know that you are quickened from the dead by the Spirit and that you are made like Jesus. Glory to God!

Oh, the word *resurrection!* I wish I could say it on the same level as the word *Jesus*. They very harmoniously go together.

Thought for today: Jesus is resurrection, and to know Jesus in this resurrection power is to see that you no longer have to be dead; you are alive unto God by the Spirit.

September 15

A New Day

Behold, I will do a new thing, now it shall spring forth;
shall you not know it? I will even make a road in the wilderness
and rivers in the desert.
—Isaiah 43:19

Scripture reading: Revelation 21

*S*ee to it that today you press on with a new order of the
Spirit so that you can never be where you were before. This
is a new day for us all. You say, "What about the people who
are already baptized in the Spirit?" Oh, this is a new day also for
those who have been baptized, for the Spirit is an unlimited source
of power. He is in no way stationary. God has no place for a person
who is stationary. The man who is going to catch the fire, hold
forth the truth, and always be on the watchtower is the one who is
going to be a beacon for all saints, having a light greater than he
would have naturally. He must see that God's grace, God's life, and
God's Spirit are a million times mightier than he.

The man who is baptized in the Holy Spirit is baptized into a
new order altogether. You cannot ever be ordinary after that. You
are on an extraordinary plane; you are brought into line with the
mind of God. You have come into touch with ideals in every way.

If you want oratory, it is in the baptism of the Spirit. If you want
the touch of quickened sense that moves your body until you know
that you are completely renewed, it is by the Holy Spirit. And while I
say so much about the Holy Spirit, I withdraw everything that
doesn't put Jesus in the place He belongs. For when I speak about
the Holy Spirit, it is always with reference to revelations of Jesus.
The Holy Spirit is the Revealer of the mighty Christ who possesses
everything for us so that we may never know any weakness. All limitations are gone. And you are now in a place where God has taken
the ideal and moved you on with His own velocity, which has a speed
beyond all human mind and thought. Glory to God!

Thought for today: Nothing in God is stationary.

September 16

Higher Heights

I will declare Your name to My brethren; in the midst of the assembly I will sing praise to You.
—Hebrews 2:12

Scripture reading: Hebrews 2:1–13

The Spirit of the Lord must have His way in everything. Oh, what would happen if we would all loosen up! Sometimes I think it is almost necessary to give an address to those who are already baptized in the Holy Spirit. I feel that, just like the Corinthian church, we may have, as it were, gifts and graces, and we may use them all, but we sit in them and do not go on beyond where we are.

I maintain that all gifts and graces are only for one thing: to make you desire gifts and graces. Don't miss what I say. Every touch of the divine life by the Spirit is only for one purpose: to make your life go on to a higher height than where you are. Beloved, if anybody has to rise up in the meeting to tell me how they were baptized with the Holy Spirit in order for me to know they are baptized, I say, "You have fallen from grace. You ought to have such a baptism that everybody can tell you are baptized without your telling how you were baptized." That would make a new day. That would be a sermon in itself to everybody, not only in here but also outside. Then people would follow you to get to know where you have come from and where you are going. (See John 3:8.) You say, "I want that. I won't settle until I get that." God will surely give it to you.

The Holy Spirit can only come into us (His temples) when we are fully yielded to Him, for the Spirit *"does not dwell in temples made with hands"* (Acts 7:48) but in *"tablets of flesh, that is, of the heart"* (2 Cor. 3:3). So it doesn't matter what kind of a building you get; you cannot count on the building being a substitute for the Holy Spirit. You will all have to be temples of the Holy Spirit for the building to be anything like Holy Spirit order.

Thought for today: The Holy Spirit never comes until there is a place ready for Him.

September 17

He Is Coming!

Therefore be patient, brethren, until the coming of the Lord. See how the farmer waits for the precious fruit of the earth, waiting patiently for it until it receives the early and latter rain. You also be patient. Establish your hearts, for the coming of the Lord is at hand.
—James 5:7–8

Scripture reading: James 5:1–12

What is the *"precious fruit of the earth"*? It is the church, the body of Christ. And God has no thought for other things. He causes the vegetation of the earth to grow and creates the glory of the flower. He gives attention to the beauty of flowers because He knows it will please us. But when speaking about the *"precious fruit of the earth,"* our Lord has His mind upon you today.

If you desire the coming of the Lord, you must certainly advocate having every believer filled with the Holy Spirit. The Holy Spirit cannot come until the church is ready. And you say, "When will the church be ready?" If believers were in an attitude of yieldedness and were in unity with God and each other, God could send the breath right now to make the church ready in ten minutes, even less than that.

So we can clearly say that the coming of the Lord is near to us, but it will be even closer to us as we are ready to receive a fuller and greater manifestation. What will be the manifestation of the coming of the Lord? If we were ready, and if the power of God were stressing that truth today, we would be rushing up to one another, saying, "He is coming; I know He is coming." Every person around would be saying, "He is coming," and you would know it to be true.

This is the only hope of the future, and nothing except the Holy Spirit can prepare the hearts of the people for His coming. Praise God, He will come! He is coming!

Thought for today: The more a person is filled with the Holy Spirit, the more he will be ready to forecast the return of the Lord and send forth this glorious truth.

Allow God to Use You

But we have this treasure in earthen vessels, that the excellence of the power may be of God and not of us.
—2 Corinthians 4:7

Scripture reading: 2 Corinthians 4

One day, in England, a lady wrote to ask if I would come and help her. She said she was blind, having two blood clots behind her eyes. I had been in London recently, and I didn't feel I wanted to go. However, I sent a letter, not knowing who she was, saying that if she was willing to go into a room with me and shut the door and never come out until she had perfect sight, I would come. She sent word, "Oh, come!"

The moment I reached the house, they brought in this blind woman. After we shook hands, she made her way to a room, opened the door, allowed me to go in, and then came in and shut the door. "Now," she said, "we are with God."

Have you ever been there? It is a lovely place.

In an hour and a half, the power of God fell upon us. Rushing to the window, she exclaimed, "I can see! Oh, I can see! The blood is gone; I can see!" Sitting down in a chair, she asked, "Could I receive the Holy Spirit?"

"Yes," I replied, "if all is right with God."

"You don't know me," she continued, "but for ten years I have been fighting your position. I couldn't bear these tongues, but God settled it today. I want the baptism of the Holy Spirit."

After she had prayed and repented of what she had said about tongues, she was filled with the Holy Spirit and began speaking in tongues.

When you put your hands upon people to pray, you can tell when the Holy Spirit is present. And if you will only yield to the Holy Spirit and allow Him to move, my word, what will happen!

Thought for today: The Lord Jesus wants those who preach the Word to have the Word in evidence in their lives.

Receive the Spirit

I thank You, Father, Lord of heaven and earth, that You
have hidden these things from the wise and prudent
and have revealed them to babes.
—Matthew 11:25

Scripture reading: Matthew 19:13–30

I wonder how many people today are prepared to be baptized. Oh, you say you couldn't be baptized? Then you have been an adult too long. You need to become childlike again. Do you know that there is a difference between being a baby and anything else in the world?

Many people have been waiting for years for the baptism, and what has been the problem? What is the wise man's difficulty? A wise man is too careful. And while he is in the operation of the Spirit, he wants to know what he is saying. No man can know what he is saying when the Spirit is upon him. His own mind is inactive. If you get into that place in which you are near God, the mind of Christ comes by the power of the Spirit. Under these conditions, Christ prays and speaks in the Spirit through you as the Spirit gives utterance. It is the mind and plan of God for us to receive the Holy Spirit.

The natural man cannot receive the Spirit of God (1 Cor. 2:14). But when you get into a supernatural place, then you receive the mind of God. Again, what is the difference between a *"wise and prudent"* man and a baby? The man drinks cautiously, but the baby swallows it all, and the mother has to hold the bottle, or some of that will go down, too. This is how God wants it to be in the Spirit. The spiritually-minded baby cannot walk. However, God walks in him. The spiritually-minded baby cannot talk, but God talks through him. The spiritually-minded baby cannot dress himself, but God dresses him and clothes him with His righteousness.

Oh, beloved, if we can only be infants in this way today, great things will take place along the lines and thought of the Spirit of God. The Lord wants us all to be so like-minded with Him that He can put His seal upon us.

Does the baby ever lose his intelligence? Does he ever lose his common sense? Does the baby who comes into the will of God lose his reason or his credentials in any way? No, God will increase your abilities and help you in everything. I am not talking here about just being a baby. I am talking about being a baby in the Spirit. Paul said in 1 Corinthians 14:20, *"In malice be babes, but in under-standing be mature."* And I believe the Spirit desires to breathe through all the attributes of the Spirit so that we may understand what the mind of the Lord is concerning us in the Holy Spirit.

Thought for today: If you will become childlike enough, if you will yield to God and let the Spirit have His way, God will fill you with the Holy Spirit.

September 20

What about Manifestations?

But the manifestation of the Spirit is given to each one
for the profit of all.
—1 Corinthians 12:7

Scripture reading: 1 Corinthians 12:1–11

We must never transgress because of liberty. What I mean is this: it would be wrong for me to take opportunities just because the Spirit of the Lord is upon me. But it would be perfectly justifiable if I clearly allow the Spirit of the Lord to have His liberty with me. However, we are not to behave inappropriately in our liberty, for the flesh is more extravagant than the Spirit.

The Spirit's extravagances are always for edification, strengthening character, and bringing us all more into conformity with the life of Christ. But fleshly extravagances always mar these things and bring the saints into a place of trial for the moment. As the Spirit of the Lord takes further hold of a person, we may get liberty in it, but we are tried through the manifestations of it.

I believe we have come to a liberty of the Spirit that is so pure it will never bring a frown of distraction over another person's mind. I have seen many people who were in the power of the Spirit, but they exhibited a manifestation that was not foundational or even helpful. I have seen people under the mighty power of the Holy Spirit who have waved their hands wildly and moved on the floor and gone on in such a state that no one could say the body was not under the power. However, there was more natural power than spiritual power there, and the natural condition of the person, along with the spiritual condition, caused the manifestation. Though we know the Spirit of the Lord was there, the manifestation was not something that would elevate or please the people or grant them a desire for more of that. It wasn't an edification of the Spirit.

If there are any here who have those manifestations, I want to help you. I don't want to hurt you. It is good that you should have the Spirit upon you; people need to be filled with the Spirit. But you never have a right to say you couldn't help doing this, that, or the other manifestation.

No manifestation of the body ever glorifies the Lord except the tongue. If you seek to be free in the operation of the Spirit through the mouth, then the tongue, which may be under a kind of subconscious control by the Spirit, brings out the glory of the Lord, and that will always bring edification, consolation, and comfort.

No other manifestation will do this. Still, I believe that it is necessary to have all these other manifestations when someone is filled with the Spirit for the first time. When the Spirit is there, the flesh must find some way out, and so, through past experience, we allow all these things at the beginning. But I believe the Holy Spirit brings a sound condition of mind, and the first thing must pass away so that the divine position may remain.

And so there are various manifestations, including kicking and waving, that take place at the incoming of the Holy Spirit, when the flesh and the Spirit are in conflict. One must decrease and die, and the other must increase and multiply. Consequently, when you come to understand this, you are in a place of sound judgment and know that now the Holy Spirit has come to take you on with God.

When the Holy Spirit is allowed full reign over the operation of human life, He always works out of divine wisdom. And when He gets perfect control of a life, the divine source flows through so that all the people may receive edification in the Spirit. If you act foolishly after you have had wisdom taught you, nobody will give you much leeway.

"We then that are strong ought to bear the infirmities of the weak" (Rom. 15:1 KJV). Some who come to church services know nothing about the power of the Holy Spirit. They get saved and are quickened, and after the Spirit comes upon them, you will see all these manifestations. In love and grace, you should bear with them as newborn babes in the Spirit and rejoice with them because that is only a beginning to an end. The Lord wouldn't want us to be anything but *"strong in the Lord and in the power of His might"* (Eph. 6:10) to help everyone around us.

Thought for today: Liberty is beautiful when we never use it to satisfy ourselves but use it in the Lord.

Living the Ascension Life

For we who are in this tent groan, being burdened, not because we want to be unclothed, but further clothed, that mortality may be swallowed up by life.
—2 Corinthians 5:4

Scripture reading: 2 Corinthians 5

I believe that, first, we must all grasp the truth that we are not our own (1 Cor. 6:19). In the second place, we belong to a spiritual order; we don't belong to the earth. And not only that, but our minds and our bodies—our whole position through the eternal Spirit—always have to be on the ascending position.

In this transforming condition, we may, by the power of the Spirit, as God gives us revelation, be lifted up into a very blessed state of fellowship with God, of power with God. And in that place of power with God, we will have power over everything else, for to have all power over the earth, we must first have power with God.

We know that we are heavenly citizens. We know that we have to exit this earth and have been preparing for our exit. Yet while we are on earth, we must live in the place where we groan over everything that binds us from being loosed from the world.

What will hold me? Association will hold me in this present world. I must hold every earthly relationship at a distance—and you know it is as natural to have earthly associations as it is to live. It must never tie me or bind me. It must never have any persuasion over me. Hear what the Scripture says, *"Being conformed to His death"* (Phil. 3:10).

What does it mean to conform to the death of Jesus? It leads me to that death of separation to God, of yieldedness, of exchange, where God takes me to Himself and leaves the old nature behind. *"While we do not look at the things which are seen, but at the things which are not seen"* (2 Cor. 4:18).

Then I may grasp some idea of what it will mean if I die to myself. I want us to see, by the grace of God, that the dissolving of our earthly bodies (see 2 Corinthians 5:1 KJV) is a great thought. There is a position in God that we must clearly understand: *"Not because we want to be unclothed, but further clothed, that mortality may be swallowed up by life."*

September 21

While mortality is necessary, it is a hindrance. While mortality has done a great deal to produce everything we see, it is a hindrance if we live with only it in mind. It is a helpful position if we live over it.

Thought for today: To descend is to be conformed. To ascend is to be transformed.

September 22

Dying Brings Life

For when I am weak, then I am strong.
—2 Corinthians 12:10

Scripture reading: 2 Corinthians 12:1–10; 13:5–9

I must understand how mortality can be *"swallowed up"* (2 Cor. 5:4). I must know how the old body, the old tendencies to the fallen nature, may be swallowed up. There is a verse we must come to. It would serve us to look at it now: *"Always carrying about in the body the dying of the Lord Jesus, that the life of Jesus also may be manifested in our body"* (2 Cor. 4:10).

What is this *"dying of the Lord"*? It is dying to desire. In the measure that we look to one another for our help, we lose faith in God. If you rely upon any man or woman, upon any human assistance, to help you, you fall out of the greater purpose God has for you.

You must learn that no earthly source can ever assist you in this. You are going to this realm of life only by mortality being swallowed up by life: *"And the life which I now live in the flesh I live by faith in the Son of God"* (Gal. 2:20). It is a process of dying and living.

This life I am speaking about absolutely ravishes you. It absolutely severs you from earthly connections. It absolutely disjoins you from all earthly help. And I can understand this word now more than ever: *"You have not yet resisted to bloodshed, striving against sin"* (Heb. 12:4).

The great striving to the point of bloodshed—blood being the very essence of life—we have not yet resisted to that degree, but we will. I know the Scripture says we have not, but I know it means that we have not arrived there yet. But thank God, we are in it in a measure.

Thought for today: You cannot get into life except through death to self.

Alive to God

Now if we died with Christ, we believe that we shall also live with Him.
—Romans 6:8

Scripture reading: Romans 6

The apostle Paul could see that if he had any communion with flesh and blood, he couldn't go forward in the Lord. (See Galatians 1:15–17.) It was even necessary for Jesus' flesh and blood ties to be put in this context. Jesus said,

> *"Who is My mother and who are My brothers?" And He stretched out His hand toward His disciples and said, "Here are My mother and My brothers! For whoever does the will of My Father in heaven is My brother and sister and mother."*
> (Matt. 12:48–50)

Flesh and blood were nothing to Jesus. God brought Him into the world as a seed of life. To Him, that obedient believer was His mother, that servant of God was His brother, that follower of Christ was His sister. But this is a higher ideal; this takes spiritual knowledge.

Let us look at another example of dying to self taken from Jesus' life. In the Garden of Gethsemane, Jesus faced His suffering from two different standpoints. His human nature instantly cried out, *"If it is possible, let this cup pass from Me"* (Matt. 26:39). The next moment, he was saying, with His divine nature, *"Nevertheless, not as I will, but as You will"* (v. 39). He also said, *"But for this purpose I came to this hour"* (John 12:27). His human nature had no more choices left. He was off to face the cross.

When God the Holy Spirit brings us to see these truths, we will deny ourselves for the sake of the Cross. We will deny ourselves of anything that would cause our brother to stumble. We will die to all fleshly indulgences, lest we should miss the great swallowing up by life (2 Cor. 5:4). We will not even mention or ever pay attention to anything along natural lines.

If we will allow God to govern us, He will lift us up into a higher state of grace than we have ever been in before. If believers could take hold of this spiritual power, they could withstand any ridicule that comes their way. When are we distracted and disturbed? When we don't reach the ideals in the Spirit. When we reach the ideals in the Spirit, what does it matter?

One reason for the trouble in churches today is people's murmuring over the conditions they are in. The Bible teaches us not to murmur (John 6:43). If you reach that standard, you will never murmur anymore. God will be purifying you all the time and lifting you higher, and you will know you are not of this world (John 15:19).

If you want to stay in the world, you cannot go on with God. If you are not of this world, your position in this life will have little effect on you. Yet you will know that everything will work for your good (Rom. 8:28) if you climb the ladder of faith with God. God will keep the world in perfect order and give you success in the end.

But God cannot work for you; you are so involved in the world that He cannot get your attention. How can someone get into this divine order when he is torn between two things: God and the world? He cannot let himself go and let God take him.

I maintain that, by the grace of God, we are so rich, we are so abounding, we have such a treasure-house, we have such a storehouse of God, we have such an unlimited faith to share in all that God has, for it is ours. We are the cream of the earth; we are the *"precious fruit of the earth"* (James 5:7). God has told us that all things will work together for our good (Rom. 8:28). God has said that we will be the *"children of the Highest"* (Luke 6:35 KJV) and that we will be the *"salt of the earth"* (Matt. 5:13). God has declared all this in His Word.

How am I to have all the treasures of heaven and all the treasures of God? Not by getting my eyes on the things that are seen, for they will fade away. I must get my eyes on the things that are not seen, for they will remain as long as God reigns.

But now a change is taking place. I read in the Scriptures: *"That you may be married to another; to Him who was raised from the dead, that we should bear fruit to God"* (Rom. 7:4).

You are joined to Another; you belong to Another. God has changed you. Is it a living fact? If it is only words, it will end there. But if it is a spiritual fact, and you reign in it, you will say, "Thank God, I never knew I was so rich!"

Thought for today: You will never reach God's blessings if you are holding on to the lower things of this world; they will keep you down.

September 24

Dissolved and Made like Christ

For we know that if our earthly house of this tabernacle
were dissolved, we have a building of God, an house not made
with hands, eternal in the heavens.
—2 Corinthians 5:1 KJV

Scripture reading: Revelation 3

The power of God can so dwell in us that it can burn up everything that is not spiritual and dissolve it to the perfection of beauty and holiness that Jesus has. Jesus was perfectly dissolved in regard to everything in His human nature, and He lived in the Spirit over everything else. As He is, so we have to be. (See 1 John 4:17.)

We shouldn't be troubled in the flesh. Was Jesus troubled in the flesh? Didn't He go forth with perfect victory? It is impossible for any avenue of flesh, or anything that you touch in your natural body, to be helpful. Even your eyes have to be sanctified by the power of God so that they strike fire every time you look at a sinner, and the sinner will be changed.

We will be clothed with a robe of righteousness in God so that wherever we walk, there will be a whiteness of effectiveness that will bring people to a place of conviction of sin. You say, "There are so many things in my house that would have to be thrown out the window if Jesus came to my home." I pray that we could understand that He is already in the house all the time. Everything ought to go out the window that couldn't stand His eyes on it. Every impression of our hearts that would bring trouble if He looked at us ought to go forever.

You ask, "What are we to do?" We are to be *"swallowed up by life"* (2 Cor. 5:4). The great I AM in perfect holiness isn't just an example, but He clothes us with His own nature.

It is impossible for us to subdue kingdoms (see Hebrews 11:33), impossible for the greater works to be accomplished (see John 14:12), impossible for the Son of God to be making sons on earth except as we stand exactly in His place.

Thought for today: There isn't a place in Scripture that God doesn't mean for us to possess and which He won't take us into.

405

Depend on God

Lord, I pray, please let Your ear be attentive to the prayer
of Your servant.
—Nehemiah 1:11

Scripture reading: Nehemiah 1

Nehemiah mourned, fasted, and prayed until his humility and yieldedness before God brought the same thing that God's Word brings to us: it dissolved him. It brought everything of his old nature into a dissolved place where he went right through into the presence of God.

Now Nehemiah was the cupbearer for the Persian king Artaxerxes. The moment the king saw Nehemiah's sad expression, he asked, "What is the matter with you, Nehemiah? I have never seen your countenance changed like this." (See Nehemiah 2:1–2.) Nehemiah was so near almightiness before the king that he could pray and move the heavens and move the king and move the world until Jerusalem was restored.

He mourned. When we reach a place where the Spirit takes us to see our weaknesses, our depravity, our failings; when we mourn before God; we will be dissolved. In the dissolving, we will be clothed with our house from heaven. We will walk in white; we will be robed with a new robe, and this *"mortality* [will] *be swallowed up by life"* (2 Cor. 5:4).

Beloved, Christ can bring every one of us, if we will, into a wholehearted dependency where God will never fail us but we will reign in life. We will travail and bring forth fruit; for Zion, when she travails, will make the house of hell shake.

Will we reach this place? Our blessed Lord reached it. Every night He went alone and reached ideals and walked the world in white. He was clothed with the Holy Spirit from heaven.

Daniel entered into the same negotiations with heaven through the same inward aspiration. He groaned and travailed until for three weeks he shook the heavens and moved Gabriel to come. Gabriel passed through all the regions of the damned to bring the message to him.

There was something so beautiful about the whole thing that even Daniel, in his most holy, beautiful state, became as corruption before the presence of Gabriel. And Gabriel strengthened Daniel by his right hand and lifted him up and gave him the visions of the world's history that are to be fulfilled. (See Daniel 9–12.)

You cannot get into life except through death, and you cannot get into death except by life. For the natural life to be swallowed up, there must be nothing there but helplessness until the life of Christ strengthens the natural life. Yet instead of the natural life being strengthened, the spiritual life comes forth with abounding conditions.

Thought for today: The only way to go into fullness with God is for the life of Christ to swallow up the natural life.

A Higher Standard

From now on, we regard no one according to the flesh.
Even though we have known Christ according to the flesh,
yet now we know Him thus no longer.
—2 Corinthians 5:16

Scripture reading: Matthew 16:1–19

To no longer know any man according to the flesh is a great thing. Beloved, we will no longer know any man along natural lines. From this moment, we will know everything only on a spiritual basis. Conversation must be spiritual. We can get distracted after we have had a really good meal; instead of no longer knowing any man according to the flesh, so that everything is in spiritual fellowship and union, we lower the standard by talking about natural things.

If you ride with me on a train, you will have to pray or testify. If you don't, you will hear a whole lot of talk that will lower the anointing, bring you into a kind of bondage, and make you wish you were riding in another part of the train. But if you break in and have a prayer meeting, you will turn the whole thing around. Go in and pray until you know everybody has been touched by it.

If you go out to dinner with anybody today, don't get side-tracked by listening to a long story about the state of their businesses. You must know only one Man now, and that is Christ, and He hasn't any business. Yet He is Lord over all businesses. Live in the Spirit, and all things will work together for good to you (Rom. 8:28). If you live for your businesses, you will not know the mind of the Spirit. However, if you live in the heavenly places, you will cause your businesses and all things to come out of their difficulties, for God will fight for you.

I won't enter into anything that is lower than spiritual fidelity. When I am preaching spiritually anointed thoughts, I must see that I lift my people into a place where I know the Spirit is leading me to know Jesus.

Suppose you know Jesus. What do you say? That He lost out? No, He didn't. But a great deal was put upon Him by the people who said,

September 26

Is this not the carpenter's son? Is not His mother called Mary? And His brothers James, Joses, Simon, and Judas? And His sisters, are they not all with us? Where then did this Man get all these things? (Matt. 13:55–56)

They said, "He is only an ordinary man. He was born the same way we all were. You see Him. So what is He?"

You will never get anything that way. He wasn't an ordinary man if He was born out of the *"loins of Abraham"* (Heb. 7:5). Two sons were born to Abraham: Isaac and Ishmael. One was the son of promise, the other wasn't. But Isaac, the son of promise, got the blessings. Isaac was a type of Christ. You can never enter into God's conditions in any way but the spiritual way.

For a time, a cloud overshadowed Jesus because of His ancestry. With the Jews, it overshadows Him today because the veil is over their eyes; but the veil will be lifted. (See 2 Corinthians 3:14–16.) With the Gentiles, the veil is already lifted.

We see Him as the Incarnation, as the Holy One of God, as the Son of God, as the *"only begotten of the Father, full of grace and truth"* (John 1:14). We see Him as the Burden-Bearer, as our Sanctifier, as our Cleanser, as our Baptizer. Know no man according to the flesh, but see Him! As we behold Him in all His glory, we will rise; we cannot help but rise in the power of God.

Know no man according to the flesh. People want holiness. People want righteousness. People want purity. People have an inward longing to be clothed with the Spirit.

May the Lord lead you to the supply of every need, far more than you can *"ask or think"* (Eph. 3:20). May the Lord bless you as you are led to dedicate yourself afresh to God this very day.

Thought for today: You will draw people if you refuse to be contaminated by the world.

Abundant Life

*I have come that they may have life, and that they may
have it more abundantly.*
—John 10:10

Scripture reading: John 10:1–18

God has a plan for us in this life of the Spirit, this abundant life. Jesus came so that we might have life. Satan comes to steal and kill and destroy (John 10:10), but God has abundance for us—full measure, pressed down, shaken together, overflowing, abundant measure (Luke 6:38). This abundance is God filling us with His own personality and presence, making us salt and light and giving us a revelation of Himself. It is God with us in all circumstances, afflictions, persecutions, and trials, girding us with truth. Christ the Initiative, the Triune God, is in control, and our every thought, word, and action must be in line with Him, with no weakness or failure. Our lives are *"hidden with Christ in God"* (Col. 3:3). When He who is our life is manifested, we will also *"appear with Him in glory"* (v. 4).

> *For we know that if our earthly house, this tent, is destroyed, we have a building from God, a house not made with hands, eternal in the heavens....For we who are in this tent groan, being burdened, not because we want to be unclothed, but further clothed, that mortality may be swallowed up by life. Now He who has prepared us for this very thing is God, who also has given us the Spirit as a guarantee.* (2 Cor. 5:1, 4–5)

God's Word is a tremendous word, a productive word. It produces what it is—power. It produces Godlikeness. We get to heaven through Christ, the Word of God; we have peace through the blood of His cross. Redemption is ours through the knowledge of the Word. I am saved because God's Word says so: *"If you confess with your mouth the Lord Jesus and believe in your heart that God has raised Him from the dead, you will be saved"* (Rom. 10:9).

If I am baptized with the Holy Spirit, it is because Jesus said, *"You shall receive power when the Holy Spirit has come upon you"* (Acts 1:8). We must all have one thought—to be filled with the Holy Spirit, to be filled with God.

September 27

The Holy Spirit has a royal plan, a heavenly plan. He came to unveil the King, to show the character of God, to unveil the precious blood of Jesus. Because I have the Holy Spirit within me, I see Jesus clothed for humanity. He was moved by the Spirit, led by the Spirit. We read of some who heard the Word of God but did not benefit from it because faith was lacking in them (Heb. 4:2). We must have a living faith in God's Word, a faith that is quickened by the Spirit.

Thought for today: Our God is a God of might, light, and revelation, preparing us for heaven.

Ready and Waiting

*The carnal mind is enmity against God; for it is not subject
to the law of God, nor indeed can be.*
—Romans 8:7

Scripture reading: Romans 8:6–25

A man may be saved and still be carnally minded. When
many people hear about the baptism of the Holy Spirit,
their carnal minds at once arise against the Holy Spirit.
One time, Jesus' disciples wanted to call down fire from heaven as
a punishment against a Samaritan village for not welcoming Him.
But Jesus said to them, *"You do not know what manner of spirit
you are of"* (Luke 9:55).

> *For we who are in this tent groan, being burdened, not be-
> cause we want to be unclothed, but further clothed, that mor-
> tality may be swallowed up by life. Now He who has prepared
> us for this very thing is God, who also has given us the Spirit
> as a guarantee.* (2 Cor. 5:4–5)

God must have people for Himself who are being clothed with a
heavenly habitation, perfectly prepared by the Holy Spirit for the
Day of the Lord. *"For in this we groan, earnestly desiring to be
clothed with our habitation which is from heaven"* (v. 2).

Was Paul speaking here only about the coming of the Lord?
No. Yet this condition of preparedness on earth is related to our
heavenly state. The Holy Spirit is coming to take out of the world a
church that is a perfect bride. He must find in us perfect yieldedness, with every desire subjected to Him. He has come to reveal
Christ in us so that the glorious flow of the life of God may flow out
of us, bringing rivers of living water to the thirsty land.

*"If Christ is in you, the body is dead because of sin, but the
Spirit is life because of righteousness"* (Rom. 8:10).

Thought for today: When we are clothed with the Spirit, our human depravity is covered and everything that is contrary to the
mind of God is destroyed.

September 29

The Plan of the Spirit

For all that is in the world; the lust of the flesh, the lust of the eyes,
and the pride of life; is not of the Father but is of the world.
—1 John 2:16

Scripture reading: 2 Timothy 1:6–14

*I*t has been a long time now since the debt of sin was settled, our redemption was secured, and death was abolished. Mortality is a hindrance, but death no longer has power. Sin no longer has dominion. You reign in Christ; you take hold of His finished work. Don't groan and travail for a week if you are in need; *"only believe"* (Mark 5:36). Don't fight to get some special thing; *"only believe."* It is according to your faith that you will receive (Matt. 9:29). God blesses you with faith. *"Have faith in God"* (Mark 11:22). If you are free in God, believe, and it will come to pass.

"If then you were raised with Christ, seek those things which are above, where Christ is, sitting at the right hand of God" (Col. 3:1). Stir yourselves up, beloved! Where are you? I have been planted with Christ in the likeness of His death, and I am risen with Christ (Rom. 6:5 KJV). It was a beautiful planting. I am seated with Him in heavenly places (Eph. 2:6). God credits me with righteousness through faith in Christ (Rom. 4:5), and I believe Him.

Why should I doubt? Why do you doubt? Faith reigns. God makes it possible. How many receive the Holy Spirit, and Satan gets a doubt in? Don't doubt; believe. There is power and strength in Him; who will dare to believe God?

Leave Doubting Street; live on Faith-Victory Street. Jesus sent the seventy out, and they came back in victory. (See Luke 10:1–18.) It takes God to make it real. Dare to believe until there is not a sick person, until there is no sickness, until everything that is not of God is withered, and the life of Jesus is implanted within.

Thought for today: We are saved, called with a holy calling—called to be saints, holy, pure, Godlike, sons with power.

September 30

Blessings of Grace and Peace

Therefore, having been justified by faith, we have peace with God through our Lord Jesus Christ, through whom also we have access by faith into this grace in which we stand, and rejoice in hope of the glory of God.
—Romans 5:1–2

Scripture reading: 1 Corinthians 1

*Y*ou are justified. You are being brought into a place of peace. And remember, the peace of God is different from any other peace. It *"surpasses all understanding"* (Phil. 4:7); it helps you to keep your composure. You are not shaken by earthly things. It is a deep peace, created by the knowledge of a living faith, which is the living principle of the foundation of all truth. Christ is in us, the hope and the evidence of glory (Col. 1:27).

See how rich you are in Christ: *"Through whom also we have access by faith into this grace in which we stand, and rejoice in hope of the glory of God."*

Peter called it a *"precious faith"* (2 Pet. 1:1). It has passed through Abraham, Jesus, the Father, and the Holy Spirit. We have access, we have a right into, we have an open door to all that the Father has, all that Jesus has, and all that the Holy Spirit has. Nothing can keep us out of it. Jesus Christ is the *"Alpha and the Omega, the Beginning and the End"* (Rev. 1:8). Through Him, we may know grace, favor, and mercy, which will lift us and take us through into grace and peace: *"Grace and peace be multiplied to you in the knowledge of God and of Jesus our Lord"* (2 Pet.1:2). Do you want grace and peace to be multiplied? You have it if you dare to believe. We have the right to the promises and the right to all the inheritance of which Christ has made us heirs.

Thought for today: Human weaknesses can spoil the effectiveness of faith. Victories become uncertain, prayers lose the anointing, and the power to take hold is hindered. But when God breathes His life into us, *"we have access by faith into this grace in which we stand."*

October 1

Spiritual Gifts

Now concerning spiritual gifts, brethren,
I do not want you to be ignorant.
—1 Corinthians 12:1

Scripture reading: Romans 11:29–12:8

*G*od wants us to enter into the rest of faith. He desires us to have all confidence in Him. He purposes that His Word will be established in our hearts; and, as we believe His Word, we will see that *"all things are possible"* (Matt. 19:26).

There is a great weakness in the church of Christ because of an awful ignorance concerning the Spirit of God and the gifts He has come to bring. God wants us to be powerful in every way because of the revelation of the knowledge of His will concerning the power and manifestation of His Spirit. He desires us to be continually hungry to receive more and more of His Spirit.

In the past, I have organized many conferences, and I have found that it is better to have a man on my platform who has not received the baptism but who is hungry for all that God has for him than a man who has received the baptism, is satisfied, has settled down, and has become stationary and stagnant. But of course I would prefer a man who is baptized with the Holy Spirit and is still hungry for more of God.

It is impossible to overestimate the importance of being filled with the Spirit. It is impossible for us to meet the conditions of the day, to *"walk in the light as He is in the light"* (1 John 1:7), to subdue kingdoms and work righteousness and bind the power of Satan, unless we are filled with the Holy Spirit.

We read that, in the early church, *"they continued steadfastly in the apostles' doctrine and fellowship, in the breaking of bread, and in prayers"* (Acts 2:42). It is important for us also to continue steadfastly in these same things.

God wants us to understand spiritual gifts and to *"earnestly desire the best gifts"* (1 Cor. 12:31). He also wants us to enter into the *"more excellent way"* (v. 31) of the fruit of the Spirit. We must implore God for these gifts. It is a serious thing to have the baptism and yet be stationary. We must be willing to deny ourselves everything to receive the revelation of God's truth and to receive the fullness of the Spirit. Only that will satisfy God, and nothing less must satisfy us.

I knew a man who was full of the Holy Spirit and would only preach when he knew that he was mightily anointed by the power of God. He was once asked to preach at a Methodist church. He was staying at the minister's house and he said, "You go on to church and I will follow." The place was packed with people, but this man did not show up. The Methodist minister, becoming anxious, sent his little girl to inquire why he did not come. As she came to the bedroom door, she heard him crying out three times, "I will not go." She went back and reported that she had heard the man say three times that he would not go. The minister was troubled about it, but almost immediately afterward the man came in. As he preached that night, the power of God was tremendously manifested. The preacher later asked him, "Why did you tell my daughter that you were not coming?" He answered, "I know when I am filled. I am an ordinary man, and I told the Lord that I did not dare to go and would not go until He gave me a fresh filling of the Spirit. The moment the glory filled me and overflowed, I came to the meeting."

Yes, there is a power, a blessing, an assurance, a rest in the presence of the Holy Spirit. You can feel His presence and know that He is with you. You do not need to spend an hour without this inner knowledge of His holy presence. With His power upon you, there can be no failure. You are above par all the time.

Thought for today: Many people today are in the midst of a great river of life but are dying of thirst because they do not dip down and take it.

October 2

Yield to God

I have come to do Your will, O God.
—Hebrews 10:9

Scripture reading: Psalm 51

As we surrender completely to God, He will be delighted to hand to us the gift that He desires us to possess. The more we realize that God has furnished us with a gift, the more completely we will be united with Jesus, so that people will be conscious of Him rather than of His gift.

If everything is not of the Holy Spirit, and if we are not so lost and controlled in the ministry of the gift that it is only to be Jesus, it will all be a failure and come to nothing. None were so self-conscious as those who said, *"In Your name, [we have] cast out demons"* (Matt. 7:22). They were so controlled by the thought that they had done it all, that God was not in it. But when He comes forth and does it, it is all right.

There is a place in the Holy Spirit where we will not allow unbelief to affect us, for God has all power in heaven and earth. I stand in a place where my faith is not to be limited because I have the knowledge that He is in me and I in Him.

Some of you have broken hearts; you have a longing for something to strengthen you in the midst of the conditions that exist in your lives, and a power to make these conditions different. You have a mighty power that is greater than all natural power. You can take victory over your homes and your spouses and children, and you must do it in the Lord's way. Suppose you do see many things that ought to be different; if it is your cross, you must take it and win the victory for God. It can be done, for He who is in you is greater than all the power of hell (1 John 4:4). I believe that anyone filled with the Holy Spirit is equal to a legion of demons any day. The Holy Spirit has His dwelling place within me and is stirring up my heart and life to adore Jesus. Other things must be left behind; I must adore Him.

Thought for today: It is worth everything to gain the Holy Spirit.

417

October 3

Pentecostal Power

Grow in the grace and knowledge of our Lord and Savior
Jesus Christ.
—2 Peter 3:18

Scripture reading: Hebrews 12:12–24

When I think about Pentecost, I am astonished from day to day because of its mightiness, its wonderfulness, and how the glory overshadows it. I think sometimes about these things, and they make me feel that we have only just touched the surface of it. Truly it is so, but we must thank God that we have touched it. We must not give in because we have only touched the surface. Whatever God has done in the past, His name is still the same. When hearts are burdened and they come face-to-face with the need of the day, they look into God's Word, and it brings in a propeller of power or an anointing that makes them know that He has truly visited.

It was a wonderful day when Jesus left the glory to come to earth. I can imagine God the Father and all the angels and all heaven so wonderfully stirred that day when the angels were sent to tell the wonderful story of "peace on earth and good will to men." (See Luke 2:14.) It was a glorious day when they beheld the Babe for the first time and God was looking on. I suppose it would take a big book to contain all that happened after that day up until Jesus was thirty years old. Everything in His life was working up to a great climax. The mother of Jesus hid many of these things in her heart. (See verse 19.)

I know that Pentecost in my life is working up to a climax; it is not all accomplished in a day. There are many waters and all kinds of experiences that we go through before we get to the real summit of everything. The power of God is here to prevail. God is with us.

Thought for today: When the Spirit of God is waiting at your heart's door, do not resist Him; instead, open your heart to the touch of God.

The Best Is Yet to Come

*Forgetting those things which are behind and reaching forward to
those things which are ahead, I press toward the goal for the prize
of the upward call of God in Christ Jesus.*
—Philippians 3:13–14

Scripture reading: Colossians 1:9–18

When Jesus was thirty years old, the time came when it was
made manifest at the Jordan River that He was the Son
of God. How beautifully it was made known! It had to be
made known first to one who was full of the vision of God. The vision comes to those who are full of God. When God has you in His
own plan, what a change; how things operate! You see things in a
new light. God is being greatly glorified as you yield from day to
day. The Spirit seems to lay hold of you and bring you further
along. Yes, it is a pressing on, and then He gives us touches of His
wonderful power, manifestations of the glory and indications of
greater things to follow. These days that we are living in now speak
of even better days to come.

Where would we be today if we had stopped short, if we had
not fulfilled the vision that God gave us? I am thinking about the
time when Christ sent the Spirit. Saul, who later became the apostle Paul, did not know much about the Spirit. His heart was stirred
against the followers of Jesus, his eyes were blinded to the truth,
and he was going to put the newborn church to an end in a short
time; but Jesus was looking on. We can scarcely understand the
whole process—only as God seems to show us—when He gets us
into His plan and works with us little by little.

We are all amazed that we are among the "tongues people."
Some of us would never have been in this Pentecostal movement if
we had not been drawn, but God has a wonderful way of drawing
us. Paul never intended to be among the disciples; he never intended to have anything to do with this Man called Jesus. But God
was working. In the same way, God has been working with us and
has brought us to this place. It is marvelous! Oh, the vision of God,
the wonderful manifestation that God has for Israel!

I have one purpose in my heart, and it is surely God's plan for
me: I want you to see that Jesus Christ is the greatest manifestation

in all the world and that His power is unequaled, but that there is only one way to minister it. Some of the people in Ephesus, after they had seen Paul working wonders by the power of Christ, began to act in human ways. (See Acts 19.) If I want to do anything for God, I see that it is necessary for me to get the knowledge of God. I cannot work on my own; I must get the vision of God. It must be a divine revelation of the Son of God. It must be that.

I can see as clearly as anything that Saul, in his mad pursuit, had to be stopped along the way. After he was stopped and had the vision from heaven and the light from heaven, he instantly realized that he had been working in the wrong way. And as soon as the power of the Holy Spirit fell upon him, he began in the way in which God wanted him to go. And it was wonderful how he had to suffer to come into the way. (See Acts 9:15–16.) A broken spirit, a tried life, and being driven into a corner as if some strange thing had happened (1 Pet. 4:12)—these are surely the ways in which we to get to know the way of God.

Thought for today: Did it ever strike you that we cannot be too full for a vision, that we cannot have too much of God?

October 5

Power in the Name of Jesus

*There is no other name under heaven given among men
by which we must be saved.*
—Acts 4:12

Scripture reading: Isaiah 42:1–13

*P*aul did not have any power of his own that enabled him to use the name of Jesus as he did. But when he had to go through the privations and the difficulties, and even when all things seemed as if they were shipwrecked, God stood by him and caused him to know that there was Someone with him, supporting him all the time, who was able to carry him through and bring out what his heart was longing for all the time. He seemed to be so unconsciously filled with the Holy Spirit that all that was needed was to bring the aprons and the handkerchiefs to him and then send them forth to heal and deliver. I can imagine these itinerant Jewish exorcists and these seven sons of Sceva in Ephesus looking on and seeing him and saying, "The power seems to be all in the name. Don't you notice that when he sends out the handkerchiefs and the aprons, he says, 'In the name of the Lord Jesus, I command the evil spirit to come out'?" (See Acts 19.)

These people had been watching, and they thought, "It is only the name; that is all that is needed," and so they said, "We will do the same." They were determined to make this thing work, and they came to a man who was possessed with an evil power. As they entered into the house where he was, they said, "We charge you in the name of Jesus, whom Paul preaches, to come out." The demon said, *"Jesus I know, and Paul I know; but who are you?"* (Acts 19:15). Then the evil power leaped upon them and tore their clothes off their backs, and they went out naked and wounded.

Oh, that God would help us to understand the name of Jesus! There is something in that name that attracts the whole world. It is the name, oh, it is still the name, but you must understand that there is the ministry of the name. It is the Holy Spirit who is behind the ministry. The power is in knowing Him.

Thought for today: The name of Jesus brings power over evil spirits.

October 6

Believe in Christ

In My name they will cast out demons; they will speak with new tongues;...they will lay hands on the sick, and they will recover.
—Mark 16:17–18

Scripture reading: Mark 16:9–19

May God help us to understand the ministry of knowing Christ. I am satisfied, first of all, that the power is in the knowledge of His blood and of His perfect holiness. I am perfectly cleansed from all sin and made holy in the knowledge of His holiness. Second, as I know Him; and as I know His power, the same power that works in me as I minister only through the knowledge of Him; and as I know the Christ who is manifested by it; such knowledge will be effective to accomplish the very thing that the Word of God says it will: it will have power over all evil. I minister today in the power of the knowledge of Him. Beyond that, there is a certain sense in which I overcome the world according to my faith in Him. I am more than a conqueror (Rom. 8:37) over everything through the knowledge that I have that He is over everything. He has been crowned by the Father to bring everything into subjection (Eph. 1:22).

Shouting won't cast out an evil spirit, but there is an anointing that is gloriously felt within and brings the act of casting out the demon into perfect harmony with the will of God. We cannot help shouting, though shouting won't do it. The power over evil spirits is in the ministry of the knowledge that He is Lord over all demons, over all powers of wickedness.

Paul went about clothed in the Spirit. This was wonderful. Was his body full of power? No! He sent forth handkerchiefs and aprons that had touched him, and when they touched the needy, they were healed and demons were cast out. Was there power in his body? No! There was power in Jesus. Paul ministered through the power of the anointing of the Holy Spirit and through faith in the name of Jesus.

Sometimes demon powers are dealt with in very different ways. But the ministry of the Spirit is administered by the power of the word *Jesus,* and His name never fails to accomplish the purpose that the one in charge has wisdom or discernment to see. This

October 6

is because, along with the Spirit of ministry, there comes the revelation of the need of the one who is bound.

The Spirit ministers the name of Jesus in many ways. I see it continually happening. I see it working, and all the time the Lord is building up a structure of His own power by a living faith in the sovereignty of Jesus' name. If I turn to John's gospel, I get the whole thing practically in a nutshell: *"This is eternal life, that they may know You, the only true God, and Jesus Christ whom You have sent"* (John 17:3). We must have the knowledge and power of God and the knowledge of Jesus Christ, the embodiment of God, in order to be clothed with God.

There are those who have come into line: they have the blessed Christ within and the power of the baptism, which is the revelation of the Christ of God within. This is so evidenced in the person who is baptized in the Spirit, and Christ is so plainly abiding, that the moment the person is confronted with evil, he is instantly sensitive to the nature of this confrontation, and he is able to deal with it accordingly.

The difference between the sons of Sceva and Paul was this: they said, "It is only the use of the name that is important." How many people only use the name; how many times are people defeated because they think it is just the name; how many people have been brokenhearted because it did not work when they used the name? If I read this into my text, "He who believes will speak in tongues; he who believes will cast out devils; he who believes will lay hands on the sick and they will recover" (see Mark 16:17–18), it seems perfectly easy on the surface of it. But you must understand this: there are volumes to be applied to the word *believe*.

Thought for today: To believe is to believe in the need of the majesty of the glory of the power of God. Believing in Christ is all power, and it brings all other powers into subjection.

What Does It Mean to Believe?

*And the evil spirit answered and said, "Jesus I know,
and Paul I know; but who are you?"*
—Acts 19:15

Scripture reading: Acts 19:11–20

What is belief? Let me sum it up in a few sentences. To believe is to have the knowledge of Him in whom you believe. It is not to believe in the word *Jesus,* but to believe in the nature of Christ, to believe in the vision of Christ, for all power has been given unto Him, and greater is He who is within you in the revelation of faith than he who is in the world. (See 1 John 4:4.) And so I say to you, do not be discouraged if every demon has not gone out. The very moment they have gone, do not think that is the end of it. What we have to see is that if all it takes is using the name of Jesus, those evil powers would have gone out in that name by the sons of Sceva. It is not that. It is the power of the Holy Spirit with the revelation of the deity of our Christ of glory; it is knowing that all power is given unto Him. Through the knowledge of Christ, and through faith in who He is, demons must surrender, demons must go out.

I say this reverently: these bodies of ours are so constructed by God that we may be filled with the divine revelation of the Son of God until it is manifest to the devils we confront, and they will have to go. The Master is in; they see the Master. *"Jesus I know, and Paul I know."* The ministry of the Master! How we need to get to know Him until within us we are full of the manifestation of the King over all demons.

Brothers and sisters, my heart is full. The depths of my yearnings are for the Pentecostal people. My cry is that we will not miss the opportunity of the baptism of the Holy Spirit, that Christ may be manifested in our human frames (2 Cor. 4:10) until every power of evil will be subject to the Christ who is manifested in us. The devils know Jesus.

Two important things are before us. First, we must surrender the mastery of ourselves to God. Then the embodiment of the Spirit gloriously covers our lives so that Jesus is glorified to the full. So first it is the losing of ourselves, and then it is the incoming of Another; it is the glorifying of Him that will fulfill all things, and when He gets hold of our lives, He can do it. When God gets hold of your life because you have yielded yourself to Him in this way, He will be delighted to allow Christ to be so manifested in you that it will be no difficulty for the Devil to know who you are.

I am satisfied that the purpose of Pentecost is to reestablish God in human flesh. Do I need to say it again? The power of the Holy Spirit has to come to be enthroned in the human life so that it does not matter where we find ourselves. Christ is manifested in the place where devils are, the place where religious devils are, the place where false religion and unbelief are, the place where formal religion has taken the place of holiness and righteousness. You need to have holiness—the righteousness and Spirit of the Master—so that in every walk of life, everything that is not like our Lord Jesus will have to depart. That is what is needed today.

I ask you in the Holy Spirit to seek the place where He is in power. *"Jesus I know, and Paul I know; but who are you?"* May God stamp this sobering question upon us, for the Devil is not afraid of us. May the Holy Spirit make us terrors of evildoers today, for the Holy Spirit came into us to judge the world of sin, of unbelief, and of righteousness; that is the purpose of the Holy Spirit. (See John 16:7–11.) Then Jesus will know us, and the devils will know us.

Thought for today: It is only when you are conquered by Christ that He is enthroned.

October 8

Christic in Us

There has not risen one greater than John the Baptist; but he
who is least in the kingdom of heaven is greater than he.
—Matthew 11:11

Scripture reading: Matthew 11:1–11

God wants to bring to us a living realization of what the Word of God is, what the Lord God means by what He says, and what we may expect if we believe it. I am certain that the Lord wishes to put before us a living fact that will, by our faith, bring into action a principle that is within our own hearts so that Christ can dethrone every power of Satan.

Only this truth revealed to our hearts can make us so much greater than we ever had any idea we could be. There is only the need of revelation and of stirring ourselves up to understand the mightiness that God has within us. We may prove what He has accomplished in us if we will only be willing to carry through what He has already accomplished in us.

For God has not accomplished something in us that should lie dormant, but He has brought within us a power, a revelation, a life that is so great that I believe God wants to reveal the greatness of it. There isn't anything you can imagine that is greater than what man may accomplish through Him.

But everything on a human basis is very limited compared with what God has for us on a spiritual basis. If man can accomplish much in a short time, what may we accomplish if we will believe the revealed Word and take it as truth that God has given us and that He wants to bring out in revelation and force?

Notice that John the Baptist was the forerunner of Jesus. Within his own short history, John the Baptist had the power of God revealed to him as probably no man in the old dispensation had. He had a wonderful revelation. He had a mighty anointing.

See how he moved Israel. See how the power of God rested upon him. See how he had the vision of Jesus and went forth with power and turned the hearts of Israel to Him. You, too, can do great things for God if you are a part of His kingdom!

Thought for today: Oh, the possibilities of man in the hands of God!

426

October 9

Looking for the Messiah

Are You the Coming One, or do we look for another?
—Matthew 11:3

Scripture reading: Matthew 11:12–24

I want you to see how satanic power can work in the mind. Satan came to John when he was in prison. I find that Satan can come to any of us.

But I want to prove that we have a greater power than Satan's—in imagination, in thought, in everything. Satan came to John the Baptist in prison and said to him, "Don't you think you have made a mistake? Here you are in prison. Isn't there something wrong with the whole business? After all, you may be greatly deceived about being a forerunner of the Christ."

I find men who might be giants of faith, who might be leaders of society, who might rise to subdue kingdoms (Heb. 11:33), who might be noble among princes, but they are defeated because they allow the suggestions of Satan to dethrone their better knowledge of the power of God. May God help us.

John sent two of his disciples to ask Jesus, "Are You the Messiah?" How could Jesus send those men back with a stimulating truth, with a personal, effective power that would stir their hearts to know that they had met Him about whom all the prophets had spoken? What would declare it? How would they know? How could they tell it?

> *Jesus answered and said to them, "Go and tell John the things which you hear and see: the blind see and the lame walk; the lepers are cleansed and the deaf hear; the dead are raised up and the poor have the gospel preached to them."*
> (Matt. 11:4–5)

And when they saw the miracles and wonders and heard the gracious words He spoke as the power of God rested upon Him, they were ready to believe.

Thought for today: Unless we are filled, or divinely insulated, with the power of God, we may be defeated by the power of Satan.

Jesus Is Our Life

From the days of John the Baptist until now the kingdom of heaven
suffers violence, and the violent take it by force.
—Matthew 11:12

Scripture reading: Matthew 11:25–30

*T*his is a message to every believer. Every believer has the life of the Lord in him. And if Jesus, *"who is our life"* (Col. 3:4), were to come, instantly our life would go out to meet His life because we exist by and consist of the life of the Son of God. (See verse 4.) *"Your life is hidden with Christ in God"* (v. 3).

If all believers understood this wonderful passage that is in the twenty-second chapter of Luke's gospel, there would be great joy in their hearts:

> Then He said to them, "With fervent desire I have desired to eat this Passover with you before I suffer; for I say to you, I will no longer eat of it until it is fulfilled in the kingdom of God." (Luke 22:15–16)

Everyone who is in Christ Jesus will be there when He sits down the first time to break bread in the kingdom of heaven. It is not possible for any child of God to remain on earth when Jesus comes. May the Lord help us to believe it.

I know there is a great deal of speculation on the Rapture and on the coming of the Lord. But let me tell you to hope for edification and comfort, for the Scripture by the Holy Spirit won't let me focus on anything except the edification, consolation, and comfort of the Spirit. (See 1 Corinthians 14:3.)

I don't mean that we are to cover up sin. God won't let us do that. But we must unveil truth. And what is truth? The Word of God is the truth. Jesus said, *"I am the way, the truth, and the life"* (John 14:6). *"You search the Scriptures, for in them you think you have eternal life; and these are they which testify of Me"* (John 5:39).

What does the truth say? It says that when Christ appears, all who are His at His coming will be changed *"in a moment, in the twinkling of an eye"* (1 Cor. 15:52). We will be presented at the same moment as all those who have fallen sleep in Him, and we will all go together.

> *We who are alive and remain until the coming of the Lord will by no means precede those who are asleep....And the dead in Christ will rise first. Then we who are alive and remain shall be caught up together with them in the clouds to meet the Lord in the air. And thus we shall always be with the Lord. Therefore comfort one another with these words.* (1 Thess. 4:15–18)

> *For I say to you, I will not drink of the fruit of the vine until the kingdom of God comes.* (Luke 22:18)

Two thousand years will soon have passed since the Lord broke bread around the table with His disciples. I am longing, the saints are longing, for the grand union when millions, billions, trillions will unite with Him in that great fellowship Supper. Praise the Lord! But now, what stimulation, what power must be working every day until that Day appears!

Thought for today: Every believer belongs to the kingdom of heaven.

October 11

Power Greater than the Enemy

Be strong in the Lord and in the power of His might. Put on the
whole armor of God, that you may be able to stand against
the wiles of the devil.
—Ephesians 6:10–11

Scripture reading: Ephesians 6:10–20

There is a power in you that is greater than any other power. By the help of the Spirit, may you come into a place of deliverance, a place of holy sanctification, where you dare to stand against the Devil's' schemings, drive them back, and cast them out. May the Lord help us!

I want God to give you an inward awakening, a revelation of truth within you, an audacity, a flaming indignation against the powers of Satan.

Lot had a righteous indignation—temporarily—but it came too late. He ought to have had it when he went into Sodom, not when he was coming out. But I don't want any one of you to be dejected because you didn't take a step in the right direction sooner. Always be thankful that you are alive to hear and to change the situation.

You must gain an inward knowledge that God is Lord over all the power of Satan. I don't doubt your sincerity about being saved, about having been justified in Christ. It is not for me to question a man's sincerity regarding his righteousness. Yet I feel I have a right to say that there is a deeper sincerity to reach for; there is a greater audacity of faith and fact to attain. There is something that you have to wake up to where you will never allow disease to have you or sin to have you or a weak heart or a pain in your back to have you. You will never allow anything that isn't perfect life to have anything to do with you. Those who try to serve two masters always lose (Matt. 6:24). If you try to join up with two things—the Lord and the Devil—the Devil will get you in the end. Allow Christ to be the Lord of your life today.

Thought for today: You are not going to oppose devils if you cannot master yourself, because you will soon find the devils to be bigger than yourself.

A God Who Saves

*Then they cried out to the LORD in their trouble, and He
delivered them out of their distresses.*
—Psalm 107:6

Scripture reading: Psalm 50

*D*oes God know all about you? Is He acquainted with you altogether? Why should you, under any circumstances, believe that you will be better off by being diseased? When disease is impurity, why should you ever believe that you will be sanctified by having a great deal of sickness?

Some people talk about God being pleased to put disease on His children. "Here is a person I love," says God. "I will break his arm. Then, so that he will love Me more, I will break his leg. So that he will love Me even more, I will give him a weak heart."

The whole thing won't stand daylight. Yet people are always talking this way, and they never think to read the Word of God, which says, *"Before I was afflicted I went astray"* (Ps. 119:67). They have never read the following words into their lives:

> *Fools, because of their transgression, and because of their iniquities, were afflicted. Their soul abhorred all manner of food, and they drew near to the gates of death. Then they cried out to the LORD in their trouble, and He saved them out of their distresses.* (Ps. 107:17–19)

Is it right to say, "You know, my brother, I have suffered so much in this affliction that it has made me know God better"? Well, now, before you agree, ask God for a lot more affliction so that you will get to know Him still better. If you won't ask for more affliction to make you still purer, I won't believe that the first affliction made you purer, because if it had, you would have more faith in it. It appears that you do not have faith in your afflictions. It is only talk, but talk doesn't count unless it is backed up by fact. However, if people can see that your words are backed up by fact, then they have some grounds for believing in them.

Thought for today: Why not trust God who knows all about you, instead of trusting in people who know only what you have told them?

Keep Looking to Jesus

For He shall give His angels charge over you,
to keep you in all your ways.
—Psalm 91:11

Scripture reading: Psalm 91

I have looked through my Bible, and I cannot find where God brings disease and sickness. I know it is the power of God that brings the glory. Yet it is the Devil and not God at all who brings sickness and disease. Why does he? I know this: Satan is God's whip, and if you don't obey God, God will stand to one side and Satan will devour you. But God will only allow him to devour so much, as was the case with Job. The Lord told Satan, "You may go only so far, and no further. Don't touch his life." (See Job 2:6.)

Why is Satan allowed to bring sickness? It is because we know better than we act. If we would be true to our convictions and walk according to the light we have been given, God would verify His presence in the midst of us, and we would know that sickness cannot *"come near* [our] *dwelling; for He shall give His angels charge over* [us]*, to keep* [us] *in all* [our] *ways"* (Ps. 91:10–11).

When Satan can get to your body, he will, if possible, make the pain or the weakness so distracting that it will affect your mind and always bring your mind down to where the pain is. When that takes place, you do not have the same freedom in your spirit to lift up your heart and shout and praise the Lord. The distraction of the pain brings the foundational power, which ought to be full of praise to God, down into the body. And through that—concerning everybody who is afflicted—*"the kingdom of heaven suffers violence"* (Matt. 11:12).

Thought for today: Anything that takes me from a position where I am in an attitude of worship, peace, and joy; where I have a consciousness of the presence of God; where there is an inward moving of the powers of God that makes me able to lift myself up and live in the world as though I were not of it (because I am not of it); anything that dethrones me from that attitude is evil, is satanic.

October 14

Let Kingdom Life Reign

Let each of us please his neighbor for his good, leading to edification.
—Romans 15:2

Scripture reading: Romans 14:12–15:2

*I*f it is only a finger or a tooth that aches, if it is only a corn on your foot that pinches you or anything in the body that detracts from the highest spiritual attainment, the kingdom of heaven is dethroned to a degree; *"the kingdom of heaven suffers violence"* (Matt. 11:12).

By the Word of God, I am proving to you that the kingdom of heaven is within you. *"Greater is he that is in you"* (1 John 4:4 KJV)—the Son of God, the kingdom of heaven within you—*"than he that is in the world"* (v. 4 KJV)—the power of Satan outside you.

Disease or weakness, or any distraction in you, is a power of violence that can take the kingdom of heaven in you by force. The same spiritual power that will reveal this to you, will relieve you.

On the authority of the Word of God, I maintain that *"greater is he that is in you"* (1 John 4:4 KJV) than any power of Satan that is around you (v. 4). How much more would be done if you would inwardly claim your rights and deliver yourselves!

I believe the Bible from front to back. If, by the power of God, I put in you an audacity, a determination, so that you won't let Satan rest, you will be victorious. Praise the Lord!

Why do I take this attitude? Because for every step of my life since my baptism, I have had to pay the price of everything for others. God has to take me through to the place so that I may be able to show the people how to do it. Some people come up to me and say, "I have been waiting for the baptism, and I am having such a struggle. I am having to fight for every inch of it. Isn't it strange?" No. A thousand to one, God is preparing you to help somebody else who is desiring to receive it.

The reason I am so firm about the necessity of getting the baptism in the Holy Spirit, and about the significance of the Spirit's making a manifestation when He comes in, is this: I fought it. I went to a meeting because I had heard people were speaking in tongues there. I forced myself on the attention of those in the meeting almost like a man who was mad. I told the people there,

433

"This meeting of yours is nothing. I have left better conditions at home. I am hungry and thirsty for something."

"What do you want?" they asked.

"I want tongues."

"You want the baptism?" they asked.

"Not I," I said. "I have the baptism. I want tongues."

I could have had a fight with anybody. The whole situation was this: God was training me for something else. The power of God fell upon my body with such ecstasy of joy that I could not satisfy the joy within with my natural tongue; then I found the Spirit speaking through me in other tongues.

What did it mean? I knew that I had had anointings of joy before this, and expressions of the blessed attitude of the Spirit of life, and joy in the Holy Spirit; I had felt it all the way through my life. But when the fullness came with a high tide, with an overflowing life, I knew that was different from anything else. And I knew that was the baptism, but God had to show me.

Thought for today: The Bible won't have an atom of power in you if you don't put it into practice in yourself.

October 15

Spiritual Warfare

For the weapons of our warfare are not carnal but mighty in God for pulling down strongholds.
—2 Corinthians 10:4

Scripture reading: 2 Corinthians

People ask, "Do all speak with tongues?" Certainly not. But all people may speak as the Spirit gives utterance—as in the Upper Room and at the house of Cornelius and at Ephesus when Jesus' followers were filled with the Holy Spirit.

There is quite a difference between having a gift and speaking as the Spirit gives utterance. If I had been given the gift of tongues when I was filled with the Holy Spirit, then I could have spoken in tongues at any time, because gifts and calling remain (Rom. 11:29). But I couldn't speak in tongues after I was baptized. Why? It was because I had received the Holy Spirit with the evidence of speaking in tongues, but I hadn't received the gift of tongues.

However, I received the Holy Spirit, who is the Giver of all gifts. And nine months afterward, God gave me the gift of tongues so that I could speak in tongues at any time. But do I? God forbid! Why? Because no man ought to use a gift; the Holy Spirit uses the gift.

I have a reason for talking like this. People come up to me all the time and say, "I have been prayed for, and I am just the same." It is enough to make you kick them. I don't mean that literally. I would be the last man to kick anybody in this place. God forbid. But if I can get you enraged against the powers of darkness and the powers of disease, if I can wake you up, you won't go to bed unless you prove that there is a Master in you who is greater than the power that is hanging around you.

Many times I have gone to a house in which an insane person lived and have been shut in with him in order to deliver him. I have gone in determined that he would be delivered. In the middle of the night chiefly, sometimes in the middle of the day, the demon powers would come and bite me and handle me terribly roughly. But I never gave in. It would dethrone a higher principle if I had to give in.

435

May the God of grace and mercy strengthen us. In the measure that we destroy these evil powers, we make it easier for weak believers. For every time Satan overcomes a saint, it gives him ferocity for another attack; but when he is subdued, he will come to the place where defeat is written against him.

In your home, with your spouse and children, you will have audacity of determination, along with a righteous indignation, against the power of disease to cast it out. That is worth more to you than anything you could buy.

Thought for today: No one can have a knowledge of an inward Christ without having a longing that there will be an increase of souls saved.

Aflame for God

[He] makes His angels spirits and His ministers a flame of fire.
—Hebrews 1:7

Scripture reading: Hebrews 1

God's ministers are to be flames of fire! It seems to me that no man with a vision, especially a vision by the Spirit's power, can read that wonderful verse without being kindled to such a flame of fire for his Lord that it seems as if it would burn up everything that would interfere with his progress.

A flame of fire! It is a perpetual fire; a constant fire; a continual burning; a holy, inward flame; which is exactly what God's Son was in the world. God has nothing less for us than to be flames! It seems to me that if Pentecost is to rise and be effective, we must have a living faith so that Christ's great might and power can flow through us until our lives become energized, moved, and aflame for God.

The important point here is that the Holy Spirit has come to make Jesus King. It seems to me that the seed, the life that was given to us when we believed—which is an eternal seed—has such resurrection power that I see a new creation rising from it with kingly qualities. Not only is the King to be within us, but also all the glories of His kingly manifestations are to be brought forth in us. Oh, for Him to work in us in this way, melting us, until a new order rises within us so that we are moved with His compassion! I see that we can come into the order of God where the vision becomes so much brighter and where the Lord is manifesting His glory with all His virtues and gifts; all His glory seems to fill the soul who is absolutely dead to himself and alive to God. There is much talk about death, but there is a death that is so deep in God that, out of that death, God brings the splendor of His life and all His glory.

An opportunity to be a flame of fire for God came when I was traveling from Egypt to Italy. What I now tell you truly happened. On the ship and everywhere, God had been with me. A man on the ship suddenly collapsed; his wife was in a terrible state, and everybody else seemed to be, too. Some said that he would die, but oh, to be a flame, to have the living Christ dwelling within you!

We are backslidden if we have to pray for power, if we have to wait until we feel a sense of His presence. The baptism of the Holy Spirit has come upon you: *"You shall receive power when the Holy Spirit has come upon you"* (Acts 1:8). Within you is a greater power than there is in the world (1 John 4:4). Oh, to be awakened out of our unbelief into a place of daring for God on the authority of the blessed Book!

So in the name of Jesus, I rebuked the devil, and to the astonishment of the man's wife and the man himself, he was able to stand. He said, "What is this? It is going all over me. I have never felt anything like this before." From the top of his head to the soles of his feet, the power of God shook him. God has given us authority over the power of the Devil. Oh, that we may live in the place where the glory excels! It would make anyone a flame of fire.

Thought for today: When we are baptized in the Holy Spirit, it is to crown Jesus King in our lives.

Faithful Servants

His lord said to him, "Well done, good and faithful servant; you were faithful over a few things, I will make you ruler over many things. Enter into the joy of your lord."
—Matthew 25:21

Scripture reading: Matthew 25:14–30

Christ, who is the express image of God (Heb. 1:3), has come to our human weaknesses in order to change them and us into a divine likeness so that, by the power of His might, we may not only overcome but also rejoice in the fact that we are more than overcomers. God wants you to be *"more than conquerors"* (Rom. 8:37). The baptism of the Spirit has come for nothing less than to possess the whole of our lives. It sets up Jesus as King, and nothing can stand in His holy presence when He is made King. Everything will wither before Him. The inheritance of the Spirit is given to every man *"for the profit of all"* (1 Cor. 12:7). Praise the Lord! In the order of the Holy Spirit, we have to *"come short in no gift"* (1 Cor. 1:7).

This same Jesus has come for one purpose: that He might be made so manifest in us that the world will see Him. We must be burning and shining lights to reflect such a holy Jesus. We cannot do it with cold, indifferent experiences, and we never will. My dear wife used to say to our daughter, "Alice, what kind of a meeting have you had?" Alice would say, "Ask Father. He always has a good time!" His servants are to be flames. Jesus is life, and the Holy Spirit is the breath. He breathes through us the life of the Son of God, and we give it to others, and it gives life everywhere.

You should have been with me in Ceylon! I was having meetings in a Wesleyan chapel. The people there said, "You know, four days are not much to give us." "No," I said, "but it is a good share." They said, "What are we going to do? We are not touching the people here at all." I said, "Can you have a meeting early in the morning, at eight o'clock?" They said they would, so I said, "We will tell all the mothers who want their babies to be healed and all the old people over seventy to come. Then after that, I will hope to give an address to the people to make them ready for the Holy Spirit."

Oh, it would have done you all good to see four hundred mothers there with their babies! It was fine! And then to see one hundred and fifty old black people, with their white hair, coming to be healed. I believe that you need to have something more than smoke to touch people; you need to be a burning light for that. His ministers must be flames of fire. There were thousands gathered outside the chapel to hear the Word of God. There were about three thousand people crying for mercy at the same time. I tell you, it was a sight.

After that, attendance at the meetings rose to such an extent that every night, five to six thousand people gathered there after I had preached in a temperature of 110 degrees. Then I had to minister to these people. But I tell you, a flame of fire can do anything. Things change in the fire. This is Pentecost. But what moved me more than anything else was this (and I say this carefully and with a broken spirit because I would not like to mislead anybody): there were hundreds who tried to touch me because they were so impressed with the power of God that was present. And they testified everywhere that with a touch, they were healed. It was *not* the power of Wigglesworth. It was because they had the same faith that was with those at Jerusalem who believed that Peter's shadow would heal them. (See Acts 5:14–15.)

What do you want? Is anything too hard for God? God can meet you now. God sees inwardly. He knows all about you. Nothing is hidden from Him, and He can satisfy the soul and give you a spring of eternal blessing that will carry you right through.

Thought for today: You can receive something in three minutes that you can carry with you into glory.

October 18

Glory

*His divine power has given to us all things that pertain
to life and godliness, through the knowledge of Him
who called us by glory and virtue.*
—2 Peter 1:3

Scripture reading: 2 Peter 1:2–17

On the Day of Pentecost, it was necessary that the disciples received not only the fire but also the rushing wind, the personality of the Spirit in the wind. (See Acts 2:1–4.) The manifestation of the glory is in the wind, or breath, of God.

The inward man receives the Holy Spirit instantly with great joy and blessedness. He cannot express it. Then the power of the Spirit, this breath of God, takes of the things of Jesus (see John 16:14–15) and sends forth as a river the utterances of the Spirit. Again, when the body is filled with joy, sometimes so inexpressible, the canvas of the mind has great power to move the operation of the tongue to bring out the very depths of the inward heart's power, love, and joy to us. By the same process, the Spirit, which is the breath of God, brings forth the manifestation of the glory.

Let us look at a few passages in the Bible that pertain to the glory. The first is Psalm 16:9: *"Therefore my heart is glad, and my glory rejoices."* Something has made the rejoicing bring forth the glory. It was because the psalmist's heart was glad.

The second one is Psalm 108:1: *"O God, my heart is steadfast; I will sing and give praise, even with my glory."* You see, when the body is filled with the power of God, then the only thing that can express the glory is the tongue. Glory is presence, and the presence always comes by the tongue, which brings forth the revelations of God. God first brings His power into us. Then He gives us verbal expressions by the same Spirit, the outward manifestation of what is within us. *"Out of the abundance of the heart the mouth speaks"* (Matt. 12:34).

Virtue has to be transmitted, and glory has to be expressed. Therefore, The Holy Spirit understands everything Christ has in the glory and brings through the heart of man God's latest thought. The world's needs, our manifestations, revivals, and all conditions are first settled in heaven, then worked out on the

441

earth. We must be in touch with God Almighty in order to bring out on the face of the earth all the things that God has in the heavens. This is an ideal for us, and may God help us not to forsake the reality of holy communion with Him, of entering into private prayer so that publicly He may manifest His glory.

Thought for today: By filling us with the Holy Spirit, God has brought into us this glory so that out of us may come forth the glory.

October 19

Hold Fast to the Vision

Where there is no vision, the people perish.
—Proverbs 29:18 KJV

Scripture reading: Acts 26:1–29

We must see the face of the Lord and understand His workings. There are things that God says to me that I know must take place. It does not matter what people say. I have been face-to-face with some of the most trying moments of men's lives, times when it made all the difference if I kept the vision and held fast to what God had said. A man must have immovable faith, and the voice of God must mean more to him than what he sees, feels, or what people say. He must have an originality born in heaven, transmitted or expressed in some way. We must bring heaven to earth.

At the end of Ephesians 3 are words that no human could ever think or write on his own. This passage is so mighty, so of God when it speaks about His being able to do all things *"exceedingly abundantly above all that we ask or think"* (v. 20). The mighty God of revelation! The Holy Spirit gave these words of grandeur to stir our hearts, to move our affections, to transform us altogether. God has never put anything up on a pole where you cannot reach it. He has brought His plan down to man, and if we are prepared, oh, what there is for us! I feel sometimes that we have just as much as we can digest. Yet such divine nuggets of precious truth are held before our hearts that it makes us understand that there are yet heights and depths and lengths and breadths of the knowledge of God stored up for us. (See Ephesians 3:17–19.) We might truly say,

> My heavenly bank, my heavenly bank,
> The house of God's treasure and store.
> I have plenty in here; I'm a real millionaire.

Thought for today: It is wonderful to never be poverty-stricken anymore, to have an inward knowledge of God's riches that are stored up, nugget upon nugget—weights of glory, expressions of the invisible Christ to be seen by men.

October 20

Victorious in Battle

Count it all joy when you fall into various trials.
—James 1:2

Scripture reading: 1 Timothy 6

*L*et the Spirit cover you so that you may be intensely earnest about the deep things of God. You should be so aligned with the Spirit that your will, your mind, and your heart are centered in God so that He may lift you into the pavilion of splendor where you hear His voice—lift you to the place where the breath of the Almighty can send you to pray and send you to preach, the Spirit of the Lord being upon you.

You are at God's banquet, a banquet at which you are never separated from Him and He multiplies spiritual blessings and fruit in your life. It is a banquet where you have to increase with all increasing, where God has for you riches beyond all things—not fleshly things, not carnal things, but spiritual manifestations, gifts, fruits of the Spirit, and beautiful beatitudes, the blessing of God always being upon you. (See 2 Corinthians 9:10–11.)

Are you ready to enter into this glorious place where you no longer live for yourself? God will take over your life and send you out to win thousands of people to Christ, so that they also may enter into eternal grace.

No person is ever able to talk about victory over temptation unless he goes through it. All the victories are won in battles.

Tens of thousands of people in Europe, America, and in other parts of the world wear badges to show they have been in battle, and they rejoice in it. They would be ashamed to wear such badges if they had not been in battle. The battle is what gives them the right to wear the badge.

It is those who have been tried to the utmost who can come out and tell you a story about it. It was only James and Peter and Paul, those who were in the front lines of the battle, who told us how we have to rejoice in our trials because wonderful blessings will come out of them. It is in the trials that we are made.

Thought for today: It is those who have been in the fight who can tell about the victories.

More Precious than Gold

That the genuineness of your faith, being much more precious than gold that perishes, though it is tested by fire, may be found to praise, honor, and glory at the revelation of Jesus Christ,
—1 Peter 1:7

Scripture reading: 1 Peter 1

Some of you wonder what is up when you are not healed in a moment. God never breaks His promise. The trial of your faith is *"much more precious than gold."*

God wants to destroy the power of the Devil. He wants to move you so that in the face of hardships, you will praise the Lord. *"Count it all joy"* (James 1:2). You have to take a leap today; you have to leap into the promises. You have to believe that God never fails you; you have to believe it is impossible for God to break His word. He is *"from everlasting to everlasting"* (Ps. 90:2).

> Forever and ever, not for a day,
> He keepeth His promise forever;
> To all who believe,
> To all who obey,
> He keepeth His promise forever.

There is no variableness with God, no *"shadow of turning"* (James 1:17). He is the same. He manifests His divine glory.

Jesus said to Mary and Martha, *"If you would believe you would see the glory of God"* (John 11:40). We must understand that there will be times of testing, but they are only to make us more like the Master. He was *"in all points tempted as we are, yet without sin"* (Heb. 4:15). He endured all things. He is our example.

Oh, that God would place us in an earnest, intent position in which flesh and blood have to yield to the Spirit of God! We will go forward; we will not be moved by our feelings.

Suppose that a man who is prayed for today receives a blessing, but tomorrow he begins murmuring because he does not feel exactly as he wants to feel. What is he doing? He is replacing the Word of God with his feelings. What a disgrace! Let God have His perfect work.

Thought for today: God has you on this earth for the purpose of bringing out His character in you.

October 22

God Will Keep You

Count it all joy.
—James 1:2

Scripture reading: Job 2:1–10

The verse does not mean "Count a bit of it as joy" but *"count it all joy."* It doesn't matter from what source the trial comes, whether it is your business or your home or what. *"Count it all joy."* Why? Because *"we know that all things work together for good to those who love God, to those who are the called according to His purpose"* (Rom. 8:28).

That is a great Scripture. It means that you have a special position. God is electrifying the very position that you hold so that the Devil will see that you have a godly character, and God can say about you what he said about Job. (See Job 1:8.)

Recall the scene. God asked, "Satan, what is your opinion about Job?" Then the Lord went on and said, "Don't you think he is wonderful? Don't you think he is the most excellent man in all the earth?"

Satan replied, "Yes, but You know, You are keeping him."

Praise the Lord! I am glad the Devil has to tell the truth. And don't you know that God can keep you, also?

"If You touch everything he has," the Devil said, "he will curse You to Your face."

God answered, "You can touch all he has, but you cannot touch him." (See Job 1:8–12.)

The Scripture says that Jesus was dead but is alive again and has power over death and hell. To this, the Scripture adds a big *"Amen"* (Rev. 1:18). The Devil cannot take your life unless the Lord allows it. "You cannot touch Job's life," God told Satan. (See Job 2:6.)

Satan thought he could destroy Job, and you know the calamity that befell this righteous man. But Job said, *"Naked I came from my mother's womb, and naked shall I return there....Blessed be the name of the LORD"* (Job 1:21). Oh, it is lovely! The Lord can give us that kind of language. It is not the language of the head. This is divine language; this is heart acquaintance.

October 22

I want you to know that we can have heart acquaintance. I learned a long time ago that libraries often create swelled heads, but nothing except the Library, the Bible, can make swelled hearts. You are to have swelled hearts because out of the heart full of the fragrance of the love of God, the living life of the Lord flows.

You must cease to be. That is a difficult thing—for both you and me—but it is no trouble at all when you are in the hands of the Potter. You are only wrong when you are kicking. You are all right when you are still and He is forming you afresh. So let Him form you afresh today into a new vessel so that you will stand the stress.

Thought for today: It is far more to speak out of the abundance of your heart than the abundance of your head.

Be Perfect

*Let patience have its perfect work, that you may be perfect
and complete, lacking nothing.*
—James 1:4

Scripture reading: Matthew 27:27–54

*I*s it possible for patience to make us *"perfect and complete"*?
Certainly, it is possible. Who was speaking in this verse? It
was the breath of the Spirit; it was also the hidden man of
the heart who had a heart like his Brother. This was James, the
Lord's brother, who was speaking. He spoke very much like his
Brother. When we read these wonderful words, we might very
likely be encountering a true kindred spirit with Christ.

James had to learn patience. It was not an easy thing for him
to understand how his Brother could be the Son of God and be in
the same family as he, Judas, and the other brothers. (See Matthew 13:55.) It was not an easy thing for him, and he had to learn
to be patient to see how it worked out.

There are many things in your life that you cannot understand, but be patient. When the hand of God is upon something, it
may grind very slowly, but it will form the finest thing possible if
you dare to wait until it is completed. Do not kick until you have
gone through the process—and when you are dead enough to yourself, you will never kick at all. It is a death we die so that we might
be alive unto God. It is only by the deaths we die that we are able
to be still before God.

Jesus said, "The cross? I can endure the cross. The shame? I
can despise it." (See Hebrews 12:2.) He withstood the bitter language spoken to Him at the cross: "If You are the Christ, come
down, and we will believe." (See Matthew 27:40, 42.) They struck
Him, but He *"did not revile in return"* (1 Pet. 2:23). He is the picture for us.

You cannot tell what God has in mind for you. As you are still
before God—pliable in His hands—He will be working out a greater
vessel than you could ever imagine in all your life.

Thought for today: Jesus knew that when He came to the end of
the Cross, He would forever save all those who would believe.

October 24

Complete, Lacking Nothing

*Let patience have its perfect work, that you may be perfect
and complete, lacking nothing.*
—James 1:4

Scripture reading: Psalm 91

To be *"complete"* means that you are not moved by anything, that you are living only in the divine position of God. It means that you are not moved, that you are not changed by what people say. There is something about divine acquaintance that is instilled; it is worked within a person by the mighty God. It becomes like intuition.

Accepting Christ as Savior builds the character of a person in purity until his inward heart is filled with divine love and has nothing but thoughts of God alone. *"That you may be perfect and complete, lacking nothing."*

When I was in New Zealand, some people came to me and said, "We would like to give you a Christmas present, if you can tell us what you would like." "I haven't a desire in the world," I said. "I cannot tell you anything I would like. I have no desire for anything except God."

One day, I was walking down the street with a millionaire. I was feeling wonderfully happy over the way the Lord was blessing in our meetings. As we walked together, I said, "Brother, I haven't a care in the world. I am as happy as a bird!"

"Oh!" he said. "Stop! Say it again! Say it again!" And he stood still, waiting for me to repeat it. "Brother, I haven't a care in the world. I am as happy as a bird!" He exclaimed, "I would give all my money, I would give everything I have, to have that!"

To be lacking nothing—hallelujah!

The Spirit of the Lord is moving us mightily to see that this is resurrection power. We were planted with Him, and we have been raised with Him (Rom. 6:5 KJV). We are from above (see Colossians 3:1–3); we do not belong to what is below. We *"reign in life"* (Rom. 5:17) by Another. It is the life of God's Son manifested in this human body.

Thought for today: The new life of God is not just on the surface.

October 25

Ask God for Wisdom

*If any of you lacks wisdom, let him ask of God, who gives to all
liberally and without reproach, and it will be given to him.*
—James 1:5

Scripture reading: James 1

Many people come to me and ask if I will pray for them to have faith. I want to encourage them, but I cannot depart from God's Word. I cannot grant people faith. But by the power of the Spirit, I can stimulate you until you dare to believe and rest on the authority of God's Word. The Spirit of the living God quickens you, and I see that *"faith comes by hearing, and hearing by the word of God"* (Rom. 10:17).

This is a living word of faith: *"If any of you lacks wisdom, let him ask of God, who gives to all liberally."* You will never find that God ever judges you for the wisdom He gives you or for the blessing He gives you. He makes it so that when you come to Him again, He gives again, never asking what you did with what He gave you before. That is the way God gives. God *"gives to all liberally and without reproach."* So you have a chance today to come for much more. Do you want wisdom? Ask of God.

You have to be in the right condition for asking. This is the condition: *"But let him ask in faith, with no doubting"* (James 1:6).

I am satisfied that God, who is the builder of divine order, never brings confusion into His order. It is only when things are out of order that God brings confusion. God brought confusion upon the men who were building the Tower of Babel because they were out of order. (See Genesis 11:1–9.) What were they doing? They were trying to get into heaven by a way that was not God's way, and they were thieves and robbers. (See John 10:1.) So He turned their language to confusion. There is a way into the kingdom of heaven, and it is through the blood of the Lord Jesus Christ.

If you want this divine order in your life, if you want wisdom, you have to come to God believing. I want to impress upon you the fact—and I am learning it more every day—that if you ask six times for anything, just for the sake of asking, it shows you are an unbelieving person. If you really believe, you will ask God and

450

know that He has abundance for your every need. But if you go right in the face of belief and ask six times, He knows very well that you do not mean what you ask, so you do not get it.

If you would really get down to business about the baptism of the Holy Spirit and ask God once and definitely to fill you, believing it, what would you do? You would begin to praise Him for it because you would know He had given it.

If you ask God once for healing, you will get it. But if you ask a thousand times a day until you do not even know you are asking, you will get nothing. If you would ask God for your healing now and begin praising Him because He never breaks His word, you would go out of here perfect. *"Only believe"* (Mark 5:36).

God wants to promote us. He wants us to get away from our own thoughts and our own foolishness, and get to a definite place, believing that He exists and that *"He is a rewarder of those who diligently seek Him"* (Heb. 11:6).

Have you reached the place where you dare to do this? Have you come to the place where you are no longer going to murmur when you are undergoing a trial? Are you going to go around weeping, telling people about it, or are you going to say, "Thank you, Lord, for putting me on the top"?

A great number of ministers and evangelists do not get checks sent to them any longer because they didn't thank the donor for the last one. A thankful heart is a receiving heart. God wants to keep you in the place of constant believing.

> Keep on believing, Jesus is near,
> Keep on believing, there's nothing to fear;
> Keep on believing, this is the way,
> Faith in the night, the same as the day.

Thought for today: God does not honor unbelief; He honors faith.

October 26

Endure Temptation

Blessed is the man who endures temptation; for when he has been approved, he will receive the crown of life which the Lord has promised to those who love Him.
—James 1:12

Scripture reading: Psalm 139

*P*eople do not know what they are getting when they are in a great place of temptation. Temptation endured brings the *"crown of life."*

There is nothing outside of purity except what is sin. All unbelief is sin. God wants you to have a pure, active faith so that you will be living in an advanced place of believing God all the time, and so that you will be on the mountaintop and singing when other people are crying.

I want to speak now about lust. I am not speaking about the base things, the carnal desires. I am not speaking so much about adultery, fornication, and such things, but I am speaking about what has turned you aside to some other thing instead of God. God has been offering you better things all the time, and you have missed them.

There are three things in life, and I notice that many people are satisfied with just one of them. There is blessing in justification, there is blessing in sanctification, and there is blessing in the baptism of the Holy Spirit. Salvation is a wonderful thing, and we know it. Sanctification is a process that takes us on to a higher level with God. Salvation, sanctification, and the fullness of the Spirit are processes.

Many people are satisfied with "good"—that is, with salvation. Other people are satisfied with "better"—a sanctified life, purified by God. Still other people are satisfied with the "best"—the fullness of God with revelation from on high. I am not satisfied with any of the three. I am only satisfied with the "best with improvement."

So I come to you not with good, but better; not with better, but best; not with best, but best with improvement—going on with God. Why? Because *"when desire has conceived, it gives birth to sin; and sin, when it is full-grown, brings forth death"* (James

452

1:15). When anything has taken me from God, it means death in some way.

When Jesus said to the disciples, "The Son of Man will be put into the hands of sinners and crucified," Peter rebuked Him (see Matthew 16:21–22), but Jesus said, *"Get behind Me, Satan! You are an offense to Me, for you are not mindful of the things of God, but the things of men"* (v. 23).

Anything that hinders me from denying myself and taking up my cross (v. 24) is of the Devil; anything that hinders me from being separated unto God is of the Devil; and anything that hinders me from being purified every day is carnal, and it is death. So I implore you today to make certain that there is no lustful thing in you that would rob you of the glory. Then God will take you to the very summit of the blessing where you can be increased day by day into all His fullness.

Thought for today: Do not neglect the Word of God. Take time to think about the Word of God; it is the only place of safety.

October 27

Unconditional Surrender

Repent, for the kingdom of heaven is at hand!
—Matthew 3:2

Scripture reading: 2 Peter 3:1–9

*P*entecost has made me rejoice in Jesus. God has been confirming His power by His Holy Spirit. I have an intense yearning to see Pentecost, and I am not seeing it. I may feel a little of the glow, but what we need is a deeper work of the Holy Spirit in order for God's message to come full of life and power and sharper than a *"two-edged sword"* (Heb. 4:12). At Pentecost, Peter stood up in the power of the Holy Spirit, and three thousand people were saved. Not long after this, he preached again, and five thousand people were saved.

I am positive that we are on the wrong side of the Cross. We talk about love, love, love, but it ought to be repent, repent, repent. John the Baptist came, and his message was *"Repent."* Jesus came with the same message: *"Repent"* (Matt. 4:17). The Holy Spirit came, and the message was the same: repent, repent, repent and believe. (See Acts 2:38.) What has all this to do with Pentecost? Everything! It is the secret of our failure.

Daniel carried on his heart the burden of the people. He mourned for the captivity of Zion, he confessed his sin and the people's sin, and he identified himself with Israel until God made him a flame of fire. (See Daniel 9.) The result: a remnant returned to Zion to walk in the despised way of obedience to God.

Nehemiah was brokenhearted when he learned of the desolation of Jerusalem. He pleaded for months before God, confessing his sin and the sin of his people (see Nehemiah 1), and God opened the way, and the walls and gates of the city were built up. It is the spirit of deep repentance that is needed.

Weeping is not repentance; sorrow is not repentance. Repentance is turning away from sin and doing the work of righteousness and holiness. What can we do to receive the baptism? Repent!

Thought for today: The baptism of the Holy Spirit brings a deep repentance and a demolished and impoverished spirit.

454

October 28

Compassion for the Lost

I heard the voice of the Lord, saying: "Whom shall I send, and who
will go for Us?" Then I said, "Here am I! Send me."
—Isaiah 6:8

Scripture reading: Isaiah 6

*I*s it possible, after we have been baptized with the Holy Spirit, to be satisfied with what we see? What made Jesus weep over Jerusalem? He had a heart of compassion. There are sin-sick souls everywhere. We need a baptism of love that goes to the bottom of the disease. We need to cry to God until He brings us up to the *"measure of the stature of the fullness of Christ"* (Eph. 4:13).

Jesus told a parable about *"a certain man [who] went down from Jerusalem to Jericho, and fell among thieves"* (Luke 10:30). Who among those who passed by and saw his predicament was his neighbor? The one who had mercy on him and helped him (vv. 36–37). Are you awake to the great fact that God has given you eternal life? With the power God has put at your disposal, how can you rest as you look out upon your neighbors? How we have sinned against God! How we lack this spirit of compassion! Do we weep as we look out upon the unsaved? If not, we are not Pentecost-full. Jesus was moved with compassion. Are you?

We have not yet grasped the plight of the heathen. Since my only daughter went to Africa, I have a little less dim idea of what it meant that God so loved the world that He gave Jesus (John 3:16). God gave Jesus. What does that mean? Compassion. *"You shall receive power when the Holy Spirit has come upon you"* (Acts 1:8). If you have no power, you have not repented. You say, "That's hard language." It is truth.

Who is your brother's keeper? (See Genesis 4:9.) Who is the son and heir? (See Galatians 4:7.) Are you salted? (See Matthew 5:13.) Do you have a pure life? Don't be fooled; don't live in a false position. The world wants to know how to be saved, and power is at our disposal. Will we meet the conditions? God says, "If you will, I will." God will do it.

Daniel knew the time in which he was living; he responded to God, and a nation was saved. Nehemiah met God's conditions for his time, and the city was rebuilt. God has made the conditions. He will pour out His Spirit.

If we do not go on, we will have it to face. It may be up to us to bring the Gospel to the nations. We can win the world for Jesus. We can turn the tap on. What is the condition? It is unconditional surrender. *"'Not by might nor by power, but by My Spirit,' says the LORD of hosts"* (Zech. 4:6). Depart from sin; holiness opens the windows of heaven. The Spirit of God will be poured out without measure, until the people say, *"What must* [we] *do to be saved?"* (Acts 16:30).

Thought for today: With the baptism of the Holy Spirit comes a demolishing of the whole man and a compassion for the world.

October 29

Holy Boldness

Now when they saw the boldness of Peter and John, and perceived that they were uneducated and untrained men, they marveled. And they realized that they had been with Jesus.
—Acts 4:13

Scripture reading: Acts 4:1–22

On the Day of Pentecost, *"they were all filled with the Holy Spirit and began to speak with other tongues, as the Spirit gave them utterance"* (Acts 2:4). What a lovely thought that the Holy Spirit had such sway that the words were all His! Jesus stands forth in the midst with such divine glory, and men are impelled, filled, and led so perfectly. Only He will meet the needs of the world.

We see that there was something beautiful about Peter and John when we read that people *"realized that they had been with Jesus."* There was something so real, so after the order of the Master, about them.

The one thing that was more marked than anything else in the life of Jesus was the fact that the people glorified God in Him. And when God is glorified and gets the right-of-way and the whole-hearted attention of His people, everyone is as He is, filled with God. Whatever it costs, it must be. Let it be so. Filled with God! The only thing that will help people is to speak the latest thing God has given us from the glory.

There is nothing outside salvation. We are filled, immersed, clothed upon with the Spirit. There must be nothing felt, seen, or spoken about except the mighty power of the Holy Spirit. We are new creatures in Christ Jesus (2 Cor. 5:17), baptized into a new nature. *"He who believes in Me, as the Scripture has said, out of his heart will flow rivers of living water"* (John 7:38). We are in the world to meet the need, but we are not of the world or of its spirit. (See John 17:15–16.) We are *"partakers of the divine nature"* (2 Pet. 1:4) to manifest the life of Jesus to the world. This is God incarnate in humanity.

Thought for today: The very life of the risen Christ is to be in everything we are and do, moving us to do His will.

New Wine

Others mocking said, "They are full of new wine."
—Acts 2:13

Scripture reading: Acts 2:13–41

*T*his new wine has a freshness about it! It has a beauty about it! It has a quality about it! It creates in others the desire for the same taste. At Pentecost, some saw, but three thousand felt, tasted, and enjoyed. Some looked on; others drank with a new faith never before seen—a new manifestation, a new realization all divine, a new thing. It came straight from heaven, from the throne of the glorified Lord. It is God's purpose to fill us with that wine, to make us ready to burst forth with new rivers, with fresh energy, with no tired feeling.

God manifested in the flesh—this is what we want, and it is what God wants. All the people said, "We have never seen anything like it." (See Acts 2:7–12.) The disciples rejoiced in its being new; others were *"cut to the heart, [crying out] to Peter and the rest of the apostles, 'Men and brethren, what shall we do?'"* (v. 37).

What shall we do? Believe! Stretch out! Press on! Let there be a new entering in, a new passion to have it. We must be beside ourselves; we must drink deeply of the new wine so that multitudes may be satisfied and find satisfaction too.

The new wine must have a new wineskin—that is the necessity of a new vessel. (See Matthew 9:17.) If anything of the old is left, not put to death, destroyed, there will be a tearing and a breaking. The new wine and the old vessel will not work in harmony. It must be new wine and a new wineskin. Then there will be nothing to discard when Jesus comes.

> *For the Lord Himself will descend from heaven with a shout, with the voice of an archangel, and with the trumpet of God. And the dead in Christ will rise first. Then we who are alive and remain shall be caught up together with them in the clouds to meet the Lord in the air. And thus we shall always be with the Lord.* (1 Thess. 4:16–17)

The Spirit is continually working within us to change us until the day when we will be like Him:

[The Lord Jesus Christ] *will transform our lowly body that it may be conformed to His glorious body, according to the working by which He is able even to subdue all things to Himself.*

(Phil. 3:21)

I desire that all of you be so filled with the Spirit, so hungry, so thirsty, that nothing will satisfy you but seeing Jesus. We are to get more thirsty every day, more dry every day, until the floods come and the Master passes by, ministering to us and through us the same life, the same inspiration, so that *"as He is, so are we in this world"* (1 John 4:17).

When Jesus became the sacrifice for man, He was in great distress, but it was accomplished. It meant *"vehement cries and tears"* (Heb. 5:7); it meant the cross manward but the glory heavenward. Glory descending on a cross! Truly, *"great is the mystery of godliness"* (1 Tim. 3:16). He cried, *"It is finished!"* (John 19:30). Let the cry never be stopped until the heart of Jesus is satisfied, until His plan for humanity is reached in the sons of God being manifested (Rom. 8:19) and in the earth being *"filled with the knowledge of the glory of the LORD, as the waters cover the sea"* (Hab. 2:14). Amen. Amen. Amen.

Thought for today: Our end is God's beginning.

Guard against Error

No one speaking by the Spirit of God calls Jesus accursed, and no one can say that Jesus is Lord except by the Holy Spirit.
—1 Corinthians 12:3

Scripture reading: John 13:1–20

*M*any evil, deceiving spirits have been sent forth in these last days who endeavor to rob Jesus of His lordship and of His rightful place. Many people are opening the doors to these latest devils, such as New Theology and New Thought and Christian Science. These evil cults deny the fundamental truths of God's Word. They all deny eternal punishment and the deity of Jesus Christ. You will never see the baptism of the Holy Spirit come upon a person who accepts these errors. Nor will you see anyone receive the baptism who puts Mary in the place of the Holy Spirit. No one can know he is saved by works. If you ever speak to someone who believes this, you will know that he is not definite on the matter of the new birth. He cannot be. And there is another thing: you will never find a Jehovah's Witness baptized in the Holy Spirit. The same is true for a member of any other cult who does not believe that the Lord Jesus Christ is preeminent.

The all-important thing is to make Jesus Lord of your life. Men can become lopsided by emphasizing the truth of divine healing. Men can get into error by preaching on water baptism all the time. But we never go wrong in exalting the Lord Jesus Christ, in giving Him the preeminent place and glorifying Him as both Lord and Christ, yes, as "very God of very God." As we are filled with the Holy Spirit, our one desire is to glorify Him. We need to be filled with the Spirit to get the full revelation of the Lord Jesus Christ.

God's command is for us to *"be filled with the Spirit"* (Eph. 5:18). We are no good if we only have a full cup. We need to have an overflowing cup all the time. It is a tragedy not to live in the fullness of overflowing. See that you never live below the overflowing tide.

Thought for today: Jesus is the Baptizer. As soon as you are ready, He will fill you.

November 1

Great Possibilities

All Scripture is given by inspiration of God, and is profitable...for instruction in righteousness, that the man of God may be complete, thoroughly equipped for every good work.
—2 Timothy 3:16–17

Scripture reading: Hebrews 10:11–31

Everyone who has received the Holy Spirit has within him great possibilities and unlimited power. He also has great possessions, not only of things that are present but also of things that are to come (1 Cor. 3:22). The Holy Spirit has power to equip you for every emergency. The reason people are not thus equipped is that they do not receive Him and do not yield to Him. They are timid and they doubt, and in the measure that they doubt, they go down. But if you will yield to His leading and not doubt, it will lead you to success and victory. You will grow in grace, and you will have not only a controlling power but also a power that reveals the mind of God and the purposes He has for you.

Many believers might be far ahead of where they are now spiritually, but they have doubted. If by any means the Enemy can come in and make you believe a lie, he will do so. We have had to struggle to maintain our standing in our salvation, for the Enemy desires to beat us out of it, if possible. It is in the closeness of the association and oneness with Christ that there is no fear, but perfect confidence all the time. I see that we should stir one another up and provoke one another to good works (Heb. 10:24).

The Pentecostal people have a "know" in their experience. We know that we have the Spirit abiding within, and if we are not moved upon by the Spirit, we move the Spirit; that is what we mean by "stirring up the Spirit." Yet it is not we but the living faith within us—it is the Spirit who stirs Himself up.

Thought for today: The child of God does not need to go back a day for his experience, for the presence of the Lord is with him and the Holy Spirit is in him, in mighty power, if he will believe.

November 2

Use the Gifts Wisely

We make it our aim...to be well pleasing to Him.
—2 Corinthians 5:9

Scripture reading: 2 Corinthians 5:1–17

While it is right to earnestly desire the best gifts, you must recognize that the all-important thing is to be filled with the power of the Holy Spirit Himself. You will never have trouble with people who are filled with the power of the Holy Spirit, but you will have a lot of trouble with people who have the gifts but no power. The Lord does not want us to *"come short"* in any gift (1 Cor. 1:7). But at the same time, He wants us to be so filled with the Holy Spirit that it will be the Holy Spirit manifesting Himself through the gifts. Where the glory of God alone is desired, you can expect that every gift that is needed will be made manifest. To glorify God is better than to idolize gifts. We prefer the Spirit of God to any gift; but we can see the manifestation of the Trinity in the gifts: different gifts but the same Spirit, different administrations but the same Lord, diversities of operation but the same God working all in all (1 Cor. 12:4–6). Can you conceive of what it will mean for our triune God to be manifesting Himself in His fullness in our assemblies?

Imagine a large locomotive boiler that is being filled with steam. You can see the engine letting off some of the steam as it remains stationary. It looks as though the whole thing might burst. You can see believers who are like that. They start to scream, but that does not edify anyone. However, when the locomotive moves on, it serves the purpose for which it was built and pulls along many cars with goods in them. It is the same way with believers when they are operating in the gifts of the Spirit properly.

When you have a good time, you must see that the spiritual conditions in the place lend themselves to it and that the people are falling in line with you. Then you will always find it a blessing.

Thought for today: We must be careful not to have a good time in the Lord at the expense of somebody else.

November 3

What Is Your Motive?

You ask and do not receive, because you ask amiss,
that you may spend it on your pleasures.
—James 4:3

Scripture reading: Ephesians 1:3–14

God says, *"Everyone who asks receives"* (Matt. 7:8). What are you asking for? What is your motive? There is a need for the gifts, and God will reveal to you what you ought to have, and you should never be satisfied until you receive it.

It is important that we know we can do nothing in ourselves. However, we may know that we are clothed with the power of God so that, in a sense, we are not in the natural man. As we go forth in this power, things will take place as they took place in the days of the disciples.

When I received the new birth at eight years of age, it was so precious and lovely. Since that time, I have never lost the knowledge of my acceptance with God. Then, brothers and sisters, God did a wonderful work in me when I waited for the baptism.

I was in a strange position. For sixteen years I had testified to having received the baptism of the Holy Spirit, but I had really only received the anointing of the Spirit. In fact, I could not preach unless I had the anointing. My wife would come to me and say, "They are waiting for you to come out and speak to the people." I would say, "I cannot and will not come without the anointing of the Spirit."

I can see now that I was calling the anointing the baptism. But when the Holy Spirit came into my body until I could not give satisfaction to the glory that was in me, God took this tongue, and I spoke as the Spirit gave utterance, which brought perfect satisfaction to me. When He comes in, He abides. I then began to reach out as the Holy Spirit showed me.

Thought for today: We must be willing to deny ourselves everything to receive the revelation of God's truth and to receive the fullness of the Spirit. Only this will satisfy God, and nothing less must satisfy us.

Claim the Gift

Please let a double portion of your spirit be upon me.
—2 Kings 2:9

Scripture reading: 2 Kings 2:1–14

*I*n the call of the prophet Elisha, God saw the young man's willingness to obey. The twelve yoke of oxen, the plow, and all soon came to nothing; all bridges had to be burned behind him (1 Kings 19:19–21). Friend, the Lord has called you, too. Are you separated from the old things? You cannot go on unless you are.

As Elisha went on with the prophet Elijah, the young man heard wonderful things about Elijah's ministry, and he longed for the time when he would take his master's place. Now the time was getting close. His master said to him, "I am going to Gilgal today. I want you to remain here." "Master," he replied, "I must go with you." Other people also knew something about it, for they said to Elisha, "Do you know that your master is going to be taken away from you today?" He said, "Hold your peace; I know it." Later on, Elijah said, "I want to go on to Bethel. You stay here." But Elisha said, "No, I will not leave you." Something had been revealed to Elisha. Perhaps, in a similar way, God is drawing you to do something; you feel it.

Then Elijah said, "The Lord has sent me to Jordan. You stay here." It was the spirit of the old man that was stirring up the young man. If you see zeal in somebody else, reach out for it; it is for you. I am coming to realize that God wants all the members of His body joined together. In these days He is making us feel that when a person is failing to go on with God, we must restore that member.

When they came to the Jordan, Elijah struck his cloak on it and they crossed. No doubt Elisha said, "I must follow his steps." And when they had gone over, the old man said, "You have done well; you would not stay back. What is the real desire of your heart? I feel I am going to leave you. Ask what you like now, before I leave you." "Master," he said, "I have seen all that you have done. Master, I want twice as much as you have."

November 4

I believe it is the fainthearted who do not get much. As they went on up the hill, down came the chariot of fire, nearer and nearer, and when it landed, the old man jumped in and the young man said, "Father, Father, Father," and down came the cloak.

What have you asked for? Are you satisfied to continue on in the old way now that the Holy Spirit has come to give you an unlimited supply of power and says, "What will you have?" Why, we see that Peter was so filled with the Holy Spirit that his shadow falling on sick people healed them (Acts 5:15).

What do you want? Elisha asked, and he got it. He came down and said, "I don't feel any differently." However, he had the knowledge that feelings are not to be counted as anything; some of you are looking at your feelings all the time. He came to the waters of the Jordan as an ordinary man. Then, in the knowledge in which he possessed the cloak (not in any feelings about it), he said, "Where is the God of Elijah?" and he struck the water with the cloak. The waters parted and Elisha put his feet down in the river and crossed to the other side. When you put your feet down and say you are going to have a double portion, you will get it. After he had crossed, there were the young men again (they always come where there is power), and they said, "The spirit of Elijah rests on Elisha." (See 2 Kings 2:1–15.)

You are to have the gifts and to claim them. The Lord will certainly change your lives, and you will be new men and women. Are you asking for a double portion? I trust that no one will *"come short"* in any gift (1 Cor. 1:7). You say, "I have asked. Do you think God will be pleased if I ask again?" Yes, do so before Him. Ask again, and we may go forth in the Spirit of the cloak. Then we will no longer be working in our own strength but in the Holy Spirit's strength, and we will see and know His power because we believe.

Thought for today: Many people miss a great many things because they are always thinking that they are for someone else.

Praying in the Spirit

*I will pray with the spirit, and I will also pray
with the understanding.*
—1 Corinthians 14:15

Scripture reading: Hebrews 7:11–28

I am going to give you a very important word about the usefulness of praying in the Spirit. Lots of people are still without an understanding of what it is to pray in the Spirit. I am going to tell you a story that will help you to see how necessary it is that you be so lost in the order of the Holy Spirit that you will pray in the Holy Spirit.

Our missionary work in the center of Africa was opened by Brothers Burton and Salter, the latter being my daughter's husband. When they went there, there were four of them: Brothers Burton and Salter, an old man who wanted to go to help them build, and a young man who believed he was called to go. The old man died on the road and the young man turned back, so there were only two left.

They worked and labored. God was with them in a wonderful way. But Burton took sick, and all hopes were gone. Fevers are dreadful there; mosquitoes swarm; great evils are there. There he was, laid out; there was no hope. They covered him over and went outside very sorrowfully, because he truly was a pioneer missionary. They were in great distress and uttered words like this: "He has preached his last sermon."

When they were in that state, without any prompting whatever, Brother Burton stood right in the midst of them. He had arisen from his bed and had walked outside, and he now stood in the midst of them. They were astonished and asked how and what had happened.

All he could say was that he had been awakened out of a deep sleep with a warm thrill that went over his head, right down his body, and out through his toes.

"I feel so well," he said. "I don't know anything about my sickness."

It remained a mystery. Later, when he was over in England visiting, a lady said to him, "Brother Burton, do you keep a diary?"

"Yes," he said.

"Don't open the diary," she said, "until I talk with you."

"All right."

This is the story she told.

"At a certain time on a certain day, the Spirit of the Lord moved upon me. I was so moved by the power of the Spirit that I went alone into a place to pray. As I went there, believing that, just as usual, I was going to open my mouth and pray, the Spirit laid hold of me and I was praying in the Spirit—not with understanding, but praying in the Spirit.

"As I prayed, I saw right into Africa; I saw you laid out helpless and, to all appearances, apparently dead. I prayed on until the Spirit lifted me, I knew I was in victory, and I saw you had risen up from that bed.

"Look at your diary, will you?"

He looked in the diary and found that it was exactly the same day.

So there are revivals to come; there are wonderful things to be done, when we can be lost in the Spirit until the Spirit prays through to victory.

Thought for today: Prayer is without accomplishment unless it is accompanied by faith.

The Word of Wisdom

To one is given the word of wisdom through the Spirit.
—1 Corinthians 12:8

Scripture reading: 1 Corinthians 2:6–16

The Scripture does not say "the gift of wisdom" but the gift of "*the word of wisdom.*" You have to "*rightly* [handle] *the word of truth*" (2 Tim. 2:15). The gift of the word of wisdom is necessary in many instances. For example, when you want to build another church building, maybe larger than the one you are in, so that everybody can speak and be heard without any trouble, a word of wisdom is needed regarding how to build the place for God's service.

When you are faced with a choice and it is difficult for you to know in what direction to go, that word can come to you in a moment and prepare you for the right way.

The gift of the word of wisdom is meant for a needy hour when you are under great stress concerning some business transaction; provided it is a godly transaction, you can ask God what to do, and you will receive wisdom.

I have been trying to show you that if you are filled with the Holy Spirit, the Holy Spirit can manifest any gift. At the same time, you are not to forget that the Word of God urges you to desire earnestly the best gifts; so while the best gift might be to you the word of wisdom, or some other gift, you should not be lacking in any gift.

This is a remarkable statement for me to make, but Scripture lends itself to me to be extravagant. When God speaks to me He says, "Anything you ask." (See John 15:7.) When God is speaking of the world's salvation He says, "Whosoever believes." (See John 3:16.) So I have an extravagant God with extravagant language to make me an extravagant person—in wisdom.

To this end, we pray that God will show us now why we really need the word of wisdom and how we may be in a place in which we will surely know it is of God.

Thought for today: The trouble with so many people is that they have never gotten out so He could get in.

November 7

A Questionable Word
Part One

To one is given the word of wisdom through the Spirit.
—1 Corinthians 12:8

Scripture reading: Ecclesiastes 7:1–12

One day I went out of my house and saw a friend of mine named John who lived opposite me. He crossed the road, came up to me, and said, "Now, Smith, how are you?"

"Very well, John," I said.

"Well," he said, "my wife and I have been praying and talking together about selling our house, and every time we think about it in any way, your name is the only one we think about."

That was a strange thing to me.

"Will you buy it?" he asked.

Now, if you remember, when David went wrong he only went wrong because he violated the holy communion and knowledge of what kept him. What was it? What was the word that would have saved him? *"You shall not covet your neighbor's wife"* (Exod. 20:17). He had to break that law to commit sin.

I was not dealing with a sin; however, looking back, I see that there were many questionable things about the situation, so that if I had thought about it for a moment, I would have been saved from many weeks of brokenheartedness and sorrow.

What was the first thing that I should have asked myself? "Can I live in two houses? No. Well, then, one is sufficient."

The next thing was, "Do I have the money to buy the house? No."

That is sufficient in itself, for God does not want any person to be in debt, and when you learn that secret, it will save you from many sleepless nights. But I was like many people; we are all learning, and none of us is perfect. However, I do thank God that we are called to perfection, whether we come into it at once or not. If you miss the mark of holiness ten times a day, fortify yourself to believe that God intends for you to be holy, and then stand again.

Thought for today: Do not give in when you miss the mark.

November 8

A Questionable Word
Part Two

To one is given the word of wisdom through the Spirit.
—1 Corinthians 12:8

Scripture reading: Ecclesiastes 7:13–29

*T*here is a saying that goes something like this: "No man fails to succeed in life because he makes a blunder; it is when he makes the blunder twice." No person who fails once loses his *"high calling"* (Phil. 3:14 KJV). Therefore, the Word of God says that when you repent with godly repentance, you will never do the same thing again. (See 2 Corinthians 7:9–11.)

It is not for you to give in; you have to fortify yourself. The day is young; the opportunities are tremendously large. May God help you not to give in. Believe that God can make you new and turn you into another person.

Now, what was the trouble with me? It was that I didn't discuss this transaction with God. Many of you are in the same place. What do we do afterward? We begin working our way out. So I began working this thing out.

"How much will you take for it?" I asked.

He named the price. I thought to myself—this was a human thought—"Now, the banking society will give me all I want. They are well acquainted with me; that will be no trouble."

So the loan officer came to look over the house.

"It is a beautiful house," he said. "It is very reasonable. You will lose nothing on this if you ever sell it. It is well worth the money. But I cannot give you within five hundred dollars of what you need."

I did not have five hundred dollars; I couldn't get it out of the business I had at that time, but I still tried a human way. I did not go to God. If I had, I could have gotten out of it. But I tried to work my way out.

The first thing I did was to try my relatives. Have you ever done that? What was wrong? They were all so pleased to see me, but I was either a bit too soon or a little bit too late; I absolutely just missed it. They all wanted to lend me the money, but I was there at the wrong time.

I had another human plan then: I tried my friends. The same thing happened.

Then I went to my lovely wife. Oh, she was a darling! She was holy! I went to her and I said, "Oh, Mother, I am in a hard place."

"I know," she said. "I will tell you what you have never done, my dear."

"What?"

"You have never gone to God once about this thing."

So then I knew she knew, and I knew what I would get if I went to prayer.

"All right, my dear, I will go pray."

It is lovely to have a place to go in which to pray—those places where you open your eyes to see if you can see Him in reality because He is so near. Ah, to walk with God!

"Father," I said, "You know all about it. If you will forgive me this time, I will never trouble you again as long as I live with anything like this."

And then came the word of wisdom. He has it. Yet it was the most ridiculous word I ever heard in all my life. The Lord said, "Go see Brother Webster."

I came downstairs. I said, "He has spoken."

"I knew He would."

"Yes, but you see He said such a ridiculous thing."

"Believe it," she said. "It will be all right. When God speaks, you know it means it is all right."

"But Mother, you could hardly think it could be right. He has told me to go see Brother Webster."

"Go," she said.

Thought for today: When you get out of the will of God, then you try your own way.

November 9

A Questionable Word
Part Three

To one is given the word of wisdom through the Spirit.
—1 Corinthians 12:8

Scripture reading: Ecclesiastes 9:13–10:10

*B*rother Webster was a man who kilned lime. The most he ever got per week, to my knowledge, was $3.50. He wore corduroy trousers and a pair of big work boots. But he was a godly man.

Early in the morning, I jumped onto my bicycle and went to his house. I got there at eight o'clock.

"Why, Brother Wigglesworth, what brings you so early?" he asked.

"I was speaking to the Lord last night about a little trouble," I said, "and He told me to come and see you."

"If that is the case," he said, "we will go down to my house and talk to the Lord."

We went to the house and he locked the door.

"Now, tell me," he said.

"Well, three weeks ago I arranged to buy a house. I found out I was short five hundred dollars. I have tried everything I know and have failed. My wife told me last night to go to God, and while I was there God said, 'Go see Brother Webster,' so here I am."

"How long have you needed it?"

"Three weeks."

"And you have never come to see me before?"

"No, God never told me."

I could have been able to know the next day if I had gone to God, but I tried my way and went to every man possible without going straight to God. I hope you won't do that now that you are to have the word of wisdom God is going to give you.

Brother Webster said to me, "For twenty years I have been putting aside a little more than half a dollar a week into a cooperative society. Three weeks ago they told me that I had five hundred dollars and that I must take it out because I was not doing business with them. I brought it home. I put it under the mattresses, under

472

the floor boards, in the ceiling, everywhere. Oh, I have been so troubled by it! If it will do you any good, you can have it."

"I had so much trouble," Brother Webster said, "that I took it to the bank yesterday to get rid of it. If I can get it out today, you can have it."

He went to the bank and asked, "How much can I have?"

"Why, it is your own," they said. "You can have it all."

He came out, gave it to me, and said, "There it is! If it is as much blessing to you as it has been trouble to me, you will have a lot of blessing."

Yes, beloved, He knows just what you need. Don't you know that if I had gone to the right place right away, I would never have been in trouble? What I ought to have known was this: there was no need for the house at all.

I could not rest. I got rid of the house and took the money back to Brother Webster and said, "Take it back; take the money back. It will be trouble to me if I keep that money; take it."

Oh, to be in the will of God!

Don't you see, beloved, there is the word, the word of wisdom. One word is sufficient; you don't need a lot. One little word from God is all you require. You can count on it; it will never fail. It will bring forth what God has desired.

May the Lord give wisdom to you so that you may *"rightly [handle] the word of truth"* (2 Tim. 2:15), walk in the *"fear of the LORD"* (2 Chron. 19:7), and be an example to other believers (1 Tim. 4:12).

I have come to a conclusion that is very beautiful, in my estimation. I once thought I possessed the Holy Spirit, but I have come to the conclusion that He has to be entirely the Possessor of me.

God can tame your tongue. God can so reserve you for Himself that your entire body will be operating in the Spirit.

Thought for today: Never take advantage of the Holy Spirit, but allow the Holy Spirit to take advantage of you.

November 10

The Power of Faith

*Above all, taking the shield of faith with which you will be able
to quench all the fiery darts of the wicked one.*
—Ephesians 6:16

Scripture reading: Galatians 5:1–15

Oh, this wonderful faith of the Lord Jesus. Our faith comes to an end. Many times I have been to the place where I have had to tell the Lord, "I have used all the faith I have," and then He has placed His own faith within me.

One of my fellow workers in ministry said to me at Christmastime, "Wigglesworth, I was never so near the end of my finances in my life." I replied, "Thank God, you are just at the opening of God's treasures." It is when we possess nothing that we can possess all things. The Lord will always meet you when you are on the edge of living.

I was in Ireland one time, and I went to a house and said to the lady who came to the door, "Is Brother Wallace here?" She replied, "Oh, he has gone to Bangor, but God has sent you here for me. I need you. Come in." She told me her husband was a deacon of the Presbyterian church. She herself had received the baptism of the Spirit while she was a member of the Presbyterian church, but they did not accept it as from God. The people of the church said to her husband, "This thing cannot go on. We don't want you to be a deacon any longer, and your wife is not wanted in the church."

The man was very enraged, and he became incensed against his wife. It seemed as though an evil spirit had possessed him, and the home that had once been peaceful became very terrible. Finally, he left home without leaving behind any money for his wife. The woman asked me what she should do.

We went to prayer, and before we had prayed five minutes, the woman was mightily filled with the Holy Spirit. I said to her, "Sit down and let me talk to you. Are you often in the Spirit like this?" She said, "Yes, and what could I do without the Holy Spirit now?" I said to her, "The situation is yours. The Word of God says that you have power to sanctify your husband. (See 1 Corinthians 7:14). Dare to believe the Word of God. Now the first thing we must do is to pray that your husband comes back tonight." She said, "I know

November 10

he won't." I replied, "If we agree together, it is done." She said, "I will agree." Then I said to her, "When he comes home, show him all possible love; lavish everything upon him. If he won't hear what you have to say, let him go to bed. The situation is yours. Get down before God and claim him for the Lord. Get into the glory just as you have gotten into it today, and as the Spirit of God prays through you, you will find that God will grant all the desires of your heart."

A month later I saw this sister at a conference. She told how her husband came home that night. He went to bed, but she prayed right through to victory and then put her hands on him and prayed. He cried out for mercy. The Lord saved him and baptized him in the Holy Spirit. The power of God is beyond all our conception. The trouble is that we do not have the power of God in a full manifestation because of our finite thoughts. But you will never get anywhere unless you are in constant pursuit of all the power of God.

Thought for today: There is no limit to what our limitless God will do in response to a limitless faith.

November 11

An Unwavering Faith

The prayer of faith will save the sick, and the Lord will raise him up.
—James 5:15

Scripture reading: James 5:7–18

One day when I came home and found that my wife was out. I was told that she was down at Mitchell's. I had seen Mitchell that day and knew that he was at the point of death. I knew that it would be impossible for him to survive the day unless the Lord undertook to heal him.

There are many who let up in sickness and do not take hold of the life of the Lord Jesus Christ that is provided for them. I hurried down to Mitchell's house, and as I got near I heard terrible screams. I knew that something had happened. I saw Mrs. Mitchell on the staircase and asked, "What is up?" She replied, "He is gone! He is gone!" I just passed by her and went into the room. Immediately I saw that Mitchell had gone. I could not understand it, but I began to pray. My wife was always afraid that I would go too far, and she laid hold of me and said, "Don't, Dad! Don't you see that he is dead?" I continued to pray and my wife continued to cry out to me, "Don't, Dad. Don't you see that he is dead?" But I continued praying. I got as far as I could with my own faith, and then God laid hold of me. Oh, it was such a laying hold that I could believe for anything. The faith of the Lord Jesus laid hold of me, and a solid peace came into my heart. I shouted, "He lives! He lives! He lives!" And he is living today.

There is a difference between our faith and the faith of the Lord Jesus. The faith of the Lord Jesus is needed. Your faith may get to a place where it wavers. The faith of Christ never wavers. When you have His faith, the thing is finished. When you have that faith, you will never look at things as they are. You will see the things of nature give way to the things of the Spirit; you will see the temporal swallowed up in the eternal.

As we remain steadfast and unmovable on the ground of faith, we will see in perfect manifestation what we are believing for.

Thought for today: It is when we are at the end of our own resources that we can enter into the riches of God's resources.

November 12

The Gift of Faith

But one and the same Spirit works all these things, distributing to each one individually as He wills.
—1 Corinthians 12:11

Scripture reading: Ephesians 3

*P*eople say to me, "Do you not have the gift of faith?" I say that it is an important gift, but that what is still more important is for us to be making an advancement in God every moment. Looking at the Word of God, I find that its realities are greater to me today than they were yesterday. It is the most sublime, joyful truth that God brings an enlargement, always an enlargement. Nothing dead, dry, or barren is in this life of the Spirit; God is always moving us on to something higher, and as we move on in the Spirit, our faith will always rise to each occasion.

This is how the gift of faith is manifested. You see something, and you know that your own faith is nothing in the situation. One day I was in San Francisco. I was sitting on a streetcar, and I saw a boy in great agony on the street. I said, "Let me get out." I rushed to where the boy was. He was in agony because of stomach cramps. I put my hand on his stomach in the name of Jesus. The boy jumped and stared at me with astonishment. He found himself instantly free of pain. The gift of faith dared in the face of everything. It is as we are in the Spirit that the Spirit of God will operate this gift anywhere and at any time.

When the Spirit of God is operating this gift within a person, He causes him to know what God is going to do. When the man with the withered hand was in the synagogue, Jesus got all the people to look to see what would happen. The gift of faith always knows the results. Jesus said to the man, *"Stretch out your hand"* (Matt. 12:13). His words had creative force. He was not living on the edge of speculation. He spoke and something happened. He is the Son of God, and He came to bring us into sonship. He was the *"firstfruits"* of the Resurrection (1 Cor. 15:20), and He calls us to be *"firstfruits"* (James 1:18), to be like Him.

Thought for today: God cannot trust some people with a gift, but He can trust those who have a humble, broken, contrite heart (Isa. 66:2).

477

November 13

A Humble Spirit

On this one will I look: on him who is poor and of a contrite spirit.
—Isaiah 66:2

Scripture reading: Romans 2:1–16

One day I was in a meeting where there were a lot of doctors and eminent men and many ministers. The power of God fell on this meeting. A humble little girl who served as a waitress opened her heart to the Lord and was immediately filled with the Holy Spirit and began to speak in tongues. All these big men stretched their necks and looked up to see what was happening. They were saying, "Who is it?" Then they learned it was "the servant." Nobody received except the servant! These things are hidden and kept back from the *"wise and prudent"* (Matt. 11:25), but the little children, the humble ones, are the ones who receive. We cannot have faith if we show undue deference to one another. A man who is going on with God won't accept honor from his fellow beings. God honors the person who has a broken, contrite spirit. How can I get to that place?

So many people want to do great things and to be seen doing them, but the one whom God will use is the one who is willing to be told what to do. And you and I will never do anything without compassion. We will never be able to remove the cancer until we are immersed so deeply in the power of the Holy Spirit that the compassion of Christ is moving through us.

I find that in everything my Lord did, He said that He did not do it but that Another who was in Him did the work (John 14:10). What a holy submission! He was just an instrument for the glory of God. Have we reached a place where we dare to be trusted with a gift from God? I see in 1 Corinthians 13 that if I have faith to move mountains and do not have love, all is a failure. When my love is so deepened in God that I only move for the glory of God, then the gifts can be made manifest. God wants to be manifested and to manifest His glory to those who are humble.

Thought for today: Let us move into the realm of faith and live in the realm of faith and let God have His way.

November 14

The Gifts of Healing

To another gifts of healings by the same Spirit.
—1 Corinthians 12:9

Scripture reading: Psalm 65

Now I will deal with the gift itself. It is actually "gifts" of healing, not the "gift" of healing. Gifts of healing can deal with every case of sickness, every disease that there is. These gifts are so full that they are beyond human expression, but you come into the fullness of them as the light brings revelation to you.

I have people continually coming to me and saying, "When you are preaching, I see a halo around you," or "When you are preaching, I have seen angels standing around you."

I hear these things from time to time, and I am thankful that people have such spiritual vision. I do not have that kind of vision; however, I have the express glory, the glory of the Lord, covering me, the intense inner working of His power, until every time I have stood before you, I have known that I have not had to choose the words I have spoken. The language has been chosen, the thoughts have been chosen, and I have been speaking in prophecy more than in any other way. So I know we have been in the school of the Holy Spirit in a great way.

The only vision I have had in a divine healing meeting is this: so often, when I have laid hands upon the people, I have seen two hands go before my hands. This has happened many, many times.

The person who has the gifts of healing does not look to see what is happening. You will notice that after I have finished ministering, many things are manifested, but they don't move me. I am not moved by anything I see.

The divine gifts of healing are so profound in the person who has them that there is no such thing as doubt, and there could not be; whatever happens could not change the person's opinion or thought or act. He expects the very thing that God intends him to have as he lays hands upon the seeker.

Wherever I go, the manifestation of divine healing is considerably greater after I leave than when I am there. Why? It is God's plan for me. God has great grace over me. Wonderful things have been accomplished, and people have told me what happened when I was there, but these things were hidden from me. God has a reason why He hides things from me.

When I lay hands upon people for a specific thing, I tell you, that thing will take place. I believe it will be so, and I never turn my ears or my eyes from the fact. It has to be so.

The gifts of divine healing are more than audacity; they are more than an unction. Those are two big things; however, the gifts of healing are the solid fact of a divine nature within the person pressing forward the very nature and activity of the Lord, as if He were there. We are in this place to glorify the Father, and the Father will be glorified in the Son since we are not afraid of taking action in this day.

The gifts of healing are a fact. They are a production; they are a faith; they are an unwavering trust; they are a confidence; they are a reliability.

People sometimes come to me very troubled. They say, "I had the gifts of healing once, but something has happened and I do not have them now."

They never had them. *"The gifts and the calling of God are irrevocable"* (Rom. 11:29), and they remain under every circumstance except this: if you fall from grace and use a gift, it will work against you. If you use tongues out of the will of God, interpretation will condemn you. If you have been used and the gift has been exercised and then you have fallen from your high place, it will work against you.

Thought for today: If you are without condemnation, you are in a place where you can pray through.

November 15

Ministering Healing

To another gifts of healings by the same Spirit.
—1 Corinthians 12:9

Scripture reading: Psalm 32

The gifts of healing are so varied. You may go to see ten people, and every case will be different. I am never happier in the Lord than when I am in a bedroom with a sick person. I have had more revelations of the Lord's presence when I have ministered to the sick at their bedsides than at any other time. It is as your heart goes out to the needy ones in deep compassion that the Lord manifests His presence. You are able to discern their conditions. It is then that you know you must be filled with the Spirit to deal with the conditions before you.

When people are sick, you frequently find that they are ignorant about Scripture. They usually know three Scriptures, though. They know about Paul's *"thorn in the flesh"* (2 Cor. 12:7); they know that Paul told Timothy to take *"a little wine"* for his *"stomach's sake"* (1 Tim. 5:23); and they know that Paul left someone sick somewhere, but they don't remember his name or the place, and they don't know in what chapter of the Bible it is found. (See 2 Timothy 4:20.) Most people think they have a thorn in the flesh. The chief thing in dealing with a person who is sick is to discern his exact condition. As you are ministering under the Spirit's power, the Lord will let you see just what will be the most helpful and the most faith-inspiring to him.

When I was in the plumbing business, I enjoyed praying for the sick. Urgent calls would come, and I would have no time to wash. With my hands all black, I would preach to these sick ones, my heart all aglow with love. Ah, your heart must be in it when you pray for the sick. You have to get right to the bottom of the cancer with a divine compassion, and then you will see the gifts of the Spirit in operation.

I was called at ten o'clock one night to pray for a young person who was dying of tuberculosis and whom the doctor had given up on. As I looked, I saw that unless God intervened, it would be impossible for her to live. I turned to the mother and said, "Well, Mother, you will have to go to bed." She said, "Oh, I have not had my clothes off for three weeks." I said to the daughters, "You will have to go to bed," but they did not want to go. It was the same with the son. I put on my overcoat and said, "Goodbye, I'm leaving." They said, "Oh, don't leave us." I said, "I can do nothing here." They said, "Oh, if you will stay, we will all go to bed."

I knew that God would not move in an atmosphere of mere natural sympathy and unbelief. They all went to bed, and I stayed, and that was surely a time as I knelt by that bed face-to-face with death and the Devil. But God can change the hardest situation and make you know that He is almighty.

Then the fight came. It seemed as though the heavens were brass. I prayed from 11:00 P.M. to 3:30 A.M. I saw the glimmering light on the face of the sufferer and saw her pass away. The Devil said, "Now you are done for. You have come from Bradford, and the girl has died on your hands." I said, "It can't be. God did not send me here for nothing. This is a time to change strength." I remembered the passage that said, *"Men always ought to pray and not lose heart"* (Luke 18:1). Death had taken place, but I knew that my God was all-powerful and that He who had split the Red Sea is just the same today. It was a time when I would not accept "No" and God said "Yes."

I looked at the window, and at that moment, the face of Jesus appeared. It seemed as though a million rays of light were coming from His face. As He looked at the one who had just passed away, the color came back to her face. She rolled over and fell asleep. Then I had a glorious time. In the morning she woke early, put on a dressing gown, and walked to the piano. She started to play and to sing a wonderful song. The mother and the sister and the brother all came down to listen. The Lord had intervened. A miracle had been worked.

The Lord is calling us along this way. I thank God for difficult cases. The Lord has called us into heart union with Himself; He wants His bride to have one heart and one Spirit with Him and to do what He Himself loved to do. That case had to be a miracle. The lungs were gone; they were just in shreds. Yet the Lord restored her lungs, making them perfectly sound.

Thought for today: After the Holy Spirit comes, you are in the place of command.

The Ministry of Longsuffering

*You, O Lord, are a God full of compassion, and gracious,
longsuffering and abundant in mercy and truth.*
—Psalm 86:15

Scripture reading: Galatians 5:19–6:3

A fruit of the Spirit that must accompany the gifts of healing is longsuffering. The person who is persevering with God must always be ready with a word of comfort. If the sick one is in distress and helpless and does not see everything eye to eye with you, you must bear with him. Our Lord Jesus Christ was filled with compassion and lived and moved in a place of longsuffering, and we will have to get into this place if we are to help needy ones.

There are some times when you pray for the sick, and you seem to be rough with them. But you are not dealing with a person; you are dealing with satanic forces that are binding the person. Your heart is full of love and compassion toward all; however, you are moved to a holy anger as you see the place the Devil has taken in the body of the sick one, and you deal with his position with a real forcefulness.

One day a pet dog followed a lady out of her house and ran all around her feet. She said to the dog, "My dear, I cannot have you with me today." The dog wagged its tail and made a big fuss. She said, "Go home, my dear." But the dog did not go. At last she shouted roughly, "Go home," and off it went. Some people deal with the Devil like that. The Devil can stand all the comfort you like to give him. Cast him out! You are not dealing with the person; you are dealing with the Devil. Demon power must be dislodged in the name of the Lord.

You are always right when you dare to deal with sickness as with the Devil. Much sickness is caused by some misconduct; there is something wrong, there is some neglect somewhere, and Satan has had a chance to get in. It is necessary to repent and confess where you have given place to the Devil (Eph. 4:27), and then he can be dealt with. It is our privilege in the power of the Holy Spirit to loose the prisoners of Satan and to let the oppressed go free.

Take your position from the first epistle of John and declare, *"He who is in* [me] *is greater than he who is in the world"* (1 John 4:4). Then recognize that it is not you who has to deal with the power of the Devil, but the Greater One who is in you. Oh, what it means to be filled with Him! You can do nothing in yourself, but He who is in you will win the victory. Your being has become the temple of the Spirit. Your mouth, your mind, your whole being may be used and worked upon by the Spirit of God.

We need to wake up and strive to believe God. Before God could bring me to this place, He broke me a thousand times. I have wept; I have groaned. I have travailed many a night until God broke me. We will never have the gifts of healing and the working of miracles in operation unless we stand in the divine power that God gives us, unless we stand believing God and *"having done all"* (Eph. 6:13), we still stand believing.

We have been seeing wonderful miracles, and they are only a little of what we are going to see. I believe that we are right on the threshold of wonderful things, but I want to emphasize that all these things will be only through the power of the Holy Spirit. You must not think that these gifts will fall upon you like ripe cherries. There is a sense in which you have to pay the price for everything you get. We must earnestly desire God's best gifts and say "Amen" to any preparation the Lord takes us through. In this way, we will be humble, usable vessels through whom He Himself can operate by means of the Spirit's power.

Thought for today: It seems to me that until God has mowed you down, you can never have this longsuffering for others.

November 17

Testimonial Prophecy

And I fell at his feet to worship him. But he said to me, "See that you do not do that! I am your fellow servant, and of your brethren who have the testimony of Jesus. Worship God! For the testimony of Jesus is the spirit of prophecy."
—Revelation 19:10

Scripture reading: Revelation 19

There is the prophecy that is the testimony of the saved person regarding what Jesus has done for him. Everyone, every newborn soul, has this kind of prophecy. Through the new birth that results in righteousness, God has given an anointing of the Spirit, a real unction of the Spirit of Christ. We felt when we were saved that we wanted everybody to be saved. That mindset has to be continuous; the whole world can be regenerated by the spirit of prophecy as we testify of our salvation in Christ.

This is the same prophecy that Paul spoke about in 1 Corinthians 14:1: *"Pursue love, and desire spiritual gifts, but especially that you may prophesy."* This verse identifies prophecy as being more important than other gifts. Think about that: prophecy is to be chosen and desired above all the other gifts; the greatest among all the gifts is prophecy.

Why prophecy? Because prophecy by the power of the Spirit is the only power that saves humanity. We are told in the Word of God that the Gospel that is presented through prophecy has power to bring immortality and light. (See 2 Timothy 1:10.) Immortality is what abides forever. Light is what opens the understanding of your heart. Light and immortality come by the Gospel.

Prophecy is to be desired above all things, and every Christian has to have it. Every believer may have gifts, though there are very few who do; however, every believer has testimonial prophecy.

Looking at Revelation 19:10, let us see what testimonial prophecy is and how it comes forth. *"I fell at his feet."* Who is this inhabitant of heaven? The one speaking to John is a man who has been on the earth. Lots of people are foolishly led by the Devil to believe that after they die, their spirits will be asleep in the grave; this is absolutely contrary to the Word of God. Don't you know that even if you live until the Lord comes, the body that you have must be put off and another must be put on, because you cannot go into heaven with your present body?

This man has been in the earth in the body and is now in heaven in the spirit, and he wants you to hear what he has to say: *"I am your fellow servant, and of your brethren who have the testimony of Jesus....For the testimony of Jesus is the spirit of prophecy."* What is the testimony of Jesus? The testimony is: "Jesus has saved me." What the world wants to know today is how they can be saved.

Testify that you are saved. Your knees may knock together, you may be trembling as you do it, but when you get it out, you enter into the spirit of prophecy. Before you know where you are, you are saying things that the Spirit is saying.

There are thousands of Christians who have never received the baptism of the Holy Spirit but who have this wonderful spirit of prophecy. People are being saved everywhere by the testimony of such believers. If you cease from testifying, you will be sorry when you give an account of your life before God (Rom. 14:12). As you testify, you will be a vessel through which the power of God can bring salvation to people (Rom. 1:16). Testify wherever you are.

Live in the place where the Lord your God moves you, not to go from house to house nor speak from person to person, but where the Lord directs you, for He has the person who is in need of truth waiting for watering with your watering can. Do not forget that you are *"ambassadors for Christ"* (2 Cor. 5:20).

Thought for today: The spirit of prophecy is the testimony that you are saved by the blood of the Lamb.

Discernment versus Judging

To another discerning of spirits.
—1 Corinthians 12:10

Scripture reading: Romans 2:1–13

*D*iscernment is a very necessary gift to understand. Most people seem to think it is a discerning of human persons. It is amazing to find that many people I come across seem to have a tremendous bent toward "discerning" others. If you carefully put this discerning of one another into real practice upon yourself for twelve months, you will never presume to try it upon another. You will see so many faults about yourself, that you will say, "O God, make me right!"

There is a vast difference between natural discernment and spiritual discernment. This statement of Jesus is remarkable:

> *How can you say to your brother, "Let me remove the speck from your eye"; and look, a plank is in your own eye? Hypocrite! First remove the plank from your own eye, and then you will see clearly to remove the speck from your brother's eye.*
> (Matt. 7:4–5)

Remember that if you begin judging, it will lead you to judgment (vv. 1–2). If you begin using your discernment to weigh people by your standards, it will lead you to judgment. Ever since God showed me Romans 2:1–3, I have been very careful to examine myself before I begin judging. Balance that in your heart. It will save you from judging.

Many notable people in the world have gotten to running another person down and finding fault. They are always faultfinding and judging people outright. I find that those people always fall in the mire. If I were to mention these people by name, you would know that what I am saying is true.

God save us from criticism! When we are pure in heart, we only think about pure things. When we are impure in heart, we speak and act and think as we are in our hearts. The pure in heart see purity.

Thought for today: May God give us that inward desire for purity so that He can take away judging.

November 19

Discerning Spirits

Beloved, do not believe every spirit, but test the spirits,
whether they are of God.
—1 John 4:1

Scripture reading: 1 John 4:1–11

From time to time, as I have seen a person under a power of evil or having a fit, I have said to the satanic force that is within the possessed person, "Did Jesus Christ come in the flesh?" and right away they have answered no. They either say no or hold their tongues, refusing altogether to acknowledge that the Lord Jesus Christ came in the flesh. It is at a time like this when, remembering that further statement of John's, *"He who is in you is greater than he who is in the world"* (1 John 4:4), you can, in the name of the Lord Jesus Christ, deal with the evil powers and command them to come out. We must know the tactics of the Evil One, and we must be able to displace and dislodge him from his position.

In Australia, I went to one place where there were disrupted and broken homes. The people were so deluded by the evil power of Satan that men had left their wives and wives had left their husbands. That is the Devil! May God deliver us from such evils in these days. There is no one better than the companion God has given you. I have seen so many broken hearts and so many homes that have been wrecked. We need a real revelation of these evil seducing spirits who come in and fascinate through the eyes, and who destroy lives, bringing the work of God into disrepute. But there is always flesh behind it. It is never clean; it is unholy, impure, satanic, devilish; and hell is behind it. If the Enemy comes in to tempt you in any way like this, I implore you to look instantly to the Lord Jesus. He can deliver you from any such satanic power. You must be separated in every way if you are going to have faith.

The Holy Spirit will give us this gift of the discerning of spirits if we desire it. Then we will be able to perceive by revelation evil powers that come in to destroy. We can reach out and get this unction of the Spirit that will reveal these things to us.

Seek the Lord, and He will sanctify every thought, every action, until your whole being is ablaze with holy purity and your one desire is for Him who has created you in holiness. Oh, this holiness!

488

Can we be made pure? We can. Every inbred sin must go. God can cleanse away every evil thought. Can we have a hatred for sin and a love for righteousness? Yes, God will create within you a pure heart. He will take away your stony heart and give you a heart of flesh. He will sprinkle you with clean water, and you will be cleansed from all your filthiness (Ezek. 36:25–26). When will He do it? When you seek Him for such inward purity.

Thought for today: To discern spirits, we must dwell with Him who is holy, and He will give the revelation and unveil the mask of satanic power, whatever it is.

November 20

Deliverance

Part One

Come out of the man, unclean spirit!
—Mark 5:8

Scripture reading: Mark 5:1–20

*L*et me tell you what may seem to be a horrible story for you to hear; nevertheless, it is a situation in which discernment is necessary. This is happening all the time, and I do thank God for it because it is teaching me how to minister to people in the Lord.

Messages came to me again and again by telegraph, letters, and other things, asking that I come to London. I wired back and wrote, but so many calls came and no hint was given in any way as to the reason I was to go there. The only thing they said was that they were in great distress.

When I got there, the dear father and mother of the needy one both took me by the hand and broke down and wept.

"Surely this is deep sorrow of heart," I said.

They led me up onto the balcony. Then they pointed to a door that was open a little, and both of them left me. I went in that door and I have never seen a sight like it in all my life. I saw a young woman who was beautiful to look at, but she had four big men holding her down to the floor, and her clothing was torn from the struggle.

When I got into the room and looked into her eyes, her eyes rolled but she could not speak. She was exactly like the man in the Bible who came out of the tombs and ran to Jesus when he saw Him. As soon as he got to Jesus, he couldn't speak, but the demon powers spoke. (See Mark 5:1–13.) And the demon powers in this young girl spoke and said, "I know you. You can't cast us out; we are many."

"Yes," I said, "I know you are many, but my Lord Jesus will cast you all out."

It was a wonderful moment; it was a moment when it was only He alone who could do it.

The power of Satan was so great upon this beautiful girl that she whirled and broke away from these four strong men.

The Spirit of the Lord was wonderful in me, and I went right up to her and looked into her face. I saw the evil powers there; her very eyes flashed with demon power.

"In the name of Jesus," I said, "I command you to leave. Though you are many, I command you to leave this moment, in the name of Jesus."

She instantly became sick and began vomiting. She vomited out thirty-seven evil spirits and gave their names as they came out. That day she was made as perfect as anybody. Praise the Lord!

Thought for today: The gift of discernment is not criticism.

November 21

Deliverance
Part Two

Come out of the man, unclean spirit!
—Mark 5:8

Scripture reading: Isaiah 58:1–12

With the gift of discernment, you are in pursuit of divine thought, divine character, and the holy, inward intuition that guides you in knowing what to do. The Lord of Hosts is in you and with you.

One time I was preaching in Doncaster, England, and a number of people were delivered. A man named Jack was greatly interested and moved by what he saw. He himself was suffering with a stiff knee. After he got home, he said to his wife, "I have taken in Wigglesworth's message, and now I am going to act on it and get deliverance. Wife, I want you to be the audience." He took hold of his knee and said, "Come out, you devil, in the name of Jesus." Then he said, "It is all right, wife." He took the yards and yards of flannel off and found he was all right without the bandage.

The next night he went to the little Primitive Methodist church where he worshipped. There were a lot of young people there who were in bad situations, and Jack had a tremendous ministry delivering his friends through the name of Jesus. He had been given to see that a great many ills to which flesh is heir are nothing else but the operation of the Enemy; but his faith had risen also, and he saw that in the name of Jesus there was a power that was more than a match for the Enemy.

Later, in a meeting in Gottenberg, Sweden, a man fell full length in the doorway. The evil spirit threw him down, manifesting itself and disturbing the whole meeting. I laid hold of this man and cried out to the evil spirit within him, "Come out, you devil! In the name of Jesus, we cast you out as an evil spirit." I lifted him up and said, "Stand on your feet and walk in the name of Jesus." I don't know whether anybody in the meeting understood me except the interpreter, but the devils knew what I said. I spoke in English, but these demons in Sweden cleared out.

Thought for today: Do not seek the gifts unless you have purposed to abide in the Holy Spirit.

November 22

Deliverance
Part Three

Come out of the man, unclean spirit!
—Mark 5:8

Scripture reading: Philippians 4:1–13

The Devil will endeavor to fascinate people through the eyes and the mind. One time a beautiful young woman was brought to me who had been infatuated with some preacher; just because he had not been interested in marrying her, the Devil had taken advantage of the situation and had made her delirious. She had been brought by friends 250 miles in that condition. She had previously received the baptism in the Spirit.

You ask, "Is there any place for the Enemy in one who has been baptized in the Holy Spirit?" Our only safety is in going on with God and in constantly being filled with the Holy Spirit. You must not forget Demas. He must have been baptized with the Holy Spirit, for he appears to have been one of Paul's right-hand workers, but the Enemy got him to the place where he loved this present world, and he fell away (2 Tim. 4:10).

When they brought this young woman to me, I discerned the evil power right away and immediately cast the thing out in the name of Jesus. It was a great joy to present her before all the people in her right mind again.

There is a life of perfect deliverance, and this is where God wants you to be. If I find that my peace is disturbed in any way, I know it is the Enemy who is trying to work. How do I know this? Because the Lord has promised to keep your mind in perfect peace when it is focused on Him (Isaiah 26:3). Paul told us to present our bodies as *"a living sacrifice, holy, acceptable to God, which is* [our] *reasonable service"* (Rom. 12:1). The Holy Spirit also spoke this word through Paul: *"And do not be conformed to this world, but be transformed by the renewing of your mind, that you may prove what is that good and acceptable and perfect will of God"* (v. 2).

Thought for today: As we think about what is pure, we become pure. As we think about what is holy, we become holy. And as we think about our Lord Jesus Christ, we become like Him. We are changed into the likeness of the object on which our gaze is fixed.

Hindrances to Discernment

*Therefore we must give the more earnest heed to the things
we have heard, lest we drift away.*
—Hebrews 2:1

Scripture reading: Hebrews 2

ou will never be able to discern or deal with evil powers as
long as there is anything in you that the Devil can touch. Before Satan can bring his evil spirits, there has to be an open
door. Hear what the Scriptures say: *"The wicked one does not touch
him"* (1 John 5:18), and *"The LORD shall preserve you from all evil;
He shall preserve your soul"* (Ps. 121:7). How does Satan get an
opening? When the believer ceases to seek holiness, purity, righteousness, truth; when he ceases to pray, stops reading the Word,
and gives way to carnal appetites. Then it is that Satan comes. So
often sickness comes as a result of disobedience. David said, *"Before I was afflicted I went astray"* (Ps. 119:67).

You will never be able to reach out your hand to destroy the
power of Satan as long as there is the vestige of human desire or
attainment in you. It is in the death of the death that you are in
the life of the life. Don't fool yourself; don't mislead yourself. Never
think that God overlooks sins. Sins have to be dealt with, and the
only way God ever deals with sin is to absolutely destroy its power.
You can be made so clean that the Devil comes and finds nothing in
you. (See John 14:30.) And then you have power by the power of
God over the powers of Satan.

Discernment is not mind or eye. Discernment is an intuition.
Your heart knows exactly what you are dealing with, and you are
dealing with it because of your heart purity against evil and uncleanness.

God continues to purify me. I can safely say that unless the
power of the Spirit purges me through and through, I cannot help
you. First of all, before I can give any life to you, the life must be in
me. And remember that the Scriptures are very clear: death works
in us so that life may work in you. (See 2 Corinthians 4:12.)

Now, the death that is working is all carnal, evil, sensual.
Don't forget the remarkable thing in the Scriptures that leads us
to this; there are sixty-six evil things listed in the Bible, such as

murder, covetousness, evil propensities. But I am here to say by the power of God that one fruit will destroy every evil thing. *"Seek first the kingdom of God and His righteousness, and all these things shall be added to you"* (Matt. 6:33).

Thought for today: You are only able to do what God desires for you to do as you have come into the depths of death to self, so that the supernatural life of Christ is abounding in you to destroy the powers of evil.

November 24

Testing the Spirits

Test the spirits, whether they are of God; because many false
prophets have gone out into the world.
—1 John 4:1

Scripture reading: John 8:31–59

elievers should try the spirits. You can see whether they are of God in this way: you will be able to tell the true revelation, and the true revelation that will come to you will always sanctify the heart; it will never have an "if" in it. When the Devil came to Jesus, he had an "if." He said, *"If You are the Son of God"* (Matt. 4:3), and *"If You will fall down and worship me"* (v. 9). The Holy Spirit never comes with an "if."

I have often dealt with people under evil powers, people in fits and other things, people so controlled by evil powers that every time they want to speak, the evil powers speak. It is a very dangerous condition, but it is true: people get possessed by the Devil.

Do you remember the biblical account of the man in the tombs who was terribly afflicted with evil powers (Mark 5:2–15)? Strong cords and chains could not hold him. Night and day, he was in the tombs, *"crying out and cutting himself with stones"* (v. 5). Jesus came on the scene, and these evil powers caused the man to run. As soon as the man got in front of Jesus, the evil spirit said, *"Have You come here to torment us before the time?"* (Matt. 8:29). This man had no power to get free, but these evil spirits were so troubled in the presence of Jesus that they cried out, *"Have You come here to torment us before the time?"*

Oh, thank God for Jesus. Jesus wants you to be so under His power, so controlled by and filled with the Holy Spirit, that the power of authority in you will resist all evil.

So many believers are not on their guard. Every believer should reach a place in the Holy Spirit where he has no desire except the desire of God. The Holy Spirit has to possess us until we are filled and divinely led by the Holy Spirit. It is a mighty thing to be filled with the Holy Spirit.

Thought for today: Do not desire to lead Jesus; if He leads you, He will lead you into truth.

496

November 25

Receiving Impressions

Follow Me.
—Matthew 9:9

Scripture reading: Psalm 63

*P*eople by the hundreds are continually pressing me with their difficulties, with their strange yet holy and noble desires, where two ways meet and they do not know which one to take. Some have received impressions in their minds and hearts, but I want to show you what comes of impressions.

A lady came to me and said, "Don't you know, the Spirit of the Lord is upon me; I have to preach the Gospel."

I said, "There is nothing wrong in that."

"I want to know where I have to go to preach, so I have come to you to see if the Lord has told you where I am to go."

"Yes, you have to begin at home. Begin at Jerusalem, and if you are successful, go to Judea; then if you are successful, God will send you to the uttermost parts of the world." (See Acts 1:8.)

God is not going to send you to the uttermost parts of the world until you have been successful around Jerusalem. We have a tremendously big job; it is well worth doing, and I want to do it well. I want to tell you the difference between the right and the wrong way to discern voices and thoughts that may come into your minds.

You have the Scriptures, and you have the Holy Spirit. The Holy Spirit has wisdom, and He does not expect you to be foolish. The Holy Spirit has perfect insight into knowledge and wisdom, and truth always gives you balance.

You always need to have one thing removed from you: being terribly afraid. When fear leaves, power and confidence come in its place. You also need to have another thing that must remain, and that is love: love in order to obey God rather than your inclinations to be something; but if God wants to make you someone, that is different.

My wife tried her best to make me someone, but she could not do it. Her heart was right; her love was right; she did her best to make me a preacher. She used to say, "Now, Father, you could do it if you wanted to, and I want you to preach next Sunday."

I did everything to get ready; I tried everything. I don't know what I did not try—it would be best not to tell you what I did try. I had as many notes as would suit a clergyman for a week.

My wife's heart, her love, her desires were all right, but when I got up to preach, I would give out my text and then say, "If anybody can preach, now is your chance, for I have finished." That did not take place once, but many times. She was determined, and I was willing. When I ministered to those who had come forward to repent and receive Jesus, I could bring them right into the kingdom. I could nurse the children while my wife preached, and I was pleased to do it. But, don't you know, when the Holy Spirit came, then I was ready. Then the preaching abilities were not mine but the Lord's. It must all be for Jesus.

Oh, I tell you, whatever you may think about it, the whole thing is that there is nothing good without Jesus. Anyone could jump on this platform and say, "I am right." But when you have no confidence, then Jesus is all the confidence you require. God must have men and women on fire for Him. God will mightily send you forth in the anointing of the Spirit, and sinners will feel convicted, but it will never be accomplished if you have it in your mind that you are going to be something. The baptism is a baptism of death, and you live only unto God.

Thought for today: To be filled with the Holy Spirit is to be filled with divine equipping.

November 26

The Holy Spirit versus Deceptive Voices

*By this you know the Spirit of God: every spirit that confesses
that Jesus Christ has come in the flesh is of God,
and every spirit that does not confess that Jesus Christ
has come in the flesh is not of God.*
—1 John 4:2–3

Scripture reading: 1 John 4:1-6

A lot of people are troubled by voices. Some are so troubled that they become very distressed. Some people take it as a great thing; they think it is very remarkable, and they go astray. Lots of people go astray by foolish prophecy, and many are foolish enough to believe that they have tongues and interpretation and that they can be told what they should do. This is altogether outside the plan of God and bordering on blasphemy.

I do not preach my own ideas. That is, I never tell you what I think, because everybody can think. I tell you what I know. Therefore, what you need to do is to listen to what I know so that you may learn it. Then you can tell others what you have learned so that they will learn also.

How can I dislodge the power of Satan? How can I deal with satanic power? How may I know whether a voice is of God or not? Are there not voices that come from God? Yes. I am here believing that I am in the right place to build you on the authority of the Word of God.

You know that a business executive is one who has a right to declare everything for the board of directors. And the Chief Executive of the world is the Holy Spirit. He is here today as a communication to our hearts, to our minds, to our thoughts, of what God wants us to know. So this Holy Executive who is in us can speak wonderful words.

I am dealing now with what you may know when you are fully in the Holy Spirit. The Spirit will teach you; He will *"bring to your remembrance all things"* (John 14:26). Now you do not need any man to teach you. But the anointing remains (1 John 2:27). This is the office of the Holy Spirit. This is the power of His communication. This is what John meant when he said, *"God is love"* (1 John

4:8). Jesus, who is grace, is with you. But the Holy Spirit is the speaker, and He speaks everything concerning Jesus.

There may be people who have been hearing voices, and it has put them in situations that have caused tremendous issues in their lives, brought a great amount of distress and brokenheartedness, and led them into confusion and trouble. Why? They did not know how to judge the voices.

If a voice comes and tells you what to do, if a person comes and says he has a special prophecy that God has given him for you, you have as much right to ask God for that prophecy as they had to give it to you, and you have as much right to judge that prophecy according to the Word of God. You need to do this, for there are people going about pretending to be tremendous people, and they are sending people nearly off their wits' end because they believe their damnable prophecies, which never are of God but are of the Devil. I am very severe on this thing. God won't let me rest; I have to deal with these things because I find people everywhere in a terrible state because of these voices. How will we get to know the difference between the voice of God and the voice of Satan? The Scripture tells us. (See 1 John 4:2-3.)

Thought for today: You do not need teachers, but you need the Teacher, who is the Holy Spirit, to bring all things to your remembrance.

Misled by a Voice
Part One

Do not believe every spirit, but test the spirits,
whether they are of God.
—1 John 4:1

Scripture reading: Judges 6:36–7:22

*T*wo sisters were saved in our meetings and were filled with the Holy Spirit. They were very lovely women, full of purity, truth, and righteousness. No one could look at them without admiring them.

Both of them worked in a telegraph office and both desired to be missionaries. They were so zealous to be missionaries that they were laying aside money and doing everything they could in order to be prepared to go to the mission field.

One of them was operating a telegraph machine when she heard a voice in her head, a voice that said something along these lines: "Will you obey me? If you will obey me, I will make you the most wonderful missionary that ever lived." Oh, beloved, try the voices, try the spirits. Only the Devil promises such a thing, but she did not know this; she did not understand. This was exactly what she wanted; it was her heart's desire, do you see? And she was so moved by this. The voice added, "And I will find you all the money you need." I have never known this kind of "leading" to come true, and you never will as long as you live.

For example, a man came to me and said, "I have in my hands a certain food for invalids that can raise millions of dollars for the missionaries." I said to him, "I will not have anything to do with it." These things are not a success. God does not work that way. If God wanted you to have gold, He could make it rain on your houses while you were away. He has all the gold, and the cattle on a thousand hills are His (Ps. 50:10).

When anybody preaches for the kingdom's sake, God will provide. Seek only God, and the rain will fall. The enduement of power will be made manifest in your mortal bodies if you are really in the Spirit.

Thought for today: Seek to be filled with the Holy Spirit not only for your sake but also for the sake of others.

Misled by a Voice
Part Two

Do not believe every spirit, but test the spirits,
whether they are of God.
—1 John 4:1

Scripture reading: Isaiah 26:1–15

Now, this young woman was so excited that her sister noticed it and went to her. "What is it?" she asked. "Oh! God is speaking to me," she said, "saying wonderful things to me."

She became so excited that her sister asked their supervisor if they could be excused for a while. So the overseer allowed them both to be excused for a time, and they went into a room. The first sister became so excited with these messages, so believing that it was of God, that her white blouse became spotted with blood as she pricked her flesh with the nails of her hand.

That is never of God. What do I read about the wisdom of God? I read that it is full of peace and gentleness; it is willing to submit; it is without partiality; it is full of goodness and truth. (See James 3:17.) And, remember, if you ever know anything about God, it will be peace. If you ever know anything about the world, it will be disorder. The peace of God, which passes all understanding (Phil. 4:7), comes to the heart after you are saved. We are *"justified by faith,"* and *"we have peace with God through our Lord Jesus Christ"* (Rom. 5:1). The peace continues until it makes us full of the *"hope of the glory of God"* (v. 2).

God showed me a long time ago, and it has not been taken out of my mind, that if I was disturbed in my spirit and was not at rest, I had missed the plan. How can you miss it? In three ways.

First of all, you can miss it because you have taken on someone else's burden. All the time you are told to cast your burden on the Lord (1 Pet. 5:7). Any number of people are overflowing with sorrow because they are taking on someone else's burden. That is wrong. You must teach them and teach yourself that you have to cast your burdens on the Lord.

Second, if you do not have peace, you have gotten out of the will of God in some way. You may not have sinned. You can be out of the will of God without sinning. You can be out of the will of God if you are not making progress. If you have not made progress since yesterday morning, you are a backslider. Everybody is a backslider who is not going on with God. You are a backslider if you do not increase in the divine character and likeness of Christ. You have to move from state to state, *"from glory to glory"* (2 Cor. 3:18), by the Spirit of the Lord.

You can lose your peace by missing some divine plan of God, and you can lose your peace because you have gotten your mind on something natural. A natural thing is a carnal thing. The Word of God says that the carnal things have to be destroyed because they are not subject to the law of God and cannot be subject to them (Rom. 8:7). Every carnal thing must be destroyed.

So you can miss the plan. Now, what is the plan? *"You will keep him in perfect peace, whose mind is stayed on You, because he trusts in You"* (Isa. 26:3). Examine yourself to see where you are. If you are not in perfect peace, you are out of the will of God.

Therefore, if these voices take away your peace, you will know they are not the will of God. But if the Spirit speaks, He will bring harmony and joy. The Spirit always brings three things: comfort, exhortation, and edification. He will make you sing *"songs in the night"* (Job 35:10). You will rise in high places, and you will not be afraid of declaring the works of the Lord. When the Spirit of the Lord is upon you and greatly active, you may *"go from strength to strength"* (Ps. 84:7), praising the Lord.

Thought for today: Nothing makes you so foolish as to turn aside from the Word of God. If you ever want to be a fool, turn away from God's Word, and you will find yourself in a fool's paradise.

November 29

Misled by a Voice
Part Three

Do not believe every spirit, but test the spirits,
whether they are of God.
—1 John 4:1

Scripture reading: Psalm 115

My wife and I were visiting at the home of these two sisters when they came in from work that day. We saw the distress. We saw the wild condition. If you are wild, that is the Devil. If you go breathlessly to the Bible, looking for confirmation of the voice, that is the Devil. The Word of God brings light. I must use it as the Word of Light. I must see it as the Light of Light. I must have it as the Light.

I must be wise, because if I say I am baptized with the Holy Spirit, if I say I am a child of God, I must act so that people will know that I have been with God. (See Acts 4:13.) If there is anything I would resound through this meeting like a trumpet, it is this: *"Do not let your good be spoken of as evil"* (Rom. 14:16)!

Well, what happened to the young woman? The voice came with such tremendous force that she could not let it go. Try the spirits. God will never do anything like that. He will never send you an unreasonable, unmanageable message.

The moment the girl became obsessed with what the voice said, what did the Devil say next? "You keep this a secret. Don't tell anybody. If you confide in anybody, let it be your sister, because she seems to understand you." So they confided in each other.

Now that is surely as satanic as anything you ever heard in your life, because every true thing, every holy thing, does not need to be kept a secret under any circumstances. Anything that is holy can be told on the housetops; God wants you to be able to tell all.

My wife and I tried to help them. "Oh, God is speaking to me!" the young woman said. And we could not change her. That night she said that the evil power continued speaking, saying to her, "Tell no one but your sister. Go to the station tonight and wait for the train. The train will come in at thirty-two minutes past seven.

Buy two tickets for Glasgow. After you have bought your tickets, you will have sixpence left."

This could be confirmed, and no one had to know but her sister. They went to the station. The train came in exactly at the right time. And there was just sixpence left after they had bought the ticket. Marvelous! Wonderful! This was sure to be right.

"See!" she said. "I have just the amount of money left after I have bought the tickets that the voice said I would." The train came in. The voice had said that a gentleman would be sitting in one of the coaches with all the money she would ever need. Directly opposite this gentleman, a woman with a nurse's cap would be sitting. The man would give her all the money, and they were to take it to a certain bank at a certain street corner in Glasgow.

Here was lack of presentation of thought. There are no banks open at half past seven, and, after investigation, it was discovered that there was no such bank in that place. Then what caused the young woman to obey the voice? It got her ear, and I will tell you what the danger is. If I had only five minutes I would say this to you: if you cannot be reasoned with, you are wrong. If you are right and everybody else is wrong, I don't care who you are, if you cannot bear examination, if what you hold cannot bear the light of the truth, you are wrong. It will save a lot of you if you will just think.

You may say, "Oh, but I know, I *know*." It is a very serious thing when nobody else knows but you. May God deliver us from such a condition. If you think you have some specialty, it is not unique; it can be repeated.

The train came in. They rushed from one end of the train to the other. There were no such people on the train. Then the voice came, "On the next platform, the next train." And they rushed over. Would you believe, those two young women were kept moving from platform to platform by those voices until half past nine at night?

Thought for today: People get outside of the plan of God when they trust solely in their own judgment.

Misled by a Voice

Part Four

Do not believe every spirit, but test the spirits,
whether they are of God.
—1 John 4:1

Scripture reading: Matthew 4:1–11

*T*he voices continued. Ah, those evil voices. How will we know whether they are of God? When God speaks, He speaks with wisdom. When the Devil came to Jesus he said, *"If You are the Son of God"* (Matt. 4:3). The Devil knew that Jesus was the Son of God, and Jesus knew and answered, *"It is written, 'You shall worship the LORD your God, and Him only you shall serve'"* (v. 10).

Was there anything wrong with what was happening with these two young women? The wrong was that the first young woman ought to have judged the spirits. If she had asked, "Did Jesus come in the flesh?" the voice would have answered no. No satanic voice in the world and no Spiritualist medium will acknowledge that Jesus came in the flesh.

The same power said to the young woman, "Now that I know you will obey me in everything, I will make you the greatest missionary in the world."

How could the two women have known at that moment that this was a false voice? Why, they could have known according to the Word of God. What does it say? *"Many false prophets have gone out into the world"* (1 John 4:1). Who are these false prophets after? Perhaps those with sincerity, earnestness, zeal, and purity. Who knows? These evil powers know. These are the questions they should have kept in their minds: What am I living for? What is the hope of my life? Do I have to be the greatest missionary in the world, or does Jesus need to be glorified in my life to do as He wills with me? The ripe grape is never as pure and perfect as it is just before it decays. The child of God is never as near to God as he is when the Devil can come and say, "You are wonderful!"

It is satanic to feel that God has a special message for you and that you are someone more special than anyone else. Every place that God brings you to in a rising tide of perfection is a place of humility, brokenness of heart, and fullness of surrender, where only God can rule in authority. It is not where you are somebody, but where God is everything and where you will be living for His glory.

It took three difficult months before these two young women were delivered from their delusion. But God did deliver them, and later He opened the door for them to go as missionaries to China. Thank God, the Devil's plan was defeated, but it was at a tremendous cost, almost of their lives.

How could they have known that it was a false voice? How can you know? When a voice comes, no matter how it seems to you, you must test it. When it is persistently pressing you to do something and you can hardly conceive how this thing could be possible, you have a position in the power of the Word of God to say to this evil power, "Did Jesus come in the flesh?" (1 John 4:3). And the satanic power will say no. But the Spirit of the living God, the Holy Spirit, always says yes. And so you can get to know the difference. We have to live in the place of knowing the Scriptures and listening to His voice so that we are able to divinely discern whether these things are of God or not.

Did Jesus come in the flesh? Yes, and now the living Christ is within you. Christ came into you the moment you believed. There is a manifestation of it. You may live in such a way that your language, your expressions, your actions, and everything speak of Christ. *"They realized that they had been with Jesus"* (Acts 4:13). You can live in such a way that the personality of Christ is exactly what Paul said: "Not I—I don't live anymore. Christ lives in me." (See Galatians 2:20.)

The Christ life, the Christ power, the personality of His presence may be in you in such a way that you cannot doubt the Word of God.

Thought for today: The workings of the Spirit are always contrary to the workings of the flesh.

December 1

Do Not Believe Every Spirit

Do not be overcome by evil, but overcome evil with good.
—Romans 12:21

Scripture reading: 2 Peter 2

*Y*ou need the Word of God in your hearts so that you might be able to overcome the world. We can so live in this divine communion with Christ that we can sense evil in any part of the world. In this present world, powers of evil are rampant. The plan of God is that we might be so in Him that we will be equal to any occasion.

"*Beloved*" (1 John 4:1). That is a good word. It means that we are now in a place where God has set His love upon us. He wants us to listen to what He has to say to us because when His beloved are hearing His voice, then they understand what He has for them.

God is dealing with us as sons; He calls us "*beloved.*" We are in the truth, but we want to know the truth in a way that will keep us free. (See John 8:32.) I want to help the people who have been so troubled with voices and with things that have happened that they have felt they had no control over them. And I want to help those who are bound in many ways and have been trying in every way to get free.

The fourth chapter of 1 John tells us specifically how to deal with evil powers, with evil voices. It tells us how we may be able to dethrone them and be in a place where we are over them. It shows us how we may live in the world not subject to fear, not subject to bondage, not subject to pain, but in a place where we are defeating evil powers, ruling over them, reigning in the world by this life of Christ. In this way, we will be from above, and we will know it. We will not be subject to the world, but we will reign over the world so that disease, sin, and death will not have dominion.

A keynote that runs through the entire Scriptures is that Jesus has vanquished and overcome all of the powers of the Devil and has destroyed his power, even the power of death. Whether we are going to believe it or not, this is for us. God sends out the challenge, and He says, "If you believe it, it will be so."

What will hinder us? Our human nature will. Gods work in us will be hindered when the human will is not wholly surrendered,

508

when there is some mixture, part spirit and part flesh, when there is a division in your own heart.

In a house where there are two children, one may desire to obey his father and mother, and he is loved and is very well treated. The other is loved just the same, but the difficulty is this: the wayward boy who wants his own way does many things to grieve his parents, and he gets the whip. They are both children in the house; one is getting the whip, the other is getting the blessing without the whip.

Any number of God's children are getting the whip who know better than they are doing. So I want you to wake up to do what you know ought to be done. Sin is never covered by your appearance, your presence, your prayers, or your tears. Sin can only be removed by repentance. When you repent deeply enough, you will find that the thing goes away forever. Never cover up sin. Sins must be judged. Sins must be brought to the blood of Christ. When you have a perfect confidence between you and God, it is amazing how your prayers rise. You catch fire, you are filled with zeal, your inspiration is tremendous, you find out that the Spirit prays through you, and you live in a place of blessing.

Thought for today: The man who lives in God is afraid of nothing.

December 2

Mediums Hindered

He who is in you is greater than he who is in the world.
—1 John 4:4

Scripture reading: John 6:47–58

One day I met a friend of mine in the street, and I said, "Fred, where are you going?"

"I am going—. Oh, I don't feel I ought to tell you," he said. "It is a secret between me and the Lord."

"Now, we have prayed together, we have had nights of communication, we have been living together in the Spirit," I said. "Surely there is no secret that could be hidden between you and me."

"I will tell you," he said. "I am going to a spiritualism meeting."

"Don't you think it is dangerous? I don't think it is wise for believers to go to these places," I said.

"I am led to go to test it according to Scripture," he replied. "They are having some special mediums from London."

He meant that they were having some people from London who were more filled with the Devil than the Spiritualists we had in our city of Bradford. They were special devils.

"I am going," he continued, "and I am going with the clear knowledge that I am under the blood of Jesus."

"Tell me the results, will you?"

"Yes, I will."

Now, beloved, I advise none of you to go to these places.

My friend went and sat down in the midst of the séance meeting, and the medium began to take control. The lights went low; everything was in a dismal state. My friend did not speak, but just kept himself under the blood, whispering the preciousness of the blood of Jesus. These more possessed devils were on the platform. They tried every possible thing they could to get under control for more than an hour, and then the lights went up. The leader said, "We can do nothing tonight; there is somebody here who believes in the blood of Christ."

Hallelujah! Do you all believe in the blood, beloved?

Thought for today: Have biblical proof for everything you have, and then you will be in a place where no one can move you.

December 3

Greater Is He Who Is in You

The LORD is my light and my salvation; whom shall I fear? The LORD is the strength of my life; of whom shall I be afraid?
—Psalm 27:1

Scripture reading: Psalm 27

*B*e ready to challenge the Devil. Don't be afraid. You will be delivered from fear if you believe. You can have *"ears to hear"* (Matt. 11:15) or ears that do not hear. Ears that hear are the ears of faith, and your ears will be so open to what is spiritual that they will lay hold of it.

When the Word of God becomes the life and nature of you, you will find that the minute you open it, it becomes life to you; you will find that you have to be joined up with the Word. You are to be the epistles of Christ (2 Cor. 3:3). This means that Christ is the Word, and He will be known in us by our fruits. (See Matthew 7:16–20.) He is the life and the nature of you. It is a new nature: a new life, a new breath, a new spiritual atmosphere. There is no limitation in this standard, but in everything else you are limited. *"He who is in you is greater than he who is in the world"* (1 John 4:4). When the Word of Life is lived out in you because it is your life, then it is enacted, and it brings forth what God has desired. When we quote something from the Scriptures, we must be careful that we are living according to it. The Word of God has to abide in you, for the Word is life and it brings forth life, and this is the life that makes you *"free from the law of sin and death"* (Rom. 8:2).

Thought for today: The Word not only gives you a foundation but also puts you in a place where you can stand and after the battle keep on standing.

511

How to Test the Spirits

You are strong, and the word of God abides in you,
and you have overcome the wicked one.
—1 John 2:14

Scripture reading: 1 John 2:14–29

*T*here are evil thoughts, and there are thoughts of evil. Evil thoughts are suggestive of the Evil One. We must be able to understand what evil is and how to deal with it. The Word of God makes us strong. All evil powers are weak. "Young men, you are strong because you know the Word." (See 1 John 2:14.)

Where do thoughts of evil come from? They come from the unclean believer, the man who is not entirely sanctified. Remember that the Devil does not know your thoughts; that is where the Devil is held. But God knows your thoughts; God knows all things. Satan can only suggest evil thoughts to try to arouse your carnal nature.

Yet if you are disturbed by evil thoughts, if you are troubled or depressed, then you are in a wonderful place. If you never tell anybody about your evil thoughts, and you are not disturbed about them, the carnal powers have never been destroyed in you. But if you tell anybody, then it is proof that you are clean; it is because you are clean that you weep. If you are not disturbed, if you have no conviction, it is because of your uncleansed heart; you have let sin come in.

How can the believer believe so that he will not be tormented? How can we be master of the situation? We must know this Scripture: *"Every spirit that confesses that Jesus Christ has come in the flesh is of God"* (1 John 4:2). Did Jesus come in the flesh? Mary produced a Son in the likeness of God. In a similar way, the eternal seed that came into us when we believed produces a life, a person, which is *"Christ in* [us]*"* (Col. 1:27) and which rises up in us until the reflection of the Son of God is in everything we do. Mary produced a Son for redemption. God's seed in us produces a son of perfect redemption, until we live in Him and move by Him, and our whole nature becomes a perfect Son of God in us (Acts 17:28). In the name of Jesus, cast self out, and you will be instantly free.

Thought for today: There is nothing strong in the Devil; the weakest believer dethrones the Enemy when he mentions Jesus.

December 5

A Ruined Life
Part One

For I say, through the grace given to me, to everyone who is among you, not to think of himself more highly than he ought to think, but to think soberly, as God has dealt to each one a measure of faith.
—Romans 12:3

Scripture reading: Mark 13:5–20

*L*ots of people are brought down by the same thing that ruined the life of a young Christian I want to tell you about. For many years after I was baptized, the Lord graciously helped me. I laid hands upon people, and they received the Holy Spirit. I thank God that that power has not stopped. I believe in asking God, in lifting up holy hands and saying, "Father, grant that whoever I place my hands upon will receive the Holy Spirit."

People have called me from various places to come and help them when they have had people they wanted to receive the Holy Spirit. Once a group from York, England, sent word saying that they had fourteen people whom they wanted to have baptized in the Holy Spirit, and would I come? They had all been saved since the last time I was there.

So I went. I have never in all my life met a group of people who were so intoxicated with the Spirit. The power of God was upon them. Right in the midst of them was a young man who had developed such a gift of teaching and leading the people forward with God through the power of the Spirit that they said they did not believe there was another man like him in all of England.

I rejoiced with them over this young man. When Jesus began His ministry, He laid hands upon eleven who turned out to be the most marvelous men, yet they were all younger then He. When Paul was brought into the knowledge of the truth, he was a young man. Jesus began the great ministry of worldwide revival with young life. World War I showed us that no man over forty years of age was good enough for that war. They had to have young blood that could stand the stress of frost, heat, and all kinds of things.

Thought for today: God wants young people filled with the power of God to go into the harvest field, because they can stand the stress.

December 6

A Ruined Life
Part Two

For I say, through the grace given to me, to everyone who is among you, not to think of himself more highly than he ought to think, but to think soberly, as God has dealt to each one a measure of faith.
—Romans 12:3

Scripture reading: Mark 13:21–37

As soon as I got to York, people came around me and said, "Oh, we've got him! We've got him! The only thing that is needed now is that we want him to receive the Holy Spirit, and as soon as he receives, we will know we have got him." They were talking about a certain young man in whom they saw unusual potential to be a great spiritual leader. When that young man spoke in tongues, they almost went wild. They shouted, they wept, they prayed. Oh, they were so excited!

The leaders said they were overjoyed at the fact of this man's baptism. I said, "Be still; the Lord will do His own work."

In a short time, he was through in the Spirit, and everybody was rejoicing and applauding. They fell into great error there. God has never yet allowed any human being to be applauded for doing the Lord's work.

This young man was in the power of the Holy Spirit, and it was lovely. But they came around him, shaking his hand and saying, "Now we have the greatest teacher there is."

Was this wrong? It was perfectly right, yet it was the worst thing they could have done; they should have been thankful in their hearts. I want to tell you that the Devil never knows your thoughts, and if you won't let your thoughts out in public, you will be safe. He can suggest a thought; he can suggest thoughts of evil. But that is not sin; all these things are from outside of you. The Devil can suggest evil things for you to receive, but if you are pure, it is like water off a duck's back.

One woman came up and said, "I wouldn't be surprised if you were another John the Baptist."

Again, before we left, this woman came up and said, "Will you believe? It is a prophecy I have received that you have to be John the Baptist."

December 6

Thank God, he put it off. But how satanic, how devilish, how unrighteous, and how untrue her words were!

That night, as he was walking home along a country road, another voice came, louder than the woman's, right in the open air: "You are John the Baptist!"

Again the young man was able to guard it off. In the middle of the night, he was awakened out of his sleep, and this voice came again: "Rise, get up. You are John the Baptist. Declare it!"

And the poor man this time was not able to deal with it. He did not know what I am now telling you. I tell you with a sorrowful heart that for hours that morning he was walking around York, shouting, "I am John the Baptist!" Nothing could be done. He had to be detained.

Who did it? Why, the people, of course.

You have no right to come around me or anybody else and say, "You are wonderful!" That is satanic. I tell you, we have plenty of the Devil to deal with without your causing a thousand demons to come and help. We need common sense.

How could that young man have been delivered? He could have said, "Did Jesus come in the flesh?" The demon power would have said no, and then the Comforter would have come.

Lord, bring us to a place of humility and brokenheartedness where we will see the danger of satanic powers.

Don't think that the Devil is a big ugly monster; he comes as an angel of light (2 Cor. 11:14). He comes at a time when you have done well, and he tells you about it. He comes to make you feel you are somebody. The Devil is an exalted demon. Oh, look at the Master.

Thought for today: May God give us the mindset of the Beatitudes (Matt. 5:3–12) where we will be broken and humble and in the dust; then God will raise us and place us in a high place.

Why Tongues?

Therefore tongues are for a sign, not to those who believe
but to unbelievers.
—1 Corinthians 14:22

Scripture reading: 1 Corinthians 14:26–40

Why has God brought this gift of tongues into operation? There is a reason. If there were not a reason, it would not be there. Why did God design it? You must see with me that the gift of tongues was never in evidence before the Holy Spirit came. The old dispensation was very wonderful in prophetic utterances. Every person, whoever he is, who receives the Holy Spirit will have prophetic utterances in the Spirit unto God or in a human language supernaturally coming forth, so that all the people will know that it is the Spirit.

This is the reason we want all the people filled with the Holy Spirit: they are to be prophetic. When a prophecy is given, it means that God has a thought, a word in season, that has never been in season before—things both new and old. The Holy Spirit brings things to pass!

So when God fulfilled the promise, when the time was appointed, the Holy Spirit came and filled the apostles. The gift that had never been in operation before came into operation that wonderful day in the Upper Room, and for the first time in all of history, men were speaking in a new order; it was not an old language, but language that was to be interpreted.

This is profound because we recognize that God is speaking. No man understands it. The Spirit is speaking, and the Spirit opens the revelation that they will have, without adulteration.

Tongues are a wonderful display of this; they are to revive the people; they are to give new depths of thought.

If you ever want to know why the Holy Spirit was greatly needed, you will find it in the third chapter of Ephesians. You will be amazed. The language is wonderful. Paul said that he was *"the least of all the saints"* (Eph. 3:8), yet God had called him to be a *"minister"* (v. 7). His language is wonderful, yet he felt in his heart and life that there was something greater, that the Spirit had him, and he bowed his knees unto the Father (v. 14).

You cannot find in all the Scriptures words with such profound fruit as those that ring through the verses of Paul's remarkable prayer in the Holy Spirit. He prayed *"that you may be filled with all the fullness of God"* (Eph. 3:19), and *"that you...may be able to comprehend with all the saints"* (vv. 17–18). He prayed that you may be able to ask and think, and think and ask, and that it will not only be abundantly but that it will also be *"exceeding abundantly above all that"* you can *"ask or think"* (v. 20). There is a man closing down and the Holy Spirit praying.

Thought for today: The Holy Spirit did not come to exalt you; He came so that you could exalt the Lord.

Yield to the Holy Spirit
Part One

Desire earnestly to prophesy, and do not forbid to speak with
tongues. Let all things be done decently and in order.
—1 Corinthians 14:39–40

Scripture reading: 1 Corinthians 14:1–25

*Y*ou are not to consider, under any circumstances, that, because you have a spiritual gift, it is right for you to use that
gift, unless the unction of the Spirit is upon you. Unless you
adhere to this word, every assembly where you are will be broken
up, and you will cause trouble. Until you come to a right understanding of the Scriptures, you will never be pleasing to God.

You have to be very careful that you never use tongues and
interpretation in confusion with prophecy. When prophecy is going
forth and the truth is being heard and all the people are receiving it
with joy and are being built up, then there is no room for tongues
or interpretation. But just at the time when the language in my
heart seems too big to express, then tongues come forth and God
looses the whole thing, and we get a new purpose in that.

So you who have this wonderful gift of tongues must see to it
that you never break in where the Spirit is having perfect
right-of-way. But when the Spirit is working with you and you
know there is a line of truth that the Lord desires to express, then
let the name of God be glorified.

You see, God wants everything to be in perfect order by the
Spirit. That is why Paul said, *"If anyone speaks in a tongue, let*
there be two or at the most three" (1 Cor. 14:27). You will never find
me speaking if three have spoken before me. And you will never
find me interpreting any word in tongues if three have spoken already. This is in order to keep the bonds of peace in the body so
that the people will not be weary, because there are some people
who have known nothing about what is right.

Unless you come to the Word of God, you will be in confusion
and you will be in judgment. God does not want you to be in confusion or in judgment, but He wants you to be built up by the Scriptures, for the Scriptures are clear.

518

December 8

If the Lord reveals truth to me, and if I have said anything previously in relation to this that has not been absolutely scriptural, I will no longer say it. I allow God's Word to be my judge. If I find that anything I have said is not scriptural, I repent before God. As God is my Judge, I never say anything unless I believe it is the sincere truth. But if I find out later that it is not exactly in the most perfect keeping with the Word of God, I never say it again.

Thought for today: May the Lord help us to be true to God first; then, if we are true to God, we will be true to ourselves.

Yield to the Holy Spirit
Part Two

Desire earnestly to prophesy, and do not forbid to speak with tongues. Let all things be done decently and in order.
—1 Corinthians 14:39–40

Scripture reading: I Thessalonians 5:11–24

*I*n 1 Corinthians 14:30 we read, *"If anything is revealed to another who sits by, let the first keep silent."* I hope that someday the church will so completely come into its beauty that if I am preaching and you have a revelation on that very thing, a deep revelation from God, and if you stand, I will stop preaching at that moment. Why? Because the Scripture says that if, when a prophet is speaking, anything is revealed to someone in the audience, let the first hold his peace and then let that other one speak.

Then the Scripture says, *"For you can all prophesy one by one, that all may learn and all may be encouraged"* (v. 31). This refers to the one who is preaching. He may be led to hold his peace while one in the midst of the congregation speaks his line of thought that is divinely appointed; then, after he finishes, another may have a prophecy, and he may get up, and so on, until you may have several who have prophesied and you have such revelations in this manner that the whole church is ablaze. I believe that God is going to help us so that we might be sound in mind, right in thought, holy in judgment, separated unto God, and one in the Spirit.

Allow me to say this, and then you judge it afterward. You are not in the right place if you do not judge what I say. You are not to swallow everything I say; you are to judge everything I say by the Scriptures. But you must always use righteous judgment. Righteous judgment is not judging through condemnation, but it is judging something according to the Word of God. In this way, the church may receive edification so that all the people may be built up according to the Word of God.

Perhaps not everyone will affirm what I have to say about this. However, I truly believe, because God has revealed it to me, that the words *"Let there be two or at the most three, each in turn"* (v. 27) mean that often the speaker will not have finished his message after giving the first insight. So often I have seen in an assembly of believers that the first person has spoken and the Spirit of the Lord has been mightily upon him, but the anointing is such that he did not finish his message with his first insight of truth, and he realizes that he is not through with that message. He speaks in the Spirit again, and we feel that the tide is higher. Then he speaks a third time, and the tide is higher still, and then he stops.

This has led me to believe that *"each in turn"* (1 Cor. 14:27) means that one person may be permitted to speak in tongues three times in one meeting. In our conferences in England, we very often have nine utterances in tongues, but there will only be three people speaking. You can have nine, but it is not necessary unless the Lord is prompting it. Sometimes I find that the Spirit will take us through in prophecy in such a way that there will not be more than one, sometimes two people speaking. If I am correct, and I believe I am correct when I say this, when we are full of prophecy, the Spirit has taken our hearts and has moved them by His power. When this happens to me, I speak as fast as I can, but I am not expressing my own thoughts. The Holy Spirit is the thought, the language, and everything; the power of the Spirit is speaking. And when the power of the Holy Spirit is speaking like this, there is no need for tongues or interpretation because you are getting right from the throne the very language of the heart and the man. Then when the person's language gives out, the Spirit will speak and the Lord will give tongues and interpretation, and that will lift the whole place.

"At the most three." Don't say four or five, but three at the most. The Holy Spirit says it.

Thought for today: Righteous judgment is not focused on criticism, but righteous judgment judges the truth of something.

A Prophet out of God's Will

Therefore let him who thinks he stands take heed lest he fall.
—1 Corinthians 10:12

Scripture reading: Philippians 3:3–21

*T*here are people today who have lived holy lives, preached sanctification, and their language of tongues has been helpful, but something has come in the way. They have lost their zeal and fire, but they still hold onto the language. This can take place in anyone's life.

I would like you to know that the speaker is no good unless he judges himself every day. If I do not judge myself, I will be judged (1 Cor. 11:31). It is no good to me if I look good to you. If there were one thing between me and God, I would not dare to speak to others unless I knew that God had made me holy, for they who bear the vessels of the Lord must be holy unto the Lord (Isa. 52:11). And I praise God because I know:

> His blood can make the vilest clean,
> His blood can make the vilest clean,
> His blood avails for me,
> His blood avails for me.

You cannot assume that someone is still living in the center of God's holy will. Because I am only a man, it is possible that I may have grieved the Spirit. If I were to speak in a formal language without unction, that would not move the people. In this type of situation, someone in the place—and this is what tongues are for— someone in the place who is hungry for God and cannot rest because he is not getting the cream of the truth would begin travailing and groaning in the Spirit and speaking in tongues. Another person would travail in the same way, receiving the interpretation of these tongues, and would arise and give that interpretation, thus lifting the people where the prophet could not because he was out of the will of God.

Thought for today: It is not sufficient for me to have your good word; I must have the Master's good word.

December 11

A More Excellent Way

Let everything that has breath praise the LORD.
Praise the LORD!
—Psalm 150:6

Scripture reading: Psalm 150

*I*f you ever get to the place where you cannot praise the Lord, it is a calamity in your life and it is a calamity to the people who are around you. If you want to take blessing into homes and make all the people around you know that you have something more than an ordinary life, you must know that God has come to supplant you and put within you a perfect praise.

God has a great place for us, so that His will may be done and we may be subject to His perfect will. When that comes to pass, no one can tell what may happen, for Jesus reached the highest place when He said, *"For I have come down from heaven, not to do My own will, but the will of Him who sent Me"* (John 6:38). So there is something in a place of yielding where God can have us for His own.

God desires that we would lose ourselves in Him in a way we have never done before. I want to provoke you to love so that you will come into this place of blessing.

Beloved, believe today that God has a way for you. Perhaps you have never come that way before. God has a way beyond all your ways of thought. He has a plan for you.

There is a great need today. People are hungry for truth. People are thirsting, wanting to know God better. There are thousands *"in the valley of decision"* (Joel 3:14), wanting someone to take them right into the depths of God.

Are you ready to pray? You say, "What should I ask for?"

You may not know what to ask for, but if you begin, the Spirit knows the desire of your heart, and He will pray according to the mind of God. You do not know, but God knows everything, and He is acquainted with you altogether and desires to promote you.

So I say, "Are you ready?" You say, "What for?" Are you ready to come promptly into the presence of God so that you may ask this day as you have never asked before? Ask in faith, doubting nothing, but believing that God is on the throne waiting to anoint you afresh today.

Are you ready? What for? Are you ready to be brought into the banquet house of God, even as Esther came in before King Ahasuerus? God will put out the scepter, and all that your heart desires He will give to you. (See Esther 5–7.)

Father, in Jesus' name we come before You believing in Your almightiness, that the power of Your hand does move us, chasten us. Build us. Let the Word of God sink into our hearts this day. Make us, O God, worthy of the name we bear, that we may go about as real, holy saints of God. Just as if You were on the earth, fill us with Your anointing, Your power, and Your grace. Amen.

Thought for today: God wants you to be blessed so that you will be a blessing.

December 12

Humility and Compassion

Being found in appearance as a man, He humbled Himself and became obedient to the point of death, even the death of the cross.
—Philippians 2:8

Scripture reading: Philippians 2:1–18

*I*t is very important to minister in the gifts of the Spirit in the proper way. There is no anointing like the unction that comes out of death, when we are dead with Christ. It is this position that makes us live with Him. If we have been conformed to His death, then, in that same death, like Paul, we will be made like Him in His resurrection power (Phil. 3:10–11).

But do not forget that Jesus was coequal with the Father and that He made Himself of no reputation when he became man and came to earth (Phil. 2:6–7). He did not come out and say that He was this, that, or the other. No, that was not His position. Jesus had all the gifts. He could have stood up and said to Peter and John and James and the rest of them, when the dead son was being carried through the gate of the city of Nain (see Luke 7:11–15), "Stand to one side, Peter. Clear out of the way, John. Make room for Me, Thomas. Don't you know who I am? I am coequal with the Father. I have all power, I have all gifts, I have all graces. Stand to one side; I will show you how to raise the dead!"

Is that how He did it? No! Never. Then what made it come to pass? He was observant. The disciples were there, but they did not have the same observance. What did He see? He saw the widow and knew that she was carrying to burial that day all her help, all her life. Her love was bound up in that son. There she was, broken and bent over with sorrow, all her hopes blighted.

Jesus had compassion upon her, and the compassion of Jesus was greater than death. His compassion was so marvelous that it went beyond the powers of death and all the powers of demons. Isn't He a lovely Jesus? Isn't He a precious Savior?

Thought for today: Observance comes from an inward holy flame kindled by God.

December 13

A Perfect Way

Though I speak with the tongues of men and of angels, but have not love, I have become sounding brass or a clanging cymbal.
—1 Corinthians 13:1

Scripture reading: 1 Corinthians 13

*D*id you ever read a verse like this? It is the state of being brought into a treasury. Do you know what a treasury is? A treasury holds or handles priceless things.

God puts you into the treasury to hold or handle the precious gifts of the Spirit. Therefore, so that you may not fail to handle them correctly, He gives you a picture of how you may handle them.

What a high position of authority, of grace, the Lord speaks about in this verse! *"Speak with the tongues of men and of angels."* Oh, isn't that wonderful!

There are men who have such wonderful qualifications for speaking. Their knowledge in the natural realm is so outstanding that many people go to hear their eloquent addresses because the language in them is so beautiful. Yet, through the baptism in the Holy Spirit, God puts you right in the midst of them and says that He has given you the capability to speak like men, with power of thought and language at your disposal, so that you can say anything.

People are failing God all the time all over the world because they are taken up with their own eloquence, and God is not in it. They are lost with the pretentiousness of their great authority over language, and they use it on purpose to tickle the ears and the sensations of the people, and it profits nothing. It is nothing. It will wither up, and the people who use it will wither up.

Yet God has said there is a way. Now, how would language *"of men and of angels"* come to prosper?

When you wept through to victory before, you were able to do anything. You were so undone that unless God helped you to do it, you couldn't do it. You were so broken in spirit that your whole body seemed to be at an end unless God reinstated you. Then the unction came, and every word was glorifying Jesus. Every sentence lifted the people, and they felt as they listened, "Surely God is in this place! He has sent His Word and healed us." (See Psalm 107:20.) They saw no man there except Jesus. Jesus was so manifested that they all said, "Oh, wasn't Jesus speaking to our hearts this morning!"

If you minister in this way, you will never become nothing. Tongues of men and angels alone will come to nothing. Yet if you speak with tongues of men and angels that are bathed in the love of God until it is to Him alone that you speak, then it will be written down forever in the history of the glory. So let the Lord help us to know how to act in the Holy Spirit.

Thought for today: When you are used only for and desire only the glory of God, your acts and life, ministry, and power will be an recorded endlessly in the glory of heaven—for the Acts of the Apostles are being recorded in the glory.

Prophecy and Goodness

And though I have the gift of prophecy, and understand all mysteries and all knowledge, and though I have all faith, so that I could remove mountains, but have not love, I am nothing.
—1 Corinthians 13:2

Scripture reading: Psalm 31

*L*ots of people desire to have faith; many desire to have prophecy; some long to know mysteries. Who knows mysteries? *"The secret of the LORD is with those who fear Him"* (Ps. 25:14). Don't change the Scriptures. *"The just shall live by faith"* (Rom. 1:17). Do not alter the Scriptures.

Do not forget that prophecy is beautiful when you understand the principle of it. Prophecy is the sixth gift mentioned in 1 Corinthians 12. What fruit or grace do you think would coincide with prophecy? Why, goodness, of course.

Why goodness? Because if you are living in holiness, entire sanctification, perfection, you would never take advantage of the Holy Spirit and would speak only as the Spirit gave prophecy. You would never say human things just because you had the gift of prophecy. You would speak according to the Spirit, giving prophecy because you had been holy.

When you speak in the natural after you have received the gift of prophecy, it is because you have come to be nothing; you are nothing; you are not counted in the great plan of the great purpose of God. But if you are hidden in Christ and your whole heart is perfected in God, and you will prophesy only when the Spirit of the Lord is upon you, then it will be something that lasts forever. People will be blessed forever and God will be glorified forever.

Suppose that I have all faith so that I could move mountains. Now, suppose that I also have a big farm, but that some of my farmland is not very profitable. It is stony; it has many rocks on it as well as some little mountains that are absolutely untillable and do no good. But because I have faith without love, I say, "I will use my faith and I will move this land. I do not care where it goes as long as my land is clean."

So I use my faith to clear my land. The next day, my poor next-door neighbor comes and says, "I am in great trouble. All your wasteland and stony, rocky land has been tipped onto mine, and my good land is ruined."

And I, who have faith without love, say to him, "You get faith and move it back!"

That profits nothing. If God brings you into a place of faith, let it be for the glory of God. Then, when you pray, God will wonderfully answer you; nothing will hinder your being used for God, for God delights to use us.

Gifts are not only given; they are also increased to those who can be used, who can keep in a place of usefulness. God keeps these yielded ones in a place of being continually supplanted—a new place that is deeper, higher, holier, richer, more heavenly.

In addition, gifts are not only usable, but God is also glorified in Jesus when you pray the prayer of faith. Jesus Himself said, "When you pray and believe, the Father will be glorified in the Son." (See John 14:12–13.)

Thought for today: It takes a just man to live by faith.

Sacrifice Is Nothing without Love

And though I bestow all my goods to feed the poor, and though I give my body to be burned, but have not love, it profits me nothing.
—1 Corinthians 13:3

Scripture reading: Mark 6:30–56

Though I can lay my hands on millions of dollars, though I can do all kinds of things with the money, and though, after I have given it all, I show the people more by giving my body to be burned, saying, "I will show what I am made of!" this is nothing, nothing! Five dollars given in the name of the Lord is of more value than thousands without acknowledging Him.

A man came to me, and we had long talks about the Lord. He told me, "I was in a very difficult place. I had been working very hard in the church and had given all my strength...."

Oh, I see such godly, holy people doing more than they ought to, thereby giving themselves away. Don't you know that your body belongs to God (1 Cor. 6:19–20), and that, if you overtax your body, God says He will judge you for it? We have to be careful because the body that is given to us is to exhibit His power and His glory, and we cannot do this if we give ourselves all the time to work, work, work and think that that is the only way. It is not the way.

The Scriptures teach us that Jesus had to go and renew His spiritual vision and power in solitude with His Father (Mark 1:35), and it was also necessary for the disciples to draw aside and rest awhile (Mark 6:30–31). Couldn't Jesus give them all they needed? My dear brother, whatever God gives you, He will never take away your common sense.

Suppose I unwisely overextended my body and knew that I had done so? How could I ask anyone to pray for me unless I repented? We must be careful. Our bodies are the temples of the Holy Spirit, and He has to dwell in them, and they have to be for His purpose in the world. We are not working for ourselves; God is to be glorified in our bodies. Many today are absolutely withered up, years before their time, because they went beyond their knowledge.

Thought for today: Your gifts will perish unless the gifts are used for the glory of Jesus.

The Gifts

Now to Him who is able to keep you from stumbling, and to present
you faultless before the presence of His glory with exceeding joy, to
God our Savior, who alone is wise, be glory and majesty, dominion
and power, both now and forever.
—Jude 24–25

Scripture reading: Jude

*I*t is very necessary that we receive the Holy Spirit in the
first place; after receiving the Holy Spirit, we must earnestly desire the gifts. Then, after receiving the gifts, we
must never forget that the gift is entrusted to us for bringing the
blessings of God to the people.

For instance, divine healing is a gift for ministering to the
needs of the people. The gift of wisdom is a word in season at the
moment of need, to show you just what to do. The gift of knowledge, or the word of knowledge, is to inspire you and to bring you
life and joy. This is what God intends.

Then there is the gift of discernment. We are not to discern
one another, but to discern evil powers and deal with them and
command them back to the pit from which they came. Regarding
the gift of miracles, God intends for us to come to the place where
we will see miracles worked. God also wants us to understand that
tongues are profitable only when they exalt and glorify the Lord.
And oh, that we might really know what it means when interpretation is given! It is not merely to have beautiful sensations and
think that is interpretation, but it is such that the man who has it
does not know what is coming, for if he did, it would not be interpretation. Interpretation is not knowing what you are going to say,
but it is being in the place where you say exactly what God says. So
when I have to interpret a message, I purposely keep my mind
from anything that would hinder, and I sometimes say "Praise the
Lord" and "Hallelujah" so that everything will be a word through
the Spirit, and not my word, but the word of the Lord!

We can have these divine gifts so perfectly balanced by divine
love that they will be a blessing all the time. However, there is
sometimes such a desire in the flesh to do something attention-
getting. How the people listen and long for divine prophecy, just as

interpretation comes forth! How it thrills! There is nothing wrong with it; it is beautiful. We thank God for the office and the purpose that has caused it to come, but let us be careful to finish when we are through and not continue on our own. That is how prophecy is spoiled. Don't fail, beloved, because the people know the difference. They know what is full of life, what is the real thing.

Then again, it is the same with a person praying. We love people to pray in the Holy Spirit; we love to hear them pray even the first sentences because the fire is there. However, what spoils the holiest person in prayer is when, after the spirit of prayer has gone forth, he continues on and people say, "I wish he would stop," and the church becomes silent. They say, "I wish that brother would stop. How beautifully he began; now he is dry!" But he doesn't stop.

A preacher was once having a wonderful time, and the people enjoyed it, but when he was through, he continued. A man came and said to someone at the door, "Has he finished?" "Yes," said the man, "long since, but he won't stop!" May God save us from that. People know when you are praying in the Spirit. Why should you take time and spoil everything because the natural side has come into it? God never intended that. God has a supernatural side; that is the true side, and how beautiful it is! People sometimes know better than we do, and we would also know if we were more careful.

May the Lord grant us revelation; we need discernment; we need intuition. It is the life inside. It is salvation inside, cleansing, filling; it is all inside. Revelation is inside. It is for exhibition outside, but always remember that it is inside. God's Son said as much when He said, "The pure in heart will see God." (See Matthew 5:8.) There is an inward sight of God, and it is the pure in heart who see God. Lord, keep us pure so that we will never block the way.

Thought for today: If you continue to prophesy on your own, at the end of the anointing, you are using false fire.

Abide in Christ

I am the vine, you are the branches. He who abides in Me, and I in him, bears much fruit; for without Me you can do nothing.
—John 15:5

Scripture reading: John 15:1–17

Beloved, it is lovely to be in the will of God. Now then, how may we be something? By just being nothing, by receiving the Holy Spirit, by being in the place where we can be directed by God and filled with His power.

What it must be to have speaking ability, to have a beautiful language, as so many men have! It is wonderful to have the tongue of an angel so that all the people who hear you are moved by your use of language. Yet how I would weep, how my heart would be broken, if I came to speak before you in beautiful language without the power.

If I had an angel's language and the people were all taken with what I said, but Jesus was not glorified at all, it would all be hopeless, barren, and unfruitful. I myself should be nothing. But if I speak and say, "Lord, let them hear Your voice. Lord, let them be compelled to hear Your truth. Lord, anyhow, any way, hide me today," then He becomes glorious, and all the people say, "We have seen Jesus!"

When I was in California, I spent many days with our dear Brother Montgomery when I had a chance. During this time, a man wrote to Brother Montgomery. This man had been saved but had lost his joy; he had lost all he had. He wrote, "I am through with everything. I am not going to touch this thing again; I am through." Brother Montgomery wrote back to him and said, "I will never try to persuade you again if you will hear once. There is a man from England, and if you will only hear him once, I will pay all your expenses." So he came. He listened, and at the end of the time he said to me, "This is the truth I am telling you. I have seen the Lord standing beside you, and I heard His voice. I never even saw you.

"I have a lot of money," he continued, "and I have a valley five hundred miles long. If you speak the word to me, I will go on your word, and I will open that valley for the Lord."

I have preached in several of his places, and God has used him wonderfully to speak throughout that valley. What I would have missed when he came the first day, if I had been trying to say something of my own instead of the Lord being there and speaking His words through me! Never let us do anything to lose this divine love, this close affection in our hearts that says, "Not I, but Christ; not I, but Christ!"

Lose all your identity in the Son of God. Let Him become all in all. Seek only the Lord, and let Him be glorified. You will have gifts; you will have grace and wisdom. God is waiting for the person who will lay all on the altar, fifty-two weeks in the year, three hundred and sixty-five days in the year, and then continue perpetually in the Holy Spirit.

Thought for today: Forget yourself and get lost in Him.

The Precious Word

Even so you, since you are zealous for spiritual gifts, let it be for the
edification of the church that you seek to excel.
—1 Corinthians 14:12

Scripture reading: Luke 8:4–18

*T*his Scripture is the Word of God, and it is most important that when we read the Word, we do so with hearts that have purposed to obey its every precept. We have no right to open the Word of God carelessly or indifferently. I have no right to come to you with any message unless it is absolutely in the perfect order of God. I believe we are in order to consider further a subject that we greatly need to be informed about in these days. So many people are receiving the baptism of the Holy Spirit, but then they do not know which way to go.

We have a great need today. It is that we may be supplied with revelation according to the mind of the Lord, that we may be instructed by the mind of the Spirit, that we may be able to rightly divide the Word of Truth (2 Tim. 2:15), and that we may not be novices, considering the fact that the Spirit of the Lord has come to us in revelation. We ought to be alert to every touch of divine, spiritual illumination.

We should carefully consider what the apostle Paul said to us: *"Do not grieve the Holy Spirit of God, by whom you were sealed for the day of redemption"* (Eph. 4:30). The sealing of the Spirit is very remarkable, and I pray to God that not one of you may lose the divine inheritance that God has chosen for you, which is greater than you could choose if your mind had ten times its normal faculties. God's mind is greater than yours. His thoughts are higher than the heavens over you (Isa. 55:9), so that you do not need to be afraid.

Thought for today: When the Word is in your heart, it will preserve you from desiring sin.

Worthy Conduct

Being confident of this very thing, that He who has begun a good work in you will complete it until the day of Jesus Christ.
—Philippians 1:6

Scripture reading: Philippians 1

I have great love for my sons and my daughter, but it is nothing in comparison to God's love toward us. God's love wants us to walk up and down the earth as His Son did: clothed, filled, radiant, with fire beaming forth from our countenances, setting forth the power of the Spirit so that the people jump into liberty.

But there is deplorable ignorance among those who have gifts. It is not right for you to think that because you have a gift, you are to wave it before the people and try to get their minds upon that, because, if you do, you will be out of the will of God. Gifts and callings in the body of Christ may be irrevocable (Rom. 11:29), but remember that God calls you to account for properly administering the gift in a spiritual way after you have received it. It is not given to adorn you, but to sustain, build, edify, and bless the church. When God ministers through a member of the body of Christ and the church receives this edification, then all the members will rejoice together. God moves upon us as His offspring, as His choice, and as the fruit of the earth. He wants us to be elegantly clothed in wonderful raiment, even as our Master is.

His workings upon us may be painful, but the wise saint will remember that among those whom God chastens, it is the one who is trained by that chastening to whom *"it yields the peaceable fruit of righteousness"* (Heb. 12:11). Therefore, let Him do with you what seems good to Him, for He has His hand upon you; He will not willingly take it off until He has performed the thing He knows you need. So if He comes to sift you, be ready for the sifting. If He comes with chastisement, be ready for chastisement. If He comes with correction, be ready for correction. Whatever He wills, let Him do it, and He will bring you to the land of plenty. Oh, it is worth the world to be under the power of the Holy Spirit!

If He does not chasten you, if you sail placidly along without incident, without crosses, without persecutions, without trials,

December 19

remember that *"if you are without chastening, of which all have become partakers, then you are illegitimate and not sons"* (Heb. 12:8). Therefore, *"examine yourselves as to whether you are in the faith"* (2 Cor. 13:5). Never forget that Jesus said this word: "They who hear My voice follow Me." (See John 10:27.)

Thought for today: Jesus wants you to have a clear ring to your testimony.

A Perfect Fit

There are diversities of gifts, but the same Spirit.
—1 Corinthians 12:4

Scripture reading: Romans 12:3–13

*T*he variation among humanity is tremendous. Faces are different, so are physiques. Your whole body may be put together in such a way that one particular gift would not suit you at all, while it would suit another person.

So the Word of God deals here with varieties of gifts, meaning that these gifts perfectly meet the condition of each believer. That is God's plan. It may be that not one person would be led to claim all the gifts. Nevertheless, do not be afraid; the Scriptures are definite. Paul said that you do not need to come short in any gift (1 Cor. 1:7). God has wonderful things for you beyond what you have ever known. The Holy Spirit is so full of prophetic operations of divine power that it is marvelous what may happen after the Holy Spirit comes.

How He loosed me! I am no good without the Holy Spirit. The power of the Holy Spirit loosed my language. I was like my mother. She had no ability to speak. If she began to tell a story, she couldn't finish it. My father would say, "Mother, you will have to begin again." I was like that. I couldn't tell a story. I was bound. I had plenty of thoughts, but no language. But oh, after the Holy Spirit came!

When He came, I had a great desire for gifts. So the Lord caused me to see that it is possible for every believer to live in such holy anointing, such divine communion, such pressed-down measure (Luke 6:38) by the power of the Spirit, that every gift can be his.

But is there not a vast and appalling unconcern about possessing the gifts? You may ask a score of believers, chosen at random from almost any church, "Do you have any of the gifts of the Spirit?" The answer from all will be, "No," and it will be given in a tone and with a manner that conveys the thought that the believer is not surprised that he does not have the gifts, that he doesn't expect to have any of them, and that he does not expect to seek them.

December 20

Isn't this terrible, when the living Word specifically exhorts us to *"earnestly desire the best gifts"* (1 Cor. 12:31)?

So in order that the gifts might be everything and in evidence, we have to see that we cease to live without His glory. He works with us, and we work with Him—cooperating, working together. This is divine. Surely this is God's plan.

God has brought you to the banquet, and He wants to send you away full. We are in a place where God wants to give us visions. We are in a place where, in His great love, He is bending over us with kisses. Oh, how lovely is the kiss of Jesus, the expression of His love!

Oh, come, let us seek Him for the best gifts, and let us strive to be wise and to rightly divide the Word of Truth (2 Tim. 2:15), giving it forth in power so that the church may be edified and sinners may be saved.

Thought for today: Look to the Holy Spirit to show you how to use the gifts so that you never use them without the power of the Spirit.

December 21

Transformed by God

Behold, I will do a new thing.
—Isaiah 43:19

Scripture reading: Titus 3

*T*hank God for His Word. Live it. Be moved by it. We will become anemic and helpless without the Word. We are not any good for anything apart from the Word. It is everything. When the heavens and earth are melted away, then we will be as bright as the day because of the Word of God.

We know it is quick and powerful and sharper than any two-edged sword, dividing soul and spirit, joints and marrow, and thoughts of the heart (Heb. 4:12). God's Word is like a sword piercing through. The Word is divinely appointed for us. Take it in; think it out; work it out. It is the truth.

When I was going to New Zealand and Australia, there were many there to see me off. An Indian doctor rode in the same car with me to the docks and boarded the same ship. He was very quiet and took in all the things that were said on the ship. I began to preach, of course, and the Lord began to work among the people. In the second class of the ship, there was a young man and his wife who were attendants for a lady and gentleman in the first class. And as these two young people heard me talking to them privately and otherwise, they were very much impressed. Then the lady they were attending got very sick. In her sickness and her loneliness, she could find no relief. They called in the doctor, and the doctor gave her no hope.

And then, when in this strange dilemma—she was a great Christian Scientist, a preacher of it, and had gone many places preaching it—they thought of me. Knowing the conditions, and what she lived for, knowing that it was late in the day, that in the condition of her mind she could only receive the simplest word, I said to her, "Now you are very sick, and I won't talk to you about anything except this: I will pray for you in the name of Jesus, and the moment I pray you will be healed."

And the moment I prayed she was healed. That was *"like precious faith"* (2 Pet. 1:1) in operation. Then she was disturbed. I showed her the terrible state she was in and pointed out to her all

540

her folly and the fallacy of her position. I showed her that there was nothing in Christian Science, that it is a lie from the beginning and one of the last agencies of hell. At best it is a lie: preaching a lie and producing a lie.

Then she came to her senses. She became so penitent and brokenhearted. But the thing that stirred her first was that she had to go preach the simple gospel of Christ where she had preached Christian Science. She asked me if she had to give up certain things. I won't mention the things; they are too vile. I said, "No, what you have to do is to see Jesus and take Jesus." When she saw the Lord in His purity, the other things had to go. At the presence of Jesus, all else goes.

This opened the door. I had to preach to all on the boat. This gave me a great chance. As I preached, the power of God fell, conviction came, and sinners were saved. They followed me into my cabin one after another. God was working there.

Then this Indian doctor came. He said, "What will I do? Your preaching has changed me, but I must have a foundation. Will you spend some time with me?"

"Of course I will."

Then we went alone, and God broke the fallow ground. This Indian doctor was going right back home but as a new man. He had left a practice there. He told me of the great practice he had. He was going back to his practice to preach Jesus.

Thought for today: It is one thing to handle the Word of God; it is another thing to believe what God says.

December 22

Our Inheritance

*His divine power has given to us all things that pertain to life
and godliness, through the knowledge of Him who called us
by glory and virtue.*
—2 Peter 1:3

Scripture reading: Matthew 21:33–44

Many people make wills and appoint someone to carry out their final requests. After the person dies, very often those people who have had property left to them never get it because of unfaithful stewards who have been left in charge. But there is one will that has been left, and He who made the whole will is our Lord Jesus Christ. After dying, He rose to carry out His own will. And now we may have all that has been left to us by Him: all the inheritance, all the blessings, all the power, all the life, and all the victory. All His promises are ours because He is risen. I believe the Lord wants us to know our inheritance.

Jesus invites you, *"Come to Me, all you who labor and are heavy laden, and I will give you rest"* (Matt. 11:28). God is willing in His great mercy to touch you with His mighty power; if He is willing to do this, how much more eager He is to deliver you from the power of Satan and to make you a child of the King! How much more necessary it is for you to be healed of your soul sickness than of your bodily ailments!

Because He is risen as a faithful High Priest, He is here to help us understand His divine principles. May God provide us with a clear knowledge of what He means for us in these days. He has called us to great banquets and wants us to bring good appetites to His table.

It is a serious thing to come to a banquet of the Lord and not be able to eat anything. We must have very thirsty conditions and hungry souls. Then we can have what is prepared for us. We can be *"strengthened with might through His Spirit in the inner man"* (Eph. 3:16). May the Lord take us into His treasures now.

Thought for today: We must experience a now power, a now blessing, a now God, a now heaven, a now glory, a now virtue.

Beyond Imagination

That Christ may dwell in your hearts through faith; that you, being rooted and grounded in love, may be able to comprehend with all the saints...the love of Christ which passes knowledge.
—Ephesians 3:17–19

Scripture reading: Romans 8

Are we children of circumstances or children of faith? In our humanity, we may be troubled by the blowing of the wind. As it blows, it whispers fearfulness; but if you are *"rooted and grounded,"* you can stand the tests, and it is only then that you *"may be able to comprehend...what is the width and length and depth and height; to know the love of Christ which passes knowledge"* (Eph. 3:18–19). It is an addition sum to meet every need, to display God's power, and to enlarge one's faith.

What does Paul mean by the width of Christ's love? It is recognizing that God is sufficient in every circumstance. The length of His love indicates that God is in everything. God is in the depths and the heights! God is always lifting you, and the truth in this verse is enough for anyone in any circumstance to triumph. He *"is able to do exceedingly abundantly above all that we can ask or think,"* not according to the mind of Paul, but *"according to the power that works in us"* (v. 20). Simplicity of heart can broaden one's perspective, but this fullness is an ideal power of God in the human soul, enlarging every part. God is there instead of you to make you full, and you are full as your faith reaches out to be filled with all the fullness of God.

The power of the Lord was present to heal. His fullness of power flowed out of the disciples to others. In Acts 1, we see the power of God revealed as Jesus was lifted up to where He was before—into the presence of God. Jesus Christ showed the power of God in human flesh. The fullness of the Godhead was bodily manifested in Jesus (Col. 2:9). John said that *"in Him was life, and the life was the light of men"* (John 1:4). His substance revealed the fullness of God. How can it be fulfilled in you? The Scripture provides the answer: He is *"able to do exceedingly abundantly above all that we can ask or think"* (Eph. 3:20). It is filled there in the glory. But it's a tremendous thing. God will have to do something.

December 23

Beloved, it is not according to your mind at all but according to the mind of God, according to the revelation of the Spirit. *"Above all that we can ask or think."* The blood has been poured out.

Truly, we are not worthy, but He is worthy. He will do more than we can even ask. How can it be possible? God puts it in your heart. He can do it. We hear much about rates of interest, but if you will faithfully follow God, He will add, enlarge, and lift you all the time, adding compound interest. Five percent? No! A thousand percent, a million percent! If you are willing, if holiness is the purpose of your heart, it will be done, for God is in His place. Will you be in the plan *"according to the power that works in* [you]*"* (Eph. 3:20)? Whatever you are at any time, it will be by His effective power, lifting, controlling, and carrying you in constant rest and peace; it is *"according to the power that works in* [you].*"* Let everyone say: *"To Him be glory in the church by Christ Jesus to all generations, forever and ever. Amen"* (v. 21).

Thought for today: Many people receive no blessing because they did not thank God for the last blessing.

December 24

Abundant Blessings

When we were still without strength, in due time
Christ died for the ungodly.
—Romans 5:6

Scripture reading: Romans 5

Through one man's disobedience, through one man's sin, death came and reigned. Then Another came. Adam was the first man; Christ, the second. One was earthly; the other, heavenly. As sin and death reigned by one, so now the New Man, the Christ-man, will make us awake to righteousness, peace, and abounding in God. Just as death had its power through a man, life has to have its power and victory. Through the God-man, we come into a new divine order.

"I cannot understand this truth, Wigglesworth." No, friend, you never will. It is a thousand times bigger than your mind. But Christ's mind replanted in your natural order will give you a vision so that you may see what you cannot understand. What you will never understand, God thoroughly understands. He blesses you abundantly.

You know how sin was abounding, how we were held, how we were defeated, how we groaned and travailed. Has sin abounded? Now grace, now life, now the ministry abounds to us.

Take a leap of faith so that you may never know what defeat is any more. Romans 5 is a real divine healing chapter; it is a real ascension chapter; it is a powerful resurrection chapter. It looses you from your limitations. It moves you from your former place into a place of coveted grace. It takes your weaknesses and sins and abounds to you with atonement. It reveals to you all that Adam ever had that bound you. It reveals all that Christ ever had or will have that abounds toward you to liberate you from all that is human and bring you into all that is divine. This is the glorious liberty of the Gospel of Christ:

> *And the gift is not like that which came through the one who*
> *sinned. For the judgment which came from one offense re-*
> *sulted in condemnation, but the free gift which came from*
> *many offenses resulted in justification.* (Rom. 5:16)

We have been condemned and lost. How human nature destroys! We all know sin had its reign, but there is justification. God works in the lower order with His mighty higher order. He touches human weaknesses with His touch of infinite, glorious resurrection power. He transforms you:

For if by the one man's offense death reigned through the one, much more those who receive abundance of grace and of the gift of righteousness will reign in life through the One, Jesus Christ. (Rom. 5:17)

How rich we are. The death-life has been replaced. Now there is a righteous life. You were in death and it was the death-life, but now you have received the righteous life. How much have you acquired of it? Have you received an *"abundance of grace"*? Your grace has run out years ago. My grace has been depleted years ago, but I realized by the revelation of the Spirit that His grace should take the place of my grace. His power should cover me where I cannot cover myself. He stands beside me when I am sure to go down. Where sin abounded, grace abounded, and His love abounded. He stretched out His hand in mercy; He never failed. He was there every time when I was sure to go down. Grace abounded. Oh, the mercy, the boundless mercy of the love of God to us!

I hope you are getting it, thriving in it, and triumphing in it. I hope you are coming to the place to see that you are a victor in it. God must give you these divine attributes of the Spirit so that you may come into like-mindedness with Him in this wonderful provision.

Thought for today: If there is an abundance of praise in your heart, your mouth cannot help speaking it.

God Is Near

"Behold, the virgin shall be with child, and bear a Son, and they shall call His name Immanuel," which is translated, "God with us."
—Matthew 1:23

Scripture reading: Matthew 1:18–25; Philippians 2:5–11

Being saved is a reality. There is a great deal of truth about having the peace of God. There is a great deal of knowledge in knowing that you are free, and there is a wonderful manifestation of power to keep you free. But I find Satan dethrones some of the loveliest people because he catches them at a time when they are unaware. I find these poor souls constantly being deceived by the power of Satan.

Hear this word: when Satan is the nearest, God is nearer with an abundant measure of His grace. When you feel almost defeated, He has a banner waving over you to cover you. He covers you with His grace; He covers you with His righteousness. It is the very nature of the Son of God.

It is impossible to remain in the natural body when you experience the life of God. When you are intoxicated with the Spirit, the Spirit life flows through the avenues of your mind and the keen perception of the heart with deep pulsations. You are filled with the passion of the grace of God until you are illuminated by the power of the new wine, the wine of the kingdom. This is rapture. No natural body will be able to stand this process. It will have to leave the body, but the body will be a preserver to it until the sons of God are marvelously manifested. Sonship is a position of rightful heirship. Sons have a right to the first claiming of the will.

I would like you to realize that redemption is so perfect that it causes you to stop judging yourself. You believe that God has a righteous judgment for you. Escape from the powers of the Devil. You can have an abundance of grace, righteousness, liberty for the soul, and transformation of the mind. You can be lifted out of your earthly place into God's power and authority.

Thought for today: Jesus left heaven though He had the right not to leave.

Waiting for the Bridegroom

Behold, the bridegroom is coming; go out to meet him!
—Matthew 25:6

Scripture reading: Matthew 25:1–13

God fascinates me with His Word. I read and read, yet it is all something so new, remarkable, and blessed. I realize the truth of that saying, "The bride rejoices to hear the Bridegroom's voice." (See John 3:29.) The Word is His voice, and as we get nearer to Jesus, we understand that He came to take out for Himself a people who would be His bride. It means not only to be saved, but also that there is an eternal destiny awaiting us in glory. God in His mercy has given us this blessed revelation of how He lived, loved, and had power to say to those disciples, "Some of you shall not see death until you see the kingdom of God coming in power." (See Mark 9:1.)

Oh, that blessed Christ, who could pray until His countenance was changed and became so glorious, until His raiment became white and glistening. He said, *"I have power to lay [My life] down, and I have power to take it again"* (John 10:18). It is true that by wicked hands He was taken and crucified, but He had to be willing, for He had all power and could have called on legions of angels to deliver Him from death. But oh, that blessed Christ had purposed to save us and bring us into fellowship and oneness with Himself. He went right through death so that He might impart to us the blessed reconciliation between God and man.

So it is that the Man Jesus Christ, who is the Atonement for the whole world, who is the Son of God, is also the sinner's Friend. *"He was wounded for our transgressions"* (Isa. 53:5). This blessed Christ gave His disciples the glory that He had with the Father before the world was. (See John 17:5.) God wants us to know that He will withhold *"no good thing...from those who walk uprightly"* (Ps. 84:11), including health, peace, joy in the Holy Spirit, and a life in Christ Jesus.

Thought for today: We must be ready for our King.

Our Helper

No one can say that Jesus is Lord except by the Holy Spirit.
—1 Corinthians 12:3

Scripture reading: John 14:16–31

The Holy Spirit has a royal plan, a heavenly plan. He came to unveil the King, to show the character of God, to unveil the precious blood. Since I have the Holy Spirit within me, I see Jesus clothed for humanity. He was moved by the Spirit and led by the Spirit. We read of some who heard the Word but did not benefit from it, because faith was lacking in them (Rom. 9:6–8). We must have a living faith in God's Word, a faith that is quickened by the Spirit.

A man may be saved and still have a human spirit. In many people who hear about the baptism of the Holy Spirit, the human spirit immediately arises against the Holy Spirit. The human spirit is not subject to the law of God, nor can it be. (See Romans 8:7.) The disciples at one time wanted to call down fire from heaven, and Jesus said to them, *"You do not know what manner of spirit you are of"* (Luke 9:55). The human spirit is not subject to the law of God.

The Holy Spirit came forth for one purpose: to reveal Jesus to us. Jesus *"made Himself of no reputation"* (Phil. 2:7), and He was obedient unto death (v. 8), that God should forever hold Him up as a token of submissive yieldedness. God highly exalted Him and gave Him a name above every name. *"Now He who has prepared us for this very thing is God, who also has given us the Spirit as a guarantee"* (2 Cor. 5:5). With the clothing upon of the Spirit, human depravity is covered, and everything that is contrary to the mind of God is destroyed. God must have bodies for Himself, perfectly prepared by the Holy Spirit, for the Day of the Lord. *"For in this we groan, earnestly desiring to be clothed with our habitation which is from heaven"* (v. 2).

Was Paul speaking here about the coming of the Lord? No! Yet this condition of preparedness is highly relevant. The Holy Spirit is coming to take back a church and a perfect bride. The Holy Spirit must find in us perfect yieldedness, with every human desire subjected to Him. *"No one can say that Jesus is Lord except by the Holy Spirit"* (1 Cor. 12:3). He has come to reveal Christ in us, so that the glorious flow of the life of God may bring rivers of living water to the thirsty land within.

The Spirit has to breathe into us a new occupancy, a new order. The Holy Spirit came to give the vision of a life in which Jesus is perfected. It is Christ *"who has saved us and called us with a holy calling, not according to our works, but according to His own purpose and grace"* (2 Tim. 1:9).

We who are saved have been called with a holy calling, called to be saints—to be pure, holy, and Godlike; to be sons with power. It is a long time now since it was settled and death was abolished. Death has no more power. This was made known through the Gospel, which brought in immortality. Mortality is a hindrance. Sin has no more dominion over you. You reign in Christ, and you make rightful use of His finished work. Don't groan and travail for a week. If you are in need, *"only believe"* (Mark 5:36). Don't fast to get some special thing, *"only believe."* It is according to your faith that God blesses you with more faith. *"Have faith in God"* (Mark 11:22). If you are free in God, believe! Believe, and it will be unto you even as you believe. (See Matthew 9:29.)

"Awake, you who sleep" (Eph. 5:14); put on light, and open your eyes. *"If then you were raised with Christ, seek those things which are above, where Christ is, sitting at the right hand of God"* (Col. 3:1). Stir yourselves up, beloved! Where are you? I am risen with Christ, planted in Him. It was a beautiful planting. I am seated with Him. God gives me the credit, and I believe Him. Why should I doubt?

Dare to believe until the life of Jesus is implanted within your soul. *"The righteous will hold to his way"* (Job 17:9). God has reserved him who is godly for Himself (Ps. 4:3). Therefore, lift up your heads.

Thought for today: The Devil makes you remember the day you failed, though you would give the world to forget about it. But God has forgotten when He forgives.

December 28

God Is All You Need

I take pleasure in infirmities, in reproaches, in needs, in persecutions, in distresses, for Christ' sake. For when I am weak,
then I am strong.
—2 Corinthians 12:10

Scripture reading: 2 Corinthians 12:1–10

*W*hen God comes into your life, you will find Him to be enough. As Israel came forth, the sun rose upon him, and he had power over all the things of the world and over Esau. Esau met him, but there was no fight now; there was reconciliation. They kissed each other. How true it is that *"when a man's ways please the LORD, He makes even his enemies to be at peace with him"* (Prov. 16:7). The material things did not count for much after the night of revelation. Who brought about the change? God did.

Can you hold on to God as Jacob did? You certainly can if you are sincere, dependent, broken, and weak. It is when you are weak that you are strong. But if you are self-righteous, if you are proud, if you are high-minded, if you are puffed up in your own mind, you can receive nothing from Him. If you become lukewarm instead of being on fire for God, you can become a disappointment to Him. And He says, *"I will vomit you out of My mouth"* (Rev. 3:16).

But there is a place of holiness, a place of meekness, a place of faith, where you can call to God, *"I will not let You go unless You bless me!"* (Gen. 32:26). And in response, He will bless you *"exceedingly abundantly above all that* [you] *ask or think"* (Eph. 3:20).

Sometimes we are tempted to think that He has left us. Oh, no. He has promised never to leave us or forsake us (Deut. 31:6). He had promised not to leave Jacob, and He did not break His promise. He has promised not to leave us, and He will not fail. Jacob held on until the blessing came. We can do the same.

If God does not help us, we are no good for this world's need; we are no longer salt, we lose our savor. But as we spend time alone with God, and cry to Him to bless us, He re-salts us. He re-empowers us, but He brings us to brokenness and moves us into the orbit of His own perfect will.

December 28

Oh, the blessedness of being brought into a life of dependence upon the power of the Holy Spirit. Henceforth, we know that we are nothing without Him; we are absolutely dependent upon Him. I am absolutely nothing without the power and anointing of the Holy Spirit. Oh, for a life of absolute dependence! It is through a life of dependence that there is a life of power. If you are not there, get alone with God. If you must, spend a whole night alone with God, and let Him change and transform you. Never let Him go until He blesses you, until He makes you an Israel, a prince with God.

Thought for today: It is those who have seen the face of God and have been broken by Him who can meet the forces of the Enemy and break down the bulwarks of Satan's kingdom.

December 29

No Condemnation

There is...now no condemnation to those who are in Christ Jesus, who do not walk according to the flesh, but according to the Spirit.
—Romans 8:1

Scripture reading: Romans 8:1–17

Nothing is going to help you attain spiritual maturity or live this higher life, except divine life, which will always help you if you yield yourself absolutely to it. Not only are we exercised by this divine life, but also we are kept in perfect rest. It is needed in this day, for people everywhere are becoming satisfied with natural things. There is no definite cry or prayer within the soul that is making people stop and cry out for God and the coming of the Son.

I am intensely eager that by some means I may inspire you to see what the Spirit has for you. Life in Christ is absolutely different from death. Life is what people long for because of its possibilities; death is what people draw back from because of its finality. God has designed for us to live in freedom from the law of sin and death.

This truth is from the divine mind of the Master. He said that He who lives for himself will die. He who seeks to live will die, but he who is willing to die will live (Luke 17:33). God wants us to see that there is a life that is contrary to this life.

The Spirit of the Lord reveals the following to us in the Word of God: *"He who believes in the Son has everlasting life; and he who does not believe the Son shall not see life"* (John 3:36). The unbelieving person is living and walking about but not seeing life. There is a life that is always brought into condemnation, which is living in death. There is a life that is free from condemnation—living in the Life.

The plan of God's Son for us is to be so much greater in this world than we have ever comprehended. God's plan is not for me to stay where I was yesterday. He desires that spiritual revelation will bring me into touch with divine harmony. God wants me to reach for something more. My eyes are looking up; my heart is looking up. My heart is big and enlarged in the presence of God, for I want to hear one word from God: "Come up higher." God will give us that—the privilege of going higher into a holy relationship with Him.

The person who is under no condemnation has the heavens opened above him. This person has the smile of God upon him. This person has come into the realm of faith and joy and knows that his prayers are answered. God the Holy Spirit would have us to understand that there is a place in the Holy Spirit where there is no condemnation. This place is holiness, purity, righteousness, higher ground, perfection, and being more perfected in the presence of God. This higher ground is perfection, where God is bringing us to live in such a way that He may smile through us and act upon us until our bodies become a flame of light ignited by Omnipotence. This is God's plan for us in the inheritance; this divine place is for us today.

There is no condemnation. God wants us to see our covering, that blessed assurance of being strengthened, that knowledge of the Rock of Ages cleft for me, that place where I know I am! And that joy unbounding where I know there are neither devils nor angels nor principalities nor powers to interfere with that life in Christ (Rom. 8:38–39)! It is wonderful!

"No weapon formed against you shall prosper" (Isa. 54:17). The power of the Most High God has put us in Christ. If we had put ourselves in, it would have been different. We were in the world, but God took us out of the world and put us into Christ. God today by His Spirit wants us to see how this regenerative power, this glorious principle of God's high thoughtfulness, is for us. God wants us to lose ourselves in His sweetness. There is a glorious power behind us when God is behind us; there is a wonderful going before when He goes before us. He said, "I will go before you, and I will be your rear guard." (See Isaiah 52:12.) And so I see that God the Holy Spirit wants me today to penetrate or bring forth or show forth the glorious joy there is in this wonderful incarnation of the Spirit for us all in Christ Jesus. Glory to God!

Thought for today: God makes us Devil-proof.

December 30

By Faith

By grace you have been saved through faith, and that not of yourselves; it is the gift of God.
—Ephesians 2:8

Scripture reading: Hebrews 11

*B*y faith Abel offered to God a more excellent sacrifice than Cain" (Heb. 11:4); *"by faith Enoch was taken away so that he did not see death"* (v. 5); *"by faith Noah...prepared an ark for the saving of his household"* (v. 7); *"by faith Abraham obeyed when he was called to go out to the place which he would receive as an inheritance"* (v. 8).

There is only one way to all the treasures of God, and that is the way of faith. All things are possible, even the fulfilling of all promises is possible, to him who believes (Mark 9:23).

There will be failure in our lives if we do not build on the base, the Rock Christ Jesus. He is the only way; He is the truth; He is the life (John 14:6). And the Word He gives us is life-giving. As we receive the Word of Life, it quickens, it opens, it fills us, it moves us, it changes us, and it brings us into a place where we dare to say amen to all that God has said. Beloved, there is a lot in an amen. You never get any place until you have the amen inside of you. That was the difference between Zacharias and Mary. When the Word came to Zacharias, he was filled with unbelief until the angel said, *"You will be mute...because you did not believe my words"* (Luke 1:20). Mary said, *"Let it be to me according to your word"* (v. 38). The Lord was pleased that she believed what He had spoken. When we believe what God has said, there will be results.

We may do much praying and groaning, but we do not receive from God because of that; we receive because we believe. Yet sometimes it takes God a long time to bring us through the groaning and the crying before we can believe.

I know that no man by his praying can change God, for you cannot change Him. Charles Finney said, "Can a man who is full of sin and all kinds of ruin in his life change God when he starts to pray?" No, it is impossible. But when a man labors in prayer, he groans and travails because his tremendous sin is weighing him down, and he becomes broken in the presence of God. When properly melted, he comes into perfect harmony with the divine plan of God, and then God can work in that clay. He could not before. Prayer changes hearts, but it never changes God. He is the same yesterday, and today, and forever: full of love, full of compassion, full of mercy, full of grace, and ready to bestow this and communicate that to us as we come to Him in faith.

Believe that when you come into the presence of God you can have all you came for. You can take it away, and you can use it, for all the power of God is at your disposal in response to your faith. The price for all was paid by the blood of Jesus Christ at Calvary. Oh, He is the living God, the One who has power to change us! *"It is He who has made us, and not we ourselves"* (Ps. 100:3). And it is He who purposes to transform us so that the greatness of His power may work through us. Oh, beloved, God delights in us, and when a man's ways please the Lord, then He makes all things move according to His own blessed purpose.

Thought for today: All people are born with a natural faith, but God calls us to a supernatural faith that is a gift from Himself.

In Tune with God

Seek first the kingdom of God and His righteousness, and all these things shall be added to you.
—Matthew 6:33

Scripture reading: 2 Peter 1

One thing that can hinder our faith is a seared conscience. There is a conscience that is spiritless, and one that is so opened to the presence of God that the smallest thing in the world will drive it to God. What we need is a conscience that is so in tune with God that not one thing can come into and stay in our lives to hinder our fellowship with God and shatter our faith in Him. And when we can come into the presence of God with clear consciences and genuine faith, our hearts not condemning us, then we have confidence toward God (1 John 3:21), *"and whatever we ask we receive from Him"* (v. 22).

In Mark 11:24 we read, *"Therefore I say to you, whatever things you ask when you pray, believe that you receive them, and you will have them."* Verse twenty-three speaks of mountains removed and difficulties cleared away. Sugarcoating won't do. We must have reality, the real working of our God. We must know God. We must be able to go in and converse with God. We must also know the mind of God toward us, so that all our petitions are always in line with His will.

As this *"like precious faith"* (2 Peter 1:1) becomes a part of you, it will make you so that you will dare to do anything. And remember, God wants daring followers who will be strong in Him and dare to do exploits. How will we reach this place of faith? Let go of your own thoughts, and take the thoughts of God, the Word of God. If you build yourself on imaginations, you will go wrong. You have the Word of God, and it is enough.

A man gave this remarkable testimony concerning the Word of God: "Never compare this Book with other books. Never think or say that this Book contains the Word of God. It is the Word of God. It is supernatural in origin, eternal in duration, inexpressible in value, infinite in scope, regenerative in power, infallible in authority, universal in interest, personal in application, inspired in totality.

Read it through. Write it down. Pray it in. Work it out. And then pass it on."

Truly the Word of God changes a person until he becomes *"an epistle of Christ"* (2 Cor. 3:3). It transforms his mind, changes his character, moves him on from grace to grace, makes him an inheritor of the very nature of God. God comes in, dwells in, walks in, talks through, and dines with him who opens his being to the Word of God and receives the Spirit who inspired it.

If you have lost your hunger for God, if you do not have a cry for more of God, you are missing the plan. A cry must come up from us that cannot be satisfied with anything but God. He wants to give us the vision of the prize ahead that is something higher than we have ever attained. If you ever stop at any point, pick up at the place where you have left off, and begin again under the refining light and power of heaven. God will meet you. And while He will bring you to a consciousness of your own frailty and to a brokenness of spirit, your faith will lay hold of Him and all the divine resources. His light and compassion will be manifested through you, and He will send the rain.

Should we not dedicate ourselves afresh to God? Some say, "I dedicated myself last night to God." Every new revelation brings a new decision. Let us seek Him.

Thought for today: Do not let one thought, one action, one thing in any way interfere with the Rapture. Ask God that every moment will be a moment of purifying.

"He who believes in Me, the works that I do he will do also; and greater works than these he will do, because I go to My Father."
– John 14:12

GREATER WORKS

Experiencing God's Power

Smith Wigglesworth

Greater Works:
Experiencing God's Power
Smith Wigglesworth

Smith Wigglesworth was extraordinarily used by God to see souls saved, bodies healed, and lives changed. Even in the face of death, Wigglesworth did not waver in his faith because he trusted the Great Physician. Your heart will be stirred as you read in Wigglesworth's own words the dramatic accounts of miraculous healings of people whom the doctors had given up as hopeless. Discover how God can enable you to reach out to a hurting world and touch all who come your way with His love.

ISBN: 0-88368-584-1 • Trade • 576 pages

ய
WHITAKER
HOUSE

proclaiming the power of the Gospel through the written word
visit our website at www.whitakerhouse.com

The Power of Faith
Smith Wigglesworth

Need a miracle? God has one for you.
Trapped in poverty? Access God's unlimited resources.
Lack vision and purpose? Discover your God-given destiny.
Feel powerless? God wants to use you in amazing ways.

Laughing at the impossible was a way of life for Smith Wigglesworth.
He trusted wholeheartedly in the words of Jesus, "Only believe."
God used a simple faith to restore sight to the blind, health to the
sick, even life to the dead. This same kind of miracle-working faith
can be yours. As you believe God, your faith will explode.
Your miracle is waiting for you—dare to believe.

ISBN: 0-88368-608-2 • Trade • 544 pages

WHITAKER HOUSE

proclaiming the power of the Gospel through the written word
visit our website at www.whitakerhouse.com